Opera & Operetta

COLLINS

Opera &
Operetta

Michael White
& Elaine Henderson

HarperCollins*Publishers*

For Patrick Brook
(*MW*)

For my father
(*EH*)

HarperCollins*Publishers*
PO Box, Glasgow G4 0NB

© HarperCollins*Publishers* 1997

ISBN 0 00 472061-X

Reprint 10 9 8 7 6 5 4 3 2 1 0

A catalogue record for this book is available from the British Library

Printed and bound in Great Britain by
Caledonian International Book Manufacturing Limited,
Glasgow G64 2QT

Contents

CONTENTS

CONTENTS

CONTENTS

CONTENTS

CONTENTS

How to Use this Book

Over 180 operas and operettas, the major works of more than 70 composers, are covered in the *Collins Guide to Opera and Operetta*, an invaluable guide to this fascinating but sometimes misunderstood artform.

The main body of the book is arranged alphabetically by composer, starting with Adams and continuing through to Zimmermann, taking in the likes of Britten, Mozart, Puccini, Strauss (Johann II and Richard), Sullivan, Verdi and Wagner along the way.

The section for each composer begins with a list of their major operatic works arranged in chronological order by year of composition. Those operas set in bold type are featured in detail on the pages within each composer section. Biographical details and information on other non-operatic works set the operas in context.

The featured operas for each composer are arranged in alphabetical order. Within the entry for each opera the presentation is exactly the same: Form, Composer, Libretto, First Performance, Principal Characters, Synopsis of the Plot, Music and Background, Highlights and Recommended Recording. The vast majority of the operas also feature an entertaining Did You Know? box including anecdotes and diverting background information.

An overview of the history and development of opera and operetta, and a glossary of musical terms round out this indispensable reference source for opera devotees and newcomers alike.

Introduction

FLORENTINE BEGINNINGS

The four-hundred-year history of opera as we know it is based on a mistake. Or at least, a mistaken assumption, made in the late 16th century by a group of Florentine intelligentsia, who were minded to re-create what they believed to be ancient classical drama. Their guide was Aristotle who, in the 4th century BC, had written about theatre and music as though such things were synonymous. Drama, said Aristotle, was the imitation of life made pleasurable by ornament and melody; and armed with this information, the Renaissance Florentines supposed that ancient drama must have been completely sung.

The first composer to put their ideas into practice was Jacopo Peri (1561–1633), whose initial attempt to 're-create' Greek mythic drama, *Dafne*, has been largely lost – leaving his subsequent *Euridice* (1600) as the first surviving opera. But in truth it only survives as a matter of academic interest: an undiverting compromise between speech and song, it's hardly ever staged.

The first opera to survive in regular performance is *La Favola d'Orfeo* (1607) by Claudio Monteverdi (1567–1643), who wasn't a Florentine at all but worked for the court at Mantua, where the ruling Gonzaga duke had witnessed the fame of *Euridice* and wanted something of his own to rival it. In the event, he got a score that outclassed Peri's capabilities, with rich and complex music partly based on the assertive style of Italian Renaissance madrigals and partly on the tradition of what were called *intermedi* – musical interludes between the acts of spoken plays which, by the late 16th century, had begun to acquire a life of their own as separate music-theatre pieces.

What Monteverdi chiefly added was a sense of how music can be used to heighten the emotional charge of a moment of theatre; and to that end he led a move away from the mythic allegories that dominated the plots of very early opera, preferring to deal with human characters and situations. 'I see the characters are winds . . .', he wrote scornfully of a libretto somebody had sent him. 'How can I imitate their speech and stir the passions?'

Stirring passions was increasingly the business of Renaissance opera composers as, with extraordinary speed, opera escaped its origins in private courtly diversion and became a public entertainment. In 1637 the world's first general-access opera house, the Teatro San Cassiano, opened in Venice. By the end of the 17th century the city housed eleven more, and the turnover of work they produced was phenomenal. It was designed to meet an insatiable demand for novelty that seems inconceivable to a time, four hundred years on, when opera has become a largely museological pursuit of the past. The repertoire was always new and ran

11

for no more than short periods before it was taken off and (usually) abandoned. Only the libretti tended to be cherished and preserved, often to be set again. The music disappeared, or was reprocessed into other scores.

WHAT DID 17TH-CENTURY ITALIAN OPERA SOUND LIKE?
Essentially it grew out of long lines of declamatory vocal music that would be embellished as appropriate and intercut with choruses and dances. Over time, and for the sake of variety, the long lines came to be divided into two types of music:

> *Recitative*: a prosaic kind of sung speech, skeletally accompanied by supporting chords on a small group of 'continuo' instruments and designed to deliver large quantities of information quickly.
> *Aria*: a more spacious, song-like melody designed for moments when the action stops and the singer has time to reflect on what has happened, how he feels, and what a splendid voice he has.

'He' is the appropriate gender here, because women had a very limited role in early opera. The vocal interest of high pitch was more often provided by castrati, who came courtesy of the Roman Catholic Church which had been castrating small boys in the cause of art for several centuries. The practice was officially illegal but an open secret, its results standardly attributed to some natural accident like 'the bite of a wild swan'.

The orchestral accompaniment to these operas would have been very modest, basically strings and one or two keyboard instruments. Woodwinds only gradually became standard, and brass instruments were reserved for grand effects.

THE ITALIAN DIASPORA
Monteverdi moved to Venice in the middle period of his life, and there he had two followers of distinction: Pier Francesco Cavalli (1602–76), remembered now for one work, *La Calisto*, and Antonio Cesti (1623–69). Cavalli went to work in Paris, Cesti in Vienna, and between them they exemplified the way Italian opera composers (not to say Italian operatic style) spread abroad.

France proved particularly welcoming, and the court of Louis XIV brokered a productive marriage between the new Italian ways and its own existing tradition of great, dance-based spectacles. Dance was the second language of the French, and, along with a general aggrandisement of scale, it became their chief gift to the operatic genre. Jean-Baptiste Lully (1632–87), the Italian-born chief composer to Louis, filled his opera scores with ballets that look and sound delightful but do nothing for the sense of drama. So did his successor, Jean-Philippe Rameau (1683–1764), who worked with Voltaire and specialised in absurdly extravagant sound-and-vision spectacles at Versailles and the Palais-Royale that no doubt played their part in the ultimate downfall of the monarchy.

12

Meanwhile, the cultural reaction to these over-opulent indulgences was the development of *opéra comique*: lighter, shorter, simpler, with a spoken text to link the arias rather than sung recitative.

England was slower to seize on the Italians, and generally content with its own version of the French dance-spectacle – the courtly masque, whose storyline, usually allegorical, was no more than a vague excuse for ceremonially scenic splendour. But Charles II's years in exile had exposed him to the magnificence of what was happening at Versailles and he was keen to have something of the sort back home, albeit more modestly funded. John Blow's *Venus and Adonis* (1682) was a development of the masque tradition that came close to opera. But England had nothing that could be called the real thing until Henry Purcell (1659–95) wrote his French-influenced (with lots of dancing) *Dido and Aeneas* (1689) for a girl's school in Chelsea. The strange thing is that having established this landmark, he took it no further and reverted to the form of writing known as semi-opera, spoken drama with musical interludes which, however substantial, is still essentially decorative and looks back to the old ways of the masque.

Germany, too, was slow to rise to the Italian bait. It imported Italian musicians who set up opera houses, but the basis of its indigenous music-making throughout the 17th century was religious and instrumental, with a new type of popular, comic speech and song mix known as *Singspiel* making an appearance around 1700. Thereafter, of course, the lure of Italy proved as strong in German-speaking countries as anywhere else; and it was to Italy that Georg Frideric Händel (1685–1759) travelled as a young man to learn his craft as a composer for the theatre.

The interesting thing is that he didn't then go back to Germany to practice it (well, not for long). He moved to London where, in 1711, when he took the town by storm with *Rinaldo*, the otherwise thriving musical life of the capital had witnessed very little Italian opera. Handel effectively created his own market, and within a short space of time it was so buoyant that London could truly be described as one of Europe's leading opera centres – a magnet for the greatest singers of the Baroque stage who came, conquered and ruled the whole process of opera production from start to finish.

THE STARS OF THE BAROQUE

It was in the 18th century that the phenomenon of star singers travelling throughout Europe in pursuit of massive fees first materialised. They tended to be Italian, ensuring that opera continued to be written and sung in their native language, even when it was being performed in England, Germany or Austria. And by now they included women in prominent roles, although the true superstars continued to be the castrati, whose abnormally high voices in roles that designated them great heroes or great lovers contributed to the pantomime-like gender anarchy of Baroque sung theatre. As men had once played women's roles, now women frequently played men. And the element of the surreal in all this was heightened by the way that standard-form Baroque opera presented Classical subjects in a bizarre synthesis of ancient and modern dress. Puffed breeches, crinolines and breastplates, plus a lot of ostrich feathers, were the uniform. But although the genre was called opera seria – meaning 'serious' – and usually involved stories of chivalric duty and high moral tone, it had no choice but to make allowances for occasional elements of comedy.

THE CONVENTIONS OF OPERA SERIA

As the singers literally called the tune in Baroque opera, its ultimate function was to flatter them with vehicles for vocal display; and the vehicles were solo arias, strung together one after another in a way that turned the whole thing into a costumed concert. Each character (there were usually six) had a specified number of arias according to his status in the piece. Each aria was meant to illustrate a particular temperament – anger, sorrow, jealously, delirium – as a calling card for the singer's sensitivity to that emotion. An aria came in three sections: part A, part B, and an embellished repeat da capo ('from the top') of part A. At the end of the aria the singer left the stage, to signify that his concert-in-miniature was over and to encourage rapturous applause. The tortuous absurdity and length of opera seria plots was largely caused by the requirement to accommodate these endless monologues-with-exit.

Otherwise, the conventions also took in freer *arioso* singing that was melodic but without the set-piece formal stature of an aria. The linking recitative came in two forms: *secco* (dry), with minimal accompaniment, and *accompagnato*, with more instruments and fuller texture. Ensembles and choruses were rarely used. For the most part, opera seria only gives you one voice at a time.

However, back in Italy not everything was seria. The ever-expanding lifelines of opera had spread from Venice to Naples, and in both cities a new kind of comic theatre emerged in the early 1700s in the form of *intermezzi*, which, like the old Florentine *intermedi*, were originally filler-pieces that played between the acts of larger works. Over time they had come to acquire an independent existence as artisan comedy (commedia dell'arte), featuring stock, low-life characters and situations. Refined into crafted opera by writers like Goldoni or composers like Giovanni Battista Pergolesi (1710–36), they established a looser kind of writing that wasn't so focused on the virtuosity of individuals and accordingly took more interest in developing ensemble style. Because of its grounding in earthy humour, it became known as opera buffa, and in its genial way it was on the attack.

REFORM

In fact, the excesses of opera seria and the singers who performed it prompted counterattacks in many quarters. In England they came with ridicule, through parody pieces like John Gay's *The Beggar's Opera*. In German-speaking countries the response was more earnest: a considered call for reform. The most celebrated reformer was Christoph Willibald

Gluck (1714–87) who, with his librettist Calzabigi, published a manifesto for the cleaning up of operatic malpractice and propagandised the ideal of 'beautiful simplicity'. No more over-decorated da capo arias. No more deadening rules to govern how a score must be constructed. Just a broad intention towards elegance and modesty.

Between them, Gluck and the Italian *intermezzi* shifted opera's goalposts at a crucial time, because around the corner, ready to exploit the consequences, was a youthful genius.

WOLFGANG AMADEUS MOZART (1756–91)

Making an early start in opera, at the age of twelve, Mozart understandably began to write according to the conventions of opera seria, complete with all their formal requirements and high tone. But he soon broke free into a less prescribed world, coloured generally by comedy and infinitely more than an embellished string of arias. The list of everything he brought to opera would be long and headed, no doubt, by his matchless gift for melody. But of hardly less significance was a dramatic energy and intelligence that rarely failed him. He created characters who lived and breathed, whose actions were dictated not by artificial rules but by the natural consequences of their situation. They are truly human (for the most part) and they truly interact, with vocal lines that interweave and build into astonishing ensembles. It's still 'number' opera, capable of analysis in terms of arias, recitatives, choruses and so on, but the numbers often merge, accumulating into long, near-seamless tracts of music like the massive finale to Act II of *Le Nozze di Figaro*, which begins about a third of the way into the Act and just rolls on – brilliantly – with barely a pause for breath.

The genius of Mozart is essentially comic, indebted to the tradition of Italian opera buffa, and most of his mature stage works explore some aspect of comedy, from the knockabout humour of *Die Entführung aus dem Serail* to the ideological pantomime of *Die Zauberflöte*. Even *Don Giovanni* is a comedy of sorts, described by the author as a 'dramma giocosa'. But Mozartian high spirits marked an end rather than a beginning in the history of Austro-German opera, not to say the whole history of Europe, because Mozart's death coincided with the French Revolution.

ROMANTIC IDEALISM

The French Revolution (1789–99) fed a new and very serious Romantic idealism into Western European consciousness. In the new France, opera was uncomfortably associated with the old order and had to reinvent itself in radical, politically high-moral terms to survive. Rescue operas involving the righting of wrongs and epic libertarian themes became the Paris fashion, championed by Cherubini and Spontini, and the fashion spread to Germany, where Beethoven's one and only opera, *Fidelio*, adopted a politically-driven rescue plot already set to music by the Frenchman Pierre Gaveau.

15

But by then, the centre of gravity in the opera world had shifted once again to Italy. The great Austro-German composers of the 19th century looked to the concert hall rather than the opera house, and those that *did* dream of operatic success, like Schubert, generally failed. The major exception was Carl Maria von Weber (1786–1826), whose fireside horror-story *Der Freischütz* became the definitive statement of German Romanticism – and, like *Fidelio*, it was written to be sung in German.

The one supreme reason for Italy's return to the top of the operatic pile in the early 19th century was Gioacchino Rossini (1792–1868), whose fame through Europe was so all-embracing that it left little room for any would-be German rivals to raise their heads. Rossini was not untouched by Romanticism, and much of his work sets grand, quasi-historical stories adapted from authors like Sir Walter Scott, whose novels had a fervent international following. But the Rossini operas that survive in repertory and are deemed his best are comedies; and they exemplify a kind of singing loosely called bel canto. What the term means is a matter of debate, but it implies the decorative virtuosity of coloratura singing, highly embellished with (in Rossini's case) a steely glitter that tends to prize exquisite technique above spontaneous emotion.

Of Rossini's two heirs and successors, Gaetano Donizetti (1797–1848) is arguably the closest in spirit, with a brilliant light-comedic touch balanced by moments of pathos, most obviously the famous (and fashionable at the time) Mad Scene in *Lucia di Lammermoor*. Donizetti set derangement so effectively that his own subsequent descent into madness was poetically appropriate.

But the master of bel canto emotion was the other heir, Vincenzo Bellini (1801–35), whose truly passionate writing found a middle way between virtuosity and expressivity that would influence Verdi and Puccini decades later. In a short life he managed to produce a body of powerful work (*no* comedies) that climaxed in *Norma*, and their truncated potential for development make him one of the great what-ifs of music history. Had he only lived to fifty, Italian opera might have taken a very different direction.

GIUSEPPE VERDI (1813–1901)

As it was, the mantle passed to a composer who emerged as *the* supreme figure in Italian opera of the later 19th century and with no rival of quite such exalted stature anywhere in the world apart from Richard Wagner. He was Giuseppe Verdi. Unlike Wagner, Verdi was not a theorist, a proselytiser or a visionary. During the 1840s his operas were read as a call to battle for the unification of Italy, but beyond that he did not write to advance radical ideas or debate abstract issues. He was a practical, straightforward man of the theatre whose work was direct and assertive, accepting sometimes crudely improbable plots for the sake of the dramatic situations they set up, but otherwise emotionally true and with a predilection for certain themes that related to his own life and about which he spoke from the heart. One of them was father-child

16

relationships, and it's no coincidence that early in his life he lost two children and a wife in traumatically rapid succession.

The breadth and compass of Verdi's work is so great that it resists summary, but in the broadest terms he introduced a new dimension to the catalogue of opera voices. Vivid, strong and sometimes as rough-edged as they are eloquent, his characters fill the ever-larger space that 19th-century opera came to expect as appropriate for its activities, following the irresistible lead of what was happening in Paris.

FRENCH OPERA

Nineteenth-century opera may have been dominated by Italian composers, but the Paris Opéra still somehow remained the Gold Standard venue from which universal trends and fashions flowed and to which everyone aspired. Wagner's early failure to be taken up by Paris was a humiliation he never forgot, generating a lifelong grievance against the man who was the undisputed monarch of the city's operatic life – Giacomo Meyerbeer (1791–1864). Meyerbeer was an expatriate German who mastered the art of monumental spectacle beloved by Paris audiences and whose works, with their Cecil B. de Mille expansiveness and crowd-pleasing ballet sequences, defined the term 'grand opera'. They set the tone, and the scale, of French stage music for decades to come, and they played their part in encouraging the massive enterprise that was *Les Troyens* by Hector Berlioz (1803–69), although Berlioz raised the artistic stakes of grand opera with elements of idealism and subtlety that were beyond Meyerbeer. Above all, Berlioz was a maverick, always his own man and never in thrall to fashion. When he wrote big, it was to please himself.

More fashion-conscious figures on the Paris circuit were Charles Gounod (1818–93), whose lighter, easier lyricism won him the fame and fortune that eluded Berlioz, and Jules Massenet (1842–1912), of whom much the same could be said. But the outstanding French opera composer of the later 19th century was Georges Bizet (1838–75) who only managed to produce one work of unarguable greatness during his brief life (another what-if?) but made it count. With a storyline of unadorned low-life realism, Carmen effectively invented verismo a decade-and-a-half before the Italians got there. In that sense it was innovative. But its *opéra comique* mix of arias and spoken dialogue was actually quite unsophisticated if you compare it with the truly epoch-making work that was emerging at the same time, across the German border.

RICHARD WAGNER (1813–83)

Born in the same year as Verdi, Wagner was the other supreme figure of 19th-century opera, and in many ways the magnitude of his achievement could be explained as a reaction against the two-and-a-half bad years he spent failing to establish himself as a young composer in Paris. French opera in general, and Meyerbeer in particular, became targets for attack, examples of the way opera had allowed itself to be debased from high art into entertainment. Wagner was to be a Messianic saviour, restoring the lyric stage to the status he imagined it once enjoyed as a temple of enlightenment – ennobling, spiritual, cleansed of all impurity – and by a stroke of luck it was during those bad years in Paris that he found solace in the German medieval myths that would prove the literary inspiration for his cultural campaign. Almost all the mature Wagner operas are based on these ancient legends, which Wagner advocated as ideal material for operatic treatment on the grounds of their timeless relevance and universality.

However ridiculous (and dangerous) some of his ideas turned out to be, Wagner was a truly revolutionary artist who changed not only the ideology of opera but its form and content. He once and for all got rid of the enduring operatic convention of 'number' opera, with the score broken down into units of aria, recitative, chorus and the like. Instead, his music was 'through-composed' in long, unbroken lines, with the vocal parts declaimed in a manner halfway between the decorative enlargement of aria and the direct narration of recitative. He set his own texts in a comparatively straightforward way, one note to a syllable. But his melodies were highly chromatic, weaving through myriad sharps and flats that undermine any clear sense of belonging to a specific key. He also set his singers the challenge of singing for long periods of time against a huge orchestra. And it's in Wagner that the orchestra really comes into its own as a distinctive force to be reckoned among the diverse elements that feed into opera. In fact, it all but takes over, with the voices sometimes reduced to an accompaniment for what's happening in the pit, rather than the more conventional reverse arrangement.

NATIONALISM

Thanks to Wagner, German was at last established as a major operatic language that could hold its own against Italian, and he spawned several generations of German disciples, starting with Engelbert Humperdinck (1854–1921), who developed and refined the process of writing stage works for their own native tongue.

But there were sporadic outbreaks of nationalistically-inspired anti-Italianism in other parts of 19th-century Europe. Spain was an example, where a tradition of folksy light opera saturated with local colour called zarzuela was gathering ground and would, at the turn of the century, prove influential on Manuel de Falla (1876–1946). But the most significant nationalist activity was taking place in Eastern Europe. In Czechoslovakia, Bedřich Smetana (1824–84) and Antonin Dvořák (1841–1904) took the lead in establishing a distinctive, folk-generated style of writing for the stage. What they began found its ultimate expression in the later, 20th-century works of Leoš Janáček (1854–1928), whose skeletal, spikily compressed approach to operatic story-telling has come to be recognised as one of the most significant contributions to the modern history of music.

The chief centre of 19th-century nationalism, though, was Russia, a land which had only recently begun to develop a distinctive musical culture after years of French and Italian domination. The father of Russian nationalism was Mikhail Glinka (1804–57), who set an enduring precedent for a grandly ceremonial kind of opera that mixed history with fairy tales but wasn't terribly well crafted in terms of its structure. These were very early days for Russian music. Composition was a semi-amateur activity, and it remained so for the generation who came after Glinka, notably a group known as the 'Mighty Handful'. The group's leading member, Modest Musorgsky (1839–81), left mighty works of startling but rough-edged originality that his more craftsmanlike compatriot Nikolai Rimsky-Korsakov (1844–1908) subsequently tied up. Pyotr Ilyich Tchaikovsky (1840–93) completed the process through which Russian opera reached mature refinement, with works which tend to be considered more Western European than those of the 'Mighty Handful', although it would be more accurate merely to describe them as less inward-looking in their Russian-ness.

THE 20TH CENTURY

Summaries of 20th-century music are invariably messier than those of earlier periods, because composers fit less easily into territorial groups or ideological movements. They tend to make their claims as individuals and resist categorisation. But the century was ushered in by one conspicuously flourishing movement in Italy known as verismo, a school of low-life realism whose first champions, Pietro Mascagni (1863–1945) and Ruggero Leoncavallo (1857–1919), found instant fame with their respective mini-masterpieces *Cavalleria Rusticana* and *I Pagliacci*, but were soon eclipsed in stature by a fellow Italian.

Giacomo Puccini (1858–1924) emerged as the next great Italian composer after Verdi. In the history of music he doesn't stand as a notable innovator, and his appeal is far from intellectual, but the strength and passion of his melodies, the quality of his orchestral writing, and his sheer theatricality (in both the best and worst senses of the word) have guaranteed his domination of the modern opera repertoire. And if Puccini doesn't always 'feel' like a 20th-century composer, remember that the majority of his mature scores, from *Madama Butterfly* onwards, came after 1900. However, the other dominant figure of early 20th-century opera was a German.

Not to be confused with the Viennese king of operetta (no relation), Richard Strauss (1864–1949) was *the* successor to Wagner in much the same way that Puccini was to Verdi, adopting the master's language, adjusting its parameters and, in the process, lightening its intensity. A young radical who, in archetypal fashion, grew into a middle-aged conservative, Strauss' early works set out to shock the bourgeoisie, his later ones to charm them. But the Wagnerian inheritance was constant in the prominence and weight he alotted to the orchestra, and in the declamatory, through-flowing style of his writing for the voice, which commonly requires the power and stamina of Wagner's *helden* singers. Through Strauss, a style of writing was fixed whose consquences can be heard today in the sometimes tough, politically driven but also sometimes romantic operas of Hans Werner Henze (born 1926) and the massively neo-Wagnerian project of Karlheinz Stockhausen (born 1928) to write an apocalyptic cycle of seven music dramas – one for each day of the week.

The excesses of Wagner and Strauss, though, led to an inevitable reaction away from opulent, well-upholstered writing on a grand scale and towards smaller, leaner alternatives. A changing world made the economics of large-scale opera harder to sustain, and while some German figures like the young Erich Korngold (1897–1957) clung to large forces and traditional trappings, more forward-looking ones like Kurt Weill (1900–50) were scaling down and rethinking the way in which opera addresses its audience. Weill's collaborations with the playwright Bertolt Brecht pioneered a new kind of music theatre, designed to be popular (with cabaret-style numbers), stripped of the top Cs and tiaras glamour of the opera house. Paul Hindemith (1895–1963) was also concerned with usefulness and, specifically, the relationship between the artist and society, although he gave operatic expression to it in a decidedly less radical manner than Weill and Brecht.

Meanwhile, the so-called Second Viennese School composers Arnold Schoenberg (1874–1951) and Alban Berg (1885–1935) had taken the Wagnerian message to its logical conclusions and beyond, with music that initially extended Wagner's exotically free harmonies to a point where key signatures became almost irrelevant, and subsequently did away with any allegiance to a key centre altogether. The resulting serial or twelve-tone music proved more viable for instrumentalists than for singers, and it hasn't found much of a following on the opera stage, even though Berg left two masterful scores of lasting importance in the modern history of the genre.

Before we leave the post-Wagnerian empire, mention has to be made of Claude Debussy (1862–1918), whose ethereally vague *Pelléas et Mélisande* is like Wagner in a whisper – perfumed, rich in symbolism, but without the bombast. *Duke Bluebeard's Castle*, the one opera of Béla Bartók (1881–1945), is another heavily symbolic score in serious debt to the master of Bayreuth.

But the Wagnerian ascendency was finally (and ironically) ended by the intervention of one of the master's most devoted admirers, Adolf Hitler, who single-handedly lost Germany its prime position in the mid-20th-century operatic league. The majority of the significant Austro-German composers went into exile as the Nazis came to power – usually with no choice in the matter – and their general direction was America, where Hindemith, Korngold, Weill and Schoenberg (among others) settled, assimilating with varying degrees of enthusiasm into the culture of their adoptive land and making their own contributions to the American musical melting-pot.

It would be wrong to describe the America of the 1930s as an operatic wasteland. It had been importing European talent (not least, Mozart's librettist Da Ponte) for more than a century and boasted flourishing lyric companies. But home-grown opera was a novelty, and native composers were struggling to find a native means of self-expression – something that wasn't merely shipped in from the old world. Marc Blitzstein (1905–64) and Virgil Thomson (1896–1989) were early experimenters, but the breakthrough came with George Gershwin (1898–1937), whose *Porgy and Bess* realised the hopes and strivings of a whole generation of American composers in the way it so successfully transcended the boundaries between 'high' and 'low' art: cultivated and vernacular. Gian Carlo Menotti (born 1911) has never been the showbiz figure that Gershwin was, and his Italian background tells in the Puccini-esque nature of his feel for melody and drama, but he was pushing at those high/low boundaries during the 1940s, with a succession of operas designed to play commercially in non-traditional Broadway-type venues. And with passing input from the racy Leonard Bernstein (1918–90) and the conservative but passionate Samuel Barber (1910–81), American opera has become a brilliantly hybrid industry, overflowing into transcendental events, such as those of Philip Glass (born 1937) and the very serious musicals of Stephen Sondheim (born 1930).

Backtracking slightly, France has had a disappointing 20th century for a country whose national house was once the spotlit focus of the opera world. After *Pelléas et Mélisande* there hasn't been much of stature apart from a couple of lightweight charmers by Maurice Ravel (1875–1937) and a religious drama by Francis Poulenc (1899–1963).

Russia has had an altogether more distinguished time with Sergei Prokofiev (1891–1953) and Dmitri Shostakovich (1906–75), whose combined works add a sharp, abrasive edge to the development of an operatic language that largely derives from Musorgsky and Tchaikovsky. The earliest operas of Igor Stravinsky (1882–1971) take their tone from the magic fantasies of Rimsky-Korsakov. But as Stravinsky became progressively less Russian and more cosmopolitan, so his music became less 'enchanted' and more austerely Neoclassical, reinventing the past and reaching back *beyond* Wagner to the delicate detachment of Mozartian and Baroque closed forms. Another displaced person in America, it's significant that Stravinsky wrote his chief opera, *The Rake's Progress*, to an English text provided by the poet W.H. Auden and set almost as though it were Latin, with wilful unconcern that the language should sound idiomatic.

And that brings us, finally, to Britain, which, in the second half of the 20th century, became a serious creative centre for opera after two hundred years of producing almost nothing of significance. The English musical renaissance that began with Elgar produced a few attempts at music theatre that attracted passing fame, like Ethel Smyth's *The Wreckers*, Delius' *A Village Romeo and Juliet* and Vaughan Williams' epic *Pilgrim's Progress*. But the spark of genius didn't quite ignite until 1945, when *Peter Grimes* put Benjamin Britten (1913–76) on the map as a figure of world stature. The thirteen original operas that followed built into a body of work unmatched by anybody of his generation. Their success inspired a torrent of work from other British composers that continues unabated, starting with Michael Tippett (born 1905) and William Walton (1902–83) and progressing down the years through the Mancunian duo of Harrison Birtwistle (born 1934) and Peter Maxwell Davies (born 1934) to Judith Weir (born 1954) and Mark-Anthony Turnage (born 1960). Turnage's blistering adaptation of the bitter social satire *Greek* by Steven Berkoff has proved one of the most powerful and most-performed operas of the last decade or so, and it crowns a period of extraordinary productivity. With the possible exception of Finland – yes, Finland – where Aulis Sallinen (born 1935) has conjured a thriving opera industry out of nothing, it's probably true to say that no country in the world could currently beat Britain's ability to generate new opera. For a political culture which does as little as possible to encourage music in general and opera in particular, this is a pleasing but bizarre state of affairs.

A Postscript on Operetta

Unlike most aspects of opera proper, operetta was a French invention, derived from the mix of song and speech practiced by composers like André Ernest Grétry (1741–1813) and Pierre Monsigny (1729–1817). 'Comique' implied lightness though not necessarily comedy, and the boundary with serious opera was fairly loosely drawn, allowing figures like François Boïeldieu (1775–1834) and Daniel Auber (1782–1871) to cross it freely.

But operetta finally came into its own in the French Second Empire with Jacques Offenbach (1819–80), whose career began on a small scale, writing for tiny Parisian theatres, but gathered international fame – which spread to Vienna in the 1860s and prompted Johann Strauss II (1825–99) to imitative action. Strauss' waltz-based shows were softer in tone than the sometimes abrasive satire of Offenbach, and they owed almost as much to the native Viennese tradition of *Singspiel* (another mix of speech and song, often heavily sentimental) as they did to the French import. But the formula was unequivocally successful, and it was soon followed by Franz Lehár (1870–1948) who took the Viennese version of the genre to the point of no return.

Meanwhile, the Offenbach phenomenon visited Britain in the 1870s and left its mark on the librettist/composer team of W.S. Gilbert (1836–1911) and Arthur Sullivan (1842–1900), whose Savoy Operas so insinuated themselves into English cultural life that its language and customs carry their imprint – not least the practice of queueing, which was introduced as a means of coping with the demand for G&S tickets.

Offenbach and G&S between them then spread to America where, reinterpreted via European exiles like the Hungarian Sigmund Romberg (1887–1951), they laid one of the foundations for the American Broadway musical. But that's another story . . .

John Adams

(1947–)

Nixon in China (1987)
The Death of Klinghoffer (1990)
I was looking at the Ceiling and then I saw the Sky
(1995)

*A*ccording to official statistics, John Adams is the most frequently performed of living American composers – his fame founded on an accessible style of writing known as Minimalism which involves the repetition of small groups of notes to a point where listeners are either mesmerised or driven crazy. An essentially West Coast American phenomenon, it was adopted by Adams in the early 1970s in reaction against an East Coast academic upbringing and meant that he was automatically associated with older Minimalist composers like Steve Reich and Philip Glass. But Adams has developed in a more eclectic way, providing himself with an escape route from what could otherwise be a restrictively dead-end musical language. *Nixon in China* and *The Death of Klinghoffer* are striking examples of newsreel opera, their stories taken from real life and presented like televisual current affairs. Nixon deals with high-level politics; *Klinghoffer* (a treatment of the *Achille Lauro* hijack) with the personal consequences of political conflict. His most recent stage work, *I was looking at the Ceiling and then I saw the Sky*, is a dramatised song-sequence in something like the popular manner of the collaborations between Bertolt Brecht and Kurt Weill earlier this century. Looking critically at the lives of young Americans at the time of the last Los Angeles earthquake, it premiered with spray-paint set-designs by radical graffiti artists.

Nixon in China

FORM: Opera in three acts; in English
COMPOSER: John Adams (1947–)
LIBRETTO: Alice Goodman
FIRST PERFORMANCE: Houston, 22 October 1987

Principal Characters

Richard Nixon, American president ✺ **Baritone**
Pat Nixon, his wife ✺ **Soprano**
Mao Tse-tung, Chinese statesman ✺ **Tenor**
Henry Kissinger, American statesman ✺ **Bass**
Chiang Ch'ing, Mao's wife ✺ **Soprano**
Chou En-lai, Chinese statesman ✺ **Baritone**

Synopsis of the Plot

Setting: China; February 1972

ACT I On their arrival in Beijing, Nixon and his wife are greeted by Chou En-lai. Nixon feels that this visit is of great symbolic significance – as much as the first moon landing, in fact, and he also expresses his pleasure that their arrival coincides with peak television viewing time in America, thus ensuring him maximum publicity. Then the President, Henry Kissinger, Mao Tse-tung and Chou En-lai each offer their individual views on world issues, during which the contrasting ideologies and philosophies of East and West become evident, and the first act closes with a banquet.

ACT II Pat Nixon is taken to visit a commune and the Summer Palace and later joins the President, Mao, Chou En-lai and Mao's wife, Chiang Ch'ing, to watch a performance of the contemporary 'political ballet', *The Red Detachment of Women*. This depicts a courageous group of women soldiers successfully battling against an unscrupulous landlord (played by Henry Kissinger). When the ballet ends, Chiang Ch'ing presents her account of the Cultural Revolution and how she sees her own place in history.

ACT III On the last night of the visit Nixon, Pat, Mao, Chiang Ch'ing and Chou En-lai are each seen in separate beds. Nixon and Mao reflect on past events in their lives and on their struggles to succeed. Nixon's wartime memories centre on the acquisition of his own hamburger stand while Mao's most vivid memories are the struggles of the Revolution. It is left to Chou En-lai to unite the past with the present by asking the question common to all political ideologies: 'How much of what we did was good?', which brings the opera to a close.

Music

Nixon in China is a mixture of exhilarating upbeat rhythms, pounding through the endless repetitions that make up a Minimalist score, and moments of reflective poignancy in which potentially cardboard characters really come to life. It isn't easy to show recent historical figures with credibility on an opera stage, and the mere idea of Nixon and Mao singing to each other raises an assumption that the tone of the piece will be satirical. But no. Despite forays into the surreal, this is straight-laced all-American drama which if anything veers toward Romanticism – with appropriately luscious music. Even the synthesiser which Adams insinuates into the orchestral textures is given a romantic treatment.

Highlight

A brilliantly energised orchestral sequence called 'The Chairman Dances', which has entered the concert repertoire as a stand-alone piece.

Did You Know?

Nixon in China is one of the most commercially successful of all modern operas. The Grammy Award-winning recording was named a 'recording of the decade' by *Time* magazine, and the whole thing broadcast on American TV as though it were a newsflash, introduced by Walter Cronkite – which is probably the only time Richard Nixon ever saw it. He declined an invitation to attend the Houston premiere, and is not known to have been present at any other live performance.

Recommended Recording

Sanford Sylvan, James Maddelena, Chorus and Orchestra of St Luke's/ Edo de Waart. Nonesuch 7559 79177-2. The only recording to date.

Samuel Barber

(1910–81)

A Hand of Bridge (1953)
Vanessa (1957)
Anthony and Cleopatra (1966)

*B*arber was an American who looked to Europe and the melodic abundance of European late-Romanticism for inspiration. Born into a WASP-ish East Coast family, he was one of the first students at the new Curtis Institute in Philadelphia where he studied singing as well as composition. Opera wasn't a preoccupation, and his few stage works have tended to be overshadowed by concert scores like the Violin Concerto, the lyrically nostalgic scena for voice and orchestra *Knoxville, Summer of 1915*, and above all by the deathless *Adagio*, which must have featured on the soundtrack to more feature films and TV documentaries than anything since Vivaldi's *Four Seasons*. But at Curtis he had met another young composer called Gian Carlo Menotti who was supremely a creature of the theatre. They went on to spend most of their lives together, and the first two of the three Barber operas were collaborations in which Menotti wrote the words. *A Hand of Bridge* doesn't actually require many words: it lasts nine minutes and is no more than a brilliant little diversion. *Vanessa*, with its darkly Ibsenesque plot, is far more substantial, while *Antony and Cleopatra* is grander still, written for the opening of the new Metropolitan Opera in New York.

Vanessa

FORM: Opera in four acts; in English
COMPOSER: Samuel Barber (1910–81)
LIBRETTO: Gian Carlo Menotti; after Isak Dinesen's story
FIRST PERFORMANCE: New York, 15 January 1958

Principal Characters

Vanessa, a baroness ❧ **Soprano**
Anatol, a young man ❧ **Tenor**
Erika, Vanessa's niece ❧ **Mezzo-soprano**
Old Baroness, Vanessa's mother ❧ **Contralto**
Doctor ❧ **Bass**

Synopsis of the Plot

Setting: A country house in an unnamed 'northern country' in the early 1900s

ACT I Vanessa waits alone in her sumptuous drawing room for a visitor to arrive. When he does at last come, Vanessa keeps her back turned to him, saying that she has waited twenty years for his return but, if he can no longer love her, then he must go immediately. As the visitor answers her, Vanessa whirls round, realizing that he cannot possibly be her lover, Anatol; he is much too young. Weak with shock she is taken to her room by Erika. Meanwhile, Anatol casts an acquisitive eye over the rich furnishings of the room. When Erika returns he explains that he is the son of Anatol, Vanessa's lover who went away twenty years ago; his father is now dead. In view of the snowstorm raging outside, he begs Erika to let him stay the night and, carefully scrutinising the girl, calmly sits down to enjoy the meal prepared for his father.

ACT II A month has gone by. Erika confesses to the old Baroness that, although she and Anatol became lovers on that first night, she does not love him and will not marry him. Vanessa, aglow with happiness, returns from skating with Anatol and announces plans for a grand New Year Ball. Later, the old Baroness questions Anatol about his behaviour towards Erika and extracts his promise to marry her. Erika, however, knowing that her aunt, Vanessa, is in love with Anatol, rejects him.

ACT III The ball is under way and Vanessa and Anatol are about to announce their engagement. The pregnant Erika, shocked and disturbed, wanders unnoticed outside into the bitter cold as the music and dancing continue in the background.

ACT IV Erika has been found unconscious and has suffered a miscarriage, kept secret from Vanessa, who is now married to Anatol and preparing to leave for their honeymoon in Paris. After they leave, Erika is alone; she orders the mirrors to be draped and the gate to be shut, just as her aunt had done: 'Now it is my turn to wait'.

Music and Background

A conservative piece for its time, *Vanessa* is richly scored in the manner of late Romanticism, owing much to Puccini and Richard Strauss, and with most of the formal ingredients of conventional 19th-century grand opera but translated into American terms. There is a fragment of a ball scene, ravishingly lyrical set-piece arias, and a sort of folk ballet – all of which contributed to the enormous success *Vanessa* enjoyed in its early years. It was the first opera in English ever to be heard at Salzburg, where it played with the Vienna Philharmonic in the pit.

Highlights

Erika's aria 'Must the winter come so soon?' is a winner, as is Vanessa's 'Do not utter a word', and the final quintet is arguably one of the most effective climaxes in modern opera.

Did You Know?

🐌 The original production of *Vanessa* was a grand event with opulent sets and costumes by Cecil Beaton. It was intended that Maria Callas should sing the title role but she declined – allegedly because she thought Erika too much a rival part.

Recommended Recording

Eleanor Steber, Rosalind Elias, Regina Resnik, Nicolai Gedda, Metropolitan Opera/Dmitri Mitropoulos. BMG/RCA GD 87899. The original cast, and the only recording.

Béla Bartók

(1881–1945)

Duke Bluebeard's Castle (1918)

Born in a part of Hungary which is now Romania, Bartók was one of the pioneer figures of 20th-century music, forging a new musical style from the folk traditions of his native country that owes nothing to the two composer-giants who are generally considered the great originators of modernity, Schoenberg and Stravinsky. Most of his work was instrumental and orchestral, with a set of six string quartets that rank as the most significant of their kind since Beethoven, and major concert scores like the *Concerto for Orchestra* and *Music for Percussion, Strings and Celesta*. His involvement with the stage was limited and *Duke Bluebeard's Castle* his only opera, although he did subsequently produce two ballet scores, *The Wooden Prince* and *The Miraculous Mandarin*. He left Hungary for America in 1940 and died there in financially straitened circumstances five years later.

Duke Bluebeard's Castle

FORM: Opera in one act; in Hungarian
COMPOSER: Béla Bartók (1881–1945)
LIBRETTO: Béla Balázs; after a fairy tale by Charles Perrault
FIRST PERFORMANCE: Budapest, 24 May 1918

Principal Characters

Duke Bluebeard ∼ Bass
Judith, his wife ∼ Mezzo-soprano

Synopsis of the Plot

Setting: Bluebeard's castle; an unknown time and country

Bluebeard enters, leading his new wife into her home, a strange, dark Gothic castle which has seven doors but no windows. He asks her if she has changed her mind about staying with him and, on her reassurance that she has not, they embrace. The door behind them is shut and bolted. Judith then notices the doors for the first time and, saying she wants to let in light and air, asks the Duke for the keys. A strange, long sighing sound is heard throughout the castle as Bluebeard, on her insistence, gives her the key to the first door. As she opens it a vivid red light streams through; it is the Torture Chamber and the walls are wet with blood. Undeterred, Judith maintains that she is not afraid and proceeds to open the next four doors: the Armoury is characterised by bronze light, the Treasury by golden light, the Garden by bluish light and the vision of Bluebeard's Kingdom by a brilliant white light. Bluebeard suggests that she has seen enough and takes her in his arms. But Judith is, by now, obsessed with knowing all his secrets and demands the sixth key. The haunting sigh is heard once more as she opens the door to find a Lake of Tears.

The final door, insists Bluebeard, must remain closed. But Judith begins to question him about his love for her. She wants to know about the women he loved before he met her, and asks what happened to them. Bluebeard stays silent and Judith opens the door, convinced that the truth lies behind it. Immediately the fifth and sixth doors swing shut and the stage darkens. Three beautiful women step out: they are his ex-wives, Bluebeard explains, and represent the morning, noon and evening of his love. Judith, he says, is his last love, that of the night, and after her is eternal darkness. Judith disappears through the seventh door and Bluebeard is alone.

Music and Background

As theatre, *Duke Bluebeard's Castle* is compact, with just one act and a playing time of an hour, but as music it has epic stature, grandly terrifying in its depiction of Duke Bluebeard's dark domain and heavy with the gloom of Gothic horror. Bartók's treatment of the story is, of course, symbolic – the opening of the doors is like an exercise in Freudian analysis, exposing the hidden secrets of the subconscious mind – and the counterbalancing of inner and outer worlds is echoed in Bartók's key structures, which gravitate between F sharp for Bluebeard and C for Judith.

Highlight

This is not an opera with stand-alone arias, and there are, after all, only two singing characters: the dead wives behind the sixth door are mute. But there is a great musical climax at the fifth door when the vision of Bluebeard's kingdom floods the stage – a heart-stopping moment that never fails in its effect.

Did You Know?

Bartók wrote this grim tale of domestic serial killing shortly after his marriage. He dedicated the score to his wife.

Recommended Recording

Samuel Ramey, Eva Marton, Hungarian State Orchestra/Adam Fischer. Sony MK 44523. Idiomatically conducted, with explosively strong performances from the two singers.

Ludwig van Beethoven

(1770–1827)

Fidelio (1805)

Born in Bonn but living and working in Vienna from his early twenties, Beethoven is one of the towering, pivotal figures of music history, with a massive output (nine symphonies, thirty-two piano sonatas, sixteen string quartets, seven concertos . . .). His work carried the Classical forms of Haydn and Mozart into the new territory of Romanticism and confirmed the potential of music to speak in spiritual as well as political terms. A radical humanitarian with revolutionary sympathies, he used his work as a public platform for the expression of personal beliefs about society and the individual, and his only opera *Fidelio* was exactly that: a statement of the power of the human spirit to triumph over tyranny and oppression which stands beside the choral finale of Beethoven's Ninth Symphony as an anthem to the ideals of universal brotherhood. Other scores express a more autobiographical struggle with human weakness: at the age of thirty he began to realise that he was going deaf, and as his hearing worsened he withdrew into a world of inner turmoil which found a mystical dimension in the late quartets.

Fidelio

FORM: Opera in two acts; in German
COMPOSER: Ludwig van Beethoven (1770–1827)
LIBRETTO: Joseph Sonnleithner and Georg Friedrich Treitschke;
after the play by Jean-Nicolas Bouilly
FIRST PERFORMANCE: Vienna, 20 November 1805

Principal Characters

Florestan, a Spanish nobleman ❧ **Tenor**
Leonore, his wife, disguised as the male Fidelio ❧ **Soprano**
Rocco, chief jailer ❧ **Bass**
Marzelline, Rocco's daughter ❧ **Soprano**
Jaquino, Rocco's assistant ❧ **Tenor**
Don Pizarro, governor of the prison ❧ **Bass-baritone**
Don Fernando, the king's minister ❧ **Bass**

Synopsis of the Plot

Setting: A fortress near Seville; 18th century

ACT I Florestan, a political prisoner and freedom fighter, has been flung into a dungeon by Pizarro and is slowly starving to death, while Pizarro spreads rumours that he has already died. Leonore, suspecting the truth, has disguised herself as a man, Fidelio, and has been taken on as an assistant by Rocco, swiftly becoming a trusted aide. Marzelline, Rocco's daughter, is unaware of the disguise and has taken a considerable fancy to Fidelio, rejecting the overtures of Jaquino, her jealous former suitor. Leonore learns that Don Fernando, the king's minister, is coming to inspect the prison, having heard that Pizarro is unlawfully locking up his own personal enemies. To Leonore's horror, Pizarro gives Rocco money and instructs him to kill Florestan. Rocco declines to commit murder, but agrees to dig a grave in the prison dungeon if Pizarro will do the deed himself. Meanwhile Leonore has urged Rocco to allow the prisoners out for some light and air, but she is heartbroken to find Florestan is not among them. Rocco then tells her that she is to help with the gravedigging so at least she will be able to see Florestan and perhaps be able to help him; if nothing else she will die with him.

ACT II Rocco and Leonore enter the dungeon where Leonore is shocked to see her emaciated and chained husband, although she is careful to control her behaviour to avoid rousing Rocco's suspicions. Leonore persuades Rocco to allow her to offer the condemned prisoner some bread and wine. Suddenly Pizarro bursts in, dagger in hand, and rushes towards Florestan – only to be stopped by Leonore who throws herself between them, declaring that she will shoot Pizarro, with a pistol she has kept hidden, before he kills Florestan. At this moment a fanfare is heard and Jaquino announces the minister's arrival. Florestan is saved and, in a symbolic gesture, he is released from his chains by Leonore. The minister orders the immediate release of all the prisoners and the arrest of Pizarro. Justice is done.

Music and Background

Fidelio is a mixture of music and speech which can prove upliftingly sublime or stodgily leaden, depending on how it's done and (critically) how much of the speech is left in. Beethoven had no previous experience of writing opera, and he took enormous trouble over it, passing through three different versions, a different name (*Leonore*) and four overtures before arriving at a final form. You could argue that the effort shows. There is also an uncomfortable relationship between the domestic and heroic elements in the opera, and a sense in which the great but static chorus of celebration at the end takes the whole thing out of the realms of theatre and into oratorio. But there is no denying the sincere depth of emotion involved, or the fact that *Fidelio* can be an exhilarating and radiantly affirmative experience – in the right hands.

Highlights

The canonic quartet 'Mir ist so wunderbar', Leonore's aria 'Komm, Hoffnung', and the prisoners' chorus 'O welche Lust' in Act I; the Leonore/Florestan duet 'O namenlose Freude!' and final chorus 'Wer ein holdes Weib errungen' in Act II.

Did You Know?

⌖ *Fidelio*'s subtitle is *Die Eheliche Liebe (Married Love)*, and Leonore is very much the idealised woman Beethoven spent his life searching for but never finding. She also represents a comparatively rare example in opera of the female lead as active heroine rather than passive victim.

⌖ *Fidelio* is said to have been based on a true incident in the French Revolution.

Recommended Recording

Christa Ludwig, Jon Vickers, Philharmonia Orchestra/Otto Klemperer. EMI CMS7 69324-2. A classic 1962 recording with a warmth and dynamism that remain unmatched.

Vincenzo Bellini

(1801–35)

I Capuleti e I Montecchi (1830)
La Sonnambula (1831)
Norma (1831)
Beatrice di Tenda (1833)
I Puritani (1835)

If Rossini was the presiding genius of Italian bel canto opera in the first half of the 19th century, Donizetti and Bellini were his two lieutenants, and like Rossini, they made their mark in Naples before moving on to Paris, which was the centre of the operatic world. Bellini was Sicilian by birth and showed an early gift for melody that got him noticed while he was still a student. His first full-length opera was staged at Naples' Teatro San Carlo when he was twenty-three and a commission from Milan followed immediately, spreading his fame beyond Italy. From then on came a steady flow of work, totalling ten operas in ten years – frantic productivity by modern standards but fairly modest by the standards of the time. In fact, Bellini took uncommon care over his work, suiting the music to specific voices (from which he nonetheless made great demands) and developing a close association with the poet Felice Romani, which became one of the most effective composer/librettist partnerships in opera history.

Norma

FORM: Opera in two acts; in Italian
COMPOSER: Vincenzo Bellini (1801–35)
LIBRETTO: Felice Romani; after Alexandre Soumet's verse tragedy
FIRST PERFORMANCE: Milan, 26 December 1831

Principal Characters

Oroveso, chief of the druids and Norma's father ⟶ Bass
Pollione, Roman pro-consul in Gaul ⟶ Tenor
Norma, high priestess of the druid temple ⟶ Soprano
Adalgisa, young priestess of the temple ⟶ Soprano
Clotilde, Norma's confidante ⟶ Mezzo-soprano
Flavio, Pollione's friend ⟶ Tenor

Synopsis of the Plot

Setting: Gaul; the Roman occupation

ACT I Oroveso comes to the sacred grove to pray to the gods to help him raise support to fight and defeat the Romans. After he has left, Pollione confides to Flavio that he no longer loves Norma, who has broken her vows of chastity for him and secretly borne his two children; he has transferred his affections to the young priestess, Adalgisa. When Adalgisa joins him, Pollione successfully persuades her to renounce her vows and go back to Rome with him. Adalgisa, in some distress, goes to see Norma to ask to be released from her vows. Norma, sympathising with her predicament, agrees to do so and asks the name of her lover. At that moment Pollione himself enters and Norma, stunned, realises the truth. She furiously denounces Pollione and the shocked Adalgisa declares that her first loyalty is to Norma, rejecting Pollione's desperate attempts to persuade her to go with him.

ACT II In her hut Norma stands over her sleeping children, dagger in hand, contemplating the shame and humiliation they will suffer in the future because of her disgrace. She cannot bring herself to harm them, however, and suggests to Adalgisa that she should leave with Pollione and take the children with her to safety. Adalgisa's response is to say that she will indeed go to Pollione – but only to try and convince him to return to Norma. In an atmosphere of gathering violence Norma learns that Pollione plans to abduct Adalgisa from the temple. Enraged, she strikes the great shield three times and declares war against Rome. Pollione is captured within the sacred temple but, to save his life, Norma offers herself, a disgraced and blasphemous priestess, as an alternative sacrifice. Confiding her children to Oroveso's care, Norma prepares to mount the funeral pyre, as Pollione, overwhelmed by her selfless love and courage, commits himself to her once more and walks beside her to the flames.

36

Music and Background

Norma is Bellini's masterpiece, written for what the composer called the 'encylopaedic' range of expression of the great bel canto singer Giuditta Pasta and closely responsive to the libretto of Felice Romani, which passed through many changes before the composer was satisfied with it. Norma herself is one of the most formidable roles in all opera, calling for extremes of tenderness and fury. Not for nothing does she get taken into the repertory of Wagner singers, and Wagner admitted a personal debt to Bellini's combination of powerful passion with spacious melodies.

Highlights

Norma's Act II 'Casta diva' is a benchmark aria for sopranos with the substance and finesse to tackle it (and there aren't many of them). Also in Act II comes a superb scene for the two sopranos – 'Mira o Norma'.

Did You Know?

ᴥ The two great Normas of modern times once appeared in the opera together, in 1952. Maria Callas took the title role, Joan Sutherland the small part of Clotilde.

ᴥ The 19th-century soprano, Therese Tietjens, playing Norma, swung her arm so wide as she struck the gong that she hit her leading man, who collapsed unconscious at her feet.

Recommended Recording

Joan Sutherland, Marilyn Horne, John Alexander, London Symphony Orchestra/Richard Bonynge. Decca 425 488-2. A classic from the 1960s, magnificently cast in the two soprano roles, with Sutherland in better voice than when she recorded *Norma* a second time, aged fifty-eight(!).

I Puritani
(The Puritans)

FORM: Opera in three acts; in Italian
COMPOSER: Vincenzo Bellini (1801–35)
LIBRETTO: Carlo Pepoli; after Ancelot and Saintine's play,
itself based on Sir Walter Scott's novel
FIRST PERFORMANCE: Paris, 25 January 1835

Principal Characters

The Puritans
Lord Walton ᔐ **Bass**
Sir George Walton, his brother ᔐ **Bass**
Sir Richard Forth ᔐ **Baritone**
Sir Bruno Robertson ᔐ **Tenor**

Lord Arthur Talbot, a Cavalier ᔐ **Tenor**
Henrietta of France, Charles I's widow ᔐ **Mezzo-soprano**
Elvira, Lord Walton's daughter ᔐ **Soprano**

Synopsis of the Plot

Setting: A fortress outside Plymouth during the English Civil War

ACT I Elvira has finally overcome her father's objection to her marriage to the Cavalier, Arthur Talbot, leaving Richard Forth a disgruntled and rejected suitor. To Elvira's joy, distant horns announce Arthur's impending arrival and he sweeps in in great style, bringing gifts that include a superb white bridal veil for his betrothed. Lord Walton gives Arthur and Elvira a safe conduct pass, saying that he cannot attend the wedding because he must escort a female prisoner, a suspected spy, to London. The prisoner is brought in and Arthur recognises her as the widow of the executed Charles I. Arthur knows that, if anyone finds out who she is, she will be murdered, and he resolves to help her escape. Draping Elvira's veil over Henrietta's head, he smuggles her out of the fortress, intercepted only by Richard, who, seeing the woman is not Elvira, is glad to see Arthur go and hopes that he may now win Elvira's love. On discovering her apparent desertion Elvira loses her reason.

ACT II Elvira's madness is observed at length in the famous Mad Scene, but the act closes on George Walton and Richard Forth as they confirm their readiness to fight to the death for the Puritan cause and, if necessary, to kill Arthur Talbot.

ACT III Arthur has now delivered Henrietta into safe keeping and is a fugitive. Nevertheless he risks his life to return to Elvira who is so shocked that she seems, partially, to regain her senses. But her obviously fragile mental state deeply disturbs Arthur and he refuses to leave her, even when he hears his Puritan enemies approaching, although he knows that capture will mean death. But, just as he is about to be summarily executed, news arrives of Cromwell's victory and the granting of a general amnesty. Elvira's joy finally restores her to sanity, Arthur is a free man and the lovers are united.

Music and Background

Written for Paris, *I Puritani* is generally considered the most sophisticated – though perhaps among the less dramatic – of Bellini's opera scores, with a finer grasp of orchestration (the composer's undeniable weak point) than he showed elsewhere. There is a pervasive militarism in the music, with prominent brass and percussion, and marching rhythms that bear out Bellini's own description of his work here as 'robust' and 'severe'. But there is also brilliance in the vocal writing, which demands a strong quartet of principal singers and, especially, a tenor with good top notes.

Highlights

Elvira's Act II 'Qui la voce' is one of the more affecting mad scenes in Italian opera; and the duet 'Suoni la tromba', also in Act II, is a famously stirring example of Bellini's martial music.

Did You Know?

～ Bellini wrote no comedies. He always chose to place his characters in what he termed *situazioni laceranti* – heart-rending predicaments.
～ George Bernard Shaw disliked the opera intensely, saying that the music 'has so little variety in its cloying rhythms that it vies for dullness with any Italian opera on the stage'.

Recommended Recording

Maria Callas, Giuseppe di Stefano, La Scala Milan/Tullio Serafin. EMI CDS7 47308-8. A 1955 recording in mono, but with Callas in superbly stylish form; not always beautiful but powerfully dramatic.

La Sonnambula
(The Sleepwalker)

FORM: Opera in two acts; in Italian
COMPOSER: Vincenzo Bellini (1801–35)
LIBRETTO: Felice Romani;
after Scribe and Aumer's ballet-pantomime
FIRST PERFORMANCE: Milan, 6 March 1831

Principal Characters

Amina, an orphan ～ **Soprano**
Teresa, her foster-mother ～ **Mezzo-soprano**
Lisa, an innkeeper ～ **Soprano**
Alessio, a villager ～ **Bass**
Elvino, a wealthy landowner ～ **Tenor**
Count Rodolfo, the local lord ～ **Bass**

Synopsis of the Plot

Setting: A Swiss village; early 19th century

ACT I The villagers have gathered together to celebrate the forthcoming betrothal of Amina and Elvino. The only one not joining in is Lisa, who loves Elvino herself, and is not mollified by the unwelcome attentions of Alessio. The marriage contract is signed; Elvino pledges Amina everything he owns and gives her a ring and a bunch of wild flowers. In return, Amina promises him her love. At that moment a handsome stranger in a soldier's uniform arrives on the scene, apparently on his way to the castle. No one recognises Count Rodolfo, who is persuaded by Lisa to stay the night at the inn. As dusk approaches, Teresa warns the villagers to go home, for fear of the white phantom that haunts the area. At the inn Lisa is flirting with Rodolfo in his room; she tells him that his identity has been discovered and the villagers will soon come to offer him their respects. They are interrupted by a noise and Lisa quickly leaves. Amina, sleepwalking, enters the room and Rodolfo realises she must be the 'phantom'. Unwilling to cause her embarrassment, Rodolfo leaves her alone (he exits through the window), just before the villagers crowd in to discover the sleeping Amina in Rodolfo's room. Lisa has thoughtfully brought Elvino and Teresa along to witness her rival's disgrace and the girl is roundly condemned by all before the wedding is cancelled.

ACT II The villagers are on their way to the castle to ask for Rodolfo's help in restoring Amina's reputation. Elvino and Amina come face to face, but he cannot believe she is innocent and furiously wrenches his ring from her finger. Back in the village square Elvino is preparing to marry Lisa when

Rodolfo arrives to try and convince him of Amina's innocence. At that moment Amina herself appears, sleepwalking on the roof before crossing a dangerous bridge, and carrying the flowers, now withered, that Elvino had given her. She speaks of her sadness at her lost love. Elvino, finally convinced, kneels before her and begs her forgiveness; Amina wakes and they are joyfully reconciled.

Music and Background

La Sonnambula is generally considered Bellini's first true masterpiece, and a fine example of the vocal style known as bel canto: a term which literally means 'beautiful song' but implies far more, including an extreme refinement of tone and technique, and an ability to deal with decorative embellishment. For a bel canto composer, Bellini's embellishments are actually rather restrained – he preferred to write in long, elegant phrases – and La Sonnambula is remarkable above all for the lyricism of the music provided for the original incumbent of the title role, Giuditta Pasta, one of the supreme singers of her age and a continuing champion of Bellini's work.

Highlights

Amina's opening cavatina 'Come per me sereno' has beguiling charm; her sleepwalking 'Ah! non credea mirarti' in the closing scene is a touching example of Bellini's extended melody; and her final 'Ah! non giunge' is a brilliant showpiece arguably unsurpassed in all bel canto writing.

Did You Know?

∾ Bel canto heroines commonly go mad, a device used to generate a sense of pathos in the character. Amina's somnambulism is a less extreme equivalent.

∾ The 'dangerous bridge' over which Amina sleepwalks was reputedly added for Jenny Lind.

Recommended Recording

Joan Sutherland, Luciano Pavarotti, National Philharmonic Orchestra/ Richard Bonynge. Decca 417 424-2. The second of Sutherland's two recordings, made in 1980 when her voice was still fresh but more expressive than before. Pavarotti is a hard-to-beat partner.

Alban Berg

(1885–1935)

Wozzeck (1922)
Lulu (1935)

*B*orn in Vienna, Alban Berg was a pupil of Schoenberg who began writing in the opulent post-Mahlerian manner of European composers early in this century and then adopted his teacher's controversial method of making music out of 'tone rows': a technique using sequences of all twelve notes of the chromatic scale in a way that allows no one note greater prominence than any of the others and denies the possibility of a key-centre to anchor the music 'in C', 'in F sharp', or whatever. Berg was never as strict an exponent of this 'serial' method as his teacher, or as his fellow-pupil Anton Webern, which makes him the most accessible of the so-called Second Viennese School of composers. *Wozzeck* and *Lulu* have accordingly acquired the status of modern classics, although they were banned in Berg's own time (the Nazi Third Reich) as degenerate. Berg's other work includes a Violin Concerto written in memory of Alma Mahler's daughter, and the Lyric Suite which contains in cryptic number-code a secret love message to his mistress.

Lulu

FORM: Opera in three acts; in German
COMPOSER: Alban Berg (1885–1935)
LIBRETTO: Alban Berg; from two plays by Frank Wedekind
FIRST PERFORMANCE: (Complete) Paris, 24 February 1979

Principal Characters

Lulu ⚮ **Soprano**
Dr Schön, a newspaper editor ⚮ **Baritone**
Alwa, his son ⚮ **Tenor**
Schigolch, an old man ⚮ **Bass-baritone**

Lulu's admirers and lovers
Countess Geschwitz ⚮ **Mezzo-soprano**
The Painter ⚮ **Tenor**
The Athlete ⚮ **Bass**
The Schoolboy ⚮ **Mezzo-soprano**
The Marquis ⚮ **Tenor**
The Banker ⚮ **Bass**
The Prince ⚮ **Tenor**

Synopsis of the Plot

Setting: Setting: Germany, Paris and London; late 19th century

ACT I Lulu is having her portrait painted as a present, but is caught in a compromising situation with the Painter by her husband, who drops dead from shock. Lulu marries the Painter and is living in some luxury; she has, as Schigolch points out, 'come a long way'. Dr Schön, one of Lulu's lovers, comes to tell her that they must stop seeing each other as he is getting engaged, at which Lulu protests vehemently. After she has gone Schön tells the Painter all about her colourful past and the many names by which she was known to her former lovers. The Painter is so distressed that he kills himself. Free again, Lulu compels Schön to call off his engagement.

ACT II Schön and Lulu are now married, but Schön is consumed with suspicious jealousy over Lulu's many admirers, including his own son, Alwa. Schön overhears Alwa declaring his love for his stepmother and suggests to Lulu that she should end her own life. Lulu, almost distractedly, takes up the gun and shoots Schön.
In a silent, filmed interlude, we learn that Lulu has been jailed for murder. She has contracted cholera, transmitted to her on purpose by Countess Geschwitz, to enable her to escape from the hospital. Lulu, Schigolch and Alwa leave for Paris.

ACT III Lulu is surrounded by a crowd of disreputable characters in a Parisian casino. The Marquis, having failed to blackmail Lulu into joining a Cairo brothel, informs the police of her whereabouts but she manages to escape just in time. Her final home is a dingy attic in a London slum where she supports herself, Alwa and Schigolch by prostitution. They are joined by the faithful Geschwitz. In this final, dark episode of her life Lulu sees Alwa killed by one of her clients before she herself, together with Geschwitz, is murdered by Jack the Ripper.

Music and Background

Lulu is a difficult, abrasive and altogether demanding piece, written for a large orchestra, with a bizarre assortment of characters who give the otherwise dark plot a surreally comic edge. It is constructed entirely from a single row of twelve notes in the closest Berg came to total Serialism. However anarchic it sounds in performance, the score actually works according to meticulously organised formal principles, and for ears accustomed to its sound-world, it presents a curious kind of beauty. Berg died before finishing the orchestration of the last act, and his widow prevented completion of the score by other hands during her lifetime. As a result, *Lulu* had no complete staging until 1979.

Highlights

For anyone less than steeped in its idiom, the big moments of *Lulu* will be dramatic rather than musical, including the pivotal film sequence in Act II (where the second half is supposed to be a palindromic mirror-image of the first), and the horrendous death of Lulu at the end (a gift for directors with a lurid imagination).

Did You Know?

🐚 Berg's widow forbade completion of the score for personal reasons: she believed Lulu – probably correctly – to be an oblique portrait of that same lover who features in the code of the Lyric Suite.

Recommended Recording

Teresa Stratas, Franz Mazura, Kenneth Riegel, Paris Opera/Pierre Boulez. DG 415 489-2. A lucid account of the complete score by the cast and conductor responsible for the 1979 premiere.

Wozzeck

FORM: Opera in three acts; in German
COMPOSER: Alban Berg (1885–1935)
LIBRETTO: Alban Berg; after Georg Büchner's play
FIRST PERFORMANCE: Berlin, 14 December 1925

Principal Characters

Wozzek, a soldier ❧ **Baritone**
Marie, his common-law wife ❧ **Soprano**
Andres, Wozzek's friend ❧ **Tenor**
Drum-Major ❧ **Tenor**
Doctor ❧ **Bass**
Captain ❧ **Tenor**
An Idiot ❧ **Tenor**

Synopsis of the Plot

Setting: Outside a garrison town; around 1820

ACT I While Wozzeck is shaving him, the Captain amuses himself by teasing the soldier who agrees with everything the officer says until the Captain suggests that Wozzeck, with a mistress and a child, has no principles. Wozzeck's response to this is that only the rich can afford principles. Later, Wozzeck and Andres are cutting sticks in a field when Wozzeck suddenly hallucinates, seeing the whole world as if on fire and hearing noises underground. Meanwhile, Marie is at their home, observing the soldiers marching by her window and, in particular, the Drum-Major. Wozzeck bursts in and tries to tell her of his experience in the field, but he frightens her and she rushes out. The next day Wozzeck relates his story to the Doctor, for whom he is acting as a paid 'guinea pig' for the Doctor's bizarre nutritional experiments. The Doctor is delighted at what he sees as the result of his experiments and foresees great fame and fortune for himself. Marie, in the meantime, has succumbed to the blandishments of the Drum-Major.

ACT II The Doctor and the Captain taunt Wozzeck with Marie's infidelity and he rushes home to confront her, threatening her with a knife, which he does not use. Wozzeck follows Marie to a crowded inn garden where he sees her dancing with the Drum-Major. Again, he is about to attack them, but the dancing stops before he can act. Alone and tormented, Wozzeck is joined by an Idiot, who tells Wozzeck that the scene before them, although apparently a happy one, is in fact reeking with blood. In his disturbed state of mind Wozzeck begins to be obsessed by the image of blood. Later, in the barracks, he and the Drum-Major fight and Wozzeck is knocked to the ground.

ACT III Marie, overwhelmed by guilt, walks with Wozzeck in the country. A blood-red moon rises over the scene as Wozzeck draws his knife and stabs her to death. He returns to the inn, where his bloodstained hands are noticed and, as a crowd gathers, he stumbles back to the murder scene to search for the knife. In his tormented mental state he imagines himself to be covered in blood and walks into the pond to clean himself, going deeper and deeper until he drowns. At their home, Wozzeck and Marie's child unconcernedly plays with his hobby-horse before, finding himself alone, he goes in search of his friends.

Music and Background

Easier on the ear than the later *Lulu*, *Wozzeck* is a dissonant score that manages to be lyrically seductive and betray little of the complex formal structures by which everything is governed. Act II is designated, rather clinically, a 'Symphony in Five Moments' and Act III a set of 'Six Inventions', but the writing is vivid, passionate, sympathetic in its treatment of the anti-hero, and disturbing in its sardonic incorporation of popular street music (a device Berg borrowed from Mahler's symphonies and song cycles).

Highlights

The entire score aches with a sense of gathering catastrophe, but Act III, Scene 2, in which Wozzeck kills Marie as the moon rises, is an especially chilling moment; the Act III, Scene 4 interlude after Wozzeck's own death is the climax of the piece; and the vignette of Wozzeck's child murmuring 'hopp hopp, hopp hopp' as he goes on playing is as unsettling an end as that of any opera.

Did You Know?

⚔ The plot of *Wozzeck* is based on a real murder which took place in 1824; a German critic at the first (incomplete) performance 'had the sensation of having been not in a public theatre but in an insane asylum. On the stage, in the orchestra, in the stalls – plain madmen.'
⚔ The opening night was preceded by no fewer than one hundred rehearsals.

Recommended Recording

Eberhard Waechter, Anja Silja, Vienna Philharmonic Orchestra/Christoph von Dohnanyi. Decca 417 348-2. A striking performance from the then husband-and-wife team Dohnanyi and Silja, with Schoenberg's *Erwartung* as a bonus filler.

Hector Berlioz

(1803–69)

Les Francs-Juges (1826)
Benvenuto Cellini (1828)
Les Troyens (1858)
Béatrice et Bénédict (1862)

Berlioz was a dreamer of dreams in the grand Romantic tradition. The son of a French country doctor, he originally studied medicine but abandoned it for music – largely under the spell of Beethoven, who ranked alongside Shakespeare, Virgil and Goethe as the composer's creative idol. Other idols included Harriet Smithson, a Shakespearian actress who became the governing inspiration for Berlioz's vividly (some might say unhealthily) imagined *Symphonie Fantastique* in 1830, his first enduringly great work. Symphonic and choral scores followed – *Harold in Italy*, the *Requiem*, *Roméo et Juliette*, the *Te Deum* – and they became the basis of his fame, which originated abroad rather than in France. But his chief interest was always the stage, and the tragedy of his creative life was that his operas failed to find support. *Les Francs-Juges* was never performed, *Benvenuto Cellini* was taken off after four nights and only the last two Acts of *Les Troyens* reached the stage. *Béatrice et Bénédict*, which was welcomed in Germany, had no Paris production until well after Berlioz's death. *La Damnation de Faust* (1846) is sometimes staged as an opera, but was written as a concert work and is probably best left as such.

Béatrice et Bénédict
(Beatrice and Benedick)

FORM: Opera in two acts; in French
COMPOSER: Hector Berlioz (1803–69)
LIBRETTO: Hector Berlioz;
after Shakespeare's play *Much Ado About Nothing*
FIRST PERFORMANCE: Baden-Baden, 9 August 1862

Principal Characters

Don Pedro, a general 〜 **Bass**
Béatrice, Don Pedro's niece 〜 **Mezzo-soprano**
Héro, Don Pedro's daughter 〜 **Soprano**
Bénédict, an officer 〜 **Tenor**
Claudio, an officer 〜 **Baritone**
Somarone, an orchestral conductor 〜 **Bass-baritone**

Synopsis of the Plot

Setting: Messina, Italy; around 1700

ACT I The townspeople gather to celebrate Don Pedro's defeat of the
Moors. Héro is joyfully anticipating the return of her beloved, Claudio, but
her cousin, Béatrice, is not so happy to contemplate the return of Bénédict,
with whom she has a much more volatile relationship, one in which neither
is willing to admit their true feelings for each other. The victorious forces
soon arrive and Héro and Claudio happily arrange their wedding for that very
evening. They encourage Bénédict to do the same, but he scoffs at the idea
of marriage and declares that, if he is ever foolish enough to do such a thing,
they can hang a banner on his roof announcing 'Here is Bénédict, the
married man'. This prompts Don Pedro and Claudio to hatch a plot to
achieve just that. Later, Bénédict, hiding behind a hedge, hears an arranged
conversation in which Béatrice confesses that she is very much in love with
him – and Béatrice subsequently hears Bénédict say the same about his
feelings for her. Their ideas on marriage now begin to change.

ACT II The wedding feast is well underway and, offstage, Somarone is
encouraged to perform a noisy drinking song. In a quiet moment Béatrice
again admits her true feelings for Bénédict and even welcomes the emotions
she had for so long denied. But old habits die hard and when Bénédict
appears she cannot resist baiting him in the usual way, although it is clear
that a new tenderness underlies their ripostes. Claudio and Héro sign the
marriage contract. The scribe has, by chance, another contract to hand and

asks if anyone else wants to make use of it. Béatrice and Bénédict agree to take each other – out of pity, of course – and the banner is duly produced!

Music and Background

Berlioz's last major work, *Béatrice et Bénédict* is nonetheless a short opera (one and a half hours), lightly written – 'with the point of a needle', as its composer said. It has brief scenes of spoken dialogue which link the musical numbers. Shakespeare's *Much Ado About Nothing* is pared down to its romantic core, and wit gives way to something like a prefiguring of balmy Hollywood enchantment in the duo-nocturne at the end of Act I.

Highlights

The two trios 'Me marier' and 'Je vais d'un coeur aimant', and the brilliant closing duet.

Did You Know?

~ *Béatrice et Bénédict* isn't the only operatic setting of Shakespeare Berlioz made. He adapted words from *The Merchant of Venice* to fit into the big love duet of *Les Troyens*.

~ The composer recounted that some critics praised the music of *Béatrice et Bénédict* 'but found the spoken dialogue "dull", even though it was taken almost word for word from Shakespeare's play!'

~ Berlioz was sent to Paris by his parents to study medicine, but he enrolled at the Conservatory of Music instead; he played no instrument professionally and supported himself through journalism, which he hated.

Recommended Recording

Susan Graham, Jean-Luc Viala, Sylvia McNair, Opéra de Lyon/John Nelson. Erato 2292 45773-2. Clean, fresh sound with light young voices, claiming a slight edge over the old Philips recording with Janet Baker and Colin Davis.

Les Troyens
(The Trojans)

FORM: Opera in five acts; in French
COMPOSER: Hector Berlioz (1803–69)
LIBRETTO: Hector Berlioz; after Virgil's *Aeneid*
FIRST PERFORMANCE: (Complete) Karlsruhe,
6–7 December 1890

Principal Characters

Aeneas, a Trojan warrior ᴥ **Tenor**
Dido, Queen of Carthage ᴥ **Mezzo-soprano**
Narbal, Dido's minister ᴥ **Bass**
Iopas, Carthaginian poet ᴥ **Tenor**
Cassandra, King Priam's daughter ᴥ **Soprano**

Note: Berlioz intended his opera to be heard on one evening (performance time is approximately four and a half hours), but it is often divided into two parts: Part I, *La Prise de Troie* (The Capture of Troy), Acts I and II; Part II, *Les Troyens à Carthage* (The Trojans at Carthage), Acts III, IV and V.

Synopsis of the Plot

Setting: Troy (Acts I and II) and Carthage (Acts III–V);
it is nine years into the Trojan War and the Greeks have retreated,
leaving behind the wooden horse on the beach

ACT I The people are celebrating their new-found freedom, ignoring Cassandra's predictions of forthcoming disaster. Even Coroebus, her lover, believes she is deranged and rejects her attempts to encourage him to leave the city. Suddenly Aeneas interrupts the merry-making and relates the dreadful events that have just taken place on the seashore. Laocoön, the priest, deeply suspicious of the wooden horse, threw a spear into its side; immediately two serpents rose out of the sea and swallowed him. Aeneas suggests that this is a sign that Pallas, to whom the horse is dedicated, was greatly displeased by Laocoön's action. King Priam orders the horse to be brought within the city walls, for safety. Cassandra, alone, is filled with misgivings as the horse, despite the unmistakable sound of the clash of weapons within it, is brought to Troy.

ACT II Aeneas is asleep in his armour but wakes on the appearance of the ghost of Hector, the dead king of Troy. Hector tells him that Troy has fallen and that Aeneas must take his son, Ascanius, to Italy to found a new empire. Pentheus, the priest, then arrives, bringing with him Troy's sacred idols, and tells Aeneas how the Greek soldiers emerged from the horse at night to sack the city; Troy is on fire and King Priam is dead. Aeneas calls his men to arms and leaves to defend the citadel. In the city Cassandra tells the Trojan women that Aeneas has escaped and has taken King Priam's treasure with him. As the Greeks storm their final refuge Cassandra stabs herself and urges the women to follow her example.

ACT III The Carthaginians are celebrating the great progress they have made in building their new city, led by their widowed queen, Dido. Iopas, the poet, interrupts their festivities to report the arrival of a foreign fleet. Dido welcomes the strangers and offers them hospitality, not recognising the disguised Aeneas. Suddenly, Narbal comes in with the news that the Numidian enemy, Iarbas, has invaded Carthaginian territory and is laying waste the countryside. Aeneas, throwing off his disguise, offers his men and weapons in Dido's service. Dido, instantly smitten by the sight of this legendary hero, accepts with alacrity.

ACT IV This act either opens or closes with The Royal Hunt and Storm, a musical interlude in which Dido, as Diana the Huntress, and Aeneas shelter in a cave where they express the ecstasy of their mutual love.
Aeneas has beaten off the Numidian threat and is celebrating his victory with Dido. The entertainments lack interest for the queen who asks Aeneas to tell her the tale of Andromache, the prisoner who yielded to her captor, Pyrrhus, and married him. The idea of remarriage, previously scorned by Dido, now seems more attractive. But as the two lovers leave, the statue of Mars, illuminated by a shaft of moonlight, breathes the one word that can ruin their hopes of a life together: 'Italy'.

ACT V Aeneas, torn between his destiny and his love for Dido, sees the ghosts of Priam, Coroebus, Cassandra and Hector – each in turn urging him to leave Carthage. He orders his men to make ready to sail and, in spite of Dido's heartbroken pleas, sets sail for Italy and the new empire. Dido's anguish turns to fury and she orders everything associated with the Trojans to be burnt on a pyre. But her bitterness soon turns again to heartbreak and she determines to die, using Aeneas's discarded sword to stab herself. As she dies she sees, prophetically, that she will be avenged by the Carthaginian hero, Hannibal, but she also has a vision of the coming Roman pre-eminence.

Music and Background

The grandest of grand operas, *Les Troyens* is in every sense an epic, and until comparatively recently it was the practice to spread the five acts over two nights. Berlioz never saw it staged on a single night as he intended – it was beyond the scope of what could be done in France at the time – and his wishes weren't fulfilled until a famous, more or less complete production at Covent Garden in 1957. Undoubtedly the composer's masterpiece, richly orchestrated and carefully plotted throughout its considerable duration, it contrasts abrasive war-music in the first two (Trojan) acts with radiant, sometimes rather lurid warmth in the next three (Carthage) and is basically the sort of music that you either love or loathe. Half-measures don't apply to anything so monumental.

Highlights

The Act IV love duet for Dido and Aeneas, 'Nuit d'ivresse et d'exstase infinie', is the great moment of the score. At the start of Act V comes an exquisite set-piece of longing for home, 'Vallon sonore', for the otherwise small role of a young sailor, Hylas. And between Acts IV and V (though Berlioz originally had it between Acts III and IV) is an orchestral intermezzo, the 'Royal Hunt and Storm', which is often played by itself as a concert piece.

Did You Know?

~ Berlioz had great difficulty in getting the opera performed, especially after rumours that it lasted eight hours, and the critics judged it severely, saying that such music could not and should not be allowed.

~ Nevertheless, people did enjoy *Les Troyens* and the composer himself recounted that, shortly after the first performance, he 'was stopped in the street by strangers who wished to shake hands with me and thank me for having composed it. Was not that ample recompense for the sneers of my enemies?'

~ Berlioz identified the young sailor, Hylas, with his own son Louis, and certainly had Louis in mind as he wrote that famous song of homesickness.

Recommended Recording

Jon Vickers, Josephine Veasy, Royal Opera Covent Garden/Colin Davis. Philips 416 432-2. A classic recording conducted by the most authoritative (and loving) Berlioz champion of modern times.

Leonard Bernstein

(1918–90)

Trouble in Tahiti (1952)
Candide (1956)
West Side Story (1957)
A Quiet Place (**1983**)

Bernstein was one of the great personalities and true bridge-builders of 20th-century music: a conducting, composing, all-round American icon whose work (usually in emotional overdrive) crossed the divide between high art and popular entertainment with a panache that only Gershwin managed before him. The son of Russian-Jewish immigrants to the United States, he made headlines after his conducting debut with the New York Philharmonic Orchestra and went on to run the NYPO for twelve exuberant years, attracting special acclaim for his uniquely heart-on-sleeve performances of Mahler. His first mature stage works were ballets (*Fancy Free, Facsimile*) and musical comedy (*On the Town*) in the 1940s. The short, one-act *Trouble in Tahiti* came out of those worlds – half-opera, half-Broadway – as did *Candide* and *West Side Story*, which contain the same sort of hybrid ingredients but in different proportions, and the *Mass* of 1971 which is the most eclectically uncategorisable score of all, uncomfortably strung between theatre, liturgy and stale '60s idealism. Jewish identity featured prominently in two of his three symphonies, and in the ballet *Dybbuk*.

Candide

FORM: Operetta in two acts; in English
COMPOSER: Leonard Bernstein (1918–90)
LIBRETTO: Lillian Hellman; after Voltaire's novel
FIRST PERFORMANCE: Boston, 29 October 1956

Principal Characters

Candide, a Westphalian youth ∾ Tenor
Cunegonde, his beloved ∾ Soprano

Dr Pangloss, Candide's tutor ～ **Baritone**
Maximilian, Cunegonde's brother ～ **Baritone**
Paquette, Cunegonde's maid ～ **Mezzo-soprano**
Old Lady ～ **Soprano**

Note: *Candide* was a critical failure when it was first produced in 1956 and there have been several revised versions. The most notable of these was the 1973 version, with a new libretto by Hugh Wheeler. New scenes were introduced, some drawn from Voltaire's novel, others invented. A 1989 concert version, conducted by Bernstein and performed in London, contains elements from various earlier revisions and is the last form of the work to which the composer gave his approval.

Synopsis of the Plot

The details of the plot vary considerably between the different versions, but in all cases the story concerns the young Candide, who has been taught by Dr Pangloss that 'everything happens for the best in the best of all possible worlds'. Armed with this unshakeable optimism, Candide sets out on his travels and experiences an endless series of disasters and difficulties, including war, rape, the apparent loss of Cunegonde, betrayal and the disappearance of Dr Pangloss at the hands of the Spanish Inquisition. Candide then leaves Europe in the company of an Old Lady and explores the New World and Eldorado. On his way back the intrepid traveller survives a shipwreck and returns, at last, to his Westphalian home. Here Candide acknowledges his disillusionment with Dr Pangloss's theories and decides that, even though the world may be full of evil, we must all try to build our own lives on good, honest principles.

Music and Background

The overture to *Candide* could almost have been Bernstein's signature tune – brilliant, up-tempo, highly charged – and it opens a piece whose hybrid nature as an up-market, philosophical, operatic operetta always caused problems in casting, staging and selling it to the public. Both words and music underwent extensive revisions over thirty years, with a conveyor belt of collaborating librettists. But the basic idea of high-spirited parody numbers survived in what amounts to an exhilarating mass-rape of European music history, buoyant with catchy, quick-change rhythms. The role of Cunegonde demands a soprano with the coloratura (i.e. embellishing) prowess of a *prima donna assoluta*; and the score is alive with character parts which are a gift to serious and maybe superannuated opera stars who want to let whatever is left of their hair down.

Highlights

Cunegonde's exquisitely decorative jewel song 'Glitter and be gay' invariably stops the show, although the demands it makes of the singer have no doubt on many an occasion stopped the show ever happening. Candide's two Act I

'Meditations' supply pathos. The big choral finale, 'Make our garden grow', is superior Hollywood and deeply moving.

Did You Know?

∼ Lillian Hellman's original libretto for *Candide* presented Voltaire's parable on the evils of paternalistic government as a veiled attack on the McCarthy witchhunt trials.

Recommended Recording

June Andersen, Jerry Hadley, Christa Ludwig, Nicolai Gedda, London Symphony Orchestra/Leonard Bernstein. DG 429 734-2. The legacy of two spectacular concert performances at the Barbican in 1989, with contributions from the Broadway veteran Adolph Green and a lot of chutzpah.

A Quiet Place

FORM: Opera in one act; in English
COMPOSER: Leonard Bernstein (1918–90)
LIBRETTO: Stephen Wadsworth
FIRST PERFORMANCE: Milan, 17 June 1983

Principal Characters

Sam, the father ∼ **Baritone**
Sam Junior, his son ∼ **Baritone**
Dede, Sam's daughter ∼ **Soprano**
François, Dede's husband ∼ **Tenor**

Synopsis of the Plot

Setting: Contemporary America

The funeral of Sam's wife, Dinah, killed in a car crash, brings together the estranged members of her family: Sam Junior, his sister and her husband,

François, who at one time was Sam Junior's lover. Underlying tensions quickly surface and Junior's mental instability becomes apparent. In the evening the four recall the history of their relationships with each other and with their dead mother. The next morning, after breakfast and games in the garden (the 'quiet place'), they find that their hostility has given way to reconciliation.

Music and Background

The operatic equivalent of a Russian doll, *A Quiet Place* is actually one piece inside another: most of the middle act is the self-contained *Trouble in Tahiti* written thirty years earlier, and its music sounds markedly different to what comes before and after. The Tahiti sections are in lyrical, near-Broadway style, with sardonic contributions from a 1950s close-harmony trio who hymn the idealised joys of suburban life while the suburban characters, Dinah and Sam, demonstrate the bleak realities. The surrounding sections are musically more complex, less direct and less memorable – although Bernstein's sense of melody is always there, not far below the surface.

Highlights

Almost all the best writing comes in the middle, Tahiti act, climaxing in a virtuoso comic monologue for Dinah, 'Island Magic', that would be pure Broadway but for its rhythmic complications, and finishing on a soaring, seriously dramatic duet, 'Is there a day or a night?', which is Bernstein at his soul-searing best.

Did You Know?

🔊 Bernstein wrote the libretto for *Trouble in Tahiti* himself, and the story is based on his own childhood memories, incorporating a peculiarly unflattering portrait of his parents.

Recommended Recording

Chester Ludgin, Beverly Morgan, Wendy White, Edward Crafts, Austrian Radio Symphony Orchestra/Leonard Bernstein. DG 419 761-1/2. The only one, recorded live at the Vienna Staatsoper.

Harrison Birtwistle

(1934–)

Punch and Judy (1967)
Down by the Greenwood Side (1969)
The Mask of Orpheus (1984)
Yan Tan Tethera (1984)
Gawain (1991)
The Second Mrs Kong (1994)

Birtwistle's tough, dense, and often abrasively loud music has made him a sort of Public Enemy for some concert-goers, a fair number of whom filled the correspondence pages of British newspapers with letters of complaint after his raucous concerto for saxophone and percussion, *Panic*, was premiered at the last night of the 1995 Proms. But others find him a grainy, granite-hard successor to the English Pastoral composers of the early 20th century, with an underlying lyricism in his writing. And no one could deny that Birtwistle's music is dramatic. Even his concert works have ritualistic theatre elements, and his stage works proper are usually based on mythical subjects which he adapts to the ritualised kind of story-telling which he has made his own, with events that repeat in cycles rather than unfold in linear terms. *The Mask of Orpheus*, for example, is a vast multimedia spectacle with electronic effects and a highly complex formal structure which recounts the myth of Orpheus in all its varying forms and different endings. Brought up in Manchester, Birtwistle was a student there at the same time as Peter Maxwell Davies and the careers of the two composers have progressed largely in tandem. Both now have knighthoods, and jockey for position as the leading creative figure in British music after Michael Tippett.

Gawain

FORM: Opera in two acts; in English
COMPOSER: Harrison Birtwistle (1934–)
LIBRETTO: David Harsent; from an anonymous 14th-century poem
FIRST PERFORMANCE: London, 30 May 1991

Principal Characters

Gawain, a knight and King Arthur's nephew ∞ **Baritone**
Morgan le Fay, a sorceress ∞ **Soprano**
Green Knight/Bertilak ∞ **Bass**
Lady de Hautdesert, Bertilak's wife ∞ **Mezzo-soprano**

Synopsis of the Plot

Setting: Arthurian Britain

ACT I While Arthur and his court are celebrating Christmas, the sorceress, Morgan le Fay, and her accomplice, Lady de Hautdesert, plan to undermine the court's complacency and self-regard. The king is bored. Morgan le Fay promises him excitement. At that moment a mysterious Green Knight arrives with a challenge: he will allow himself to be beheaded but the knight who does the deed must present himself at the Green Chapel in a year and a day, and submit to a similar blow. Gawain accepts the challenge; he decapitates the Green Knight who, to everyone's amazement, gets up and leaves with his head under his arm. The act concludes with a masque during which Gawain is prepared, spiritually, for his journey to the Green Chapel and his potentially fatal meeting with the Green Knight.

ACT II Gawain, on his way to the Green Chapel, finds shelter in the castle of Bertilak de Hautdesert. Bertilak issues him with another challenge: he will hunt for three days and exchange all he has caught for what Gawain can acquire in the castle. Spurred on by Morgan le Fay, Lady de Hautdesert tries to seduce Gawain while her husband is away. She gives him a sash with magical properties to protect him from death; he keeps it for his forthcoming confrontation with the Green Knight. Gawain is struck three times by the Knight, but is only grazed, and the Knight reveals himself to be Gawain's host, Bertilak de Hautdesert. Gawain returns to Arthur's court to be greeted as a hero. But knowing the truth to be otherwise – that he only survived the ordeal through the magic of the sash – he rejects the court's empty praise and demands for tales of bravery and valour. The collective morale of the Round Table is punctured, and Morgan le Fay, who plotted all this, rejoices in her victory.

Music and Background

It's no use pretending that this is easy listening. It isn't; and the orchestral textures are so Wagnerian in scale and weight that you have to pay very careful attention to catch any of the words in performance. There are times when the whole score seems like a great machine grinding relentlessly away in an unbroken flow of (very noisy) sound. But repeated listening helps to sort out what's going on – as is the case with any opera – and reveals the poetry within the punishment. Otherwise, *Gawain* packs a massive punch on stage; and the ritual theatre of the turning of the seasons at the end of Act I is a good example of the cyclic, ceremonial preoccupations of the composer.

Highlights

The arrival of the Green Knight on what Birtwistle calls a 'noble pantomime horse' is bizarre but breathtaking: you hear clip-clopping noises from the orchestra and in any other circumstance they might make you laugh. But not here. The effect is spine-tingling and awesome. For an example of how memorably melodic Birtwistle *can* be when he chooses, try Gawain's repeated cries of 'I'm not that hero' in the final scene.

Did You Know?

≈ Many commentators consider *Gawain* one of the supreme achievements of late 20th-century opera.

Recommended Recording

Francois Le Roux, John Tomlinson, Marie Angel, Royal Opera, Covent Garden/ Elgar Howarth. Collins Classics 7041-2. The only recording, taken live from the Covent Garden performances.

Punch and Judy

FORM: Opera in one act; in English
COMPOSER: Harrison Birtwistle (1934–)
LIBRETTO: Stephen Pruslin
FIRST PERFORMANCE: Aldeburgh, 8 June 1968

Principal Characters

Punch ～ High baritone
Judy/Fortune Teller ～ Mezzo-soprano
Pretty Polly/Witch ～ High soprano
Choregos/Jack Ketch ～ Baritone
Lawyer ～ High tenor
Doctor ～ Deep bass

Note: *Punch and Judy* takes the form of a prologue, four scenes and an epilogue, during which a violent re-enactment of the traditional Punch and Judy puppet story takes place.

Synopsis of the Plot

PROLOGUE The Choregos welcomes the audience.

SCENE 1 Punch rocks the baby and sings it a somewhat threatening lullaby before tossing it on the fire. When Judy comes in, Punch leads her to the Altar of Murder where he stabs her before the Choregos takes her to the gibbet. Punch then sets off on Horsey to find Pretty Polly, whom he discovers sitting on a pedestal under a green spotlight. Punch serenades Polly and presents her with a huge sunflower, but she is unimpressed, especially as the sunflower is damaged by the fire in which the baby died.

SCENE 2 Punch is confronted with his crime by the Lawyer and the Doctor. But Punch is too clever for them and leads them both to the Altar of Murder where he stabs the Doctor with a gigantic syringe and the Lawyer with a quill pen. They are both taken to the gibbet and Punch resumes his search for Pretty Polly. This time he finds her under a red spotlight, but again she refuses his gift, a jewel, because it is tainted by the suffering of Punch's victims.

SCENE 3 The Choregos enters into the action and confronts Punch, but he, too, must die – sawn to death inside a double bass case. The death of the Choregos precipitates Punch into a nightmare, at the end of which he is beaten and taunted as he is confronted with his crimes. Resuming his search, Punch finds Pretty Polly's pedestal, empty, under a blue spotlight.

SCENE 4 Punch is imprisoned and under sentence of death, but he tricks the Choregos, disguised as Jack Ketch, the hangman, into putting his own head into the noose. For this unintentional good deed Punch is reunited with Pretty Polly (bathed in white light), the gallows is transformed into a maypole and everyone (except the Choregos) is happy.

EPILOGUE The Choregos brings the proceedings to a close.

Music and Background

Punch and Judy tells a violently anarchic story in terms of the stylised ritual order of ancient Greek drama – hence the presence of a 'Choregos' (i.e. the Punch and Judy man) to present and stage-manage the action. All the music comes in self-contained, sometimes extremely short numbers strung together in the manner of Baroque opera and oratorio, with Bach's *St Matthew Passion* as an admitted model. But the ultimate sound world of *Punch and Judy* is abrasively remote from Bach, with the small, on-stage band of just fifteen instruments often screaming shrilly at the far extremities of their pitch. Determined listeners appreciate its brilliant game-like invention and the sheer energy with which Birtwistle batters their ears.

Highlights

Hard to say, except that you need to catch onto the repeating patterns and sequences that work like aural signposts through the score. And there *are* windows of lyricism, as well as the relief of genuine jokes.

Did You Know?

At *Punch and Judy*'s first performance, in the 1968 Aldeburgh Festival, Benjamin Britten and Peter Pears famously walked out.

Recommended Recording

Phyllis Bryn-Julson, Jan de Gaetani, Philip Langridge, Stephen Roberts, London Sinfonietta/David Atherton. Decca Headline HEAD 24/5.

Georges Bizet

(1838–75)

La Maison du Docteur (1855)
Le Docteur Miracle (1857)
Don Procopio (1859)
Ivan IV (1863)
Les Pêcheurs de Perles (1863)
La Jolie Fille de Perth (1867)
Djamileh (1872)
Carmen (1875)

*B*izet's short life – he died at thirty-six – was beset by disasters, disappointments, self-destroyed scores and abandoned projects, and although he wrote one of the most celebrated operas in the history of the medium, he never lived to see the measure of *Carmen*'s success. His interest in opera began early, while he was still studying in Paris with Halévy and (privately but influentially) Gounod, and his first stage works were more Italianate than French, modelled after Donizetti and Rossini. Later scores attracted the criticism that they were 'Wagnerian', although it's hard to see why. Apart from *Carmen*, only one other opera, *Les Pêcheurs de Perles*, has survived in repertory, along with a mere handful of concert scores, including the youthful Symphony in C (which must be one of the most effective things ever written by a teenager), the suite of incidental music to the play *L'Arlésienne*, and the piano pieces *Jeux d'Enfants*.

Carmen

FORM: Opera in four acts; in French
COMPOSER: Georges Bizet (1838–75)
LIBRETTO: H. Meilhac and L. Halévy; after Prosper Mérimée's story
FIRST PERFORMANCE: Paris, 3 March 1875

Principal Characters

Carmen, a gypsy girl ✒ **Soprano**
Don José, a corporal ✒ **Tenor**
Micaëla, a country girl ✒ **Soprano**
Zuniga, Don José's lieutenant ✒ **Bass**
Escamillo, a toreador ✒ **Baritone**

Synopsis of the Plot

Setting: Seville, Spain; about 1820

ACT I In the square, dominated by a cigarette factory, a group of soldiers are lazily mounting guard when Micaëla arrives, looking for her soldier sweetheart, Don José, and is told to come back later. As Don José and Zuniga march in with the relief guard, the girls emerge from the factory for a break and Carmen is quickly surrounded by admirers. With her eye firmly fixed on José, she warns that loving her is a dangerous game and she tosses him a rose. When everyone has gone, José retrieves the rose and hides it in his tunic. Micaëla returns and is telling José news about his mother when José is informed that Carmen has attacked another girl, and he must arrest and guard her. Left alone with José, Carmen charms him into allowing her to escape.

ACT II Carmen is the centre of admiration at the local inn. Escamillo, the toreador, is particularly captivated by her, as is Zuniga. But when Carmen learns that José, who has been demoted and imprisoned for helping her, is about to be released, she warns them both to go away and not return. José arrives, delighted to be back with his beloved Carmen, who tries to persuade him to throw in his lot with some smugglers with whom she is working. José refuses, but when Zuniga returns and is attacked by Carmen's new friends, he has no alternative but to escape with them.

ACT III In the smugglers' hideaway Carmen and José are becoming increasingly disillusioned with each other. Escamillo comes looking for Carmen and José is forced to fight him. Micaëla, who has been searching for José, pleads with him to go with her to see his dying mother. José agrees, but he warns Carmen that the affair is not yet over.

ACT IV A grand bullfight is about to take place and Carmen enters triumphantly on Escamillo's arm, ignoring warnings that José is in the crowd. Confronted by her rejected lover, she refuses to return to him and throws his ring in his face. Consumed by jealous rage, José stabs her to the heart before giving himself up.

Music and Background

Carmen is written in a form known as *opéra comique*, which means not that it's a comedy but that it mixes song with spoken dialogue, and would have surprised audiences of its time in that it takes the otherwise straightforward 'comique' style to unprecedented levels of perfection and sophistication. Spain was an abiding obsession of French composers from the later 19th century onwards, and *Carmen* is saturated in local colour, with set-piece Spanish dances like the habanera and seguidilla. The orchestration is especially fine – it was praised by later composers like Tchaikovsky and Richard Strauss – and the emphasis on orchestral sound is the one vaguely understandable reason why contemporary critics thought of it as Wagnerian.

Highlights

Arguably every thirty bars! Act I has Carmen's habanera 'L'amour est un oiseau rebelle' and seguidilla 'Près des ramparts de Séville'. Act II introduces Escamillo with his bullish 'Toréador, en garde', and gives Don José his first real chance to shine with the Flower Song: 'La fleur que tu m'avais jetée'. Act III has Carmen's fatalistic foresight of death, 'En vain pour éviter', and Micaëla's enchanting 'Je dis que rien', with a dramatic highlight in José's 'Dût-il m'en coûter la vie'. Act IV begins with the procession to the bull ring.

Did You Know?

The opera was a critical failure at its first performance but Tchaikovsky predicted that within ten years it would be the most popular opera in the world.

Oscar Hammerstein II turned the opera into an American wartime musical called *Carmen Jones*. Adapted for cinema in 1954, the title role was played by Dorothy Dandridge miming to the voice of Marilyn Horne.

Recommended Recording

Agnes Baltsa, José Carreras, Katia Ricciarelli, José van Dam, Berlin Philharmonic Orchestra/Herbert von Karajan. DG 410 088-2. A hard choice when there are so many alternatives – including Maria Callas (EMI), Marilyn Horne (DG) and Teresa Berganza (DG) – but this is a near-flawless cast, with Baltsa on devastating form, before the voice got raw.

Les Pêcheurs de Perles
(The Pearl Fishers)

FORM: Opera in three acts; in French
COMPOSER: Georges Bizet (1838–75)
LIBRETTO: M. Carré and E. Cormon
FIRST PERFORMANCE: Paris, 30 September 1863

Principal Characters

Leïla, a Brahman priestess ◈ **Soprano**
Zurga, the fishermen's leader ◈ **Baritone**
Nadir, a fisherman ◈ **Tenor**
Nourabad, a Brahman high priest ◈ **Bass**

Synopsis of the Plot

Setting: Ceylon (Sri Lanka); ancient times

ACT I The fishermen have gathered on the beach to choose their new leader and to celebrate the occasion with singing and dancing. Zurga is chosen as their chief and, to his delight, his old friend Nadir arrives on the scene. Zurga and Nadir recall old times together, particularly their rivalry for the love of Leïla. They are pleased, however, that in spite of this, their sworn oath of friendship for each other has never been broken. A boat arrives, bringing with it a heavily-veiled priestess, who has come to undertake a vigil and to pray for the fishermen's safety at sea. The priestess is sworn to strict vows of chastity, on pain of death, and Zurga forbids anyone to approach her. The priestess is, of course, Leïla, and she and Nadir recognise each other, rekindling their lost love.

ACT II Leïla and Nourabad are in a ruined temple and Nourabad reminds her of her vows. Leïla reassures him that she will not break her promises, reminding him of how she once risked death to protect a fugitive, whose gold chain she still wears. But when Nourabad leaves, she sings of her love for Nadir. In a moment he is beside her and they acknowledge their passion, before Leïla persuades Nadir to leave. Unfortunately he is seen by Nourabad and quickly captured. Leïla and Nadir are brought before Zurga who is inclined to be lenient – until he recognises Leïla and accuses Nadir of further treachery.

ACT III The storm outside echoes Zurga's restlessness as he tries to decide what to do. Leïla begs him to pardon Nadir, but Zurga's jealousy prevents him from doing so. Finally Leïla gives Zurga her gold chain and asks him to send it to her mother, after she is dead. The funeral pyre is ready and Leïla and Nadir are about to die, when someone sees the glow of fire in the distance – the camp is in flames! In the commotion Zurga admits that he set fire to the camp because Leïla saved his life once – it was he who gave her the chain long ago. Zurga releases Leïla and Nadir and they go, leaving him alone to face Nourabad, who has overheard everything, and the wrath of the people.

Music and Background

This is an opera that exists in varying editions made after Bizet's death, and it isn't hard to understand why the score fell prey to other hands. Its quality is uneven – Bizet called it an 'honourable, brilliant failure' – and there are longueurs that combine with a lamentably feeble plot to make the piece, in parts, almost unbearable. But there are also moments of luxuriant, Gounod-indebted melody that show the composer at his lyrical best. You just have to take the rough with the smooth.

Highlights

The Act I tenor-baritone duet , 'Au fond du temple saint', ranks high among the all-time favourite opera pops items. Nothing else in the score quite compares with it, but Nadir's Act I romance, 'Je crois entendre encore', is a hypnotic melody, magically orchestrated.

Did You Know?

 Les Pêcheurs de Perles was the last thing Hector Berlioz reviewed before resigning his job as a Parisian music critic. He wrote that it did Bizet 'the greatest honour'.
 On the other hand, George Bernard Shaw thought little of the opera, dismissing it as a 'pretty poem'.

Recommended Recording

Barbara Hendricks, John Aler, Gino Quilico, Toulouse Capitole Choir and Orchestra/Michel Plasson. EMI CDS7 49837-2. Not the *most* exciting performances imaginable, but nothing better has emerged on disc in recent years.

Arrigo Boito
(1842–1918)

Mefistofele (1867)
Nerone (1918)

*B*oito was the very model of a literate, late 19th-century Italian polymath, and his lasting significance to opera is as much a matter of his words as of his music. As a young man he provided Verdi with the text for a 'Hymn of the Nations', and some twenty years later (after a falling-out and reconciliation between them) wrote the libretti for three of Verdi's greatest operas: the revised *Simon Boccanegra*, *Otello* and *Falstaff*. It proved a collaboration almost without equal in opera history; and you could argue that Boito's treatment of the Othello story is dramatically more effective than the original Shakespeare. As a composer he was never on such sure ground. *Mefistofele* occupied him for years, from when he was a student, and its premiere was a fiasco, undermined by its own ambitions. *Nerone* was similarly a work-in-progress for years, and left incomplete at his death.

Mefistofele

FORM: Opera in a Prologue, four acts and an Epilogue; in Italian
COMPOSER: Arrigo Boito (1842–1918)
LIBRETTO: Arrigo Boito, after Goethe's play
FIRST PERFORMANCE: Milan, 5 March 1868

Principal Characters

Mefistofele ∿ Bass
Faust, a scholar ∿ Tenor
Margherita, a young girl ∿ Soprano
Marta, her neighbour ∿ Mezzo-soprano
Elena (Helen of Troy) ∿ Soprano

Synopsis of the Plot

Setting: Heaven, 16th-century Frankfurt, Classical Greece

PROLOGUE In heaven Mefistofele wagers with God that he can gain possession of Faust's soul.

ACT I It is Easter Sunday and Faust is observing the celebrations. Among the crowds he notices a strange, grey monk, who, unseen by Faust, follows him to his home. As Faust begins to study his Bible, the monk makes himself known and, as Mefistofele, quickly persuades Faust to promise him his soul in exchange for renewed youth and Mefistofele's services.

ACT II Faust meets Margherita and successfully seduces her, giving her a sleeping potion to give to her mother so that they will not be disturbed. Then Faust accompanies Mefistofele to the frenzied *Walpurgisnacht* (Witches' Sabbath) celebrations in the Harz mountains. But as the dancing becomes wilder and wilder Faust suddenly sees a vision of Margherita with a red ring round her neck.

ACT III Margherita is in a condemned cell, convicted of drowning the baby she has borne Faust and poisoning her mother. Mefistofele brings Faust to see her and they talk of escaping, but when she recognises Mefistofele as the Devil, Margherita rejects Faust and dies, praying for forgiveness, and Mefistofele drags Faust away.

ACT IV Mefistofele transports Faust back to classical Greece where he spends a rapturous time with the beautiful Helen of Troy.

EPILOGUE Now aged and alone, Faust reflects on the pointlessness of his experiences; he turns to the Gospels to give him strength and courage to resist Mefistofele, who offers him ever more attractive adventures. As Faust dies, praying for salvation, heaven claims its victory over the Devil, who shouts his continuing defiance.

Music and Background

As originally planned, *Mefistofele* was a very long and very radical score, intended to fix Italian opera on what Boito thought should be its true path. But the devastating failure of the premiere caused him to subject the piece to massive revisions, scaling it down in every way and leaving something more conventional. A general response is that the music is uneven and doesn't convincingly knit the piece into a whole, but it makes a strong vehicle for a good bass, and has been associated with some of the greatest bass voices of modern times – notably Chaliapin in the first years of this century.

Highlights

Faust's 'Dai campi, dai prati' and Mefistofele's 'Son lo spirito' dominate Act I. Margherita's lament 'L'altra notte' makes a poignant opening to Act III, whose Prison Scene is arguably the best-written section of the whole score.

Did You Know?

✏ At the disastrous opening night the opera continued until well after midnight.

✏ *Mefistofele* treats the same subject as Gounod's *Faust* but includes more of the philosophical context which Goethe originally gave to the central love-interest.

Recommended Recording

Nicolai Ghiaurov, Luciano Pavarotti, Mirella Freni, Montserrat Caballé, National Philharmonic Orchestra/ Oliviero de Fabritiis. Decca 410 175-2. A hard-to-beat cast on good form, and the last recording Fabritiis made before he died in 1982.

Alexander Borodin

(1833–87)

Prince Igor (1869–87)

The illegitimate son of a Russian prince, Alexander Borodin was one of the group of composers known as 'The Mighty Handful' or 'The Five' who were largely self-taught and combined their creative work with other careers. Borodin, who described music as 'a pastime, a relaxation from more serious pursuits', was an academic chemist; which explains why his one surviving opera, *Prince Igor*, remained incomplete at his death, despite seventeen years of intermittent work on the score. It was subsequently completed by Rimsky-Korsakov and Glazunov. Apart from *Prince Igor*, Borodin's best-known compositions are his symphonies (two complete, one unfinished) and string quartets, whose tunes were ambushed and recycled into the 1950s musical *Kismet*.

Prince Igor

FORM: Opera in a Prologue and four acts; in Russian
COMPOSER: Alexander Borodin (1833–87)
LIBRETTO: Alexander Borodin; after a sketch by Stasov
FIRST PERFORMANCE: St Petersburg, 4 November 1890

Principal Characters

Igor, Prince of Seversk ☙ **Baritone**
Prince Galitsky, his brother-in-law ☙ **Bass**
Vladimir, Igor's son by his first wife ☙ **Tenor**
Yaroslavna, Igor's second wife ☙ **Soprano**
Khan Konchak, Polovtsian prince ☙ **Bass**
Konchakovna, Khan Konchak's daughter ☙ **Mezzo-soprano**
Ovlur, a Christian Polovtsian soldier ☙ **Tenor**

Synopsis of the Plot

Setting: Putivl, a town in the Seversk region,
and in the Polovtsian camp; 1185

PROLOGUE Igor is preparing to leave with his son, Vladimir, on a campaign against the pagan Polovtsian khans. He says a sorrowful farewell to his wife, Yaroslavna, and appoints Prince Galitsky to govern in his absence.

ACT I Yaroslavna misses Igor greatly, but Galitsky and his friends are enjoying themselves – even to the extent of kidnapping a young girl. Yaroslavna, coming to hear of this, argues fiercely with Galitsky and finally forces him to release the girl. After he leaves she receives bad news; Igor has been captured and the Polovtsians are marching on Putivl.

ACT II In the Polovtsian camp Konchakovna is looking forward to seeing the man she loves, Vladimir, who, like his father, has been captured. When he is brought in, under guard, they reaffirm their love for each other, unobserved by all except Ovlur, the Christian convert. Ovlur then offers to help Igor escape, but such a thing is against Igor's code of honour and he refuses. Igor is well-treated by Konchak who tries to persuade him to become an ally; failing in this, Konchak offers him his freedom, in return for his promise not to fight the Polovtsians in future. Igor refuses. Nevertheless, Igor's principles impress Konchak greatly and he entertains him with singing and dancing.

ACT III The Polovtsians are celebrating the victory of an allied army and the Russians realise that their countrymen's situation is becoming desperate. So when Ovlur once again offers to help Igor escape, he accepts. Vladimir, however, is torn between love for his country and love for Konchakovna, who, having failed to persuade him to stay, raises the alarm as Igor and Vladimir are escaping. Igor evades capture but Vladimir does not. However, Konchak is prepared to be magnanimous; he offers Vladimir his freedom and gives him permission to marry Konchakovna.

ACT IV Sitting sadly on the town walls at Putivl, Yaroslavna suddenly sees Prince Igor approaching and is overjoyed. The bells announce his safe return and Igor emerges with his wife to general acclaim, ready once more to lead his people.

Music and Background

The sound-world of *Prince Igor* is colourful, bold, and a striking mix of Russian-Asian influences, with melodies that seem folk-like but are actually original to the composer. Much of the music was written by later hands, especially in Act III, which was left with large sections missing at Borodin's death; and Rimsky-Korsakov's orchestrations add a gloss that wouldn't otherwise have been there. But the impact of this epic, tableau-like piece is undeniable, and it contains some of the best-loved melodies in all opera.

Highlights

More or less the whole of Act II which contains superb arias for most of the principal soloists, including Konchakovna's lovely 'Medlenno dyen ugasal', and finishes with the celebrated 'Polovtsian Dances'.

Did You Know?

⌘ Glazunov's supreme achievement in the completion of *Prince Igor* was to have written out the overture (never committed to manuscript) from his memory of Borodin's improvisation in private performances.

Recommended Recording

Boris Martinovich, Nikola Ghiuselev, Nicolai Ghiaurov, Alexandrina Milcheva, Sofia National Opera/Emil Tchakarov. Sony S3K 44878. The only current recording to include the whole of Act III, and very effective even though it doesn't offer the star names (like Boris Christoff) of rival versions.

Benjamin Britten

(1913–76)

Paul Bunyan (1941)
Peter Grimes (1945)
The Rape of Lucretia (1946)
Albert Herring (1947)
The Little Sweep (1949)
Billy Budd (1951)
Gloriana (1953)
The Turn of the Screw (1954)
Noye's Fludde (1957)
A Midsummer Night's Dream (1960)
Curlew River (1964)
The Burning Fiery Furnace (1966)
The Prodigal Son (1968)
Owen Wingrave (1970)
Death in Venice (1973)

*A*rguably the greatest English composer and certainly one of the
greatest opera composers of the 20th century, Benjamin Britten
was born, raised and effectively spent his whole life on the Suffolk coast
in small-town circumstances which influenced his work – most
obviously *Peter Grimes*, *Albert Herring* and *The Little Sweep*, which are
all set geographically within a few miles of where he lived. The sea is a
recurring theme in his music, along with the world of sleep and dreams,
the sacrifice of innocence, and the idea of the social outcast. But the
determining factor behind almost all these subject choices was his
homosexuality, which found expression – as both a source of anguish
and of profound creative energy – just below the surface of so many
scores. From *Peter Grimes* onwards, his operas usually have a leading
tenor role written originally for his lifelong partner, Peter Pears. Even
beyond the opera stage, Britten was principally a vocal rather than
symphonic composer. Major scores include the *War Requiem*, several
song cycles (of which the best known is the *Serenade for Tenor, Horn
and Strings*), the early *Variations on a Theme of Frank Bridge*, and a
superb sequence of string quartets.

73

Albert Herring

FORM: Opera in three acts; in English
COMPOSER: Benjamin Britten (1913–76)
LIBRETTO: Eric Crozier; after Guy de Maupassant's story
FIRST PERFORMANCE: Glyndebourne, 20 June 1947

Principal Characters

Albert Herring, a greengrocer's assistant ✌ **Tenor**
Mrs Herring, his mother and owner
of the greengrocer's shop ✌ **Mezzo-soprano**
Lady Billows, an elderly lady ✌ **Soprano**
Florence Pike, her housekeeper ✌ **Contralto**
Miss Wordsworth, a schoolteacher ✌ **Soprano**
Mr Gedge, the vicar ✌ **Baritone**
Mr Upfold, the mayor ✌ **Tenor**
Superintendent Budd ✌ **Bass**
Sid, the butcher's assistant ✌ **Baritone**
Nancy, the baker's assistant ✌ **Mezzo-soprano**

Synopsis of the Plot

Setting: Loxford, a Suffolk market town; spring 1900

ACT I The festival committee meet at Lady Billows' house to choose a suitable local girl as Queen of the May. Unfortunately none of the young ladies proposed meets Lady Billows' exacting moral standards, so a revolutionary solution is put forward: the committee will elect a May King instead, and the honour falls on Albert Herring. Albert, meanwhile, is working in his mother's shop where he is being roundly teased by Sid and Nancy for his innocence and his subservience to his domineering mother. Lady Billows and the committee arrive to give him the good news of his election as May King. Albert scoffs at the notion but his mother, her eye on the £25 prize, shouts down his protests.

ACT II The day of Albert's coronation has arrived and, after a church service, he is entertained, fêted and offered advice by everyone from the schoolchildren to Lady Billows. Sid and Nancy, meanwhile, have spiked Albert's lemonade with rum and, the formalities over, he drains his glass as the festivities begin. By the evening Albert is thoroughly tipsy and, encouraged by Sid and Nancy, he sets off in search of some fun.

ACT III It is the afternoon of the following day, but Albert has not returned home. His orange-blossom May King crown has been found, crushed, on the road. Everyone assumes he is dead, gathering dejectedly at Mrs Herring's shop to offer condolences. Suddenly Albert's head appears round the door – and the 'mourners' turn on him and berate him for his behaviour. Albert's account of his drinking and fighting scandalises the worthies, who leave in disgust, but is applauded by Sid and Nancy who recognise Albert's new-found emancipation.

Music and Background

This is a comedy, as alive with musical jokes (like the love-potion motif from Wagner's *Tristan und Isolde* that accompanies the drinking of the lemonade) as with theatrical high spirits. Much of the writing parodies the Englishness of English music, with a virtuosic brilliance in the depiction of character and an extraordinary resourcefulness in what it extracts from a mere thirteen instruments in the orchestra.

Highlights

The love music for Sid and Nancy in Act I; the entire May King Scene in Act II; and the mock threnody 'In the midst of life is death' in Act III.

Did You Know?

🐌 This quintessentially English piece began life as a French short story called *Le Rosier de Madame Husson*.

Recommended Recording

Sylvia Fisher, Peter Pears, April Cantelo, English Chamber Orchestra/ Benjamin Britten. Decca 421 849-2. A period piece but still fresh, and a fine record of British singing in the 1960s.

Billy Budd

FORM: Opera in two acts; in English
COMPOSER: Benjamin Britten (1913–76)
LIBRETTO: E.M. Forster and Eric Crozier;
after Herman Melville's story
FIRST PERFORMANCE: London, 1 December 1951

Principal Characters

Billy Budd, an able seaman ❧ **Baritone**
Captain Vere ❧ **Tenor**
Claggart, Master-at-Arms ❧ **Bass**

Synopsis of the Plot

Setting: At sea on *The Indomitable*; 1797, during the French wars

ACT I Captain Vere, now an old man, reflects on the inseparability of good and evil, recalling in particular the case of Billy Budd.
Billy is one of three men impressed from a passing merchant ship, significantly named *The Rights of Man*, to serve on *The Indomitable*. Both officers and men take to the handsome, cheerful and lively Billy, except for Claggart who takes an instant, and envious, dislike to him and determines to destroy him. Claggart's sadistic ways terrify the weaker members of the crew, who will do anything to avoid further floggings, including carrying out Claggart's instructions to persecute Billy. Billy is warned to be wary of the Master-at-Arms, but he brushes the warning aside, even when he is told that Claggart is fomenting a rumour that Billy wants to start a mutiny.

ACT II As mists swirl around the ship, Claggart warns the captain that there is talk of mutiny, but before he can implicate Billy the mists lift to reveal a French ship. Instantly the crew rushes to battle stations, but the mists close round again before any significant damage can be inflicted. Claggart again approaches the captain, claiming Billy as the instigator of a mutiny, and although Vere is incredulous he agrees to interview Billy in Claggart's presence. Billy, stunned at the charges, is afflicted by his childhood stammer and, unable to speak, strikes Claggart in anger and frustration and kills him with a single blow. Taken before a drumhead court, Billy is sentenced to hang for murder and the captain refuses to intervene on his behalf.
Back in the present, Captain Vere asserts that he could indeed have saved Billy, although he no longer questions why he did not do so. He claims to have found peace and contentment, but his vivid recollection of these powerful events long ago casts doubt on this assertion.

Music and Background

Many Britten enthusiasts find this his most rewarding opera score, and it is certainly one of his biggest, calling for large forces which are used in grand, near-Verdian terms. The cast is all-male but with voice-types so precisely specified for contrast that the music never feels locked in a limited world of sound. And just as the story describes a symbolic conflict between good (Billy) and evil (Claggart), so the music carries an associated symbolism of conflicting keys – heard at the outset when the curtain rises to an accompaniment of two string groups, one playing in B flat Major, the other in B Minor.

Highlights

Claggart's credo 'Would that I never encountered you' is the dark focus of Act I, with the below-decks shanty 'Blow her away' its moment of most haunting lyricism. In Act II the Chase Scene is an exhilarating operatic spectacle; Billy's pre-execution ballad, 'Look! Through the port comes the moonshine', a conventional but moving monologue; and the cathartic sequence of thirty-four chords that follows the killing of Claggart manages to say more than words ever could.

Did You Know?

∼ Modern readings of the piece (and of the Herman Melville novel on which it is based) surmise that, rather than hating Billy, Claggart is in love with him.

Recommended Recording

Peter Glossop, Peter Pears, Michael Langdon, London Symphony Orchestra/Benjamin Britten. Decca 417 428-2. A classic, handsomely done (as Claggart actually sings, rather than speaks) and without rival.

Death in Venice

FORM: Opera in two acts; in English
COMPOSER: Benjamin Britten (1913–76)
LIBRETTO: Myfanwy Piper; after Thomas Mann's story
FIRST PERFORMANCE: Snape, 16 June 1973

Principal Characters

Gustav von Aschenbach, a writer ∼ Tenor
The Traveller (multiple role) ∼ Bass-baritone
Voice of Apollo ∼ Countertenor
Tadzio, a Polish youth ∼ Choreographed role
His mother ∼ Silent role

Synopsis of the Plot

Setting: Munich and Venice; 1911

ACT I At home in Munich Aschenbach is weary and disillusioned with his work and unable to write. He decides to travel south to Venice, to try and regain his creative powers. On the boat Aschenbach is surrounded by several young, lighthearted passengers, among whom, incongruously, is an elderly man with rouged cheeks and dyed hair. At his hotel on the Lido, Aschenbach notices a Polish family, including Tadzio, a boy of immense physical beauty to whom he is immediately attracted. On a trip into Venice, Aschenbach finds the city suffocating and claustrophobic, and he decides to cut short his stay. But when his luggage is mistakenly sent to Como instead of back to Germany, he changes his mind and agrees, not unhappily, to stay on. Aschenbach slowly becomes obsessed with Tadzio, barely able to take his eyes off him as he plays games on the beach, and finally admitting to himself that he loves the boy.

ACT II Aschenbach hears rumours of a fever in Venice, but the hotel barber is evasive, and Aschenbach is anxious to conceal the truth from Tadzio's family in case they leave. As the rumours grow more insistent, Aschenbach's behaviour becomes more bizarre as he starts to follow Tadzio's family wherever they go. At last the cholera epidemic is generally acknowledged and the visitors are advised to leave before the city is sealed off. Still Aschenbach does not tell Tadzio's family; all he cares about is that they will not leave. His thoughts become more heated and intense; he convinces himself that Tadzio understands and even returns his love. To make himself more attractive he has his hair dyed and his face rouged in a ghastly travesty of youth. By now the hotel is almost empty and Aschenbach learns that the Polish family are about to leave. He goes to the beach one last time to watch Tadzio. When the boy falls during a game, Aschenbach calls out his name in anguish before he collapses, dying, in his chair.

Music and Background

This is Britten's last opera, written with extraordinary refinement for the specific vocal qualities of Peter Pears in the final stage of his singing career. The central role is all-important, rivalled only by that of the baritone who, in a virtuoso performance, takes on seven different characters – all of them agents in the process of advancing Aschenbach towards his death. The orchestration is especially striking: economical, precise but deep-dyed with exotic oriental colouring inspired by the sound of Javanese gamelan music and used to suggest the fatal allure of the boy Tadzio.

Highlights

The power of *Death in Venice* is cumulative rather than dependent on 'big' moments; but the Beach-games Scene at the end of Act I is peculiarly evocative, and the Dream Scene in Act II a disturbing example of stage-trauma. Listen for the rocking, barcarolle motif that literally ferries Aschenbach to his grave.

Did You Know?

Visconti's film of *Death in Venice* came out while Britten was planning his opera, and the composer determined not to see it lest he be accused of plagiarism. In any event, Britten stayed closer to the book than Visconti did, including the academic debate on the nature of attraction that makes *Death in Venice* more than just a love story.

Recommended Recording

Peter Pears, John Shirley-Quirk, James Bowman, English Chamber Orchestra/Steuart Bedford. The original cast recording made in 1974 after the premiere at Snape Maltings, Suffolk.

Gloriana

FORM: Opera in three acts; in English
COMPOSER: Benjamin Britten (1913–76)
LIBRETTO: William Plomer; after Lytton Strachey's biography
FIRST PERFORMANCE: London, 8 June 1953

Principal Characters

Elizabeth I ~ Soprano
Earl of Essex ~ Tenor
Frances, Countess of Essex ~ Mezzo-soprano
Lady Penelope Rich, Essex's sister ~ Soprano
Lord Mountjoy ~ Baritone
Sir Walter Raleigh, captain of the guard ~ Bass
Sir Robert Cecil, secretary of the council ~ Baritone

Synopsis of the Plot

Setting: London and Norwich; the later years of Elizabeth's reign

ACT I The queen is at a tournament when Essex, hot-blooded and ambitious, provokes a quarrel with Mountjoy, the tournament victor, whom he sees as a rival for the queen's favour. Elizabeth is displeased at this and urges them to become reconciled. Later, Robert Cecil cautions the queen about showing too much affection for Essex, who is trying to persuade Elizabeth to let him go to Ireland to repress the Tyrone rebellion.

ACT II Elizabeth is making a state visit to Norwich, attended by Essex, who seems impatient of the ceremonials. He is still anxious to set off for Ireland and complains to his wife, Frances, of the queen's unwillingness to let him go. Frances urges caution, but Essex is confident that he has Elizabeth's affection and that his power and influence will increase accordingly. Once more in London, Essex instructs his wife to attend a ball in her most extravagant dress, even though Frances knows that this will antagonise the queen. Elizabeth orders some energetic dancing, after which the ladies retire to change their linen. When Frances returns she is in a much more subdued outfit, complaining that her dress has been stolen. And when Elizabeth next appears it is clear who stole it – but the dress is much too small for her and she looks grotesque. Essex's anger mounts higher and higher at this insult, but the queen mollifies him by finally agreeing that he can go to Ireland as the Lord Deputy.

ACT III Essex has failed to quell the Irish rebellion and is trying to put the blame on his enemies at court. Cecil tells the queen that Essex is stirring up revolt in England and, reluctantly, she orders that he be kept under guard. The evidence against Essex begins to accumulate and the councillors, led by Cecil, try to persuade the queen to sign his death warrant. Frances comes to appeal for his life and elicits a sympathetic response from the queen, but when her companion, Lady Rich, arrogantly tells Elizabeth that she should pardon Essex because she needs him, Elizabeth promptly calls for the death warrant and signs it.

Music and Background

A ceremonial piece, written for the coronation of Queen Elizabeth II, *Gloriana* proceeds in a sequence of tableaux with much spectacle – in sound as well as vision – and cleverly contemporised allusions to the music of the Tudor court. But the writing balances these grand public statements against intimate scenes in which Elizabeth gives voice to her private feelings with touching poignancy. Everything hangs on the central role which is accordingly long, taxing and in every sense a *tour de force*.

Highlights

The Earl of Essex's hauntingly beautiful second lute song, 'Happy were he' in Act I; the sequence of ceremonial dances and choral numbers that comprise the masque in Act II; the courtly dances of the Act II Ball Scene; the queen's final monologue as a dream-sequence of episodes from her life and reign pass before her.

Did You Know?

~ *Gloriana* drew muted applause at its premiere, partly because the glittering audience of diplomats, royalty and other coronation guests didn't know what to make of it but largely because they were wearing full court dress, including white gloves.

Recommended Recording

Josephine Barstow, Philip Langridge, Della Jones, Welsh National Opera/Charles Mackerras. Decca 440213-2. The only full recording, produced in 1993, with a superb roster of latterday British voices that features in Barstow the finest modern exponent of the central role.

A Midsummer Night's Dream

FORM: Opera in three acts; in English
COMPOSER: Benjamin Britten (1913–76)
LIBRETTO: Benjamin Britten and Peter Pears,
after Shakespeare's play
FIRST PERFORMANCE: Aldeburgh, 11 June 1960

Principal Characters

Oberon, King of the Fairies ~ **Countertenor**
Titania, Queen of the Fairies ~ **Coloratura soprano**
Puck ~ **Spoken role**
Hermia, in love with Lysander ~ **Mezzo-soprano**
Helena, in love with Demetrius ~ **Soprano**
Demetrius, in love with Hermia ~ **Baritone**
Lysander, in love with Hermia ~ **Tenor**
Theseus, Duke of Athens ~ **Bass**

Hippolyta, betrothed to Theseus ❧ **Contralto**
Bottom, a weaver ❧ **Bass-baritone**
Peter Quince, a carpenter ❧ **Bass**
Flute, a bellows mender ❧ **Tenor**
Snug, a joiner ❧ **Bass**
Snout, a tinker ❧ **Tenor**
Starveling, a tailor ❧ **Baritone**

Synopsis of the Plot

Setting: A wood near Athens and Theseus' palace

ACT I Oberon and Titania have quarrelled over the possession of an Indian boy stolen by the fairies. Oberon plots revenge and instructs Puck to fetch the magic herb which, squeezed into the eyes, will make the recipient fall instantly in love with the next person they see. Oberon also plans to use the magic herb to help Helena, in love with Demetrius, who has eyes only for Hermia. Puck, however, confuses Demetrius with the sleeping Lysander, so that when he wakes and sees Helena, Lysander falls instantly in love with her (and out of love with Hermia), and chases after her, leaving a bewildered Hermia alone and frightened.

ACT II The Athenian craftsmen are rehearsing a play, their contribution to the duke's forthcoming wedding celebrations. Titania, asleep nearby, awakes to see Bottom, whom Puck has disguised with an ass' head on his shoulders, and falls immediately in love with him. Oberon is delighted with Puck's mischief-making – until he sees that Puck has squeezed the juice into Lysander's eyes by mistake. He makes amends by administering the juice himself to Demetrius, but now both men are in love with Helena; Helena and Hermia quarrel and the men decide to fight a duel. Exasperated, Oberon orders Puck to ensure that the men come to no harm and that the four lovers are appropriately reconciled.

ACT III Oberon now possesses the Indian boy, the cause of his quarrel with Titania, so he releases both Titania and Bottom from the spell. The four lovers, asleep in the wood, have been suitably positioned so that, on waking, they see the 'correct' partner. They make their way, somewhat bemused, to Athens, where the duke gives them his blessing and arranges a joint wedding, alongside his own. The craftsmen perform their tragic play with intense seriousness – but their incompetence and confusion turn it into high farce. At midnight the celebrations stop and the humans retire, leaving the fairies once more to their own world.

Music and Background

Britten's favoured themes of sleep and dreams inspired a score of pure enchantment that creates three distinctive sound-worlds for the three categories of character at large in the wood: lovers, rustics and fairies. The supernatural comes with high voice-types (Oberon is a countertenor, the fairies' chorus a group of boy trebles) and the delicate accompaniment of harps, keyboards and percussion, while the rustic play-within-a-play of *Pyramus and Thisbe* is a wicked parody of 19th-century bel canto opera – and especially of the way Joan Sutherland used to sing it!

Highlights

Oberon's exquisitely antique-style aria 'I know a bank' in Act I; in Act III the lovers' quartet, the entire *Pyramus and Thisbe* Scene, and the final fairy chorus, 'Now until the break of day', with its serene and somehow ceremonial rhythmic lilt.

Did You Know?

The libretto is Shakespeare's own text, cut down by Pears and Britten to roughly half its original length. So skilful is the reduction that they had to invent only one line of new text to cover the joins.

Recommended Recording

Alfred Deller, Elizabeth Harwood, Peter Pears, Josephine Veasy, Owen Brannigan, London Symphony Orchestra/Britten. Decca 425 663-2. An unbeatable classic, not least for the spectral artistry of Alfred Deller, who effectively inspired this whole opera.

Peter Grimes

FORM: Opera in a Prologue and three acts; in English
COMPOSER: Benjamin Britten (1913–76)
LIBRETTO: Montague Slater;
after the narrative poem by George Crabbe
FIRST PERFORMANCE: London, 7 June 1945

Principal Characters

Peter Grimes, a fisherman **Tenor**
Hobson, a carrier and the village policeman **Bass**
Swallow, a lawyer and village coroner **Bass**
Mrs Sedley, a widow **Mezzo-soprano**

Ellen Orford, a widowed schoolmistress ✿ **Soprano**
Auntie, landlady at the Boar Inn ✿ **Contralto**
Balstrode, a retired sea captain ✿ **Baritone**
Ned Keene, a 'quack' chemist ✿ **Baritone**

Synopsis of the Plot

Setting: The Borough, a fishing village on the east coast of England

PROLOGUE An inquest has been held on the death of Grimes' apprentice, lost at sea in suspicious circumstances. In spite of the villagers' doubts, Grimes has been exonerated, but advised not to take another boy.

ACT I Keene comes to see Grimes to tell him that he has found him another apprentice. Several objections are raised to this and Hobson refuses point-blank to fetch the boy from the workhouse until Ellen Orford, who sympathises with Grimes, agrees to accompany him. As a storm approaches, the villagers retire to the Boar, leaving Grimes alone with Balstrode, who advises the unpopular fisherman to leave the village altogether. In a rare moment of optimism, Grimes confides to Balstrode his hopes of acquiring money, respect from the villagers and, eventually, Ellen Orford as his wife. Later, Grimes joins the villagers in the Boar as the storm lashes around them, but he makes them uneasy. Indeed they become positively angry when Hobson, Ellen and the new boy arrive, soaked and exhausted, and Grimes insists on taking the boy out again immediately.

ACT II Ellen is disturbed to see a bruise on the boy's neck and remonstrates with Grimes when he insists, on a Sunday, that the boy must work. Grimes' response is to hit her, an act grimly noted by the villagers who are, at that moment, emerging from church. Feelings against Grimes are rapidly rising and a deputation is sent to his hut to find out the truth. Hearing the villagers approaching, Grimes hustles the boy out of the hut and on to the cliff path; minutes later he falls to his death.

ACT III Grimes seems to have disappeared and the boy's sweater has been found on the beach. Hysteria and suspicion dominate the atmosphere and a full-scale manhunt is launched. But it is Ellen and Balstrode who find the half-demented Grimes. Ellen wants to take him home but Balstrode advises him that he has no alternative but to take his boat out to sea and sink it. Grimes accepts the inevitable.

Music and Background

This is the opera that put Britten, and British opera, on the map; and it remains the most popular work in the composer's stage catalogue. Using a big orchestra with Verdian force, and sometimes methods, it has all the ingredients of traditional grand opera (including a Mad Scene) recast in 20th-century terms. The chorus scenes can be electrifying, the central role (one of the great tenor parts of modern times) a fascinatingly ambivalent synthesis of lyric beauty and brute force, and there is a memorable sequence of 'sea interludes' which function as orchestral entr'actes but also, in the manner of Berg's *Wozzeck*, chart Grimes' descent into mental breakdown.

Highlights

The storm interlude and Grimes' unnerving one-note soliloquy 'Now the Great Bear and Pleiades' in Act I. Ellen's radiant and archetypally Brittenesque aria 'Glitter of waves', the manhunt chorus 'Now is gossip put on trial' and orchestral passacaglia in Act II. The second manhunt, with its devastating chorus cries of Peter's name, and Grimes' Mad Scene in Act III.

Did You Know?

Peter Grimes is the product of homesickness. The setting is Aldeburgh, close to where Britten had been brought up, but he took the idea for the opera from a magazine item on George Crabbe that he read while he was living in America. The article was by E.M. Forster, and it began: 'To think of Crabbe is to think of England'.

Recommended Recording

Peter Pears, Claire Watson, Geraint Evans, Royal Opera, Covent Garden/ Benjamin Britten. Decca 414 577-2. Made in 1958 and now with a number of rival versions, including Jon Vickers in the title role for Philips, but still without equal.

The Rape of Lucretia

FORM: Opera in two acts; in English
COMPOSER: Benjamin Britten (1913–76)
LIBRETTO: Ronald Duncan; after André Obey's play, itself based on Livy and Shakespeare
FIRST PERFORMANCE: Glyndebourne, 12 July 1946

Principal Characters

Lucretia, Collatinus' wife Mezzo-soprano
Collatinus Bass

Tarquinius, ruler of Rome ❧ **Baritone**
Junius ❧ **Baritone**
Male Chorus ❧ **Tenor**
Female Chorus ❧ **Mezzo-soprano**

Synopsis of the Plot

Setting: Rome; 510 BC

ACT I In the army camp Tarquinius, Collatinus and Junius are drinking steadily and complaining about the general untrustworthiness of women, with the exception of Collatinus' wife, Lucretia, who is known to be absolutely and unshakeably faithful. This assertion provokes Tarquinius, who rides furiously to Rome with the sole intention of destroying Lucretia's reputation. When Tarquinius arrives at her home, Lucretia welcomes him, rather uneasily, and offers him hospitality.

ACT II Tarquinius creeps into Lucretia's room and she, sleepily imagining it to be her husband, responds to him before realising the truth and struggling, in vain, to prevent him from raping her. The next day Lucretia sends for Collatinus, who quickly learns the truth from her attendants. Collatinus reassures his wife of his love for her but Lucretia's shame is too great for her to bear and she stabs herself to death.

Music and Background

The Rape of Lucretia followed *Peter Grimes* in Britten's output but was written for far more modest resources – eight voices and a chamber ensemble of thirteen instruments – which reflect a concern for the practical problems of getting opera onto the stage in the years of austerity immediately after the Second World War. The tone of the writing is itself austere, stiff with an emotional restraint that limits the opera's popularity. But the brilliance with which Britten draws from these small resources ingenious effects like the opening evocation of a sultry Italian night – complete with bullfrogs and cicadas – is undeniable, and the vividness of this sound-painting more than compensates for moments of monochrome dryness elsewhere.

Highlights

The Male Chorus account of Tarquinius' night-ride in Act I is tense with excitement. In Act II the most purely beautiful music comes, oddly perhaps, as Tarquinius steals upon the sleeping Lucretia, singing 'Within this frail crucible of light'.

Recommended Recording

Janet Baker, Peter Pears, Heather Harper, English Chamber Orchestra/ Benjamin Britten. Decca 425 666-2. Discs that captured Janet Baker on peak form in 1970, with singing of depth and dignity.

The Turn of the Screw

FORM: Opera in a Prologue and two acts; in English
COMPOSER: Benjamin Britten (1913–76)
LIBRETTO: Myfanwy Piper; after the story by Henry James
FIRST PERFORMANCE: Venice, 14 September 1954

Principal Characters

The Prologue 🔊 Tenor
The Governess 🔊 Soprano
Miles 🔊 Boy Treble
Flora 🔊 Soprano
Mrs Grose, the housekeeper 🔊 Soprano
Miss Jessel, the former governess 🔊 Soprano
Peter Quint, the former servant 🔊 Tenor

Synopsis of the Plot

Setting: Bly, an English country house; mid-19th century

PROLOGUE A narrator introduces the story, telling us of how the young Governess has been engaged by the guardian of the two children, Miles and Flora. There is only one condition attached to the post: she must not trouble him.

ACT I The Governess is warmly welcomed at Bly and soon settles in. Slowly, however, she becomes aware of the increasing strangeness of the children's behaviour and of a sinister atmosphere in the house, culminating in the momentary sighting of an unknown man at a window. On consulting the housekeeper, the Governess learns that this is Quint, the former manservant, now dead. Quint, she is told, was very close to Miles and had a relationship with Miss Jessel, the previous governess, who is also now dead. When the Governess finds both Flora and Miles communicating with these ghostly manifestations, she becomes seriously worried.

ACT II The Governess' apprehensions reach a climax when she is confronted herself by Miss Jessel's ghost and, despite Mrs Grose's assurances that the children are in no danger, she determines to break the one condition of her employment and write to their guardian. Miles is deeply disturbed by this and, encouraged by Quint, he steals the letter before it can be sent. Flora disappears and is found by Mrs Grose and the Governess by the lake, communicating with Miss Jessel, whom Mrs Grose cannot see. Flora denies Miss Jessel's presence and turns bitterly on the Governess before Mrs Grose takes the girl back to the house. That night Mrs Grose stays with Flora and is horrified by the child's dreams; she decides to take her right away. Left alone with Miles, the Governess urges him to tell her what is in his mind but Quint appears, uttering warnings, and the boy is torn between the two of them. The conflict is too great and he collapses and dies in the Governess' arms.

Music and Background

The most elegantly organised of all Britten's operas, *The Turn of the Screw* is a small-scale chamber piece with thirteen instruments in the orchestra and a chilling intensity that delivers powerful emotions in a controlled way. The story is organised into short scenes linked by instrumental interludes and, musically, each scene is a variation on a twelve-note theme whose constant adaptations 'turn the screw' of the score in just the manner of Henry James' title. As so often in Britten, the story concerns the corruption of innocence, but the (literally) haunting beauty of the highly embellished writing for the male ghost, Peter Quint, presents him as an ambiguously attractive character with whom the audience is clearly meant to feel some sympathy.

Highlights

Miles' unsettlingly innocent solo in the Act I Lesson Scene, 'Malo I would rather be'; the ghosts' duet at the beginning of Act II, culminating in the line (borrowed from Yeats) 'The ceremony of innocence is drowned'.

Recommended Recording

Peter Pears, Jennifer Vyvyan, David Hemmings, English Opera Group/ Benjamin Britten. Decca 425 672-2. The original cast recording made in 1955 and never bettered.

Alfredo Catalani
(1854–93)

Dejanice (1882)
Loreley (1879)
La Wally (1891)

orn in Lucca, educated in Paris and settling finally in Milan,
where he became professor of composition at the conservatoire,
Catalani had the misfortune to be a slightly older contemporary of
Puccini who outclassed and overshadowed him. A lifelong invalid, his
early death at thirty-nine left him with just one opera which survives in
(fairly) regular repertory, *La Wally*. Its Nordic theme is typical of the
German Romantic interests that make the music of this Italian
composer unusual for its place and time.

La Wally

FORM: Opera in four acts; in Italian
COMPOSER: Alfredo Catalani (1854–93)
LIBRETTO: Luigi Illica; after W. von Hillern's story
FIRST PERFORMANCE: Milan, 20 June 1892

Principal Characters
Wally ᴇ Soprano
Stromminger, her father and a rich landowner ᴇ Bass
Hagenbach ᴇ Tenor
Gellner ᴇ Baritone
Afra, proprietress of the inn ᴇ Contralto
Walter, a wandering player ᴇ Soprano

Synopsis of the Plot
Setting: The Swiss Tyrol; 1800

ACT I Wally has fallen in love with Hagenbach, the son of her father's old
enemy, although her feelings are not reciprocated. Gellner, who wants to
marry Wally, warns Stromminger of his daughter's feelings towards

Hagenbach, and Stromminger's response is to order Wally to marry Gellner within the month or leave his house. Wally leaves to live on the mountain.

ACT II Some time has passed, during which Stromminger has died and Wally has inherited his fortune. She returns to the village for a festival and, believing that Afra is now engaged to her beloved Hagenbach, insults her. Hagenbach, hearing of this, decides to avenge Afra. He dances with Wally, kisses her and swears undying love, and she is enraptured – until the mocking laughter of the onlookers alerts her to the truth. Furious and humiliated, she promises to marry Gellner if he kills Hagenbach.

ACT III Wally goes home and, reflecting more calmly on the situation, realises that she must stop Gellner from harming Hagenbach. But before she can act he bursts in, telling her he has pushed Hagenbach into a ravine. Wally, spurred on by guilt and remorse, goes down a rope into the ravine and rescues Hagenbach. Wally gives him into Afra's care and leaves.

ACT IV Living alone and isolated on the mountainside, Wally resigns herself to her fate. Suddenly Hagenbach, fully recovered, appears and says he has come to tell her he loves her. Wally confesses her part in his 'accident' but he reassures her of his love. As they make their way down to the village the sound of an approaching avalanche is heard. Hagenbach is swept away by the snow and, distraught, Wally throws herself after him.

Music

Set in the Swiss Alps, *La Wally* is notable for its incursions into local colour, including Tyrolean dances in Act II. But at the end of the day this is Italian opera, looking forward to the kind of through-composed verismo writing of Puccini (whose *Manon Lescaut* appeared the following year) and quite well characterised. Its weakness is a story which, for all its momentous happenings, makes less than powerful theatre.

Highlight

Wally's poignant farewell at the end of Act I, 'Ebben? Ne andrò lontana', is the most celebrated item in all Catalani's output and a tune made still more famous by extensive use in the 1981 film *Diva*.

Did You Know?

➤ This opera became known largely through the efforts of the conductor Toscanini; he saddled his daughter with the heroine's name.

Recommended Recording

Renata Tebaldi, Mario del Monaco, Monte Carlo Opera/Fausto Cleva. Decca 425 417-2. A finer cast than it probably deserves.

Gustave Charpentier
(1860–1956)

Louise (1900)

Not to be confused with the earlier Marc-Antoine Charpentier who wrote a famous *Messe de Minuit* and several less-famous pastoral operas in French Baroque taste, Gustave Charpentier was a student of Massenet at the late 19th-century Paris Conservatoire. He began work on the one and only score for which he is known, *Louise*, while still studying there. An urban low-life forerunner of *La Bohème*, *Louise* was an instant success and Charpentier rested on its laurels ever after, writing little in the last half-century of his life beyond a sequel, *Julien*, that reworked already-written music and never caught on.

Louise

FORM: Opera in four acts; in French
COMPOSER: Gustave Charpentier (1860–1956)
LIBRETTO: Gustave Charpentier (and, possibly, Saint-Pol-Roux)
FIRST PERFORMANCE: Paris, 2 February 1900

Principal Characters

Louise, a young Parisian working-class girl ∾ Soprano
Her mother ∾ Soprano
Her father ∾ Baritone
Julien, a young poet ∾ Tenor

Synopsis of the Plot

Setting: Montmartre, Paris

ACT I Louise and Julien are in love, but Julien has failed to gain Louise's parents' approval for their marriage. He tells Louise that he has written again to her parents but, if they still refuse to let them marry, she must elope with him. Louise's mother mocks Julien, saying he is a lazy good-for-nothing who drinks too much, and they argue violently until Louise's father comes home and opens Julien's letter. He tries to be reasonable but his wife becomes increasingly vituperative about Julien, and Louise collapses in tears.

ACT II Early in the morning Julien and his friends are waiting near Louise's workplace. When she arrives he manages to talk to her, but is angered by her refusal to leave her parents, without their blessing, to live with him. At work, the other girls tease Louise and then discuss the glories of love and romance. When Julien appears outside the window to serenade her, Louise can bear no more and abruptly leaves the workroom to join him.

ACT III Now happily living together and very much in love, Julien and Louise take part in the local carnival procession, during which Louise is crowned Muse of Montmartre. But when Louise's mother appears it is as a very different person from the termagant of Act I; looking sad and anxious, she explains that Louise's father is very ill and desperate to see his daughter. On the understanding that she can leave when she wants to, Louise finally agrees to go and see him, despite Julien's suspicions.

ACT IV Louise's father has recovered but he has changed and become irritable and dissatisfied with his life. Both he and Louise's mother refuse to let her go back to Julien, in spite of her obvious sadness and longing. In the end Louise insists on leaving, pushing past her father as he tries to bar the way, and leaving him to curse Paris, which has stolen his daughter from him.

Music and Background

Bustling with the atmosphere of Montmartre street life, Charpentier's score is rich in local colour and memorable for the avant-garde incorporation of sewing-machine noise, in the interests of realism. Otherwise, the music is more conventional for its time than is the Zola-esque story of free-living and loving it sets. Influences are basically Gounod and Massenet.

Highlights

This is effectively a one-number opera and the (very celebrated) number is the Act III romance with which Louise celebrates her happiness with Julien, 'Depuis le jour'.

Did You Know?

Louise was sensationally successful on its first night and was performed one thousand times in Paris alone during Charpentier's lifetime.

Recommended Recording

Ileana Cotrubas, Plácido Domingo, New Philharmonia Orchestra/Georges Prêtre. Sony S3K 46429. Nicely done and no real competition.

Luigi Cherubini

(1760–1842)

Lodoïska (1790)
Eliza (1794)
Médée (1797)
Les Deux Journées (1800)

Born in Florence to a musical father, Cherubini was a prodigy who began writing stage works in his teens, came to London in his twenties, and finally settled in Paris where he founded an opera company that somehow survived the traumas of the Revolution. A survivor himself, Cherubini perfected a genre of heroic rescue-opera with spoken dialogue, designed to please post-Revolutionary tastes after the old style of grand, static and completely sung Classical stories lost favour as a relic of the royal past. His influence in France was short-lived, but in Austro-Germany it was considerable and fed through to Beethoven's rescue-opera *Fidelio*.

Médée
(Medea)

FORM: Opera in three acts; in French
COMPOSER: Luigi Cherubini (1760–1842)
LIBRETTO: F-B. Hoffman
FIRST PERFORMANCE: Paris, 13 March 1797

Principal Characters

Medea, former wife of Jason ~ **Soprano**
Jason, leader of the Argonauts ~ **Tenor**
Creon, King of Corinth ~ **Bass**
Dirce, Creon's daughter ~ **Soprano**
Neris, Medea's servant ~ **Mezzo-soprano**

Synopsis of the Plot

Setting: Creon's palace and Corinth; mythological Greece

ACT I Jason has abandoned the murderous Medea and, with their two sons, has made his home in Corinth. He now wishes to marry Creon's daughter, Dirce, but she has considerable doubts about the wisdom of the union, despite reassurances from her father that Medea will not harm them. A few moments later a stranger is admitted, to be revealed as Medea herself. Creon orders her to leave or suffer imprisonment. Left alone with Jason, Medea tries every means in her power to persuade him to come back to her, but he stands firm.

ACT II By the next morning the people, hearing of Medea's presence, are demanding her blood. Creon warns her to escape while she can, but she begs him to let her stay just one more day so that she can see her children, and he agrees. Left alone, Medea plans her revenge as the sound of wedding music is heard in the distance.

ACT III Medea calls on the gods of the underworld to help her as a storm rages round the temple and the palace. Medea's children are brought to her by Neris and, firmly repressing any faint stirrings of maternal feeling, she drags them into the temple and stabs them. From the palace come the horrifying cries of the dying Dirce, poisoned by the wedding presents Medea had contrived to give her. Jason and the crowd come after Medea, but it is too late: before he can reach the temple she appears in the doorway, surrounded by the Furies, and curses Jason, holding aloft the knife with which she has killed the children. Terrorstricken, the people scatter as the temple bursts into flames.

Music and Background

Médée is a work of highly charged musical drama, focused on two characters, Jason and Medea, and two subjects, revenge and death. The grand, Classical story may look back to the old, aristocratic manner of opera before the Revolution, but the fierceness of the story-telling puts it in a different league, and *Médée* is in fact the only Revolutionary-period opera to have found a lasting place in the repertory. The title role is towering, an exhausting challenge for the singer. And although the score was written with spoken dialogue in the manner known as *opéra comique*, there are decidedly no laughs.

Highlights

The Jason/Medea duet that closes Act I is classical drama at its best, and Neris' Act II aria 'Ah, nos peines' has touching beauty; but the musical dynamism in this opera comes in Act III, whose furious temper is set by the opening orchestral storm and escalates throughout into the final conflagration.

Did You Know?

æ. The death of the first soprano to tackle Medea was widely thought to be a consequence of the strain of singing the part.

Recommended Recording

Sylvia Sass, Veriano Luchetti, Budapest Symphony Orchestra/Lamberto Gardelli. Hungaraton HCD 11904/5. A better all-round performance than the legendary but flawed 1950s recording with Maria Callas.

Francesco Cilea
(1866–1950)

Adriana Lecouvreur (1897)
L'Arlesiana (1902)

Cilea began writing operas when he was still a student at the Naples Conservatory but had lasting success with only one, *Adriana Lecouvreur*, and with the tenor aria known as Federico's Lament from another, *L'Arlesiana*. The championship of the famous Enrico Caruso was instrumental in both cases. Much of Cilea's life was devoted to teaching, and he ultimately became director of the conservatory where he studied. A member of the verismo school of composition, his musical language was more refined than most but tended to be limited in the development of ideas.

Adriana Lecouvreur

FORM: Opera in four acts; in Italian
COMPOSER: Francesco Cilea (1866–1950)
LIBRETTO: Arturo Colautti; from the play by Scribe and Legouvé
FIRST PERFORMANCE: Milan, 6 November 1902

Principal Characters
Adriana, an actress ❦ **Soprano**
Maurizio, Count of Saxony ❦ **Tenor**
Michonnet, stage director ❦ **Baritone**
Prince de Bouillon ❦ **Bass**
Princess de Bouillon, his wife ❦ **Mezzo-soprano**
Abbé de Chazeuil ❦ **Tenor**

Synopsis of the Plot
Setting: Paris; 1730

ACT I At the theatre, Adriana confides to Michonnet, who adores her, that she loves an officer in the Count of Saxony's service. They are interrupted by the officer himself (actually the Count in disguise) who immediately declares his love for Adriana; before leaving for the performance, Adriana gives him some violets for his buttonhole. The Prince and the Abbé then enter, discussing a letter they have intercepted, addressed to Maurizio and arranging an assignation at the villa of the Prince's mistress, Adriana's actress rival, Duclos. The two men allow the letter to be delivered to Maurizio, who realises that the writer is not Duclos, but the Princess, a former lover. He decides to keep the appointment for political reasons. Adriana, meanwhile, is invited by the Prince to join an after-theatre party at the villa.

ACT II Maurizio and the Princess meet, but the Princess is upset to see the violets he is wearing and accuses him of having another lover; with great presence of mind he says they are a gift for her. At that moment they are surprised by the arrival of her husband and the Abbé, and the Princess hides in the next room. When Adriana arrives she recognises Maurizio as her 'officer' and they reaffirm their love. Maurizio asks Adriana to help the woman in the next room to escape. Later, in the dark, the two women discover that they are rivals for Maurizio's love.

ACT III The Prince and Princess are holding a party. Among the guests is Adriana, whose voice the Princess recognises as that of her rival for Maurizio. When Maurizio himself comes in, the two rivals resort to charge and countercharge, ending with Adriana declaiming a passage from Racine's *Phèdre* about lustful women while looking the Princess straight in the eye.

ACT IV Adriana is deeply depressed, believing that Maurizio no longer loves her. Her misery is compounded by the delivery of a box 'from Maurizio' containing the violets that she had given him. Sadly, Adriana kisses them and throws them on the fire. At that moment Maurizio himself comes in and asks her to marry him. Adriana is overjoyed. But suddenly she turns pale and faint. She accuses Maurizio of sending her poisoned flowers, which he denies, before dying in his arms. Michonnet, broken-hearted, knows that this is the work of the Princess, who has exacted the ultimate revenge.

Music and Background

Adriana Lecouvreur is generally said to be a fine opera for a fine soprano past her prime: in other words, the title role makes enough demands to be challenging but without too many top notes. As verismo writing goes, it is comparatively restrained and subtle.

Highlights

Adriana's Act I 'Io son l'umile ancella' is sort of motto theme that recurs throughout the score. Her Act IV 'Poveri fiori' is the other show-stopper.

Recommended Recording

Joan Sutherland, Carlo Bergonzi, Welsh National Opera/Richard Bonynge. Decca 425 815-2. Sutherland in peak, grand-tragic form.

Domenico Cimarosa
(1749–1801)

Il Matrimonio Segreto (1792)

Most of his eighty stage works are forgotten now, but in his time, Cimarosa was probably the most prolific and successful opera composer in Europe, notwithstanding the fact that he was a contemporary of Mozart. After studies in Naples he moved to St Petersburg as court composer to Catherine the Great, but failed to please his patron. Moving on to Vienna, he took a similar position with Emperor Leopold II, and it was there that his most enduring work, *Il Matrimonio Segreto*, was premiered. Cimarosa had the added distinction of being sentenced to death for revolutionary tendencies. The sentence was reduced to imprisonment and exile, and he died in Venice, allegedly from poisoning.

Il Matrimonio Segreto
(The Secret Marriage)

FORM: Opera in two acts; in Italian
COMPOSER: Domenico Cimarosa (1749–1801)
LIBRETTO: Giovanni Bertati; after Colman and Garrick's play
FIRST PERFORMANCE: Vienna, 7 February 1792

Principal Characters
Geronimo, a rich merchant ~ Bass
Carolina, Geronimo's daughter ~ Soprano
Elisetta, another daughter ~ Soprano
Fidalma, Geronimo's widowed sister ~ Mezzo-soprano
Paolino, Geronimo's clerk ~ Tenor
Count Robinson ~ Bass

Synopsis of the Plot
Setting: Bologna; 18th century

ACT I Paolino and Carolina have been secretly married and Carolina feels it is now time to break the news to her father, Geronimo, particularly as he has just heard that the aristocratic Count Robinson is on his way to propose to her sister, Elisetta. Geronimo is, of course, delighted to learn of the Count's imminent arrival and Elisetta effortlessly assumes the airs of a countess, thus provoking a quarrel with her sister. Fidalma tries to make peace between the girls. All this talk of marriage has made her think of her own situation, and she reflects on her secret love for Paolino. Count Robinson arrives, but mistakes first Fidalma, then Carolina, for his future bride; when he is finally introduced to Elisetta, the least attractive of the three, he announces that he would rather have Carolina instead. Elisetta is furious and the act ends in pandemonium.

ACT II Geronimo is confronted by the Count who proposes that, instead of marrying Elisetta, he will take Carolina – for half the originally agreed dowry. Geronimo agrees and tells Paolino, who decides, reluctantly, to tell the truth to Fidalma in the hope that she will help them. Fidalma mistakes his reticent behaviour for the bashfulness of a lover and accepts the proposal of marriage she thinks he is about to make! Paolino is so shocked he faints and Fidalma is trying to revive him when Carolina comes upon them and demands an explanation. Meanwhile, Elisetta and Fidalma have hatched a plot to get Geronimo to send Carolina to a convent; Paolino and Carolina decide that they must run away. They are hiding in Carolina's room when Elisetta bursts in, claiming Carolina is up to no good with the Count, who then emerges from his own room to ask what the fuss is about. At last Paolino and Carolina admit they are married and are forgiven; the Count agrees to marry Elisetta and harmony is restored.

Music and Background

A sparkling, romantic buffo comedy, *Il Matrimonio Segreto* straddles the worlds of Mozart (who died just two months before its first performance) and composers-to-come Rossini and Donizetti. The fast-moving patter songs certainly look foward to Italian bel canto writing, as does the needle-sharp clarity of the more lyrical numbers.

Highlights

Geronimo's wide-ranging Act I aria 'Udite tutti' is a piece of evergreen operatic comedy; and the following female voice trio for Carolina, Elisetta and Fidalma, 'Le faccio un inchino', sustains the fun. Act II brings Paolino's lyrical 'Pria che spunti' as the lovers resolve to run away.

Recommended Recording

Dietrich Fischer-Dieskau, Arleen Augér, Julia Varady, Julia Hamari, English Chamber Orchestra/Daniel Barenboim. Immaculately characterised performances, directed with great spirit.

Peter Maxwell Davies

(1934–)

Eight Songs for a Mad King (1969)
Taverner (1968)
The Martyrdom of St Magnus (1976)
The Lighthouse (1979)
The Doctor of Myddfai (1996)

orn in Manchester, Peter Maxwell Davies was one of a small circle of composers (including Harrison Birtwistle) who studied there together and collectively reacted against the broad conservatism that prevailed in 1950s British music. Davies established himself as a leading figure of the avant-garde with works which subjected medieval borrowings to highly complex 20th-century processes derived from the twelve-tone systems of Schoenberg and his followers. From the first he was interested in writing for the theatre; and with his own performance group The Fires of London he developed a style of small-scale but hard-hitting music theatre typified by *Eight Songs for a Mad King*, which is effectively a miniature opera for one voice and accompanying instruments. Davies' earlier works specialise in extreme emotional states and shock tactics, their subject matter homing in on issues of betrayal and the exposure of hypocrisy. But he has also written many, gentler works for children; and since he made his base the remote Scottish Orkney Islands his music has been influenced by the natural features of a bleakly beautiful landscape. Hugely prolific, his output includes six symphonies and large, programmatic orchestral scores.

The Lighthouse

FORM: Chamber opera in a Prologue and one act; in English
COMPOSER: Peter Maxwell Davies (1934–)
LIBRETTO: Peter Maxwell Davies
FIRST PERFORMANCE: Edinburgh, 2 September 1980

Principal Characters

The lighthouse keepers/relief officers
Sandy Tenor
Blazes Baritone
Arthur Bass

Synopsis of the Plot

Setting: An Edinburgh courtroom and the Flannan Isle lighthouse;
December 1900

PROLOGUE In the courtroom, the three officers who arrived at the
lighthouse to relieve the keepers and found it abandoned give their version
of events.

ACT I In a flashback to the lighthouse we are introduced to the three
lighthouse keepers. It is their last evening and they eat, play cards and sing to
amuse themselves. Slowly, however, underlying tensions and mutual
enmities begin to surface and their characters become more clearly defined:
the Bible-thumping hypocrite, Arthur; the rough, uncultivated Blazes; and
the gentler, wistful Sandy. As thick fog slowly blankets the lighthouse,
emotional tensions are heightened to breaking point and each man sinks
into despair, haunted by his own personal demon. Suddenly the blinding
lights of an oncoming ship appear through the fog, to be mistaken for the
eyes of a great beast. The three keepers are replaced by the three relief
officers who indicate that the keepers, driven to insanity by their isolation,
had attacked them and had to be killed. The mystery surrounding the
lighthouse (did the keepers abandon it or were they killed?) is never solved;
the light is made automatic but the three men can still be seen, forever
reliving their final hours.

Music and Background

The courtroom prologue suggests parallels with Britten's *Peter Grimes*, and
something of the tough, man-against-the-elements atmosphere of that
earlier piece transfers to this operatic psycho-drama, although the forces are
much smaller and the music more tightly written, using mathematical
systems in the way that much of Davies' work does. The more lyrical

moments tend to be parodies of popular musical forms – another Davies fingerprint. All the roles are taken by the same three voices.

Highlights

The arrival of 'the Beast' is memorable, and so is the mechanically repeated figure, 'The lighthouse is now automatic', that plays out the score.

Did You Know?

The opera is based on a true story of three keepers who disappeared from the Flannan Isle lighthouse in 1900. On the very night the opera premiered in 1980, the Flannan Isle lighthouse (now automatic) mysteriously, and for the first time ever, went out.

Recommended Recording

Neil Mackie, Christopher Keyte, Ian Comboy, BBC Philharmonic/ Peter Maxwell Davies. Collins Classics 14152. The only one.

Claude Debussy
(1862–1918)

Pelléas et Mélisande (1902)

Born near Paris, Debussy was fascinated by the theatre all his life and had a celebrated relationship with the impresario Diaghilev, who turned scores like the *Prélude à l'Après Midi d'un Faune* into ballets. He was also interested in the human voice, and matured into one of the greatest of French song-writers, with incomparable settings of Verlaine and Baudelaire. But he only completed one opera, *Pelléas et Mélisande*, and although he devoted later years to attempts at an operatic adaptation of Edgar Allan Poe's *The Fall of the House of Usher*, they survive as little more than sketches. Principally, the composer is remembered for his piano, chamber and orchestral music – written largely in an imagistic way that earned him the label 'impressionist', though 'symbolist' might be more accurate. With atmospherically suggestive scores like *Prélude à l'Après Midi d'un Faune* and the orchestral *Images*, he introduced a new language of sound and was undoubtedly one of the founding fathers of modern music.

Pelléas et Mélisande

FORM: Opera in five acts; in French
COMPOSER: Claude Debussy (1862–1918)
LIBRETTO: Maurice Maeterlinck's play, slightly adapted by Debussy
FIRST PERFORMANCE: Paris, 30 April 1902

Principal Characters

Arkel, King of Allemonde ~ Bass
Geneviève, Arkel's daughter-in-law and mother of Golaud and Pelléas
~ Mezzo-soprano
Golaud, Arkel's grandson ~ Baritone
Pelléas, Arkel's grandson and Golaud's half-brother ~ Tenor
Mélisande ~ Soprano
Yniold, Golaud's son by his first marriage ~ Soprano/Boy treble

Synopsis of the Plot

Setting: The imaginary kingdom of Allemonde; medieval times

ACT I While out hunting, Golaud finds a mysterious girl, Mélisande, weeping in a forest; nearby is a well with a golden crown at the bottom, fallen from her head. Golaud marries Mélisande and, some time later, takes her to Arkel's castle to ask his grandfather's forgiveness for the unplanned marriage; Arkel had a different bride in mind for Golaud. On her arrival, Mélisande meets Pelléas and it is clear that they have fallen in love with each other.

ACT II Pelléas and Mélisande are together by a well when Mélisande drops her ring into the water; at that moment Golaud falls from his horse. Later, lying injured in bed, Golaud notices that the ring is missing and Mélisande replies, falsely, that she lost it by the sea. Golaud sends her, with Pelléas, to look for it.

ACT III Mélisande is sitting at the castle window, talking to Pelléas; she allows her long hair to fall over his shoulders and he plays with it. They are surprised in their game by Golaud who warns Pelléas to leave Mélisande alone. Golaud then questions his little son, Yniold, about the relationship between Pelléas and Mélisande and even holds him up to the window so that he can see what they are doing: just sitting together, answers the boy.

ACT IV Pelléas tells Mélisande that he is leaving and they plan one last meeting. Golaud is by now furiously jealous and attacks Mélisande, dragging her across the room by her hair until he is stopped by Arkel. The two lovers meet by the well, as arranged. In the distance they hear the castle doors being locked and barred – there is no going back. Golaud, hiding nearby, hears and sees their declarations of love; he leaps at them, killing Pelléas while Mélisande escapes.

ACT V Mélisande has given birth to a child and now lies, ill and dying, at the castle. Golaud begs her forgiveness, which she grants, but his desperate pleas to know whether she was unfaithful go unanswered as her life ebbs away.

Music and Background

One of the greatest and most beautiful of 20th-century operas, *Pelléas et Mélisande* can also be one of the most maddening, in that it sets Maeterlinck's story in such muted, enigmatic and elusive terms. As the short, often inconclusive scenes waft delicately by, you feel you want to shake the characters into livelier reactions and the music into more obvious climaxes. But then, this is symbolist drama: a thing of dream-like nuance rather than emphatic statement. With motifs tied to specific characters and orchestral interludes (not always played) between the scenes, it owes a debt to Wagner, whose influence Debussy tried and failed to resist. *Tristan und Isolde* is a clear point of reference. But the Wagnerism in *Pelléas et Mélisande* is purified, its opulence refined down to more modest, simple terms and a kind of unadorned word-setting, halfway between speech and chant, with one note per syllable. The role of Pelléas requires a peculiarly light, high-lying baritone to bring it off stylistically.

Highlights

With no arias and such general restraint, it would be misleading to call anything here a 'highlight', but the loss of the ring in Act II and Golaud's use of the child Yniold to spy on Mélisande are, in different ways, disturbing moments.

Did You Know?

A row with Maeterlinck over the casting of Mélisande (he wanted the part to go to his mistress) meant that Maeterlinck dissociated himself from the premiere and had hostile notes printed for distribution to the first night audience, which helped provoke uproar in the theatre.

Recommended Recording

Francois Le Roux, Maria Ewing, José van Dam, Vienna Philharmonic Orchestra/Claudio Abbado. DG 435 344-2. The best all-round cast, the best orchestral sound, and conducting of clear, focused elegance.

Léo Delibes

(1836–91)

Lakmé (1883)

Brought up in Paris, Delibes studied at the Conservatoire there and felt the lure of the theatre early on as a boy chorister at the Paris Opéra. But it was as a composer for the ballet that he made a lasting reputation, with works like *Coppélia* (1870) and *Sylvia* (1876), which remain classics of the genre. His vocal style was formed in operetta, writing for Offenbach's theatre the Bouffes-Parisiens, and its hallmarks remained lightweight elegance and wit. Only one serious opera survives in repertory.

Lakmé

FORM: Opera in three acts; in French
COMPOSER: Léo Delibes (1836–91)
LIBRETTO: Edmond Gondinet and Philippe Gille; after Loti's novel
FIRST PERFORMANCE: Paris, 14 April 1883

Principal Characters

Lakmé ⚘ Soprano
Mallika, her slave ⚘ Mezzo-soprano
Hadji, her servant ⚘ Tenor
Nilakantha, Lakmé's father, a Brahmin priest ⚘ Bass-baritone
Gérald, a British officer ⚘ Tenor
Frédéric, a British officer ⚘ Baritone

Synopsis of the Plot

Setting: Imperial India; 19th century

ACT I Gérald, his fiancée and other friends, are wandering near Nilakantha's home when they come across the temple, breaking down a bamboo fence to gain access. Gérald is left behind, sketching, as the others move on and is seen by Lakmé and Mallika. Gérald is instantly entranced by the beautiful Lakmé, who responds to his fervour, although her main concern is his safety; her father harbours an implacable hatred for the

British occupiers of India. Gérald disappears through the broken fence as they hear Nilakantha returning. Nilakantha notices the damage and swears vengeance on those who had dared to profane his sacred ground.

ACT II While visiting the market Gérald hears Lakmé singing – a trap devised by her father to catch the man who desecrated his garden, attracted there, he believes, by Lakmé's beauty. When Lakmé sees Gérald she faints and he rushes to her side. Nilakantha stabs him.

ACT III Helped by Hadji, Lakmé has taken Gérald to a secret hideaway. But Frédéric has followed the wounded officer and, when Lakmé goes to fetch water from the sacred spring, he appeals to Gérald to leave with the regiment that night. Gérald agrees. When she returns, bringing the water that, when drunk by lovers, assures them of everlasting love, Lakmé senses his change of heart. She takes a leaf from the poisonous datura tree and bites it, before they drink the water together. Gérald is broken-hearted when she dies, but her father, knowing that his beloved daughter will have eternal life, accepts her death with equanimity.

Music and Background

While *Lakmé*'s plot has the sort of exotic setting fashionable at that time, the music is uncommonly well-written and fresh-sounding for a score that doesn't attempt anything particularly radical. The models are Massenet and Bizet, and its decorous melodies sing out in strictly formal, self-contained numbers as though Wagner had never existed. But no matter. With appealingly restrained touches of oriental colour and enchanting lyricism it remains a winner with audiences and singers alike. Most of the great sopranos with a claim to coloratura – the ability to negotiate highly decorative vocal lines – have been drawn to the title role.

Highlights

The famous Act I 'Flower Duet' for Lakmé and Mallika is a celebration of the female voice, spinning embroidered skeins of song in long, unbroken, creamily seductive measures. Lakmé's Act II 'Bell Song' is a showpiece aria.

Did You Know?

The famous 'Flower Duet' became still more famous when British Airways borrowed it as the theme to their long-running TV commercial. They use the less commendable EMI recording with Mady Mesplé.

Recommended Recording

Joan Sutherland, Alain Vanzo, Monte Carlo Opera/Richard Bonynge. Decca 425 485-2. Sutherland in glorious form, even if you don't get the consonants.

Gaetano Donizetti

(1797–1848)

Anna Bolena (1830)
L'Elisir d'Amore (1832)
Lucrezia Borgia (1833)
Maria Stuarda (1834)
Lucia di Lammermoor (1835)
L'Assedio Calais (1836)
La Fille du Régiment (1839)
La Favorite (1840)
Linda di Chamounix (1842)
Don Pasquale (1843)

Enormously prolific, with some seventy operas to his name, Donizetti was born in Bergamo, built his career in Naples and moved on to triumph in Paris and Vienna as a leading exponent of the style of vocal writing known as bel canto: a style where, in performance, beauty of line and virtuosity of embellishment are paramount. At his death (from syphilis) in 1848, about a quarter of the Italian operas in regular European repertory were by him – an achievement rivalled only by his slightly older contemporary, Rossini. It wasn't to last, and by the turn of the century most of his work had been forgotten, leaving in performance only the comedies for which he is still principally known: *L'Elisir d'Amore, Don Pasquale* and *La Fille du Régiment*. But Donizetti considered himself above all else a composer of romantic drama, and with the revival of interest in 'display' singing, encouraged from the middle of this century by stars like Callas and Sutherland, his serious works have resurfaced, led by *Lucia di Lammermoor* which is now a well-established vehicle for coloratura sopranos with a gift for pathos.

Don Pasquale

FORM: Opera in three acts; in Italian
COMPOSER: Gaetano Donizetti (1797–1848)
LIBRETTO: Giovanni Ruffini and Gaetano Donizetti
FIRST PERFORMANCE: Paris, 29 June 1843

Principal Characters

Don Pasquale, an old bachelor ⁓ **Bass**
Dr Malatesta, his friend ⁓ **Baritone**
Ernesto, his nephew ⁓ **Tenor**
Norina, a young widow ⁓ **Soprano**
A notary ⁓ **Baritone**

Synopsis of the Plot

Setting: Rome

ACT I Don Pasquale, a wealthy old bachelor, disapproves of his nephew's choice of the widowed Norina as his future wife. To punish Ernesto he decides to take a wife himself, produce his own son and heir and thus deprive Ernesto of his expected inheritance. Dr Malatesta has agreed to try and find the old man a suitable wife and suggests his own sister – young, innocent and fresh from the convent – as the perfect choice. Don Pasquale is overjoyed. But Dr Malatesta is a friend of the young lovers as well as of Don Pasquale, and he tells Norina of his scheme to disguise her as his sister and trick the old man into marriage; she will then make his life such a torment that he will gladly return to the single life. Norina is delighted with the idea.

ACT II Malatesta introduces the heavily-disguised 'Sofronia' to Pasquale and he is much taken by her simplicity and demureness. The marriage, he announces, must be immediate and, fortunately, Dr Malatesta has had the forethought to bring his notary with him so that the contract can be drawn up. Ernesto, who arrives just in time to be a witness, is thunderstruck when he recognises Norina, but Malatesta quickly explains the deception. The instant the ceremony is over, the sweet, docile 'Sofronia' becomes rude, domineering and very keen to spend her new husband's money.

ACT III 'Sofronia' enters, expensively dressed, and tells Pasquale she is off to the theatre. On the way out she deliberately drops a letter arranging an assignation with an unknown lover. Pasquale consults Malatesta who advises him to wait in the garden and catch the lovers unawares. This he does, but Ernesto slips away and 'Sofronia' denies everything. Malatesta tells Pasquale that the best solution would be to allow Ernesto and Norina to marry; Norina will then be installed as mistress of the house, instead of 'Sofronia'. On hearing this, 'Sofronia' declares that she will never sleep under the same roof as Norina. Pasquale, having found a way of ridding himself of his tormentor, gives his consent to Ernesto's marriage. 'Sofronia' joyfully throws off her disguise, the lovers are reunited and there is nothing left for Pasquale to do but accept the situation with as much grace as he can muster.

Music and Background

A sparkling comedy that crowns the great tradition of Italian opera buffa, this is music whose flawless brilliance belies the speed with which it was written: roughly two weeks to complete the short score, with the orchestration done during rehearsals. Act II in particular has a Mozartian perfection, running numbers together in a near-seamless flow, and it comes with more heart to the comedy than buffo opera often allows. It also comes with a distinctive style of 'floating' recitative, accompanied by occasional string chords rather than the more obtrusive (and normal) keyboard cadences.

Highlights

Virtually the whole of Act II, as the comedy builds to its side-splitting climax; otherwise, Ernesto's soaring Act I 'Sogno soave casto' and Act III serenade 'Comè gentil'. There is also a celebrated duet for Pasquale and Malatesta in Act III, 'Cheti, cheti, immantinente'.

Did You Know?

🎵 The speed with which *Don Pasquale* was written is partly explained by the inclusion of material which Donizetti lifted (after the manner of the time) from previous works, but the borrowings only increase the admiration you have to have for the apparent integrity of a score where every element fits so perfectly into the whole.

Recommended Recording

Sesto Bruscantini, Mirella Freni, Philharmonia Orchestra/Riccardo Muti. EMI CDS7 47068-2. Admirably cast, stylishly conducted, and with fine orchestral sound.

L'Elisir d'Amore
(The Elixir of Love, The Love Potion)

FORM: Opera in two acts; in Italian
COMPOSER: Gaetano Donizetti (1797–1848)
LIBRETTO: Felice Romani;
after Scribe's libretto for Auber's *Le Philtre*
FIRST PERFORMANCE: Milan, 12 May 1832

Principal Characters

Nemorino, a young countryman ∞ Tenor
Giannetta, a country girl ∞ Soprano
Adina, a rich farm owner ∞ Soprano
Belcore, a sergeant ∞ Baritone
Dulcamara, a 'quack' doctor ∞ Bass

Synopsis of the Plot

Setting: A small Italian village; 19th century

ACT I Nemorino is trying desperately, if shyly, to win the heart of rich, beautiful Adina, but he is firmly upstaged by the confident, masterful Belcore, who mocks Nemorino's efforts. Nemorino has been reading the story of Tristan and Isolde and, like Tristan, forlornly accepts that his only hope of winning his beloved lies in his acquisition of a love potion. Just at that moment Dulcamara and his colourful waggon appear. Nemorino outlines his problem and Dulcamara assures him that he has exactly the same potion that Tristan used. He sells him (for Nemorino's last coin), a small bottle of Bordeaux wine, with the proviso that the magic takes twenty-four hours to work. Nemorino's happiness is assured and he settles down to wait for Adina to fall in love with him – only to have his dreams shattered by the news that Belcore's detachment must leave immediately and he and Adina have decided to marry that very day.

ACT II The wedding feast is under way at Adina's farm and the happy couple depart to sign the marriage contract. A disconsolate Nemorino is offered another bottle of elixir, this time one that has an instant effect. To pay for the potion Nemorino enlists with Belcore's regiment. Meanwhile, news has arrived that Nemorino has just inherited a large sum of money and the village girls all flock around him. Nemorino, unaware of his luck, supposes this to be the effect of the elixir. Adina, who has postponed the signing of the contract, learns from Dulcamara that Nemorino has bought the potion and this, together with the fact that he even enlisted so that he could pay for it, touches her very much. Nemorino, seeing a tear in her eye, pours out his heart to her and she, in turn, tells him that she has bought his discharge from the army. The happy couple are united and Dulcamara does a roaring trade in elixirs – proved to bring not only love but money too! Even the rejected Belcore accepts the situation philosophically, and comforts himself with the thought that the world is, after all, full of girls.

Music and Background

This 'male Cinderella' opera may be full of stock comic characters, but their music rises above the predictable and blossoms into some of the most engaging melodies of the bel canto repertoire. Essentially a tenor's opera in which Nemorino inevitably steals the show with his romanza 'Una furtiva lagrima' (oddly but effectively accompanied by solo bassoon), it nonetheless offers all the principal characters their moment, and even allows them some opportunity for character development. Not all bel canto operas bother with such things.

Highlights

'Una furtiva lagrima' in Act II is the turning point of the opera (when Nemorino realises that Adina loves him) and the moment everybody waits for. But Nemorino's opening Act I cavatina 'Quanto è bella' is almost equally famous; Dulcamara has an irresistible song of sales patter 'Udite, udite'; and the duet 'Esulti pur la barbara', when Adina finds Nemorino drinking the potion, is the spirited high point of Act I.

Did You Know?

⚖ In Donizetti's lifetime, this was his most popular score.

Recommended Recording

Joan Sutherland, Luciano Pavarotti, English Chamber Orchestra/Richard Bonynge. Decca 414 461-2. A young Pavarotti, captured in his prime in 1971.

La Fille du Régiment
(The Daughter of the Regiment)

FORM: Opera in two acts; in French
COMPOSER: Gaetano Donizetti (1797–1848)
LIBRETTO: J-H. Vernoy de Saint-Georges and J-F-A. Bayard
FIRST PERFORMANCE: Paris, 11 February 1840

Principal Characters

Marie, the 'daughter of the regiment' ⁓ **Soprano**
Sulpice, a sergeant in the grenadiers ⁓ **Bass**
Tonio, a Tyrolean youth, in love with Marie ⁓ **Tenor**
Marquise de Birkenfeld ⁓ **Mezzo-soprano**
Hortensio, her steward ⁓ **Bass**

Synopsis of the Plot

Setting: The Swiss Tyrol and the Marquise's château; around 1810

ACT I The Marquise and her steward, Hortensio, have been interrupted in their journey by a skirmish between Swiss and French troops nearby. Tonio brings them the good news that the French have been defeated and he is soon followed by Sergeant Sulpice, who reassures them of their safety. When Marie herself arrives on the scene, Sulpice reminds her of how she was found, as a baby, on the battlefield and raised by the soldiers as their 'daughter'. He then questions her about the young man she has recently been seen with. Marie tells him that, while picking flowers, she nearly fell over a cliff and was rescued by a young Tyrolean, with whom she has fallen in love. Sulpice reminds her that she may only marry a grenadier. Suddenly Tonio is dragged in, accused of spying; Marie successfully pleads for him and, to be near her, Tonio enlists as a grenadier. Meanwhile, the Marquise has asked the soldiers to give her safe passage home and on hearing the name Birkenfeld, Sulpice gives her papers, addressed in that name, found on the baby Marie. The Marquise declares Marie to be her long-lost niece and insists that she goes to live with her, leaving behind the regiment and her beloved Tonio.

ACT II The Marquise is training Marie to be a lady and has decided that she should marry the future Duke of Krakenthorp. Marie dreads the marriage and confesses to Sulpice, who is recuperating from a wound at the château, that she still loves Tonio. At that moment the grenadiers are heard marching outside and several of them, including Tonio, crowd into the Marquise's salon. The two lovers decide to elope, but Tonio says that such a drastic step is not really necessary: the Marquise had no sister, so Marie

113

cannot be her niece and can marry whom she will. The Marquise has no choice but to admit that Marie is her illegitimate daughter. Now, however, Marie feels it is her duty to obey her mother and is about to sign the marriage contract when several grenadiers burst in and reveal her military upbringing, to the scandalised disapproval of the assembled wedding guests. Marie tells them all how much she owes to the regiment and the Marquise, touched by her simplicity and generosity, gives her permission to marry the man she loves.

Music and Background

This is Donizetti taking on a change of style – from Italian opera buffa (with sung recitatives) to French *opéra comique* (with spoken dialogue to link the musical numbers). Just *how* French it is was proved by the composer's later and considerably less successful attempts to rewrite the score as an Italian piece – a version which is almost never heard today. With rousing military tunes, graceful arias, and opportunites for vocal display – not least a good number of high Cs for the tenor – *La Fille du Régiment* has always been a bel canto favourite. Its only weak point, the Act II finale, is usually pepped up by the insertion of some extraneous aria as a sort of party piece.

Highlights

Marie's regimental song in Act I, 'Chacun le sait', is an exuberant number, and her farewell aria at the end of the act, 'Il faut partir', is deeply touching. Tonio's best numbers are his Act I 'Pour mon âme' (with its nine top Cs) and his Act II address to the Marquise, 'Pour me rapprocher de Marie'.

Did You Know?

~ Mendelssohn admired the opera so much he said he wished he'd written it himself; it was an immediate success, with forty-four performances in 1840 alone.

~ During World War II the great soprano Lily Pons used to insert as her extra Act II aria the 'Marseillaise' and carry a flag with the cross of Lorraine.

Recommended Recording

Joan Sutherland, Luciano Pavarotti, Royal Opera Covent Garden/Richard Bonynge. Decca 410 193-2. An absolute classic of its period (and any other) with Sutherland and Pavarotti in top form.

Lucia di Lammermoor

FORM: Opera in three acts; in Italian
COMPOSER: Gaetano Donizetti (1797–1848)
LIBRETTO: Salvatore Cammarano; after Sir Walter Scott's novel
FIRST PERFORMANCE: Naples, 26 September 1835

Principal Characters

Lord Enrico Ashton of Lammermoor ✺ Baritone
Lucia Ashton, his sister ✺ Soprano
Raimondo, the family chaplain ✺ Bass
Edgardo, Master of Ravenswood ✺ Tenor
Arturo Bucklaw ✺ Tenor

Synopsis of the Plot

Setting: Scotland; the end of the 17th century

ACT I Enrico Ashton has arranged for his sister, Lucia, to marry Arturo Bucklaw, a union through which he hopes to restore the family's declining fortunes. But Lucia, to his fury, has been seen secretly meeting his enemy, Edgardo of Ravenswood, whose title and estates Enrico has already taken over. Lucia, hearing of her brother's plans to destroy Edgardo, decides to warn him that his life is in danger but, when they meet, Edgardo tells her that he is being sent away on a political mission to France. He promises to write to her and they part, assuring each other of their undying love.

ACT II Enrico is more determined than ever that Lucia should marry Arturo, so he tricks her by showing her a forged letter, supposedly from Edgardo, in which he says that he is marrying another woman. Still she resists until her brother tells her that he needs this marriage to restore him to royal favour. Finally Lucia resigns herself to his will. The marriage is arranged and, as the guests assemble to witness the signing of the marriage contract, Edgardo suddenly interrupts the ceremony. On being shown the signed marriage contract, Edgardo curses Lucia, accusing her of treachery, and she collapses.

ACT III The wedding celebrations are in full swing when the horrified chaplain bursts in with the news that Lucia has lost her reason and has stabbed Arturo to death. Lucia herself then appears, her wedding dress stained with blood. At first she appears to believe that she is living happily in the future with Edgardo before returning to reality, reliving the terrible scene at the wedding and collapsing unconscious. Meanwhile Edgardo, gazing bitterly up at the blazing windows of Ravenswood Castle, curses his fate. A group of people pass by and tell him, to his incredulous astonishment, that Lucia is insane and dying – a fact soon confirmed by the chaplain. Overcome with grief and hopelessness, Edgardo kills himself.

Music and Background

Lucia di Lammermoor passes through moments of dramatic ineptitude and musical conventionality, but it also offers some surprisingly effective musical psychology where what you hear has something real to say about the emotions and mental state of the characters. Lucia's Mad Scene (probably the most celebrated of its kind in all opera) offers a telling reflection of the heroine's distress in the way it throws out fragmentary reminiscences of past themes – all of them distorted except for her memory of her Act I duet with Edgardo. Many commentators regard *Lucia di Lammermoor* as Donizetti's overall masterpiece. Its brand of high Romantic drama (and use of a high baritone for Enrico) proved a major influence on Verdi.

Highlights

The Mad Scene, with its blood-sports contest between voice and flute for the most brilliant embellishment, has always dominated this opera – to such an extent that it used to be common to jettison the following scene and end the whole piece there and then. Act II opens with a fine three-part duet between Lucia and Enrico and culminates in one of the most celebrated ensembles in all opera, the sextet 'Chi mi frena'.

Did You Know?

 Flaubert set a famous passage of *Madame Bovary* during a performance of *Lucia di Lammermoor*, using the opera as a symbol of his heroine's decline.
 Donizetti also wrote an opera with the rather less exotic-sounding title *Emilia di Liverpool*.

Recommended Recording

Joan Sutherland, Luciano Pavarotti, Sherrill Milnes, Royal Opera Covent Garden/Richard Bonynge. Decca 410 193-2. The second of Sutherland's two Decca recordings, made in 1971 and demonstrating why she was the Lucia of her time. Perhaps of all time.

Maria Stuarda
(Mary Stuart)

FORM: Opera in three acts; in Italian
COMPOSER: Gaetano Donizetti (1797-1848)
LIBRETTO: Giuseppe Bardari; after Schiller's play
FIRST PERFORMANCE: Milan, 30 December 1835

Principal Characters

Mary, Queen of Scots ⌒ **Soprano**
Elizabeth I, Queen of England ⌒ **Soprano**
Earl of Leicester ⌒ **Tenor**
Earl of Shrewsbury (Talbot) ⌒ **Baritone**
Lord Burleigh (Cecil) ⌒ **Bass**

Synopsis of the Plot

Setting: London and Fotheringhay; 1587

ACT I Mary, imprisoned by her cousin, Elizabeth, writes to Leicester, the queen's favourite, imploring him to help her. Leicester, sympathetic to the unfortunate queen and much taken by the portrait accompanying the letter, determines to help her. Elizabeth demands to see the letter and, in spite of her suspicions of Mary's ambitions, she agrees to Leicester's request that she should meet her cousin at Fotheringhay.

ACT II At Fotheringhay, the imprisoned queen walks in the grounds, nostalgically reflecting on the past and longing for freedom. Leicester arrives in advance of the royal party and urges Mary to take a submissive attitude towards her cousin; he swears that he will avenge her if Elizabeth should injure her and even asks her to marry him. Elizabeth arrives, accompanied by Cecil, who deeply mistrusts Mary. Face to face the two queens survey each other; Mary forces herself to kneel before Elizabeth and ask for mercy, but Elizabeth is so infuriated by the sight of the proud, still beautiful Queen of Scots that she taunts her and goads her until Mary's resolution gives way and she calls her cousin a 'vile bastard'.

ACT III Mary's cause is lost and Elizabeth, urged on by Cecil and angered by Leicester's continuing support for Mary, signs the death warrant, ordering Leicester to witness the execution. Mary receives the news calmly, and, praying for all those who have wronged her, is led towards her death as Leicester stands helplessly by.

Music and Background

This is one of the Donizetti operas which has been rediscovered in modern times after a century of neglect. From the start, the piece had trouble with the censors – stories about royal personages usually did – and first appeared in an adapted version that moved the plot to Renaissance Florence. The manuscript was subsequently lost, only resurfacing in modern times. The writing is uneven but at its best powerfully dramatic, building into forceful climaxes like the encounter between the two queens at the end of Act II where Mary calls Elizabeth a 'vil bastarda'. This is theatre fantasy: in history the two queens never met.

Highlights

The Act II 'Dalogo delle due regine', as the score calls it, stands out if only for its situation. Otherwise the finest moments come in Act III, from the confessional duet between Mary and Talbot to her execution aria, which many listeners think the finest dramatic music in Donizetti's entire output.

Did You Know?

❧ At rehearsals for the premiere in 1834, the two queens got carried away during their 'Dialogo' and ended up in a fist fight – won by Mary. Elizabeth collapsed and had to be taken home.

Recommended Recording

Joan Sutherland, Huguette Turangeau, Luciano Pavarotti, Teatro Comunale di Bologna/Richard Bonynge. Decca 425 410-2. Sutherland yet again establishing her supremacy among Donizetti sopranos.

Antonin Dvořák
(1841–1904)

Dimitrij (1882)
The Jacobin (1888)
The Devil and Kate (1898)
Rusalka (1900)

Dvořák is principally remembered as a composer of symphonies (nine) and instrumental chamber music (including fourteen string quartets). Only one of his ten operas – *Rusalka* – has achieved any currency outside his homeland. But opera was a recurring preoccupation throughout his life, and his early professional experience in music was as a violist in Prague's National Theatre orchestra, playing under Smetana. His stage works fall broadly into two groups – heroic nationalist scores and rustic folk fantasies – and they work well enough in practice, with fluent writing for the voices. But considered as a whole, they give the listener no real sense of a developing technique or style, and individual works have little to compare with the popular melodic appeal of, say, the 'New World Symphony'.

Rusalka

FORM: Opera in three acts; in Czech
COMPOSER: Antonin Dvořák (1841–1904)
LIBRETTO: S.J. Kvapil; after de la Motte Fouqué,
Hans Christian Andersen and Hauptmann
FIRST PERFORMANCE: Prague, 31 March 1901

Principal Characters

Rusalka, a water nymph ~ Soprano
Prince ~ Tenor
Vodník, the Spirit of the Lake and Rusalka's father ~ Bass
Ježibaba, a witch ~ Mezzo-soprano
Foreign Princess ~ Soprano

Synopsis of the Plot

Setting: The lake shore, the castle grounds

ACT I Rusalka tells Vodník, her father, that she has fallen in love with the Prince and wishes to become human. Vodník is very distressed, but he cares deeply for his daughter and advises her to consult the witch, Ježibaba. Ježibaba is willing to use her powers to enable Rusalka to walk on land – but she will be forever dumb in the Prince's presence and, if he should prove unfaithful to her, they will both be damned. The spell is cast and Rusalka waits as the Prince, hunting nearby, is irresistibly drawn to the lake. He sees Rusalka, is enchanted by her beauty and takes her home to his castle.

ACT II The Prince and Rusalka are to be married, but the bridegroom is becoming dissatisfied with his silent consort and passes much of his time with the Foreign Princess. He decides to give a ball to celebrate his forthcoming nuptials, but spends most of the evening with the Foreign Princess. Rusalka, distraught, rushes out to the grounds, where she finds her father and begs him to help her. Rusalka's fears are confirmed by the appearance of the Prince, bringing his new love with him; Rusalka hears him assure the Foreign Princess that he is tired of Rusalka and now loves only her. Rusalka throws herself into his arms, but is rejected; Vodník curses the Prince.

ACT III Rejecting Ježibaba's suggestion that she can redeem herself by murdering the Prince, Rusalka resigns herself to her lonely fate as a wandering wraith. Meanwhile, the Prince has fallen ill and, delirious, staggers to the lake to search for Rusalka. She tells him that she is now cursed by his rejection and, if she were to kiss him, he would die. He begs her to give him peace; she kisses him and he dies in her arms before she sinks, for the last time, into the waters of the lake.

Music and Background

The haunting beauty of this atmospheric score stands head and shoulders above anything else Dvořák produced for the stage, and quite apart from the opportunities it offers a pure-voiced young soprano to shine in her big solo, it also makes a good company piece.

Highlights

Rusalka's Act I 'Invocation to the Moon' takes precedence over all else as one of Dvořák's most beguiling tunes. The Act I finale would be a love duet if only Rusalka hadn't been struck dumb, but Dvořák gets round the problem by making the Prince's closing measures speak for both.

Recommended Recording

Gabriela Beňačková, Wieslaw Ochman, Czech Philharmonic Orchestra/ Vaclav Neumann. Supraphon 10 3641-2. Authentically Slavonic singing without the standard drawbacks.

Gottfried von Einem

(1918–96)

Dantons Tod (1946)
Der Prozess (1952)
Der Besuch der Alten Dame (1970)

Gottfried von Einem's largely tonal, often tuneful eclecticism has made him one of the most popular 'new' composers in Germany since the Second World War, although his work has had limited exposure elsewhere. Born to Austrian parents, his earliest years as a musician were spent in quiet resistance to the Third Reich, studying with the composer/writer Boris Blacher who subsequently provided libretti for most of von Einem's operas. They began with *Dantons Tod*, commissioned immediately after the war by the Salzburg Festival, and continued with *Der Prozess*, an adaptation of Kafka's *The Trial*. Other works, like the so-called 'mystery play' *Jesu Hochzeit*, have created passing shock-waves and notoriety, but von Einem was essentially a conservative figure whose music proved summatory rather than revolutionary.

Dantons Tod
(Danton's Death)

FORM: Opera in two acts; in German
COMPOSER: Gottfried von Einem (1918–96)
LIBRETTO: B. Blacher and Gottfried von Einem;
after Georg Büchner's play
FIRST PERFORMANCE: Salzburg, 6 August 1947

Principal Characters

Danton, a deputy ✺ Baritone
Robespierre, a deputy ✺ Tenor
Camille Desmoulins, a deputy ✺ Tenor
Lucile Desmoulins, his wife ✺ Soprano
Hérault de Sechelles, a deputy ✺ Tenor
Saint-Just, a deputy ✺ Bass
Simon, a theatrical prompter ✺ Buffo-bass

Synopsis of the Plot

Setting: Revolutionary Paris in 1794

ACT I A group of deputies and their friends are sitting around a gaming table discussing the political situation, particularly the absolute power of Robespierre and his current Reign of Terror. Camille Desmoulins, a young, revolutionary friend of Danton, makes it clear that he feels the killing should stop now and that Danton should oppose the ruthless, bloodthirsty Robespierre. Danton, however, seems tired and disillusioned and is disinclined to make a stand. The scene changes to the street, where Simon, suspecting that his daughter has become a prostitute, castigates the rich men who can buy the bodies of the poor. The mob agrees with him and a hapless young man, assumed to be an aristocrat, is almost strung up from the nearest lamp post. Robespierre himself now arrives and announces new death sentences, to general acclaim. The crowd disperses and Robespierre is left alone with Danton, who cannot conceal his distaste for Robespierre's methods; after he has gone Robespierre decides that he has no choice but to eliminate Danton and his supporters. Danton and Camille are arrested.

ACT II Danton and Desmoulins are in prison. Outside, the people at first support Danton but Robespierre, through Simon, puts about rumours that Danton has lived like an aristocrat while he, Robespierre, has stayed true to the principles of the Revolution. Danton is brought to trial on false charges of conspiracy against the people, which he strongly and eloquently denies.

Support for him is definitely growing when Saint-Just brings forward new 'evidence' against him. At this point Danton accuses Robespierre of treachery and the trial collapses in uproar. The final scene takes place in the square: crowds are singing and dancing in anticipation of the coming executions, their favourite form of entertainment. Danton, Desmoulins and Hérault are brought in; the people shriek abuse at them before they are guillotined. Only Lucile is left, sadly grieving over what she, and France, have lost that day.

Music and Background

This opera adapts Büchner's story in ways that enlarge the role of the crowd, who become like the turbulent, commentating masses of the Bach Passions. Written in seventeen separate numbers, partly linked by instrumental interludes, it makes an interesting comparison with Britten's more or less contemporary *Peter Grimes* – although von Einem shows nothing of Britten's gift for melody. Most of the solo vocal writing comes in speech-like *parlando* style.

Highlight

The exhilarating, complex choral writing in the Part II Tribunal Scene.

Did You Know?

🐎 Von Einem's original inspiration for the opera was the unsuccessful plot on Hitler's life in 1944.

Recommended Recording

Theo Adam, Werner Hollweg, Kurt Rydl, Kristina Laki, Austrian Radio Symphony Orchestra/Lothar Zagrosek. Orfeo C102 842H. A live recording from the 1983 Salzburg Festival.

Manuel de Falla
(1876–1946)

La Vida Breve (1904)
El Retablo de Maese Pedro (1922)
Atlántida (1946, unfinished)

The best-known of all modern Spanish composers – not least for his orchestral fantasy *Nights in the Gardens of Spain* – Falla was born in Cadiz, studied in Madrid, and learnt his craft writing the sort of light operas (zarzuelas) that commanded theatrical taste there. He subsequently moved to Paris where he joined the glittering circle of composers like Debussy and Ravel and found outlets for his work that didn't exist in Spain. His first true opera, *La Vida Breve*, finally reached the stage – nine years after composition – in France. And *El Retablo de Maese Pedro*, an ingenious puppet opera taken from one of the *Don Quixote* stories, with a boy treble as narrator, was written for a private performance in the house of the celebrated Parisian salon hostess Princess de Polignac. Falla's last intended stage work, a spectacular opera-oratorio on the last days of Atlantis called *Atlántida*, was left unfinished at his death. His final years were spent in Argentina.

La Vida Breve
(Brief Life, The Short Life)

FORM: Opera in two acts; in Spanish
COMPOSER: Manuel de Falla (1876–1946)
LIBRETTO: C. Fernández Shaw
FIRST PERFORMANCE: Nice, 1 April 1913 (in French)

Principal Characters
Salud, a gypsy ❧ **Soprano**
Paco, a young man ❧ **Tenor**
Carmela, a young girl ❧ **Mezzo-soprano**
Uncle Salvador ❧ **Bass**
Grandmother ❧ **Mezzo-soprano**

124

Synopsis of the Plot

Setting: Granada; early 20th century

ACT I Salud is anxiously awaiting the arrival of her beloved, Paco, whom she is to marry. Her grandmother tells her of the dangers of loving too much, but Salud takes no notice. She is overjoyed when at last he comes, professing eternal love. The two lovers are grimly observed by Salud's Uncle Salvador, who tells her grandmother that he has heard rumours that Paco is to marry a girl from his own class, Carmela, the very next day.

ACT II Paco and his bride, Carmela, are enjoying a party to celebrate their wedding. Salud observes the festivities from the street outside and is heartbroken to see the man she loves laughing and talking with his new bride. The guests are mingling in the courtyard when Salvador and Salud appear. Salvador offers to sing and dance for the company but Salud, clearly in a highly-charged state of mind, approaches Paco and, sadly and movingly, accuses him of betraying her. But her emotions prove too much for her to bear and she falls dead at his feet, the air ringing with the sound of gypsy curses against the faithless Paco.

Music and Background

With its wealth of local colour, dances, feasting and flamenco, this is nationalist music with a vengeance, often described as a Spanish *Cavalleria Rusticana* without the melodrama. The score is largely a vehicle for the soprano Salud, the only fully fleshed-out character in what isn't always totally compelling drama, but there's a general freshness and vitality that sustains the piece through its short duration.

Highlights

Salud's 'Vivan los que rien' in Act I; the flamenco singer in Act II.

Did You Know?

At the time of writing this vivid evocation of Granada street-life, the composer had never been there.

Recommended Recording

Teresa Berganza, José Carreras, London Symphony Orchestra/Garcia Navarro. DG 435 851-2. Strong, earthy singing with a young Carreras in a small role.

John Gay
(1685–1732)

The Beggar's Opera (1728)

John Gay was never actually a composer but a self-educated poet and playwright who began life as an apprentice to a silk merchant and wrote the libretto for Handel's *Acis and Galatea*. His claim to fame is that he developed the idea of 'ballad opera': taking pre-existing tunes, adding new words, and weaving them into an extended story which played in plain English as an early 18th-century equivalent to mid-20th-century kitchen-sink drama. The subjects concerned 'low' life, and involved satirical allusions to contemporary politics. They also pilloried the fashion for grand, high-minded Italian opera which, under the leadership of Handel, had been the chief entertainment of London society. The enormous success of *The Beggar's Opera* contributed to Handel's problems in maintaining his operatic livelihood through future years. Ironically, the income from *The Beggar's Opera* helped establish a new theatre at Covent Garden which subsequently became the national focus for Italian opera in Britain, and continues so to this day.

The Beggar's Opera

FORM: Ballad opera in three acts; in English
COMPOSER: Music collected and arranged
by J.C. Pepusch (1667–1752)
LIBRETTO: John Gay (1685–1732)
FIRST PERFORMANCE: London, 29 January 1728

Principal Characters

Captain Macheath, highwayman and womaniser ✎ Baritone
Peachum, a 'fence' ✎ Bass
Mrs Peachum, his wife ✎ Soprano
Polly Peachum, his daughter and Macheath's wife ✎ Soprano
Lockit, a corrupt jailer ✎ Baritone
Lucy Lockit, his daughter ✎ Soprano
The Beggar ✎ Speaking role
The Player ✎ Speaking role

Synopsis of the Plot

Setting: London; 18th century

ACT I The Beggar explains his 'opera' to the Player, emphasising the equal status of the two female leads and the 'wonderfully pathetic' prison scene. The story begins with Peachum, who is examining the present state of his business affairs and contemplating the likely fortunes of several members of his gang who have been arrested. He is joined by his wife, who wants to discuss their daughter; Polly, she thinks, has taken a fancy to Macheath but Peachum is horrorstruck at the idea that Polly should marry anyone. Mrs Peachum determines to find out more, and soon returns, having discovered, to her fury, that Polly has already secretly married Macheath. Polly protests that she loves her new husband, but her parents ignore her and determine to turn the unfortunate affair to their own advantage. They arrange to have Macheath arrested (he will surely be hanged for his crimes) and warn Polly to expect imminent widowhood. Polly, who has hidden Macheath in her room, advises him to leave and they part sadly.

ACT II Macheath joins his men at a tavern and tells them he must go into hiding. But he delays too long, singing and dancing, and is arrested. Languishing in Newgate prison, Macheath is confronted by Lucy Lockit, the jailer's daughter, who blames him for her pregnancy. Macheath manages to persuade her that he loves her, refers to her as his 'wife' and pleads for her help. Lucy promises to do what she can. Later, having elicited no support from her father, Lucy goes to visit Macheath and is aghast when Polly comes in and throws her arms around her husband's neck. The two women roundly insult each other before Peachum appears to drag his daughter away. After they leave, Macheath persuades Lucy to help him escape, which she does.

ACT III Peachum and Lockit have been informed of Macheath's whereabouts and they plan his capture. Meanwhile, Lucy has invited Polly on a social visit and has prepared the 'rat's bane' for her. The two women spar warily, if outwardly affably, with each other, but are interrupted by the sudden entry of Macheath, once more in chains. Polly and Lucy visit the miscreant in the condemned cell – but when they are joined by four more women, each with a child, Macheath protests that he has had enough and is ready to be hanged. At this point the Beggar and the Player reappear; the former is all for the hanging to go ahead, but the latter thinks that this would be a tragedy and, after all, the opera must end happily. The Beggar capitulates and Macheath is reprieved.

Music and Background

The sixty-nine short numbers which make up the score are borrowings from Handel, Purcell, Jeremiah Clarke and many others, along with anonymously written folk-songs. Linked by spoken text, they were intended for performance by actors rather than trained singers, and originally delivered with minimal accompaniment – no more than an added instrumental bass-line or two, supplied by a minor London-based composer called Johann Christoph Pepusch. Most modern performances beef up the score with latterday arrangements. A notable example is that made by Benjamin Britten in 1948, which elaborates the music into something of true operatic stature – fascinating but remote from what 18th-century audiences heard.

Highlights

The chorus for Macheath and his gang 'Let us take the road' (a borrowing from Handel's *Rinaldo*); the adaptation of Purcell's 'Lilliburlero' into 'The modes of the court'.

Did You Know?

֍ The most celebrated of all modern *Beggar's Opera* rewrites was undertaken in 1928 when Kurt Weill turned it into *Die Dreigroschenoper*.

Recommended Recording

Kiri Te Kanawa, James Morris, Joan Sutherland, Warren Mitchell, Angela Lansbury, Alfred Marks, National Philharmonic Orchestra/Richard Bonynge. Decca 430 066-2. A confection of stars, singing and otherwise, that sort of works. If you prefer the Britten version, the one complete (and very good) recording is on Decca 436 850-2.

George Gershwin
(1898–1937)

Porgy and Bess (1935)

*I*n a short life – he died from a brain tumour, aged thirty-eight –
George Gershwin established himself as the archetype of modern
American creativity, with a genius that crossed all boundaries of music-
making. Born into a Russian-Jewish immigrant family in Brooklyn, he
began writing songs as a teenager then graduated to entire Broadway
revues and shows, setting lyrics by his brother Ira. Their collaborations
produced some of the most durably successful vocal music of the 20th
century. But his ambitions extended beyond Broadway towards large-
scale works that would carry the bedrock of American vernacular music
– black jazz – into the concert hall and opera house. His first triumph in
that direction was *Rhapsody in Blue* (1924), followed by a Piano
Concerto the next year. But the crowning achievement of all his work
was *Porgy and Bess* (1935) which proved to be the first true, viable
American opera, and the only one so far to have maintained a place at
the heart of the repertory.

Porgy and Bess

FORM: Opera in three acts; in English
COMPOSER: George Gershwin (1898–1937)
LIBRETTO: DuBose Heyward and Ira Gershwin;
after the play by DuBose and Dorothy Heyward
FIRST PERFORMANCE: Boston, 30 September 1935

Principal Characters

Porgy, a cripple ✎ **Baritone**
Crown, a stevedore ✎ **Bass**
Bess, Crown's girlfriend ✎ **Soprano**
Jake, a fisherman ✎ **Baritone**
Clara, Jake's wife ✎ **Soprano**
Sportin' Life, a drug dealer ✎ **Tenor**
Robbins, a neighbour ✎ **Tenor**
Serena, Robbins' wife ✎ **Soprano**
Peter, the honeyman ✎ **Tenor**

Synopsis of the Plot

Setting: Catfish Row, Charleston, USA; the 'recent past'

ACT I The colourful nightlife of Catfish Row is in full swing when Crown arrives with Bess and attempts to join a crap game, although he is too drunk to play properly. When the others mock him, he loses control and kills Robbins. Bess gives him money and tells him to run away; she herself is sheltered by Porgy. As Robbins' body is laid out – with a saucer on his chest to collect contributions for the funeral – a detective arrests Peter for the murder, in spite of the mourners' protests.

ACT II Life has returned to normal in Catfish Row: the fishermen mend their nets, Sportin' Life peddles drugs, and Porgy and Bess, an unlikely couple, have found contentment together. Bess goes on a picnic to Kittiwah Island where Crown suddenly appears and reasserts his influence over her: she misses the boat back home. Two days later, Bess is back with Porgy but in a highly emotional state. The sound of a hurricane bell warns everyone of an approaching storm when suddenly Crown bursts in and violently throws Porgy to the ground. Further violence is forestalled by Clara, who, at that moment, sees her husband's boat floating upside down in the river. Clara rushes out, followed by Crown, who vows to return for Bess.

ACT III Clara, Jake and Crown are all believed to have been killed in the storm. Suddenly Crown appears but, as he passes Porgy's window, is stabbed then strangled. The subsequent police investigation is hampered by the noncooperation of the Catfish Row residents. Porgy is arrested for contempt of court, but released a week later. He joyfully returns to Catfish Row, but finds that Bess has gone to New York with Sportin' Life. Undaunted, he resolves to follow her and bring her back.

Music and Background

It's tempting to devalue *Porgy and Bess* as a sequence of hit songs held together by surrounding music which is less than technically complete, and there are certainly moments where Gershwin seems to swim beyond his depth. But the emotional candour of the writing, its vigour and its impact more than compensate, and no other opera in the whole history of the genre has more memorable melodies. It's also worth remembering that although *Porgy and Bess* was written for operatically trained voices, it premiered not in an opera house but in a New York theatre. Gershwin called it 'folk opera', signalling a hybrid status and retreating from direct comparison with the great works of opera proper. That it doesn't reach the stage all that often is simply down to the problem of assembling an all-black cast (as it really does have to be) who can deal with both the operatic and the Broadway aspects of the piece.

Highlights

Where do you start? The solo songs – Clara's 'Summertime', Porgy's 'I got plenty o' nuttin', Serena's 'My man's gone now' – are almost all classics of their kind, as is the duet 'Bess, you is my woman', and a fair number of the larger ensembles like 'It ain't necessarily so'.

Did You Know?

∾ Under the terms of his will, Gershwin specified that all productions of the opera in English-speaking countries must use all-black artists; productions in translation may employ non-black singers in appropriate makeup.

∾ Gershwin once asked Maurice Ravel for lessons in the technique of composition. Ravel replied that, since Gershwin earned so much, Ravel should be the one to ask for lessons.

Recommended Recording

Willard White, Cynthia Haymon, Damon Evans, London Philharmonic/ Simon Rattle. EMI CDS7 49568-2. The celebrated Glyndebourne production with a largely African-American cast: as authentic an experience as you'll get.

Umberto Giordano
(1867–1948)

Andrea Chénier (1896)
Fedora (1898)
La Cena delle Beffe (1924)

G iordano's ten operas all equivocate between what was at the time old-fashioned romantic melodrama and the new, usually low-life, often vulgar realism of Italian verismo which took hold after the runaway success of Mascagni's *Cavalleria Rusticana*. The success of his own *Andrea Chénier* (after a couple of more questionable projects failed to hold the stage) propelled him into the front rank of the verismo composers, and *Fedora* kept him there. But not for long. His musical language coarsened, his invention waned, and apart from passing recognition for *La Cena delle Beffe* (*The Feast of the Jesters*) which attracted notoriety for its gruesome plot, he offered little more to music history, settling down instead with a rich wife.

Andrea Chénier

FORM: Opera in four acts; in Italian
COMPOSER: Umberto Giordano (1867–1948)
LIBRETTO: Luigi Illica
FIRST PERFORMANCE: Milan, 28 March 1896

Principal Characters

Andrea Chénier, a poet ∾ Tenor
Maddalena de Coigny ∾ Soprano
La Contessa de Coigny, her mother ∾ Mezzo-soprano
Bersi, her maid ∾ Mezzo-soprano
Carlo Gérard, a servant ∾ Baritone
Incredibile, a spy ∾ Tenor

Synopsis of the Plot

Setting: Paris, at the time of the French Revolution

ACT I During the preparations for a grand party at the Château de Coigny, Gérard, who is in love with the Contessa's daughter, Maddalena, bitterly denounces the luxurious living of the aristocracy and the system that represses the poor. The guests begin to arrive, among them the poet, Chénier, who is prevailed upon by Maddalena to improvise a poem. Chénier's lines extol the beauty of France, but compare it to the misery of the poor. The wealthy guests are insulted, but the Contessa quickly orders the band to strike up a lively dance. Hardly has it begun, however, when Gérard bursts in, leading a motley group of beggars. The Contessa, furious, orders them out and the party goes on as if nothing had happened.

ACT II Three years have passed and the first phase of the Revolution is over. Chénier sits alone in a busy Parisian café, carefully watched by the spy, Incredibile. He is brought a passport and told to leave the city immediately, as he has powerful enemies. Chénier refuses: he is intrigued by several anonymous letters he has received, signed Hope. Convinced that the writer is a beautiful woman, he longs to find her. Gérard enters with other revolutionary leaders and, from his conversation with Incredibile, it is clear he is searching for Maddalena. Later, Bersi tells Chénier that he can meet 'Hope' that evening. When he arrives at the rendezvous, the woman, Maddalena, reveals her true identity, and, as one of the hated aristocrats, begs him for help. Incredibile, who has been watching, fetches Gérard; the two men fight and Gérard is wounded. He urges Chénier to save himself and to protect Maddalena.

ACT III A crowd has gathered at the Revolutionary Tribunal to observe the proceedings. Chénier has been arrested and is to be tried, but Gérard is troubled by his conscience: can he denounce Chénier as an enemy of the Revolution? But jealousy and desire overpower Gérard's scruples; with Chénier gone, Maddalena will surely be his. He signs the indictment. Maddalena herself comes to see him and offers herself in return for Chénier life. Gérard promises to do what he can. At the trial, Gérard astonishes everyone by defending Chénier but, inevitably, the death sentence is passed.

ACT IV Chénier is in prison, writing his last poem, when Gérard and Maddalena arrive at the gate. Maddalena bribes the jailer to let her take the place of one of the condemned prisoners and, together, she and Chénier are taken to the guillotine.

Music and Background

At its best this is a passionate score bearing comparison with Puccini and offering moments of heroic grandeur to the tenor in the title role. It is certainly the finest music the composer ever wrote, with an effective mixture of heightened drama, historical reference (revolutionary songs, 18th-century dances), naturalism (screaming choruses, conversational exchanges) and a handful of distinctive arias.

Highlights

Chénier's so-called *improvviso* 'Un dì, all'azzurro spazio' contrasts natural joys with man-made miseries and is the high point of Act I. Gérard's conscience aria 'Nemico della patria' and Maddelena's confessional 'La mamma morta' crown Act III, and the final duet, 'Vicino a te', ends the opera on a peak of exultant lyricism.

Did You Know?

❧ Andrea Chénier was a real-life poet, although the librettist here was at pains to point out that the events of the opera are fictional.
❧ 'La mamma morta' was used in the 1993 film *Philadelphia*, starring Tom Hanks.

Recommended Recording

Plácido Domingo, Renata Scotto, Sherrill Milnes, Maria Ewing, National Philharmonic Orchestra/James Levine. RCA GD 82046. A strong cast, fierily conducted and at mid-price!

Fedora

FORM: Opera in three acts; in Italian
COMPOSER: Umberto Giordano (1867–1948)
LIBRETTO: Arturo Colautti; after Sardou's play
FIRST PERFORMANCE: Milan, 17 November 1898

Principal Characters

Princess Fedora, a rich widow ❧ **Soprano**
Count Loris Ipanov ❧ **Tenor**
Jean de Siriex, a French diplomat ❧ **Baritone**
Countess Olga ❧ **Soprano**
Grech, a police officer ❧ **Bass**

Synopsis of the Plot

Setting: St Petersburg, Paris and Switzerland; late 19th century

ACT I Count Vladimir Andreyevich is engaged to the wealthy widow, Princess Fedora. At his home his servants gossip about the Count's gambling, drinking and womanising and imply that his forthcoming marriage is more for money than love. They are interrupted by the arrival of Fedora herself, looking for her fiancé. Suddenly there is a commotion and the Count, shot and gravely wounded, is brought in and carried to his room, where he soon dies. Grech begins an investigation which focuses on the delivery that morning of a letter, later removed, which led to the assignation resulting in Count Vladimir's death. A servant remembers seeing Count Loris Ipanov in the house at that time and Fedora is instantly convinced that he is the murderer. Loris has fled the country and Fedora swears revenge.

ACT II Fedora has caught up with Loris in Paris, where she has taken a house. She gives a reception, inviting Loris, who has fallen in love with her. When Fedora tells him that she is returning to Russia, Loris admits that he cannot return; he is wanted for the murder of Count Vladimir. Fedora can barely hide her triumph, but Loris maintains his innocence and promises to bring her documentary proof that evening. After he has gone, Fedora contacts Grech, who stations officers in the garden ready to catch Loris after he has given his evidence to Fedora. When Loris returns, he tells Fedora that, even though Count Vladimir was engaged to her, he was having an affair with Loris's wife, Wanda. He shows Fedora their letters and says that when he confronted the guilty lovers, Vladimir shot and injured him; he returned the shot and fatally wounded his adversary. Fedora begins to doubt her past belief in his guilt and insists that Loris remains in the house.

ACT III Loris and Fedora are living happily together in Switzerland when news arrives that Count Vladimir's father had arranged for the arrest of Loris' brother, Valerian. Imprisoned in a cell on the banks of the Neva, Valerian drowned as the waters slowly rose; the shock has killed their mother. Fedora confesses to Loris her part in initiating the persecution of Loris and his family and begs for forgiveness. But Loris curses her and, distraught, she takes poison and dies, leaving Loris, too late, to understand and to forgive.

Music and Background

The sometimes thin plot set to sometimes flimsy music leaves you wondering whether this opera isn't just an excuse for stylish decor and a catalogue of 'effects': not least, an electric bell and an onstage bicycle. But there are some touches of local colour, including alpine music and Chopin parodies.

Highlights

Loris' Act II aria 'Amor ti vieta' provides one of the main themes. The other, representing Fedora's love for her dying count, is heard in the opening prelude.

Recommended Recording

Magda Olivero, Mario del Monaco, Tito Gobbi, Monte Carlo Opera/ Lamberto Gardelli. Decca 433 033-2. A vintage recording from 1969.

Philip Glass
(1937–)

Einstein on the Beach (1975)
Satygraha (1980)
***Akhnaten* (1983)**
The Making of the Representative for Planet 8 (1986)
The Voyage (1992)

*P*hilip Glass is a love-or-hate composer, and even those who hate him can't ignore him. One of the founding figures of the American Minimalist movement (see also John Adams), he has become an icon of the contemporary avant-garde in opera, working with theatre gurus like Robert Wilson on epically enigmatic projects that attract adulation and contempt in roughly equal measure. Born in Baltimore, he studied in Europe and India before settling into the world of experimental, cross-disciplinary performance art that flourished in New York in the 1960s. Out of that experience came his first big stage work, *Einstein on the Beach*, which has surprisingly little to say about Einstein, beaches or anything else that appeals to reason. Its admirers find in it religious qualities, and hypnotic transcendence is the one obvious potential in Glass' endlessly repeating patterns of notes. Much of his music is scored for the forces of his own stage band, which carries the textures of rock culture (amplified instruments, mostly woodwind, and synthesiser) into concert and opera venues. To any sensitive ear it registers as crude, crass, tedious and loud.

Akhnaten

FORM: Opera in three acts; in English, Egyptian and Hebrew
COMPOSER: Philip Glass (1937–)
LIBRETTO: Philip Glass, Shalom Goldman,
Robert Israel, Richard Riddell
FIRST PERFORMANCE: Stuttgart, 24 March 1984

Principal Characters

Akhnaten, King of Egypt ❧ **Countertenor**
Nefertiti, his wife ❧ **Mezzo-soprano**
Queen Tye, his mother ❧ **Soprano**
Horemhab, general and future king ❧ **Baritone**
Aye, Nefertiti's father and Akhnaten's adviser ❧ **Bass**
High Priest ❧ **Tenor**

Synopsis of the Plot

Setting: Egypt; from the 14th century BC to the present

ACT I King Amenhotep III's funeral takes place, marked by the religious rites and rituals accorded to the worship of the great gods Isis, Osiris and Horus. The new king, Amenhotep IV, is crowned and duly recognised as the incarnation of Horus, son of Isis and Osiris. But after the coronation, Amenhotep rejects his father's religion and imposes the worship of Aten, changing his name to Akhnaten. The confused High Priest leaves them as the king, Nefertiti and Tye dance blasphemously through the temple.

ACT II The new god, Aten, is the only god to be worshipped and Akhnaten has also abolished polygamy, preferring to remain faithful to the beautiful Nefertiti. Akhnaten builds a city, Akhetaten, to the glory of the new religion and, when it is complete, he sings a hymn to the sun.

ACT III Akhnaten, his wife and their six daughters are living contentedly in the new city. But the king's neglect of his state affairs is causing unrest outside, and hostile forces are threatening the country's security. Akhnaten will not listen and, eventually, is deserted by the faithful Aye, who takes his daughter, Nefertiti, with him. Aye joins forces with the High Priest of Amon and Horemhab, and they overthrow Akhnaten. The new city is destroyed and the king disappears. The old religion is reinstated. Centuries later, present-day tourists are guided round the remains of Akhetaten, still haunted by the spirits of Akhnaten, Tye and Nefertiti.

Music and Background

Glass describes this an a opera about 'religion, orthodoxy and reaction'; its most notable feature in sound terms is a ritual stasis. The infinitely repeating figures in the orchestra (full-sized but without violins) are a test of endurance and alertness. For this reason – and this alone – *Akhnaten* is a difficult score.

Highlights

The Act I funeral music and Akhnaten's Act II 'Hymn to the Sun'.

Recommended Recording

Paul Esswood, Stuttgart Opera/Dennis Russell Davies. Sony M2K 42457. The only one, and more than enough.

Mikhail Glinka
(1804–57)

A Life for the Tsar (1836)
Ruslan and Lyudmila (1842)

Mikhail Glinka was the first Russian composer to find world fame and is regarded as the founding father of his country's nationalist school – although his music was actually influenced by sources far and wide and owes almost as much to past precedents from France, Germany and (above all) Italy as it does to anything in his native tradition. Born into a wealthy landowning family, he was typical of the self-taught dilettantes who dominated Russian musical life at the time. Much of his musical knowledge was picked up from involvement with an orchestra of serfs owned by his uncle! As a young man, he also spent some time in Italy, establishing friendships with Donizetti and Bellini. Back in Russia, there can be no doubt of the hold his two operas – the grandly patriotic *A Life for the Tsar* and chaotic but magical *Ruslan and Lyudmila* – exerted over the composers who came after him. But *Ruslan and Lyudmila* was actually a failure at its premiere, and the subsequent years of his life were spent in barren disillusion.

A Life for the Tsar

FORM: Opera in four acts and an Epilogue; in Russian
COMPOSER: Mikhail Ivanovich Glinka (1804–57)
LIBRETTO: Gyorgy Fyodorovich Rozen and others
FIRST PERFORMANCE: St Petersburg, 9 December 1836

Principal Characters
Susanin, a peasant 〜 **Bass**
Antonida, his daughter 〜 **Soprano**
Sobinin, Antonida's betrothed 〜 **Tenor**
Vanya, an orphan adopted by Susanin 〜 **Mezzo-soprano**

Synopsis of the Plot

Setting: Russia and Poland; 1613

ACT I Antonida is awaiting the return of her betrothed, Sobinin, and dreams of their approaching wedding day. But her father, Susanin, is very concerned about the unsettled state of the country and refuses to allow his daughter to marry until a new tsar is chosen. When Sobinin arrives he brings good news – a Polish attack on Moscow has been repelled and the assembly has elected a new tsar, none other than their own landlord, Romanov, who is hiding in a nearby monastery.

ACT II At the Polish headquarters, a ball is in progress and the Poles talk confidently of their forthcoming campaign against the Russians. News arrives of their defeat at Moscow and of the election of Romanov as tsar. The Poles decide to take him prisoner before he can be installed.

ACT III Susanin, Antonida and Vanya are at home, happily preparing for the wedding, and pleased that the political situation has been resolved. Vanya is worried that the Poles may try and kidnap the new tsar, but he is reassured by Susanin who says that no one would betray him. Suddenly a party of Polish troops enter and demand to know the whereabouts of Romanov. Susanin at first refuses to help them, but then agrees: he manages to indicate to Vanya that he must warn the tsar while he, Susanin, leads the Poles out of their way. Antonida is distraught, realising that her father is sure to be killed when his deception is discovered. Sobinin returns and, after hearing the news, gathers a group together and sets out to rescue Susanin.

ACT IV By nightfall Sobinin and his men have lost their way in the snowbound woods; the exhausted Vanya has managed to reach the monastery and warn the tsar to escape, and Susanin has led the Poles deep into the freezing, impenetrable forests, where they light a fire and fall asleep. Susanin knows they are beginning to suspect the truth and he realises that he will die; all he wants to do is to be able to keep the Poles in the forest until dawn, thus giving the tsar time to escape. The Poles are roused by a storm and they question Susanin, who admits he deliberately led them astray. He taunts his enemies and they kill him, just as the first rays of the sun shine through the trees. Sobinin and his men rush in and fall upon the Poles.

EPILOGUE In Moscow, the crowds are celebrating the tsar's coronation, although Susanin's family's joy is mixed with grief. The tsar, they are assured, will not forget this sacrifice.

Music and Background

This opera lives deep in the Russian psyche – to the extent that after the 1917 Revolution it was widely argued that the chief melody of the final scene should be adopted as the new Soviet national anthem. But most of the music in the score is a measured synthesis of East and West, matching European ideas to Russian folk-inspired material. With stirring emotions and grand, historically-based tableaux in which the chorus play a major part, it set a precedent for Russian operas of the future.

Highlights

The most impressive moments come with massed singing – in the Act III Bridal Chorus and Act V ensemble of praise 'Glory to our Russian Tsar'.

Did You Know?

☙ When Glinka the great nationalist left Russia for the last time (he died in Germany) he reportedly spat on the ground and hoped 'never to see this vile country again'.

Recommended Recording

Boris Martinovich, Alexandrina Pendachanska, Chris Merritt, Sofia National Opera/Emil Tchakarov. Sony S3k 46487. Authentic but idiomatic and fresh singing from a largely Eastern European cast.

Ruslan and Lyudmila

FORM: Opera in five acts; in Russian
COMPOSER: Mikhail Glinka (1804–57)
LIBRETTO: Valerian Fyodorovich Shirkov, with minor contributions by Markevich, Kukolnik, Gedeonov and Glinka; after Pushkin
FIRST PERFORMANCE: St Petersburg, 9 December 1842

Principal Characters

Svetozar, Prince of Kiev ☙ Bass
Lyudmila, his daughter ☙ Soprano
Ruslan, a knight ☙ Baritone
Ratmir, an eastern prince ☙ Contralto
Farlaf, a warrior ☙ Bass
Gorislava, Ratmir's slave ☙ Soprano
Finn, a good sorcerer ☙ Tenor
Naina, an evil sorceress ☙ Mezzo-soprano
Chernomor, an evil dwarf ☙ Silent role
The Head ☙ Chorus

Synopsis of the Plot

Setting: Kiev and fantasy lands; legendary times

ACT I A grand wedding feast has been prepared in Svetozar's palace. His daughter, Lyudmila, is to be married to the knight, Ruslan, and a minstrel sings of the coming trials and wonders that their union will bring. But Lyudmila's happiness is mixed with sadness – sadness that she must leave her father's home and pity for her two rejected suitors, Ratmir, a prince from the East, and Farlaf, a warrior. Suddenly a loud clap of thunder is heard and the palace is plunged into darkness. When light is restored and the stunned company recover, they see, to their horror, that Lyudmila has vanished. Svetozar promises her hand in marriage and half his kingdom to the one who finds her.

ACT II Ruslan consults Finn, the sorcerer in his mountain cave. Finn tells him that Lyudmila has been abducted by Chernomor, an evil dwarf, whose strength lies in his great beard; Finn also warns him against the evil powers of Naina, a sorceress. Next we see Farlaf consulting Naina, who promises the warrior her help and sends him home to await her instructions. The scene changes to a battlefield where a disconsolate Ruslan picks his way over broken and discarded weaponry and the remains of dead soldiers. As the mist clears, Ruslan sees a mighty sleeping Head before him; the eyes open and the giant tries to blow him away, but Ruslan strikes the Head with his lance and the Head, defeated, gives him a magic sword with which to destroy Chernomor, explaining that he is Chernomor's brother and his present predicament is a result of his brother's evil actions.

ACT III Ratmir and the faithful Gorislava have arrived at Naina's magic castle; the prince is soon enchanted by the seductive charms of the sorceress' maidens, forgetting Lyudmila altogether. Ruslan is the next to arrive and, in turn, soon succumbs to the maidens, but Finn intervenes and the spell is broken. The castle disappears and the two men find themselves in a forest. Ratmir realises he truly loves Gorislava and the three continue their search for Lyudmila.

ACT IV Lyudmila, imprisoned by Chernomor, is tormented by her captivity and refuses to capitulate to the dwarf. News arrives that Ruslan is on his way and Chernomor casts a spell over Lyudmila before leaving to fight her rescuer. Ruslan is soon victorious and, waving aloft Chernomor's beard, comes to release Lyudmila, only to find, to his horror, that he cannot wake her. He calls on Ratmir and Gorislava to help him and, together, they take her back to Kiev.

ACT V On the way home, Farlaf abducts Lyudmila and is pursued by Ruslan. Farlaf brings her to Svetozar, hoping to claim her and his reward, but he is unable to rouse her. Suddenly the sound of galloping horses announces the arrival of Ruslan, Ratmir and Gorislava and Farlaf runs away. Ruslan, with the help of a ring given to him by Finn, wakes Lyudmila and, to general rejoicing, the wedding feast is resumed.

141

Music and Background

The composition of this piece was messy, with a libretto provided by a collection of amateur writers and random efforts by Glinka to set it. The process took five years, working at different scenes in no particular order, and the result was a chaotically uneven score that doesn't fit together well and sinks to levels of risible weakness. But at best it transcends the problems: deeply Russian in a way that set enduring precedents for Russian music through to Stravinsky, and sometimes surprisingly inventive. Glinka's richly-coloured orchestration conjures up a world of magic fantasy, and although the story moves with ponderous slowness, it somehow sets its own timescale. You don't sit looking at your watch.

Highlights

Act I: the minstrel Bayan's second song 'There is a desert land'; Lyudmila's farewell 'I am sad'; and the abduction. Act II: Ruslan's 'O field bestrewn with bones'. Act III: the Persian Song of the Slave Girls; Ratmir's 'Sultry heat supplants the shade of night'. Act IV: Lyudmila's 'Far from my beloved'; and the Oriental Dances. Act V: Ratmir's romance 'She is life and joy to me'.

Did You Know?

🎵 One of Glinka's many gifts to Russian music was a convention, found in *Ruslan and Lyudmila*, of portraying humans by standard, key-based diatonic music and supernatural creatures by freer, chromatic music – in other words, awash with sharps and flats.

Recommended Recording

Vladimir Ognovienko, Anna Netrebko, Mikhail Kit, Larissa Diadkova, Galina Gorchakova, Kirov Opera/Valery Gergiev. Philips 446 746-2. One of Gergiev's splendid reappraisals of core Russian repertory, vividly played and characterfully sung.

Christoph Willibald Gluck
(1714–87)

Orfeo ed Euridice (1762)
La Rencontre Imprévue (1764)
Alceste (1767)
Iphigénie en Aulide (1773)
Iphigénie en Tauride (1778)

Gluck was the great reformer of opera history: a sober, serious-minded figure who took in hand the display-oriented stage traditions of the early 18th century and cleaned them up, taking as his goal the ideal of noble simplicity. His intentions were made clear in his preface to the score of *Alceste*, in which he talks about confining music to its 'true purpose of serving poetry with expression and following a story without interrupting the action or stifling it with pointless ornament . . . in short, I have tried to abolish all the abuses against which good sense and reason have long cried out in vain'. Born in Bohemia, he was active in Vienna then Paris, and worked on his so-called 'reform' operas with the poet Raniero de Calzabigi, forming one of the most effective composer/librettist partnerships of all time.

Alceste

FORM: Opera in three acts; in Italian and French (see note)
COMPOSER: Christoph Willibald Gluck (1714–87)
LIBRETTO: R. de Calzabigi; revised version by Roullet;
after Euripides
FIRST PERFORMANCE: Vienna, 26 December 1767;
revised version Paris, 23 April 1776

Principal Characters
Alceste, Queen of Thessaly ❧ **Soprano**
Admète, King of Thessaly ❧ **Tenor**

High Priest of Apollo ➤ **Bass**
Evandre, leader of the people of Pherae ➤ **Tenor**
Hercules ➤ **Bass**
Apollo ➤ **Baritone**
Thanatos ➤ **Bass**

Note: The Synopsis of the Plot and Highlights sections follow the French version of the opera.

Synopsis of the Plot

Setting: Mythological Thessaly

ACT I Admète lies seriously ill and Alceste is desperate to find a way of saving her husband, the father of their two children. The High Priest consults Apollo and the Oracle confirms that Admète must die, unless someone can be found to die in his place. Alceste resolves to die for her husband and calls upon the gods of the underworld to do their worst – she is not frightened of dying for the one she loves best.

ACT II Admète begins to recover and asks how this could have happened. When Evandre tells him that someone has agreed to die in his place, he is horrified and refuses to accept such a sacrifice. Alceste and Admète are joyfully reunited, but Alceste cannot repress her feelings as the time comes for her to leave for the underworld. Admète senses her unhappiness and presses her to name the victim who is to die in his place. Alceste finally admits that she is the one.

ACT III Admète has followed his wife to the entrance of the underworld and the people, left behind, are mourning the loss of their much-loved king and queen. At that moment Hercules arrives, just back from his labours, and reassures the people that he will save them both and defeat the powers of death. Alceste approaches the Altar of Death and Admète joins her, wishing only to die alongside her. But Thanatos warns them that only one can die and Alceste refuses to go back on her decision to die in place of her husband. Hercules challenges Death, and at the moment of his victory Apollo himself appears and announces that Hercules has won both Admète and Alceste their lives, and himself a place among the gods.

Music and Background

The 'reform' opera *par excellence*, *Alceste* is music of extreme solemnity which transforms a story originally told by Euripides with elements of humour into unremitting tragedy. The instrumental colouring is dark, with prominent trombones to add a morose dignity to the scenes that concern death and the underworld. The story-telling is simple and slow, and the moral tone of the piece is loftily high. In anything but strong, intense performances it can, in fact, be dull. But Gluck reformed his own reforms, and nine years after the premiere of the first, Italian-language, version of the score, a second, French, version appeared with substantial changes that enhance its dramatic potential. This later version has become more usual in practice, although it's a matter of contention which is best.

Highlights

The famous aria is Alceste's Act I awesome challenge to the gods to do their worst, 'Divinités du Styx'. In Act II she crowns a particularly grand scene with her farewell to life, 'Ah! malgré moi'.

Did You Know?

🜚 This was one of the first full-scale Italian operas not to ask for a castrato in the cast.

Recommended Recording

Jessye Norman, Nicolai Gedda, Tom Krause, Bavarian Radio Symphony Orchestra/Serge Baudo. Not ideal but the best you'll find.

Iphigénie en Tauride
(Iphigenia in Tauris)

FORM: Opera in four acts; in French
COMPOSER: Christoph Willibald Gluck (1714–87)
LIBRETTO: Nicolas-François Guillard; after Euripides
FIRST PERFORMANCE: Paris, 18 May 1779

Principal Characters

Iphigenia, Priestess of Diana 🜚 Soprano
Orestes, her brother 🜚 Baritone
Pylades, his friend 🜚 Tenor
Thoas, King of Tauris 🜚 Bass
Diana, Goddess of Hunting 🜚 Mezzo-soprano

Synopsis of the Plot

Setting: Legendary Tauris (Scythia); after the Trojan War

ACT I A great storm is followed by the entrance of Iphigenia who, clearly shaken, tells of her dream the previous night in which she saw her father, Agamemnon, murdered by her mother, his wife Clytemnestra. She also saw her brother, Orestes, but in the dream she was forced to kill him. Her fellow-priestesses are commiserating with her when Thoas arrives to tell her that the oracles have decreed that she must offer the gods a sacrifice, the life of a stranger, to ward off evil. At that moment people rush in dragging two young Greeks with them, Orestes and Pylades, found shipwrecked on the shore.

ACT II Orestes and Pylades are in chains. Pylades is taken away and Orestes, on the verge of madness and pursued relentlessly by the Furies, blames himself for his friend's capture and probable death. At last, sleep overcomes him and he dreams of his mother, waking to see her, as he thinks, in front of him. But it is Iphigenia who stands there; so many years have passed that they do not recognise each other. Orestes tells her of events in Mycenae, of how Clytemnestra killed Agamemnon and was, in turn, killed by Orestes, himself now dead. Iphigenia is grief-stricken and performs funeral rites for her supposedly dead brother.

ACT III Iphigenia now wishes to save Orestes and orders him to take a letter to her sister, Electra, the last member of her family alive in Mycenae, but Orestes will not leave Pylades and threatens suicide unless Iphigenia allows Pylades to take the letter. She reluctantly agrees.

ACT IV The time has come for the sacrifice and Iphigenia, praying for strength, is about to plunge the knife into Orestes when, with astonished joy, they recognise each other. Thoas bursts into the temple, having heard that one of the captives has left Tauris, and is about to sacrifice Orestes himself when Pylades returns with a Mycenean army and kills Thoas. The subsequent fighting is cut short by Diana herself who pardons Orestes and sends him, with her statue which the people of Tauris had stolen, back to Mycenae as king, accompanied by Iphigenia.

Music and Background

This is arguably Gluck's finest opera: noble and heroic but with more life and considerably greater vigour than *Alceste* or *Orfeo ed Euridice*. It breathes new life into his otherwise severe 'reform' ideas, and even attempts an early example of operatic psychology in providing a character, Orestes, with music that meaningfully contradicts the words of his Act II aria 'Le calme rentre dans mon coeur'. Agitated strong accompaniments make clear that his heart is anything but calm. The opera exists in two versions, the first in French, the second in German (which recasts the role of Orestes as a tenor).

Highlights

Iphigenia's Act II lament 'O malheureuse Iphigénie' is probably the most celebrated number, along with the two Orestes arias in Act II: 'Le calme' (as above) and the furiously motivated 'Dieux qui me poursuivez'.

Did You Know?

 Iphigénie en Tauride is effectively a post-Trojan War sequel to Gluck's earlier *Iphigénie en Aulide*, where the heroine is narrowly rescued from a fiery end.

 The opera had a profound effect on the young Berlioz, who commented, 'I vowed as I left the Opéra that in spite of father, mother, uncles, grandparents, friends, I would be a musician', thus initiating a bitter rift with his family, who had sent him to Paris to be a medical student.

Recommended Recording

Diana Montague, John Aler, Thomas Allen, Lyon Opera/John Eliot Gardiner. Philips 416 148-2. An award-winning issue with clean, well-focused but powerful singing from a largely Anglo-American cast.

Orfeo ed Euridice
(Orpheus and Eurydice)

FORM: Opera in three acts; in Italian and French
COMPOSER: Christoph Willibald Gluck (1714–87)
LIBRETTO: Ranieri de Calzabigi; revised version
by Pierre-Louis Moline; after the classical myth
FIRST PERFORMANCE: Vienna, 5 October 1762;
revised version Paris, 2 August 1774

Principal Characters

Orpheus, a poet and singer
 Countertenor/Mezzo-soprano/Tenor
Eurydice, his wife Soprano
Eros, God of Love Soprano

Synopsis of the Plot

Setting: Ancient Greece, Hades and the Elysian Fields

ACT I Orpheus is so overcome with grief at the death of his wife, Eurydice, that Zeus takes pity on him. The god sends Eros to Orpheus to tell him that Zeus will allow him to go down to Hades, the underworld, and, through the power of his music, charm its guardians into letting Eurydice come back with him. But there is one condition: Orpheus must not look at Eurydice. Orpheus is confident that he can meet this condition and sets out immediately.

ACT II Orpheus arrives at the gates of Hades to be confronted by Furies and demons, but he soon placates them and they drift away. The gates of the Elysian Fields open and Orpheus goes in. Eurydice is led to him and he prepares to leave with her as the Blessed Spirits encourage her to come back.

ACT III Orpheus has so far avoided looking at Eurydice, but she finds his behaviour disturbing and is convinced he no longer loves her. Orpheus tries vainly to reassure her, and finally he turns to her and takes her into his arms. Instantly she dies. Orpheus, heartbroken at his loss, is on the point of killing himself, when Eros comes to him and says that his faithfulness and constancy have won Eurydice's life, and she is restored to him once again.

Music and Background

Featuring the most celebrated of all opera stories – because the central character represents the persuasive potency of music – this is yet another Gluck opera which exists in two versions. Written in Italian for performance in Vienna, it set Orpheus as a castrato. Later, rewritten in French for Paris, where castrati were not the custom, it set him as a peculiar kind of high tenor known as an *haute-contre*. Orpheus is usually sung, these days, by a mezzo-soprano or (if the performance has any claim to period style) a countertenor.

Highlights

Orpheus' Act III lament 'Che farò senza Euridice' is a classic of its kind and the number by which the title role will be judged. The Act I lament 'Chiamo il mio ben così' and delectable Act II 'Che puro ciel' complete the test.

Did You Know?

✎ 'Che farò' became particularly famous in the mid-20th century through performances by Kathleen Ferrier available on Decca 433 468-2.

Recommended Recording

Anne Sofie von Otter, Barbara Hendricks, Lyon Opera/John Eliot Gardiner. EMI CDS7 498 34-2. Gardiner uses Berlioz's mixture of the two versions, with a French text and a mezzo-soprano Orpheus.

Charles Gounod
(1818–93)

Faust (1859)
Mireille (1864)
Roméo et Juliette (1867)

Born and raised in Paris, Charles Gounod was a spiritually inclined classicist whose early ambitions were to write religious choral music and train for the priesthood. Both these interests fed into *Faust* which was his first (and never quite to be repeated) operatic success. Most of his other stage works failed, and in the course of a messy life involving wrangles with wives, women and publishers, he came to live in England during the 1870s, sustaining his reputation with thoroughly Victorian oratorios for the British market.

Faust

FORM: Opera in five acts; in French
COMPOSER: Charles Gounod (1818–93)
LIBRETTO: Jules Barbier and Michel Carré; after Goethe's drama
FIRST PERFORMANCE: Paris, 19 March 1859

Principal Characters

Faust, a doctor ❧ **Tenor**
Mephistopheles ❧ **Baritone**
Marguerite ❧ **Soprano**
Valentin, Marguerite's brother ❧ **Baritone**
Siebel, a youth, in love with Marguerite ❧ **Mezzo-soprano**
Wagner, a student ❧ **Bass**

Synopsis of the Plot

Setting: Germany; 16th century

ACT I Bitterly disillusioned and cursing his life and work, old doctor Faust calls on the powers of darkness. Instantly Mephistopheles materialises in front of him and offers him anything he wants. Faust wants to be young again and, although he hesitates about promising Mephistopheles his soul in return for such a gift, Mephistopheles convinces him by conjuring up a vision of beautiful young Marguerite, assuring Faust that he will possess her.

ACT II A happy crowd is singing and drinking at a local festival when Mephistopheles joins them. At first he is welcomed, but his strange powers disturb the people and they recognise the evil before them. Left alone, he is joined by Faust, who is anxious to meet Marguerite. A crowd of dancers comes along, Marguerite among them, and Faust introduces himself to her.

ACT III Siebel, who is desperately in love with Marguerite, leaves her some flowers, but Mephistopheles produces a much grander gift for Faust to present to her: a casket of jewels. Marguerite is delighted. Later, Mephistopheles contrives to leave her alone with Faust and they find themselves falling in love. In the evening, the two lovers part, but Mephistopheles stops Faust as he is leaving, pointing out the accessibility of Marguerite's window. Faust climbs in, to the sound of Mephistopheles' mocking laughter.

ACT IV Marguerite sits wretchedly in her room; she has been betrayed and abandoned by Faust, the father of her child. Valentin, arriving back from war, is told of his sister's disgrace and he challenges Faust. Faust, with Mephistopheles' assistance, mortally wounds Valentin who dies angrily cursing his sister.

ACT V Mephistopheles has taken Faust to the Harz mountains for the infernal *Walpurgisnacht* celebrations. But Faust's enjoyment is interrupted by a sudden vision of Marguerite with blood on her neck, and he orders Mephistopheles to take him to see her. Marguerite is now in prison, deranged and condemned to death for killing her baby. Faust tries to persuade her to leave, but she rejects him and is saved, her soul taken to heaven, leaving Faust to be dragged down to hell.

Music and Background

The most enduringly successful of all French operas, *Faust* is buoyant with the sort of melodies people know without realising where they come from. Originally written as *opéra comique* with spoken dialogue, the score was aggrandised over time with sung recitatives and extra music, including the celebrated ballet, but it remains essentially a lightweight response to Goethe, concentrating on love rather than philosophy. Wagner thought it emotionally facile and dismissed the score as 'face-powder music'. However, the characters have won their way into the very heart of the repertory, with Marguerite a charming and rewarding role that gears up to extraordinary dramatic stature at the end.

Highlights

Many. Act I has Faust's celebration of renewed youth 'À moi les plaisirs'. Act III brings Faust's 'Salut! demeure chaste et pure', a text-book example of

French Romantic tenor writing with crowd-pleasing top Cs, plus Marguerite's brilliantly decorative Jewel Song 'Ah! Je ris de me voir'. Act IV has the Soldiers' Chorus 'Gloire immortelle', and finishes with a spiritual march to heaven in Marguerite's rousing 'Anges purs, anges radieux'.

Did You Know?

ㅇ One of the most successful operas ever written, *Faust* had received 1000 performances in Paris alone by 1894. Singing translations exist in at least twenty-five languages.

Recommended Recording

Richard Leech, Cheryl Studer, José van Dam, Thomas Hampson, Capitole de Toulouse Orchestra/Michel Plasson. EMI CDS7 54228. Spirited, unslushy conducting, with fine if sometimes lightweight voices.

Roméo et Juliette
(Romeo and Juliet)

FORM: Opera in five acts; in French
COMPOSER: Charles Gounod (1818–93)
LIBRETTO: Jules Barbier and Michel Carré; after Shakespeare
FIRST PERFORMANCE: Paris, 27 April 1867

Principal Characters

Romeo, a Montague ㅇ **Tenor**
Mercutio, his friend ㅇ **Baritone**
Juliet, a Capulet ㅇ **Soprano**
Gertrude, her nurse ㅇ **Mezzo-soprano**
Tybalt, a Capulet ㅇ **Tenor**
Friar Lawrence ㅇ **Bass**

Synopsis of the Plot

Setting: Verona; 14th century

ACT I A group of masked Montagues, among them Romeo, gain access to a grand Capulet ball. Romeo and Juliet meet and instantly fall in love. They are surprised together by Tybalt, who recognises Romeo, but before he can be challenged, Romeo and his friends quickly leave. Juliet realises with shock that Romeo's family are the sworn enemies of the Capulets.

ACT II Romeo has secretly made his way into the Capulet garden. He hides near Juliet's balcony and, when she appears, they reaffirm their feelings for one another, pledging undying love and longing to be together.

ACT III The two lovers persuade Friar Lawrence to perform a secret marriage service, which he does with only Gertrude, Juliet's nurse, as witness. Later, a street brawl between the Montagues and Capulets results in the death of Mercutio at the hands of Tybalt. In revenge, Romeo kills Tybalt and, as a consequence, is banished from Verona.

ACT IV The lovers are together in Juliet's room, but when day breaks Romeo has to leave. Juliet's father tells her that she is to marry Paris that day and, in despair, she pleads with the friar to help her. He suggests that she swallows a special potion which will make her appear to be dead; her body will be transported to the family tomb where she will wake, and Romeo will come to her. Juliet takes his advice.

ACT V Romeo has heard of Juliet's death. He should have received word from the friar explaining the plan, but the letter has failed to reach him. He breaks into the tomb and, believing Juliet to be dead, takes poison. Juliet wakes and, unable to contemplate life without him, stabs herself to death.

Music and Background

This is one of the few operas based on Shakespeare to follow its Shakespearian original closely, although the focus of the action has been taken close in to the lovers, cutting much of the extraneous action, and Gounod couldn't resist a small adaptation at the end – reviving Juliette just in time for a final duet with Romeo before he dies. The score was much revised by the composer over twenty years, and modern performances vary in what they retain or delete.

Highlights

Apart from Romeo's Evening Song 'Ah! lève-toi soleil' which ranks in the French tenor repertory alongside Faust's 'Salut! demeure', the main interest comes in four great love duets, especially 'O nuit divine' in Act II and 'Nuit d'hyménée' in Act IV.

Recommended Recording

Alfredo Kraus, Catherine Malfitano, Capitole de Toulouse Orchestra/ Michel Plasson. EMI CDS7 47365-8. Not easy to find, but worth the search for the style and elegance of the singing – even if Kraus isn't so youthful.

George Frederick Handel

(1685–1759)

Agrippina (1709)
Rinaldo (1711)
Il Pastor Fido (1712)
Giulio Cesare (1724)
Tamerlano (1724)
Rodelinda (1725)
Partenope (1730)
Ariodante (1734)
Alcina (1735)
Serse (1738)
Semele (1743)

Handel was the leading opera composer of the Baroque period and devoted most of his working life and energies to music for the stage – a fact which until fairly recently has been obscured by his fame as a composer of orchestral works and oratorios. Born in Halle, Germany, his first experience in opera came as a violinist and harpsichord player in Hamburg, where his earliest operas were staged. A three-year trip to Italy steeped him in the conventions of Italian opera seria, of which he became an unequalled master. From there he moved to Hanover and then, rapidly, to London where he settled and responded to the rising demand for Italian opera, starting with *Rinaldo* in 1711. But opera in London was a commercial as opposed to courtly proposition, driven by box office, and he found himself in constant problems as an impresario-composer. By the 1730s he was on the retreat, transferring his interest to oratorios, which were cheaper to do, in vogue, in English, and accessible to a wider audience. The appearance of *Messiah* in 1741 fixed the focus of his reputation for the next two hundred years as the requirements of opera seria made it an increasingly impracticable proposition. While the oratorios found deathless fame, the operas died; not one received a staging anywhere from 1754 to 1920. It is only in the last thirty years that their stature has been widely recognised.

Alcina

FORM: Opera in three acts; in Italian
COMPOSER: George Frederick Handel (1685–1759)
LIBRETTO: Antonio Marchi; after Ariosto
FIRST PERFORMANCE: London, 16 April 1735

Principal Characters

Alcina, an enchantress ❧ Soprano
Morgana, her sister ❧ Soprano
Bradamante ❧ Contralto
Ruggiero, a knight ❧ Countertenor/Mezzo-soprano
Oronte, Alcina's general ❧ Tenor
Melisso, Bradamante's guardian ❧ Bass

Synopsis of the Plot

Setting: Alcina's magic island

ACT I Bradamante and her guardian, Melisso, are searching for Ruggiero, Bradamante's betrothed, and have been shipwrecked on Alcina's island. Alcina welcomes the strangers and her sister, Morgana, is very attracted to Bradamante, who is dressed as a man and pretending to be her own brother, Ricciardo. Bradamante and Melisso discover that Ruggiero is also on the island and, in fact, has become Alcina's latest lover. Oronte, Alcina's general and Morgana's former suitor, is jealous of the attention that Morgana pays to 'Ricciardo'. He tells Ruggiero that Alcina is very taken by this new young man and that Ruggiero may soon find himself cast aside by Alcina and, possibly, transformed into a wild animal or a tree, this being her customary way of dealing with cast-off lovers! The situation is becoming dangerous for Bradamante/Ricciardo but, even when she reveals her true identity to Ruggiero, he will not leave Alcina's island and she refuses to leave without him.

ACT II Melisso manages to put a magic ring on Ruggiero's finger which breaks Alcina's spell, and her enchanted palace becomes a desert. Ruggiero, now returned to his senses, pretends still to love Alcina to prevent her from casting a spell over Bradamante (as 'Ricciardo'). Alcina, heartbroken at losing Ruggiero, but nevertheless determined on revenge, calls on her magic to help her, but her powers all but desert her.

ACT III Morgana now learns that 'Ricciardo' is in fact Bradamante and shares her sorrow with the faithful Oronte. Meanwhile, Ruggiero and Bradamante plan to leave the island but are afraid of what Alcina might do to them, especially as Bradamante has decided that she must restore Alcina's stricken former lovers to their rightful shapes. Alcina tries to dissuade the lovers by pretending friendship for them, but Ruggiero is not taken in, and he smashes the urn which contains the essence of Alcina's powers. Instantly Alcina and Morgana vanish and Alcina's rejected lovers return joyfully to life.

Music and Background

Stories of enchantresses and captured lovers turn up frequently in Handel operas, not least for the scenic opportunities they offer. This one comes fixed in all the conventions of the period, with a castrato hero (usually sung, now, by a countertenor) and static display arias where any action stops dead and the singer expounds, at length and with the repetitions standard to what was called da capo form, on a single emotion – love, fear, anger, or whatever. The chorus would have been very small – just a handful of singers supporting the principal roles – and the running time long (with the result that the score is often cut in modern stagings), but it remains one of the popular favourites in the Handel canon, largely because of its ravishing main tunes.

Highlights

The big number is Ruggiero's farewell to the enchanted island, 'Verdi prati', in Act II, rivalled only by Alcina's beguiling 'Mi restano le lagrime' in Act III.

Did You Know?

⁂ The original castrato in *Alcina* was Giovanni Carestini, one of the international superstars of his voice-type, with a career that stretched across most of Europe. Castrati were the singers the 18th-century public wanted above all to hear, and they were accordingly the biggest earners.

Recommended Recording

Arleen Augér, Della Jones, John Tomlinson, City of London Sinfonia/Richard Hickox. EMI CDS7 49771-2. A magnificent, British-based cast originally assembled for the Spitalfields Festival.

Giulio Cesare
(Julius Caesar)

FORM: Opera in three acts; in Italian
COMPOSER: George Frederick Handel (1685–1759)
LIBRETTO: Nicola Francesco Haym; after G.F. Bussani
FIRST PERFORMANCE: London, 20 February 1724

Principal Characters

Giulio Cesare ～ Countertenor
Curio, a tribune ～ Bass
Cornelia, Pompeo's wife ～ Mezzo-soprano
Sesto, Pompeo's son ～ Mezzo-soprano/Tenor
Achilla, Egyptian general ～ Bass
Tolomeo, King of Egypt and Cleopatra's brother ～ Countertenor
Cleopatra ～ Soprano
Nireno, Cleopatra's attendant ～ Countertenor/Contralto

Synopsis of the Plot

Setting: Alexandria; 48 BC

ACT I Cesare has defeated Pompeo and is thus the unchallenged emperor of Rome and all its territories. Pompeo's wife and son, Cornelia and Sesto, come to Cesare to ask for mercy for the defeated Pompeo, but before Cesare can act, Achilla comes in with Pompeo's severed head in a basket – sent as a gift by Tolomeo to ingratiate himself with the conqueror. Cesare is revolted by this act and Sesto swears to take revenge on his father's killer. Meanwhile, Cleopatra disguises herself as her maid, Lydia, and sets out to win Cesare's support against her brother. Cesare, much taken with her beauty, agrees to help her. Tolomeo, in his turn, is attracted to Cornelia, but is rebuffed by her.

ACT II Cesare and Cleopatra, still disguised as Lydia, are together in the garden when Curio rushes in to say that Tolomeo's soldiers are on their way. Cleopatra, revealing her true identity, begs Cesare to escape but he refuses to run away and goes out to face his enemies. Alone, Cleopatra is in despair over the safety of the man she now loves. Later, Achilla brings Tolomeo the news that Cesare was forced to leap into the sea and is now presumed to have drowned.

ACT III Achilla has transferred his allegiance to Cleopatra and has been mortally wounded in the battle in which she has been taken prisoner by her brother, Tolomeo. But before he dies, Achilla gives Sesto his official ring, enabling him to gain access to the palace. Cesare, who has swum to safety and has been hiding and waiting for an opportunity, observes Achilla's act and now reveals himself, taking control of the situation. Cleopatra is quickly rescued by Cesare, Tolomeo is killed by Sesto and, in a grand ceremony, Cleopatra is crowned Queen of Egypt by her lover.

Music and Background

This was the supreme achievement of Handel's time with the London opera company known as the Royal Academy of Music, and it transforms the conventions of opera seria into music of profound emotional power. Conceived on a grand scale for no fewer than three castrati, it originally featured two of the greatest singers of their age, the castrato Senesino in the title role and the soprano Francesca Cuzzoni as Cleopatra. Needless to say, it proved a hit, and on a grand scale, with the most elaborate and richly scored writing in any of Handel's operas up to that time.

Highlights

Cleopatra's Act II seduction aria 'V'adoro pupille' is arguably the most ravishingly beautiful music Handel ever wrote; and her two laments, 'Se pietà' in Act II and 'Piangerò la sorte mia' in Act III, rank not so far behind.

Did You Know?

 Francesca Cuzzoni was a *prima donna assoluta* in every sense of the term. Handel was on one occasion so irritated by her behaviour during rehearsals that he threatened, before witnesses, to 'fling her out of the window'.

Recommended Recording

Jennifer Larmore, Barbara Schlick, Derek Lee Ragin, Concerto Köln/René Jacobs. Harmonia Mundi HMC 901 385/7. A slowly paced but altogether recommendable, award-winning issue.

Semele

FORM: Opera in three acts; in English
COMPOSER: George Frederick Handel (1685–1759)
LIBRETTO: William Congreve; after Ovid
FIRST PERFORMANCE: London, 10 February 1744

Principal Characters

Cadmus, King of Thebes ❧ Bass
Semele, his daughter ❧ Soprano
Ino, her sister ❧ Contralto
Athamas, Prince of Boeotia ❧ Countertenor
Jupiter ❧ Tenor
Juno, his wife ❧ Contralto
Iris, Juno's messenger ❧ Soprano
Apollo ❧ Tenor

Synopsis of the Plot

Setting: Legendary Thebes

ACT I Cadmus and his family have gathered in the temple of Juno to solemnise the marriage of Semele and Athamas. But Semele is secretly in love with the god Jupiter, who appears to her in human form, and delays the ceremony as long as possible. Suddenly, the fire on the altar dies down, thunder is heard and everyone runs away in fear, leaving only Ino and Athamas; Ino tells Athamas she is in love with him. Cadmus returns and tells how Semele was lifted up to the heavens by a great eagle; the priests interpret this as a great favour from the gods and they all rejoice, including Semele, whose voice can be heard from a distant cloud extolling the joys of love.

ACT II Iris has told her mistress, Juno, about the beautiful new palace that Jupiter, Juno's husband, has built for Semele. Juno is furious and decides to call on the services of Somnus, the God of Sleep, to help her gain access to the palace. Meanwhile, Semele is becoming discontented with the disparity between her status as a mortal and Jupiter's status as a god, despite the reassurance of his love. Jupiter, alarmed at this development, sends for Ino, Semele's sister, to distract her and keep her company.

ACT III Somnus has agreed to make the palace guards and Ino stay asleep, so that Juno can enter in Ino's guise; he will also provide Jupiter with an erotic dream that will leave him vulnerable to any demand Semele might make. Juno then appears to Semele and shows her a magic mirror which makes Semele seem more beautiful than she is. Semele is overcome with admiration for herself and Juno suggests she should refuse to sleep with Jupiter until he promises her immortality and shows himself to her in his full glory as a god. When Jupiter enters, anxious to take her in his arms, Semele refuses him; Jupiter's response is to promise her anything she wants and Semele makes her demands. Jupiter, realising the consequences of appearing before her in his true form as a god, tries to dissuade her, but Semele insists. Jupiter transforms himself into a fiery cloud and, too late, Semele realises that she will be scorched to death by his flames. Ino returns to Thebes to tell the tale and she and Athamas agree to marry. Apollo himself appears and announces that Bacchus, the God of Wine, will rise from Semele's ashes, and the Thebans rejoice.

Music and Background

Semele's right to be considered as an opera is questionable. Handel wrote it for performance in a theatre (Covent Garden) but 'in the manner of an oratorio', without dramatic action. The libretto is in English, and much of it comes in the form of stand-and-sing chorus numbers that get in the way if the piece *is* staged. But the libretto is based on a pre-existing opera text, and there are clear indications that Handel thought of it in dramatic terms – which latterday stage directors take as licence for themselves to move in on. Apart from anything else, a staging helps to define the tone of the piece, which is a distinctly secular, un-oratorio-like mix of seriousness and comedy.

Highlights

The most celebrated number is Jupiter's Act II 'Where'er you walk', which has a thriving life beyond its theatrical context. Semele's Act III aria 'I shall myself adore' is a brilliant showpiece of comic vanity as the not-quite heroine admires her face in the magic mirror.

Did You Know?

❧ The self-regarding character of Semele, chasing the favour of the king of the gods, would have been understood by contemporary audiences as a satirisation of King George III's mistress, Lady Yarmouth.

Recommended Recording

Kathleen Battle, Marilyn Horne, Samuel Ramey, English Chamber Orchestra/John Nelson. DG 435 782-2. Kathleen Battle typecast, with superb support and an orchestral accompaniment which may not use period instruments but outclasses John Eliot Gardiner's rival version which does.

Serse
(Xerxes)

FORM: Opera in three acts; in Italian
COMPOSER: George Frederick Handel (1685–1759)
LIBRETTO: Anonymous; from earlier versions
by Stampiglia and Minato
FIRST PERFORMANCE: London, 15 April 1738

Principal Characters

Serse, King of Persia ❧ **Mezzo-soprano**
Arsamene, his brother ❧ **Mezzo-soprano/Countertenor**
Amastre, a foreign princess ❧ **Mezzo-soprano**
Ariodate, commander of the army ❧ **Bass**
Romilda, his daughter ❧ **Soprano**
Atalanta, her sister ❧ **Soprano**
Elviro, Arsamene's servant ❧ **Bass**

Synopsis of the Plot

Setting: Ancient Persia, King Serse's court

ACT I Serse, wandering in the gardens, has been eulogizing a plane tree(!), when he overhears Romilda singing and is so captivated by her voice that he instructs Arsamene to tell her that he wishes to marry her. Arsamene, who is Romilda's lover, is dumbstruck and refuses. He warns Romilda of his brother's intentions, much to the gratification of Atalanta, Romilda's sister, who is in love with Arsamene herself and hopes that this turn of events will remove the competition. Romilda rejects Serse and, discovering Arsamene's relationship with her, Serse temporarily banishes his brother. Meanwhile, Amastre, Serse's rejected former lover, appears at the court, disguised as a man, determined on revenge.

ACT II Arsamene has entrusted Elviro with a letter for Romilda but Elviro gives it to Atalanta instead. Atalanta shows Serse the letter, saying it is addressed to her, not to Romilda, whom Arsamene is only pretending to love. Serse confronts Romilda with the letter but she insists that she will always love Arsamene and rejects Serse once again. Meanwhile, Atalanta has told Arsamene that Romilda has yielded to Serse and Arsamene is brokenhearted. When Serse sees Arsamene in such a depressed state, he promises to pardon him and to allow him to marry the woman he really loves, namely Atalanta! Arsamene replies that he only loves Romilda, and later Serse advises Atalanta to forget about Arsamene. When Romilda comes in, Serse again declares his love for her, but Romilda stands firm. They are

160

interrupted by Amastre, who accuses Serse of treachery and draws her sword; royal guards arrest her, but Romilda persuades Serse to let her go.

ACT III Atalanta has admitted her deception and withdraws from the fray. But Serse still presses Romilda, who tells him, to Arsamene's fury, that she will obey her father's wishes in the matter. Serse has already promised Ariodate, Romilda's father, that she shall marry a person equal in status to himself, of royal blood. Ariodate, knowing nothing of all the foregoing complications, naturally assumes that this means that Romilda can marry Serse's brother, Arsamene, not Serse himself, and arranges the wedding on this assumption. Serse is enraged when he finds out what Ariodate has done, and his fury is exacerbated when he receives a letter from Amastre, accusing him of betraying her. Amastre throws off her disguise and Serse asks her to forgive him; she does so gladly. Serse blesses the marriage of Romilda and Arsamene and everything ends happily.

Music and Background

No opera about a king infatuated with a plane tree could be entirely serious, and the tone of this piece is heavy – or, more accurately, buoyant – with tongue-in-cheek irony that gives a comic edge to not entirely comic situations. It departs from the formalities of opera seria more readily than most of Handel's stage works, with arias that tend to be short and without the repetitions of the da capo form that was standard for the time.

Highlights

Serse's opening arietta 'Ombra mai fù' – addressed to the plane tree – has found fame beyond its operatic context as 'Handel's Largo'. In Act II, Serse's 'Se bramate d'amar' is a striking outburst of vocal fury stirred by unrequited love.

Did You Know?

⚓ Handel's so-called Largo (which means slow and dignified) is actually marked Larghetto (slow-ish) in the score.

Recommended Recording

Barbara Hendricks, Paul Esswood, Cheryl Studer, La Grande Écurie/ Jean-Claude Malgoire. CBS SM3K 36941. The best of limited and not so distinguished alternatives.

Tamerlano
(Tamburlaine)

FORM: Opera in three acts; in Italian
COMPOSER: George Frederick Handel (1685–1759)
LIBRETTO: Nicola Francesco Haym;
after Piovene, Pradon and Ducas
FIRST PERFORMANCE: London, 31 October 1724

Principal Characters

Tamerlano, Emperor of the Tartars ᧞ Countertenor
Bajazet, Emperor of the Turks ᧞ Tenor
Asteria, his daughter, in love with Andronico ᧞ Soprano
Andronico, Greek prince, in love with Asteria
᧞ Contralto/Countertenor
Irene, Princess of Trebizond, engaged to Tamerlano ᧞ Mezzo-soprano
Leone, friend of Tamerlano and Andronico ᧞ Bass

Synopsis of the Plot

Setting: Bithynia; 1402

ACT I Tamerlano has defeated Bajazet and now holds him and his
daughter, Asteria, captive. Andronico, Tamerlano's Greek ally, brings Asteria
(whom he loves) with him to plead for Bajazet's life. Tamerlano instantly falls
in love with Asteria and offers Bajazet his freedom if he consents to their
marriage; in addition he offers Andronico his fiancée, Irene, in return for
Andronico's help in achieving his wish. Asteria is dismayed when Tamerlano
tells her that her beloved Andronico is to marry Irene but, alone, she reveals
that, although hurt and sad at his apparent betrayal of her, her feelings for
him have not changed. Irene arrives, to be told that she is now to marry
Andronico, not Tamerlano; she is refused permission to see Tamerlano and
is advised, by Andronico, to disguise herself as one of her own messengers
and thus gain access to the emperor to plead her case.

ACT II Tamerlano has decided to marry Asteria with or without her father's
consent. Andronico and Bajazet are horrified at the prospect of Asteria
becoming Tamerlano's wife and, when she prepares to mount the throne, her
father disowns his daughter in shame. Asteria responds by drawing a dagger,
saying that she had intended to use it on her husband as soon as they were
alone together. Tamerlano, furious, threatens Asteria and Bajazet with
death.

ACT III Bajazet and Asteria resolve to commit suicide by poison, rather than submit to the tyrant. Tamerlano, meanwhile, decides to make another attempt to marry Asteria, and enlists Andronico's help. Andronico, finally, finds the courage to defy Tamerlano, and admits his love for Asteria. Tamerlano's initial rage turns to thoughts of revenge and he decides to behead Bajazet and marry Asteria to the meanest slave. He orders Asteria to serve him at a banquet, but Irene sees her pour poison into Tamerlano's cup and warns him, throwing off her disguise as she does so. Tamerlano orders Asteria to be given to the slaves and Bajazet to watch her violation. Bajazet takes poison and dies, cursing the tyrant. Asteria begs for death herself but Tamerlano, encouraged by Irene who has resumed her rightful place at his side, chooses mercy over cruelty; he frees Asteria and allows her to marry her beloved Andronico.

Music and Background

Tamerlano is unusual in that although the title role and technical male lead, Andronico, were both conventionally written for castrati (one of them the superstar castrato Senesino), the character who dominates the action is the tenor Bajazet, and tenors did not usually get such prominent treatment in Handelian opera. It is also unusual in being one of the few Handel stage works to count as a genuine tragedy, without comic input, and it certainly ranks alongside the very best of the others in terms of musical quality, even if it hasn't managed to match their audience appeal.

Highlights

The strengths here tend to be the dramatic confrontational numbers rather than solo arias: above all, the death of Bajazet in Act III and the sustained tension of the Throne-room Scene in Act II.

Did You Know?

🐾 Registering surprise that the hero-role of Bajazet had not been given to a castrato, the *Weekly Journal* (a London newspaper) couldn't resist the sly comment that the substitute tenor ' was never *cut out* for a singer'.

Recommended Recording

Derek Lee Ragin, Nigel Robson, Michael Chance, English Baroque Soloists/John Eliot Gardiner. Erato 2292 45408-2. Sometimes harsh sound, but superb singing from the two countertenors.

Joseph Haydn

(1732–1809)

La Infedeltà Delusa (1773)
L'Incontro Improvviso (1775)
Il Mondo della Luna (1777)
La Vera Constanza (1778)
La Fedeltà Premiata (1780)
Orlando Paladino (1782)

Haydn's enduring reputation rests with his vast output of symphonies, oratorios and masses, string quartets and keyboard sonatas – anything but opera. But during his thirty years of service to the aristocratic Esterhazy family, living and working on their estates, he completed some twenty operas for performance in the family's private theatres and counted some of them among his proudest achievements. That history has judged otherwise is due to the problems of making these, usually very long, scores live effectively on stage. Haydn's theatre-sense compares poorly with that of his contemporary, Mozart; and living in remote isolation with the Esterhazys, he never had the chance to learn the craft from direct experience of how other composers – especially Italians – practised it. Nor did he have access to inspired librettists. The result is a large quantity of music that makes fascinating study and can be superbly written, but can also be supremely tedious in performance. Recent years have seen a revival of interest – notably at the English country-house opera venue Garsington – but it remains sporadic.

La Fedeltà Premiata
(Fidelity Rewarded)

FORM: Opera in three acts; in Italian
COMPOSER: Joseph Haydn (1732–1809)
LIBRETTO: Giambattista Lorenzi
FIRST PERFORMANCE: Esterháza, 25 February 1781

Principal Characters

Celia, in love with Fileno ᴥ **Mezzo-soprano**
Fileno, in love with Celia ᴥ **Tenor**
Amaranta ᴥ **Mezzo-soprano**
Count Perrucchetto ᴥ **Baritone**
Melibeo, high priest ᴥ **Bass**
Nerina, a nymph ᴥ **Soprano**
Lindoro, Amaranta's brother and temple assistant ᴥ **Tenor**
Diana, Goddess of Hunting ᴥ **Soprano**

Synopsis of the Plot

Setting: Legendary Cumae

ACT I Cumae is suffering under a curse which demands that, every year, two faithful lovers must be sacrificed to a sea monster; the curse can only be lifted when a noble hero offers his own life instead. Naturally, Melibeo, the devious high priest, keeps a close eye on the romantic liaisons around him, for to be in love can mean death. Indeed, he is not above manipulating events to suit himself, such as advising Lindoro, who loves Nerina, to switch his affections to Celia, while Melibeo himself pursues Amaranta. But when the absurd Count Perrucchetto arrives on the scene, Amaranta decides that he is a much more interesting prospect and sets her sights firmly on becoming a countess. The annual search is on for the lovers to be sacrificed and Melibeo gives Celia an ultimatum: marry Lindoro or go to her death with Fileno. She is about to submit to his demands when Nerina rushes in, pursued by satyrs, one of whom carries Celia away.

ACT II Melibeo devises a plan to pair the Count and Celia together, thus despatching them both to the sea monster and leaving Amaranta for himself. Fileno decides to kill himself, but his arrow breaks while he is carving his last message on a tree trunk. Celia, alone and depressed, finds refuge in a cave, but she has been observed by Melibeo, who sends Perrucchetto in after her. When they emerge together, the high priest names them as the sacrificial couple.

ACT III Perrucchetto and Celia are prepared for the sacrifice. But Fileno cannot bear the idea of Celia being devoured by the sea monster and steps forward, as a hero, to offer his own life instead. Suddenly the great goddess, Diana, appears amid thunder and lightning, to save him. She lifts the curse and brings together Celia and Fileno, Nerina and Lindoro, and Amaranta and the Count. The manipulative Melibeo, however, she takes as her victim.

Music and Background

This is pastoral opera at its most charming, although the well over three hours running time of the original version stretches the point. The music is of as high an order as you find in Haydn's stage works, and the characters are well drawn in a plot that balances serious and comic elements side by side. But as with all Haydn operas, the dramatic structure gets absurdly complicated, losing shape and thrust. Haydn quarried some of his score for later works, turning the overture, for example, into the finale of his Symphony No.73.

Highlight

The emotional range of Celia's 'Ah come il core' as she contemplates death in Act II provides the finest moments of the whole score and was later published by Haydn as a free-standing cantata for concert performance.

Did You Know?

Asked in 1787 to write an opera for public performance in Prague, Haydn declined on the grounds that 'scarcely any man could stand comparison with the great Mozart'.

Recommended Recording

Lucia Valentini Terrani, Tonny Landy, Frederica von Stade, Ileana Cotrubas, Lausanne Chamber Orchestra/Antal Dorati. Philips 432 430-2. Part of a distinguished Haydn opera series recorded in the 1970s with choice casts.

Hans Werner Henze

(1926–)

König Hirsch (1955)
Der Prinz von Homburg (1958)
Elegy for Young Lovers (1961)
Der Junge Lord (1964)
The Bassarids (1965)
We Come to the River (1976)
The English Cat (1983)
Das Verratene Meer (1989)

Through a prodigious catalogue of work, Henze has established himself as the leading post-war composer of opera in Germany – although much of his life has been spent in voluntary exile in Italy where, since the 1950s, he has found Mediterranean warmth a healing antidote to sore memories of his north German background. Brought up during the Third Reich and unwillingly conscripted into its army, he embraced radical socialism and produced a number of works during the 1960s and '70s that carry a committed political agenda, like the oratorio *The Raft of the Medusa* (1968). Politics also infiltrated his operas, through collaborations with the writer Edward Bond (*We Come to the River, The English Cat*), and earned him a reputation for polemical dogma. But musically Henze has always been a free spirit, embracing styles and languages of writing from severe serialism to luxuriant tonality. His eclecticism and bias toward theatre music has long prompted comparison with Britten, although most listeners would find Henze's music tougher going.

The Bassarids

FORM: Opera in one act (four movements); in English
COMPOSER: Hans Werner Henze (1926–)
LIBRETTO: W.H. Auden and Chester Kallman; after Euripides
FIRST PERFORMANCE: Salzburg, 6 August 1966 (in German)

Principal Characters

Dionysus, a Greek god 🙰 Tenor
Tiresias, an old, blind prophet 🙰 Tenor
Cadmus, former King of Thebes 🙰 Bass
Autonoe, Cadmus's daughter 🙰 Soprano
Agave, Cadmus's daughter 🙰 Mezzo-soprano
Pentheus, King of Thebes and Agave's son 🙰 Baritone

Note: Bassarids are adherents of Dionysus, whose cult involves sensual pleasures, intoxication and violence.

Synopsis of the Plot

Setting: Thebes and Mount Cithaeron; mythological times

MOVEMENT I Pentheus, the new King of Thebes, is alarmed at the influence of the Dionysian cult over his people, who are irresistibly drawn away to Mount Cithaeron. Dionysus is said to be the son of Cadmus's dead daughter, Semele, and of Zeus himself, but there are grave doubts about his divinity. Pentheus has banned the cult in Thebes and has even gone so far as to extinguish the flame on Semele's tomb.

MOVEMENT II Pentheus has sent his guards after the runaways and they return with Agave, Autonoe, Tiresias and a Stranger. Pentheus questions Agave, his mother, about events on Cithaeron, but she makes little sense to him, and he turns to the Stranger.

MOVEMENT III An earthquake allows Agave, Autonoe and Tiresias to escape from prison and return to Cithaeron. Meanwhile, the Stranger (Dionysus himself, of course) begins to cast his seductive spell over the ascetic Pentheus. He shows the king a lively vision of Dionysian rites through Agave's mirror, after which the half-bewitched king decides to go to Cithaeron to see for himself, disguised, on Dionysus' advice, as a woman. Once there Pentheus hides in a tree to watch the rites, but Dionysus warns the Bassarids, who pull him down. Even Agave does not recognise her own son. The Bassarids tear him apart and she decapitates him.

MOVEMENT IV The Bassarids are celebrating and Agave is holding aloft her son's head, believing it to be a lion. Cadmus forces her back to reality and she is horrified at what has happened. Now Dionysus appears, dressed as a king, and orders the palace to be burnt to the ground. He calls on Persephone, Goddess of the Underworld, and Zeus to release his mother, Semele. Two gigantic fertility symbols spring out of the ground and the people fall down and worship them.

Music and Background

Henze's most successful opera to date, *The Bassarids* comes in one huge and powerful Act, structured like a symphony in four movements and starting with a huge sonata-like conflict between abrasive ideas representing Pentheus and softer, pliant ones for Dionysus. The second movement is a dance scherzo, the third an adagio with intermezzo, and the fourth a passacaglia on a forty-three-note theme. For all this apparent formality, though, the music flows unbroken, in the manner of Wagner; and the whole opera could be described as an attempt to come to terms with the Wagnerian tradition – to which Henze was not naturally sympathetic. He described the mood of the score as 'ecstatic pessimism'.

Highlights

Impossible to say: this is a cumulative score that makes its mark through sustained tensions rather than contained events.

Did You Know?

Before the librettists Auden and Kallman agreed to work on this piece they insisted that Henze should see a performance of *Götterdämmerung* and 'make peace' with Wagner.

Recommended Recording

Kenneth Riegel, Andeas Schmidt, Robert Tear, Berlin Radio Symphony Orchestra/Gert Albrecht. Koch Schwann 314 006-2. A handsome account of one of the strongest modern opera scores around.

Elegy for Young Lovers

FORM: Opera in three acts; in English
COMPOSER: Hans Werner Henze (1926–)
LIBRETTO: W.H. Auden and Chester Kallman
FIRST PERFORMANCE: Schwetzingen, 20 May 1961 (in German)

Principal Characters

Gregor Mittenhofer, a poet ❧ Baritone
Dr Wilhelm Reischmann, his doctor ❧ Bass
Toni Reischmann, Dr Reischmann's son ❧ Tenor
Elisabeth Zimmer, Mittenhofer's mistress ❧ Soprano
Carolina, Gräfin von Kirchstetten, Mittenhofer's secretary
❧ Contralto
Hilda Mack, a widow ❧ Soprano

Synopsis of the Plot

Setting: The Austrian Alps; 1910

ACT I At an alpine hotel Hilda Mack awaits the return of her husband, who disappeared on the mountain forty years ago on the first day of their honeymoon. She is joined by the poet, Mittenhofer, and his entourage; Mittenhofer visits the hotel annually, to observe Hilda's behaviour, and to take inspiration from her hallucinations. Almost immediately, Hilda goes into one of her visions and Mittenhofer makes copious notes; Toni finds the whole thing distasteful, but Mittenhofer is delighted. Shortly afterwards a mountain guide reports that the body of a young man has been found, preserved in a glacier. It is almost certainly that of Hilda's husband. Elisabeth agrees to tell Hilda, and her gentleness and tact impress Toni, who finds himself falling in love with her.

ACT II Toni and Elisabeth are deeply in love and Toni urges her to leave Mittenhofer. They are observed by Carolina, who reports back to the poet. Mittenhofer invites Elisabeth to tea and tries to make her feel sorry for him; she feels she cannot tell him about her new love, but Toni has no such compunction and leaves Mittenhofer in no doubt about his feelings for Elisabeth. They are interrupted, however, by a rather tipsy Hilda, who now fully understands the situation and demands 10 per cent of Mittenhofer's future royalties! Mittenhofer manages to calm everyone down and asks Dr Reischmann for his blessing on the young couple; he then introduces his

170

new poem, *The Young Lovers*. He asks Toni and Elisabeth to stay on for a few days until his sixtieth birthday, and to pick him some edelweiss from the mountain. Everything appears to be happy and calm but, once alone, Mittenhofer explodes with fury, castigating everyone and wishing them all dead. When Hilda returns to confront him, he rushes out, to the sound of her hysterical laughter.

ACT III The next day the lovers depart for the mountain and Hilda leaves, bestowing on Carolina the enormous scarf she has been knitting for the last forty years. After a while the mountain guide comes in, anxiously reporting that a blizzard is imminent, and asking if anyone is on the mountain. Mittenhofer says he knows of no one and, when questioned by a horrified Carolina, suggests she goes away, as she needs 'a change of scene'. Inevitably, Toni and Elisabeth are caught in the blizzard and, exhausted, die together on the mountain. Later, Mittenhofer is about to give a public reading of his poem, *Elegy for Young Lovers*, dedicated to Toni and Elisabeth. He mouths the words as we hear the wordless voices of Hilda, Elisabeth, Carolina, Toni and Dr Reischmann in the background.

Music and Background

A chamber opera for just six singing voices and a small orchestra, *Elegy for Young Lovers* nonetheless uses an extensive array of percussion to create a cold but sparkling sound-scape appropriate to the mountain setting. Intricately structured into thirty-four short scenes, each one individually titled, the score links different characters with different orchestral colours. Mittenhofer, for example, has horn, trumpet and trombone, Reischmann a bassoon, Hilda Mack a flute, and Carolina a cor anglais.

Highlights

Hilda Mack's extravagant, coloratura singing in Acts I and II; the violent Blizzard Scene in Act III.

Did You Know?

The florid visionary music for Hilda Mack and its association with the flute is modelled after the example of the Mad Scene in Donizetti's *Lucia di Lammermoor*.

Recommended Recording

Dietrich Fischer-Dieskau, Thomas Hemsley, Berlin Deutsche Oper/Hans Werner Henze. DG 449 874-2. Excerpts only, but authoritatively recorded under the composer in 1964.

Paul Hindemith
(1895–1963)

Mörder, Hoffnung der Frauen (1919)
Cardillac (1926)
Neues vom Tage (1929)
Mathis der Maler (1935)
Die Harmonie der Welt (1957)

Hindemith was an essentially conservative composer whose mature work took a strong moral stand, not least against totalitarianism and the Third Reich. But his early operas – a trio of deliberately provocative one-acters in the spirit of German Expressionism, starting with *Mörder, Hoffnung der Frauen* – won him notoriety as a radical, free-thinking *enfant terrible*; and in many ways his musical outlook was innovative. He dedicated much of his life to what he called *gebrauchsmusik*, designed to be of practical use to professionals and amateurs alike. He also took an interest in jazz. But eventually his writing settled into the language of neoclassicism, heard in the opera *Cardillac* which follows the sort of structural patterns Handel might have used two hundred years earlier. A story about the role of artists in society, *Cardillac* was a natural precursor to *Mathis der Maler*, which takes a similar theme and attracted condemnation by the Nazis even before its premiere (which was proscribed). Hindemith left Germany in 1937 and went to America where he taught at Yale. A distinguished performer as well as composer, he was the soloist for the premiere of Walton's Viola Concerto in 1929.

Mathis der Maler
(Matthias the Painter)

FORM: Opera in seven scenes; in German
COMPOSER: Paul Hindemith (1895–1963)
LIBRETTO: Paul Hindemith
FIRST PERFORMANCE: Zürich, 28 May 1938

Principal Characters

Mathis ⚬ **Baritone**
Albrecht, Archbishop of Mainz and Mathis' employer ⚬ **Tenor**
Riedinger, a wealthy citizen ⚬ **Bass**
Ursula, Riedinger's daughter ⚬ **Soprano**
Schwalb, leader of the peasants' army ⚬ **Tenor**
Regina, his daughter ⚬ **Soprano**
Sylvester, an officer ⚬ **Tenor**
Countess von Helfenstein ⚬ **Contralto**

Synopsis of the Plot

Setting: Mainz during the Peasants' War; c.1525

SCENE 1 Mathis is quietly painting a fresco in a monastery when Schwalb and his daughter burst in, on the run from the soldiers. Schwalb reproaches Mathis for painting when he could be helping in the struggle for freedom. The soldiers are heard approaching and Mathis gives Schwalb his horse, promising his support.

SCENE 2 The citizens of Mainz are awaiting Albrecht's return, meanwhile arguing about the relative merits of Protestantism and Catholicism. When Albrecht arrives, Riedinger protests about the Catholic order to burn Protestant books; Ursula and Mathis, however, talk of love. Suddenly Sylvester enters and accuses Mathis of allowing Schwalb to escape; Albrecht tells Mathis to stay out of politics, at which Mathis resigns from his service.

SCENE 3 The Catholics are burning Lutheran books and, in his house, Riedinger and his fellow Protestants are hiding as many as they can. Riedinger is shown a letter, supposedly from Luther to Albrecht, urging him to renounce celibacy and marry a Protestant, thus bringing reconciliation. Riedinger's hints that Ursula might be the one chosen for this honour makes her uneasy, and she begs Mathis to take her away. Mathis assures her that he loves her, but feels impelled to take up the peasants' cause and cannot take her with him.

SCENE 4 The peasants have captured a village; they execute the local count and threaten the countess with rape. Mathis intervenes on her behalf but is struck down. The peasants are themselves then attacked and Schwalb is killed. The countess saves Mathis' life and the soldiers depart, leaving Regina weeping over her father's body.

SCENE 5 Albrecht's financial problems are now severe and he is advised to marry a wealthy woman as soon as possible. When he realises his bride is to be Ursula, he is astonished, and upbraids her for taking part in such an affair. Ursula's reply, that she is only doing it to help reconcile the two opposing religions, awakens Albrecht's conscience; he too will devote himself to religious reconciliation – but through his own church and according to its laws.

SCENE 6 Mathis and Regina are running away from the fighting and take refuge in a forest. Mathis' sleep is disturbed by a series of visions, in which (as St Anthony) he is confronted by people and incidents from his past, concluding with Albrecht (as St Paul) urging him to return to his painting and thereby exercise his true gifts from God.

SCENE 7 Mathis is in his studio, filled with paintings and drawings. Near him is Ursula, tending to the dying Regina. After an interlude, we see Mathis alone, his studio almost bare; following a visit from Albrecht, Mathis slowly and methodically puts his last remaining possessions into a chest. His life's work is over and the time has come for him to face death in a spirit of acceptance.

Music and Background

This opera is based on the real-life 16th-century painter Matthias Grünewald whose chief work, the magnificent Isenheim altarpiece, is widely regarded as a statement of political solidarity with the poor and oppressed. From its opening prelude (entitled 'Concert of Angels' after another of Grünewald's altarpieces), the score gathers period atmosphere through references to folk and medieval music and by recurring use of the techniques of counterpoint associated with bygone times. It is generally slow-moving, sometimes static, and suffers unfairly from the reputation Hindemith has latterly acquired as an 'academic' composer. But for anyone who takes the trouble to study it, *Mathis der Maler* proves a powerful and passionate piece, conceived by the composer in autobiographical terms and the crowning achievement of his creative life.

Highlights

The opening prelude with its soaring principal melody; the dramatic excitement of the book-burning in Scene 3 and Mathis' visions in Scene 6.

Did You Know?

Hindemith wrote a free-standing concert score, the 'Mathis der Maler Symphony', as a prefatory exercise for the opera. It was the embarrassing success of the symphony that prompted the Nazis to ban the larger work.

Recommended Recording

Dietrich Fischer-Dieskau, James King, Bavarian Radio Symphony Orchestra/Rafael Kubelík. EMI 7243 5 55237 23. Reissue of a solidly-cast 1979 performance.

Engelbert Humperdinck

(1854–1921)

Hänsel und Gretel (1893)
Königskinder (1897)

A student of architecture who gave it up for music, Humperdinck met Wagner as a young man and helped him prepare the score of *Parsifal* for its premiere, which proved a life-determining experience. Thereafter, his music moved in Wagner's shadow, albeit with a lighter touch and considerable input from folk song. *Hänsel und Gretel* was an immediate and enduring success which brought Humperdinck fame and fortune. None of his remaining operas found a place in popular repertoire, with the possible exception of *Königskinder*, another fairy-tale score which attracted a big following in America.

Hänsel und Gretel

FORM: Opera in three acts; in German
COMPOSER: Engelbert Humperdinck (1854–1921)
LIBRETTO: Adelheid Wette; after the Brothers Grimm
FIRST PERFORMANCE: Weimar, 23 December 1893

Principal Characters

Hänsel ∾ Mezzo-soprano
Gretel ∾ Soprano
Gertrud, their mother ∾ Soprano
Peter, their father, a brushmaker ∾ Baritone
The Sandman ∾ Soprano
The Dew Fairy ∾ Soprano
The Witch ∾ Mezzo-soprano

Synopsis of the Plot

Setting: A hut and the witch's house in a wood

ACT I Hänsel and Gretel are working alone in a hut: Hänsel is making brooms and Gretel is knitting. They are hungry and, to keep up their spirits, they begin to play, dancing energetically around the room. When Gertrud returns, she is angry to find them playing, not working, and, in her annoyance, knocks over a jug of milk which was to have been their supper. She sends them out into the woods to pick strawberries. After they have gone, Peter returns, a little the worse for drink, having had a profitable day. He produces a large basket of food and asks for the children. He is horrorstruck when Gertrud tells him she has sent them to the woods, because he has heard of a Witch who rides there on a broomstick, and catches and eats children. They both rush out of the house.

ACT II The two children have wandered deep into the woods and are getting very tired and afraid of the growing darkness and strange noises. Suddenly the Sandman appears and calms them, so that they settle down to sleep, protected by fourteen white angels.

ACT III After having been woken by the Dew Fairy, Hänsel and Gretel see that they are not far from a gingerbread house. Inevitably they are attracted towards it and start to break off pieces to eat. Suddenly the Witch emerges and casts a spell to prevent them from moving. Hänsel is taken away to be fattened up; Gretel, set moving once more, is put to work in the house. While the Witch feeds Hänsel, Gretel cancels the spell cast over him (using the words she had heard the Witch use), and together they push the Witch

176

into the oven. As they eat their fill of the house, the oven explodes and they are surrounded by several motionless children, baked into cakes by the Witch. Hänsel frees the children from the Witch's spell; Peter and Gertrud are overjoyed to find them safe and well, and even the Witch herself reappears – now transformed into a cake!

Music and Background

This opera grew out of a sequence of songs written for domestic performance at the suggestion of Humperdinck's sister, who had made her own adaptation of the Brothers Grimm story, softening its nightmare qualities. The opera that finally resulted came at just the right time when German audiences, still dazed from Wagnerian fallout, were craving something nationalist and popular as an alternative to the rush of new works flooding in from Italy. The Wagnerian qualities in *Hänsel und Gretel* are its use of leitmotifs – recurring melodies associated with particular characters, emotions or situations – and its allocation of prominence to the orchestra, which is used symphonically, not just as a secondary accompaniment. But the Wagnerianisms are also tempered by a simplicity and charm that comes from children's folk songs. This is sweet-toothed music: comfortable and loving where Wagner can be severe and grand.

Highlights

In Act I the delightful little dance-number for the children, 'Brüderchen komm tanz mit mir'. In Act II the children's evening prayer, 'Abends will ich schlafen gehn', which leads into a deliriously rich orchestral fantasy known as the Dream Pantomime. Act III has the jubilant duet of triumph 'Juchhei! Nun ist die Hexe tot', and the grand finale which reprises most of the big tunes and frames the final children's duet 'Ihr Englein die uns so treu'.

Did You Know?

 The Witch and Gertrud are often sung by the same soprano, suggesting Freudian implications to the piece.

Recommended Recording

Anne Sofie von Otter, Barbara Bonney, Marjana Lipovsek, Bavarian Radio Symphony Orchestra/Jeffrey Tate. EMI CDS7 54022-2. Good modern and not too sentimental reading with an unbeatable witch from Ms Lipovsek.

Leoš Janáček

(1854–1928)

Jenůfa (1903)
Fate (1905)
The Excursions of Mr Brouček (1917)
Kátya Kabanová (1921)
The Cunning Little Vixen (1923)
The Makropulos Case (1925)
From the House of the Dead (1928)

Janáček was born in the mid-19th century but counts as a 20th century composer in that nearly all the major works for which he is remembered were written late in life – and they then took time to attract widespread interest. Only in the last thirty or so years has he come to be recognised as one of the great opera composers, largely through the efforts of the conductor Charles Mackerras. Born in a remote part of Moravia, Janáček spent the first half of his life teaching obscurely in Brno and trying, without success, to get his music played in Prague. The breakthrough came in 1916 when the Prague Opera finally accepted *Jenůfa*. Janáček was sixty-two, but took on a new lease of life – confirmed the following year when he met and fell in love with a young, married woman. His feelings weren't returned, but they developed into a fantasy obsession that proved directly responsible for his greatest stage works: *Kátya Kabanová, The Cunning Little Vixen* and *The Makropulos Case*. Other well-known scores include the *Glagolitic Mass* (1926), two major string quartets (1923 and 1928) and the classic *Sinfonietta* (1926).

The Cunning Little Vixen

FORM: Opera in three acts; in Czech
COMPOSER: Leoš Janáček (1854–1928)
LIBRETTO: Leoš Janáček; after Těsnohlídek
FIRST PERFORMANCE: Brno, 6 November 1924

Principal Characters

Sharp Ears, the Vixen ◆ **Soprano**
Golden-mane, the Fox ◆ **Soprano**
Badger ◆ **Bass**
Cock ◆ **Mezzo-soprano**
Forester ◆ **Baritone**
Schoolteacher ◆ **Tenor**
Priest ◆ **Bass**
Harašta, a poulterer ◆ **Bass-baritone**

Synopsis of the Plot

Setting: A forest near Brno, the Forester's lodge and the inn; about 1920

ACT I It is a warm, sunny afternoon in the forest and the Forester, tired and hot, lies down for a sleep. Immediately the animals and insects resume their business; the dragonfly dances, the cricket and the grasshopper join in a waltz and a frog tries to catch a mosquito. But the frog has attracted the attention of a young foxcub, the Vixen, who chases him. Inadvertently he lands on the Forester's nose, who wakes, seizes hold of the Vixen and carries her off. Time passes and the Vixen is living miserably in the Forester's yard. One day the Forester's son teases her and she nips him; the Forester punishes her by chaining her up. The next morning the Vixen tries to foment a revolution among the hens, urging them to free themselves from the Cock's domination. But she gets little response from them and, in disgust, she digs a hole and lies in it, feigning death. When the Cock investigates, she springs up and bites off his head. In the turmoil that follows the Vixen snaps the chain and escapes back into the woods.

ACT II The Vixen ousts the Badger from his sett and makes her home there. Meanwhile, the Forester, the Schoolteacher and the Priest are drinking at the inn, and the Forester is teased about losing the Vixen. Later, the Schoolteacher is staggering home when, observed by the Vixen, he mistakes a sunflower for his lost love, and falls on his face, much to her amusement; he is succeeded by the Priest, also drunk, whose bitter memories of love and betrayal are interrupted by the Forester, searching for the Vixen and determined to shoot her. But the Vixen has gone back to her earth, where she meets the Fox; they fall in love and marry.

ACT III The Fox and the Vixen are now proud parents. One day Harašta comes along with a basket full of chickens and the Vixen lures him away by pretending to be injured. Harašta falls over, she escapes and joins her family, who are devouring the chickens. But Harašta shoots at them and they scatter, leaving the Vixen lying dead. Time passes, the Priest goes away and the Forester muses on his past and on his love for the forest and its spiritual qualities. Again he falls asleep among the trees and, in a dream, sees the Vixen; he stretches out towards her and takes hold – but it is only the frog he has caught this time, not the Vixen.

Music and Background

The idea for this curious fantasy opera came from a comic-strip series in a Brno newspaper, which Janáček adapted (using his own libretto) into a philosophical reflection on the cycle of life in the natural world. Much of the music is purely orchestral, with long sequences designed for choreography; but the singing zoo of animals is beautifully characterised, with children taking the parts of the smallest creatures, and with a touching pathos in the contrast between the sterile ageing of the humans and the youthful vigour of the wildlife all around them.

Highlights

The evocative orchestral music for Vixen's dream in Act I, the Vixen's wedding celebrations in Act II, and the Forester's final, nostalgic monologue in Act III.

Did You Know?

~ The opera's focus on passing time acquires a peculiar poignancy when you remember that Janáček completed the score on the eve of his seventieth birthday.

Recommended Recording

Lucia Popp, Eva Randová, Vienna State Opera/Charles Mackerras. Decca 417 129-2. Radiant sound and passionately played, with Lucia Popp a natural (Czech-born) choice for the title role.

The Excursions of Mr Brouček

FORM: Opera in two parts; in Czech
COMPOSER: Leoš Janáček (1854–1928)
LIBRETTO: Part 1, Janáček, Gellner, Dyk, Procházka;
after Čech's novel; Part 2, Procházka; after Čech's novel
FIRST PERFORMANCE: Prague, 23 April 1920

Note: The opera consists of two parts, each representing one of Mr Brouček's two dreams: Part 1, 'Mr Brouček's Excursion to the Moon' and Part 2, 'Mr Brouček's Excursion to the Fifteenth Century'. The same characters appear in different guises in both parts.

Principal Characters

Mr Brouček (Mr Beetle), a landlord ❧ **Tenor**
Málinka ❧ **Soprano**
Domšík ❧ **Bass-baritone**
Mazal, a painter ❧ **Tenor**
Würfl, a publican ❧ **Bass**

Synopsis of the Plot

Setting: 19th-century Prague, the moon, 15th-century Prague

PART 1: ACT I Brouček leaves his friends and staggers out of the pub. He is greatly impressed by the moon he sees on his way home, imagining life there to be much less problematic than on earth. Suddenly and mysteriously Brouček is borne aloft and wakes to find himself addressed by a moonbeam, Blankytný, wearing the face and clothes of Brouček's tenant, the painter Mazal. But Blankytný is affronted by Brouček's familiarity and bursts into lyrical poetry in praise of his lady love. The object of Blankytný's affections, Etherea (who looks like Málinka), soon arrives, but she falls instantly in love with Mr Brouček and flies away with him on Blankytný's winged horse.

ACT II Etherea and Brouček arrive at the Temple of the Arts, a star-shaped creation, with each point of the star representing a different branch of the arts. Here Brouček is welcomed by the refined artists, but they are increasingly appalled by his matter-of-fact ways, particularly his use of the word 'nose', which is especially shocking. Feeling hungry, Brouček takes a string of sausages from his pocket and begins to eat one, listing its contents to the vegetarian, flower-eating artists, thus provoking a storm of horrified protest. Brouček has, by now, had enough; he makes a getaway on the

181

winged horse and arrives back on the earth, where he finds himself being carried home.

PART 2: ACT I The voices of Brouček and his companions at the pub can be heard offstage. Once again Brouček stumbles out and this time finds that he has fallen into a treasure chamber. He eventually makes his way out and wanders into the street, where, because of his strange 19th-century speech and clothes, he is arrested as a spy. He pretends to be a Czech just returned home after many years abroad.

ACT II Taken into Domšík's home and given medieval clothes to wear, Brouček begins to understand that he has been transported back to the 15th century and, in fact, is caught up in the religious Hussite wars. Brouček's indifference to the situation angers his host and his guests, but a sudden emergency forestalls an ugly scene; Brouček is given a pike and told to go and fight. Shortly, however, he sneaks back, puts his own clothes back on and lights a cigar – to the horror of Domšík's daughter (bearing a striking resemblance to Málinka) – who takes the cigar as a sign of the devil and rushes out into the street shrieking 'Anti-Christ!' Brouček is denounced as a liar and a coward. He is thrust into a beer barrel to be burnt to death, but the flames of the fire are transformed into the flame of a candle held in Würfl's hand as he peers inside the barrel into which Brouček had tumbled on his way out of the pub. Brouček is rescued and gives a highly edited account of his adventure, but 'Not a word to anyone!'

Music and Background

Like many of Janáček's operas, *The Excursions of Mr Brouček* accommodates the eccentric and the downright perverse within its odd two-part narrative; and it doesn't work easily on stage. Part 1 was written years before Part 2, with an intervening break during which Janáček resolved to abandon opera altogether, and there are stylistic disparities between them in just about every sense, dramatic as well as musical. But the music of Part 1 has much charm, and although Part 2 can be long-winded, it offers stirring moments in the Hussite choruses.

Highlights

The local atmosphere of the Part 1 opening scene with its lyrical waltz tune 'Love, love, magical flower', and the Hussite chorales in Acts I and II of Part 2.

Recommended Recording

Vilém Přibyl, Czech Philharmonic Orchestra/František Jílek. Supraphon 11 2153-2. A rounded and delightful reading, with an all-Czech cast.

From the House of the Dead

FORM: Opera in three acts; in Czech
COMPOSER: Leoš Janáček (1854–1928)
LIBRETTO: Leoš Janáček; after Dostoyevsky
FIRST PERFORMANCE: Brno, 12 April 1930

Principal Characters

Alexander Petrovič Gorjančikov ∾ Baritone
Prison Governor ∾ Bass
Šiškov ∾ Baritone
Luka ∾ Tenor
Skuratov ∾ Tenor
Aljeja, a Tartar boy ∾ Mezzo-soprano
Small Prisoner ∾ Baritone
Elderly Prisoner ∾ Tenor

Synopsis of the Plot

Setting: A Siberian prison; about 1860

ACT I A new prisoner, Alexander Petrovič, arrives at the prison on a bitterly cold winter morning. The Governor tells him to behave while he's there and questions him about his crime; on learning that he is a political prisoner, he orders Petrovič to be flogged. After he is taken away, the other prisoners talk about a captured eagle which they keep in a cage, before being sent off to work, leaving Skuratov and Luka to tell of their past lives and crimes. Alexander Petrovič is brought back, more dead than alive.

ACT II Several months have gone by; it is a summer evening by the river and the prisoners are about to stop work. Alexander Petrovič asks Aljeja, the young Tartar boy, about his family and offers to teach him to read and write. The prisoners eat their evening meal, dominated by Skuratov's recounting of how he murdered his sweetheart's fiancé. After the meal, the prisoners perform and enjoy two short plays. Later, Alexander Petrovič is drinking tea with Aljeja when the Small Prisoner begins to bait Alexander about his 'refined' ways, finally smashing a jug over the boy's head. Aljeja collapses and the guards rush in.

ACT III Aljeja lies delirious in the prison hospital, watched over by Alexander Petrovič, and Luka lies dying in the next bed. Šiškov tells a long, brutal story of his abused and beaten wife, whom he finally murdered for her supposed faithlessness. Luka dies as the story ends and, as his body is taken

183

away, Šiškov recognises him as his wife's lover, masquerading under another name. Beside himself with rage, he curses the dead man, ignoring the Elderly Prisoner's comment that Luka is a man, just like any other. The Governor calls Alexander to see him and, apologising for the flogging on his arrival, says he is to be freed. His shackles are struck off and, as he leaves, the prisoners release the eagle and celebrate its freedom, before they are ordered back to work.

Music and Background

Short but severe, *From the House of the Dead* is a work of extreme concision which carries to the limits the tendency to terse, clipped statements and a kind of shorthand story-telling in Janáček's scores. It was his last opera, and because the score was still on his desk when he died, musicologists assumed that it must have been left unfinished. But no, the thin textures and fragmented episodes were meant to be exactly as they are: stark, sketchy, sometimes little more than a string of unrelated monologues in which prisoners recount their own experiences. For its time *From the House of the Dead* amounts to something like experimental opera. There are no 'star' roles; rather, the soloists seem to emerge from (and return to) the community of everyone on stage.

Highlights

Petrovič's return from the flogging at the end of Act I and the long monologue for Šiškov in Act III, plus the release of the eagle at the end.

Did You Know?

✎ This opera began its life as a projected violin concerto, hence the prominence of the solo violin writing in the overture.

Recommended Recording

Dalibor Jedlička, Jiri Zaharadníček, Vienna State Opera/Charles Mackerras. Decca 430 375-2. Grimly atmospheric, with a vivid Eastern European cast.

Jenůfa

FORM: Opera in three acts; in Czech
COMPOSER: Leoš Janáček (1854–1928)
LIBRETTO: Leoš Janáček; after Gabriela Preissová
FIRST PERFORMANCE: Brno, 21 January 1904

Principal Characters

Grandmother Buryjovka, the millowner ∾ **Contralto**
Laca Klemeň, step-grandson of Grandmother Buryjovka
and half-brother to Steva ∾ **Tenor**
Števa Buryja, grandson of Grandmother Buryjovka
and half-brother to Laca ∾ **Tenor**
Kostelnička Buryjovka ∾ **Soprano**
Jenufa, her step-daughter and granddaughter of Grandmother Buryjovka
∾ **Soprano**

Synopsis of the Plot

Setting: A village in Moravia; 19th century

ACT I Grandmother Buryjovka, Laca and Jenůfa are working together at
the mill when Jenůfa hears the news that she has anxiously been waiting for:
Števa, her lover and father of her secret, unborn child, has not been
conscripted into the army after all and is expected back in the village at any
moment. But when Števa and his friends arrive, they are very drunk and
their carousing outrages Kostelnička so much that she forbids Števa to talk
any more of marriage to Jenůfa until he has been sober for at least one year.
Jenůfa, left alone with Števa, tells him of the baby and pleads with him to
help her in her terrible situation, but he is largely unresponsive and leaves
her. When Laca returns he torments Jenůfa by ridiculing Števa's feelings for
her and, enraged by her constant defence of his half-brother, slashes her
across the face.

ACT II Jenůfa's baby has been born, but Števa has lost interest in her now
that she is scarred. Kostelnička, who is deeply ashamed of the disgrace this
event has brought to the family, tries to persuade Števa to marry Jenůfa, but
he admits he is now engaged to Karolka, the mayor's daughter. She then
turns to Laca who, she knows, loves Jenůfa, but he is unwilling to take on
Števa's child. After much agonising Kostelnička tells Laca the baby has died,
then takes the child and drowns it in the lake. She tells Jenůfa, who has been
ill, that she was delirious for two days, during which time the child died and
was buried.

ACT III Jenůfa has agreed to marry Laca, but the ceremony is interrupted by the dreadful news that a baby's body has been found under the ice. Jenůfa recognises the baby as hers and, as the crowd turns dangerously against her, Kostelnička comes forward and confesses her guilt. Jenůfa, with a great effort, forgives her stepmother, who is taken away. Jenůfa now feels bound to offer Laca his freedom, but he refuses to go and Jenůfa, recognising his constancy, joyfully admits she now loves him.

Music and Background

This opera, which took ten years to write, was the turning point in Janáček's career and it remains his most popular stage work. Written over a period of nearly ten years, it charts a stylistic development from simple folk-like tunes to more sophisticated musical procedures, although the composer was at pains to say that there isn't a *real* folk tune in the whole score: everything is original, and this is effectively the piece where the *Bartered Bride* tradition of central European opera steps boldly into the modern world. The orchestration too has a transitional quality: richer and more conventionally lyrical than Janáček's later operas, but introducing striking touches of modernity like the insistent use of the xylophone in Act I, associated with the turning of the mill-wheel.

Highlights

The finest moments are dramatic: the knifing in Act I; Kostelnička's decision to kill the child in Act II; and the discovery of the frozen corpse in Act III.

Did You Know?

So little faith did the Czech musical establishment have in Janáček that the Prague Opera only agreed to stage *Jenůfa* if the score was reorchestrated by the company's music director. The reorchestration remained the standard way to present the piece until fairly recently.

Recommended Recording

Elisabeth Söderström, Eva Randová, Vienna State Opera/Charles Mackerras. Decca 414 483-2. Far and away the best recording: vividly intense with a superb cast.

Kátya Kabanová

FORM: Opera in three acts; in Czech
COMPOSER: Leoš Janáček (1854–1928)
LIBRETTO: V. Červinka; after Ostrovsky
FIRST PERFORMANCE: Brno, 23 November 1921

Principal Characters

Marfa Ignatĕvna Kabanová (Kabanicha), a wealthy merchant's widow
Contralto
Tichon Ivanyč Kabanov, her son *Tenor*
Katĕrina (Kátya) Kabanová, his wife *Soprano*
Varvara, the Kabanov family's adopted daughter *Mezzo-soprano*
Boris Grigorjevič, his nephew *Tenor*
Váňa Kudrjáš, a teacher and chemist *Tenor*

Synopsis of the Plot

Setting: The Russian town of Kalinov; 1860s

ACT I The Kabanovs are returning from church, observed by Boris, who confesses that he is in love with Kátya. Kátya's mother-in-law, a powerful and dominating woman, is jealous of her son Tichon's new wife, and tells him that he treats her much too leniently. She orders Tichon to go away on business and insists that he instructs his wife how to behave while he is away, much to Kátya's embarrassment and humiliation.

ACT II In the evening, Kátya, Kabanicha and Varvara are working at their embroidery. After Kabanicha leaves, Varvara says she has obtained the key of the garden gate and is going to meet her sweetheart, Kudrjáš; she offers to send for Boris to meet Kátya. Kátya, although she is drawn to Boris, is determined to remain faithful, and initially refuses, but later she succumbs to her feelings and goes out to meet him.

ACT III During a violent thunderstorm, several people, including Kátya, Tichon and Kabanicha, take shelter in a ruined building by the river Volga. Kátya is in a volatile state of mind, overwrought and tormented by guilt. Suddenly she sees Boris among the crowd and bursts out with a confession of her faithlessness, before rushing out into the storm. Kátya wanders alone in a desolate place by the river; she longs half for death and half to see Boris again. But when he comes, it is only to say he has been sent away by his rich uncle, Dikoj. Abandoned by her lover, Kátya cannot bear the thought of her public shame and the misery of living with the taunts of her triumphant mother-in-law, and she throws herself in the river as the voices of the searchers are heard nearby.

Music and Background

Kátya Kabanová is the first of the four 'Indian summer' operas, written late in life, on which Janáček's reputation largely rests. The cast of characters bears similarities with that for *Jenůfa*, but their music is sparer, more concise, and indicative of Janáček's mature interest in the pitched sound-patterns of ordinary speech as a starting point for setting words to music. A repeating motif of eight timpani strokes, representing the ominous, ever-present hand of fate, sounds throughout, from the overture onwards.

Highlights

The summer's evening Love Scene in Act II has the most endearingly evocative music in all Janáček's output, plus a passionate top C for the tenor. The humiliation of Kátya at the end of Act I and her confession in Act III are moments of compelling drama; and her monologues in the same acts are vocal high points.

Did You Know?

🔊 The tender portrait of the central character was inspired by Kamila Stösslová, the young married woman for whom Janáček in old age developed an unrequited, fantasy-based love.

🔊 This was the first of Janáček's operas to be performed in the UK (April 1951).

Recommended Recording

Elisabeth Söderström, Peter Dvorský, Vienna State Opera/Charles Mackerras. Decca 421 852-2. Yet another winner in the Mackerras Janáček series. Unmatchable.

The Makropulos Case

FORM: Opera in three acts; in Czech
COMPOSER: Leoš Janáček (1854–1928)
LIBRETTO: Leoš Janáček; after Karel Čapek
FIRST PERFORMANCE: Brno, 18 December 1926

Principal Characters

Emilia Marty, an opera singer ✖ **Soprano**
Albert Gregor ✖ **Tenor**
Kristina (Krista), in love with Janek ✖ **Soprano**
Kolenatý, a lawyer ✖ **Baritone**
Jaroslav Prus ✖ **Bass**
Janek, his son ✖ **Tenor**
Count Hauk-Šendorf ✖ **Baritone**

Synopsis of the Plot

Setting: Prague; 1922

ACT I Emilia Marty, a famous opera singer, unexpectedly arrives at Dr Kolenatý's law offices and reveals an astonishingly detailed knowledge of an inheritance case, Gregor v. Prus, which has been unresolved for ninety-five years. Indeed she goes so far as to give the precise location of a will in the Prus house, which leaves the estate to Ferdinand Gregor, Albert's forebear. Kolenatý returns with the will, and Jaroslav Prus, who demands further proof of Albert Gregor's entitlement to inherit; this Emilia promises to supply.

ACT II At the opera house, Emilia behaves rudely to all her admirers, except for the elderly and half-senile Count Hauk-Šendorf, who says she reminds him of Eugenia Montez, a great Spanish beauty, beloved by him fifty years ago. After she sends him away with a kiss, Emilia turns to Prus' son, Janek, and persuades him to bring her a sealed envelope from his father's house. But Janek is intercepted by his father, who takes the envelope instead.

ACT III The next morning Emilia is confronted in her hotel room by Kolenatý and several others who have become deeply suspicious of her motives. When she leaves them alone they investigate her luggage and are intrigued to find that her possessions all carry different 'E.M.' names – Eugenia Montez, Ellian MacGregor, Elsa Müller. Emilia returns, bringing a bottle of whisky and, steadily drinking, gives an account of her extraordinary life. She was born Elina Makropulos, daughter of a Greek doctor at the Habsburg court of Rudolf II. Commanded to produce a potion to prolong life, her father tried it first on his young daughter; she has, therefore, survived over three hundred years, disguising her longevity by changing her name. She had an illegitimate child by Joseph Prus, with whom she left the formula for the potion in a sealed envelope, the very one that she asked Janek to bring to her, so that she can renew herself again. Emilia's story is greeted sceptically, but as she collapses, mumbling Greek prayers, the truth is acknowledged. Offering the formula to Krista, Emilia recognises her life as cold, lonely and futile and longs only for death. Krista burns the formula and Emilia dies.

Music and Background

Janáček's own libretto adapted a pre-existing philosophical comedy into theatre of searing emotional power that ranks among the most striking operas of the 20th century. Most of its musical energy is focused into confrontational duets between Emilia and her admirers. The central role is a gift for a true singing actress with *femme fatale* potential – like Anja Silja in the recent Glyndebourne production – so long as she can bring the right degree of chilling weariness to her encounters with prolonged life and still command the audience's sympathy.

Highlights

Emilia's final monologue in which she describes the emptiness of her life against a ghostly offstage choir that mirrors her words.

Did You Know?

  The aloofness of Emilia Marty is another of Janácek's operatic responses to his fantasy lover Kamila Stösslová.

Recommended Recording

Elisabeth Söderström, Peter Dvorský, Vienna Philharmonic Orchestra/ Charles Mackerras. Decca 430 372-2. The Decca Mackerras team yet again providing the best Janáček on disc, with a magnificent central performance from Söderström.

Oliver Knussen
(1952–)

Where the Wild Things Are (1983)
Higglety Pigglety Pop! (1985)

*T*he British conductor/composer Oliver Knussen came to public attention at a young age, conducting the London Symphony Orchestra in his own music at the age of fifteen. Since then he has written mostly concert scores, and built a reputation for himself in Britain and America (where he studied) as an authoritative voice in the contemporary music world. His output is steady, and reveals the influence of such diverse figures as Musorgsky and Elliott Carter. His two operas are both short one-acters based on picture-books by the American children's author/illustrator Maurice Sendak and made an instant impression through pictorially enchanting Glyndebourne productions designed by Sendak himself.

Where the Wild Things Are

FORM: Opera in one act; in English
COMPOSER: Oliver Knussen (1952–)
LIBRETTO: Maurice Sendak
FIRST PERFORMANCE: Brussels, 28 November 1980

Principal Characters

Max, a small boy ~ **Soprano**
Mama ~ **Mezzo-soprano**
The Wild Things
Tzippy ~ **Mezzo-soprano**
Wild Thing with Beard ~ **Tenor**
Goat Wild Thing ~ **Tenor**
Wild Thing with Horns ~ **Baritone**
Rooster Wild Thing ~ **Bass-baritone**
Bull Wild Thing ~ **Bass**

Synopsis of the Plot

Setting: Max's room

Spoilt Max is cheeky to his mother and, sent to bed supperless, is pursued by a vacuum cleaner. Max's imagination takes over and his room becomes a forest; then he gets into a boat and is borne away. He arrives at an island and moors the boat. Strange noises herald the arrival of the Wild Things, huge monsters who try their best to scare the wits out of this unwelcome intruder. But they fail and, when Max stamps his foot and looks them in the eye, they cower before him, only taking the opportunity of creeping up on him when his back is turned. Max is crowned their king and, after the ceremony, orders the Wild Rumpus to begin. After much noise and cavorting, Max orders them to stop and to go to bed – much as his mother had ordered Max himself. Max gets back into the boat and sets off back to his room, where everything is reassuringly familiar.

Music and Background

In a total duration of no more than forty minutes, Knussen creates a childhood fantasy that bears comparison with Ravel's *L'Enfant et les Sortilèges* – not only in its subject matter but in its combination of charm, magic, ingenuity and exuberance. Something for children from eight to eighty.

Highlights

Max's fur songs and journey-music, which Knussen has extracted from the score and published separately as a concert piece.

Did You Know?

➤ Through his association with Tanglewood, the summer residence of the Boston Symphony Orchestra and celebrated teaching centre, Knussen is one of the few British composers of his generation to have made much headway with the American public.

Recommended Recording

Rosemary Hardy, Mary King, London Sinfonietta/Oliver Knussen. Unicorn DKPCD 9044. The only one, using the Glyndebourne cast.

Erich Korngold
(1897–1957)

Die Tote Stadt (1920)
Das Wunder der Heliane (1926)

Korngold was a prodigy who had a ballet and two operas premiered in Vienna while he was still a teenager – encouraged and promoted by his father who happened to be Vienna's leading music critic. *Die Tote Stadt*, his most enduring work, was written in his early twenties and was an immediate success that would probably have secured him a lasting celebrity in the German-speaking world but for the rise of Hitler. Korngold was a Jew, and in 1934 fled to America where he wrote Hollywood film scores. Commercially he did well, but the luxuriant late-Romanticism of his writing didn't develop, and when he returned to Vienna after the war he found that time had moved on, leaving him behind. Korngold believed the extravagantly scored, post-Straussian *Das Wunder der Heliane* to be his best work, but the piece was largely forgotten until a recent recording reminded listeners of its outrageous but endearing excesses.

Die Tote Stadt
(The Dead City)

FORM: Opera in three acts; in German
COMPOSER: Erich Korngold (1897–1957)
LIBRETTO: Erich Korngold and Julius Korngold
(together using the pen-name, Paul Schott); after Rodenbach
FIRST PERFORMANCE: Hamburg and Cologne (simultaneously),
4 December 1920

Principal Characters
Paul ✍ **Tenor**
Marie, his wife ✍ **Soprano**
Marietta, a dancer ✍ **Soprano**
Frank, Paul's friend ✍ **Baritone**
Brigitta, Paul's housekeeper ✍ **Mezzo-soprano**

Note: The roles of Marie and Marietta are traditionally taken by the same singer.

Synopsis of the Plot
Setting: Bruges; late 19th century

ACT I Paul is mourning his young wife, Marie, who has recently died, and even keeps a room specially dedicated to her in their home. The room holds all the items which remind Paul of Marie, the most precious of which is a plait of her golden hair. One day, when Frank, his friend, arrives, Paul excitedly tells him he has met a woman who looks very like Marie; he has, in fact, invited her to the house so that he can see her walk through Marie's room, thereby bringing her back to life. When Marietta comes, Paul is so taken by her resemblance to Marie that he tries to kiss her; she pulls away and accidentally knocks the cover from a portrait of the dead woman. Marietta is astonished to see what she supposes to be her own portrait, but almost immediately leaves for a rehearsal. After she has gone, Paul is struggling with his conflicting emotions when he seems to see the figure in the portrait step out and, after telling him he must live his own life, transform itself into the dancing form of Marietta.

ACT II Paul's strange dream-vision continues and he finds himself wracked by guilt, torn between loyalty and love for Marie and his new passion for Marietta. These emotions reach a crisis point when he watches Marietta and her fellow performers rehearse a scene from Meyerbeer's *Robert le Diable*, which calls upon Marietta to rise from the tomb. Paul is outraged at what he sees as a mockery of Marie's death, and shouts abuse at Marietta,

194

telling her he is only attracted to her because she looks like Marie. Marietta decides that she should confront the situation directly by staying the night with him at his home, thereby laying the ghost to rest.

ACT III In Paul's vision, the two have spent the night together and Marietta is triumphant. But when a religious procession passes by under the window, Marietta mocks Paul's piety and they argue. She takes up Marie's band of hair and drapes it round her neck. Paul, furious, strangles her. At this point the vision disappears and Paul is suddenly interrupted by his housekeeper, Brigitta, who announces that the lady visitor has returned to collect her umbrella and some flowers which she left behind on her visit. When they meet it is clear that Marietta would like the relationship to go further, but, disillusioned by his dream, Paul says nothing. After she has gone he decides to leave Bruges, the decaying city of death; the dead cannot be reclaimed.

Music and Background

A voluptuously scored symbolist dream, saturated with the damp gloom of its setting, *Die Tote Stadt* does not often reach the stage but is known for the wilting beauty of its principal motif: one of a collection of short but pervasive not-quite themes that run through the opera and suggest lingering memories of the past. Korngold writes on a grand scale for a large orchestra whose power tends in practice to drown the singers, but a good performance can nonetheless be overwhelming, especially for lovers of melancholia.

Highlights

In Act I the vision of Marie, in which she sings 'Gluck, das mir verblieb'; Act II has the serenade for the imagined Marietta.

Did You Know?

With a cult-kitsch reputation, the composer has always been revered and reviled in equal measure. His American Violin Concerto was dismissed as 'more corn than gold'.

Recommended Recording

René Kollo, Carol Neblett, Hermann Prey, Munich Radio Orchestra/Erich Leinsdorf. RCA GD 87767. Leinsdorf making the most of a very rich score.

Franz Lehár

(1870–1948)

Die Lustige Witwe (1905)
Der Graf von Luxemburg (1909)
Das Land des Lächelns (1929)

Franz Lehár grew up in the world of Austro-Hungarian military bands (his father was a bandmaster) but also studied the violin and had composition lessons in Prague (with Fibich and Dvořák) which were to stand him in good stead. For a composer of light music, he had an uncommonly good technique and feel for orchestration, and was certainly the most proficient (as well as the most successful) exponent of Viennese operetta this century. The hits began with *Die Lustige Witwe*, which became the mainstay of his reputation ever after, and fell into abeyance during the First World War when new kinds of popular music started to infiltrate the European market from America. But the 1920s brought Lehár into contact with the tenor Richard Tauber and there followed a succession of operettas, written specifically to exploit Tauber's vocal gifts and personality, that returned Lehár to the forefront of public esteem in his native land. A mark of Lehár's stature is that his music has always attracted the interest of great singers with serious 'operatic' careers.

Die Lustige Witwe
(The Merry Widow)

FORM: Operetta in three acts; in German
COMPOSER: Franz Lehár (1870–1948)
LIBRETTO: Viktor Léon and Leo Stein; after Meilhac
FIRST PERFORMANCE: Vienna, 30 December 1905

Principal Characters

Baron Zeta, Pontevedrin envoy ⁓ **Baritone**
Valencienne, his wife ⁓ **Soprano**
Camille, in love with Valencienne ⁓ **Tenor**
Count Danilo Danilowitsch, secretary to the Pontevedrin legation
⁓ **Tenor**
Hanna Glawari, a rich Pontevedrin widow ⁓ **Soprano**
Njegus, clerk to the legation ⁓ **Spoken role**

Synopsis of the Plot

Setting: Paris; early 19th century

ACT I A party is in progress at the Pontevedrin legation, and one of the guests is the fabulously wealthy Hanna Glawari. On her entrance the widow is immediately surrounded by solicitous French noblemen, observed anxiously by the Pontevedrin envoy, Baron Zeta, who is greatly concerned that her millions should remain in impoverished Pontevedro and not be transferred to France in the event of her marrying a Frenchman. Zeta sees a definite possibility of resolving the situation in the person of Danilo, the legation secretary, and he arranges to have Danilo forcibly brought to the party from his revels in a Parisian nightclub. The reluctant Danilo falls asleep on his arrival but his snores are overheard by Hanna; the two recognise each other as former lovers, but Danilo recoils from the fact that Hanna is the target of gold-diggers, and assures her he will never be one of them. He is shocked, therefore, to be told by Zeta that he is required to marry Hanna, and refuses point-blank. When Hanna chooses him – he is the only man ignoring her – as a dancing partner, Danilo reacts by attempting to auction the dance for 10,000 francs to go to charity; but the other men melt away and Danilo takes her in his arms and sweeps her into the ballroom.

ACT II Hanna is hosting a party at her home, and the guests include Camille, in love with Zeta's wife, Valencienne, and Danilo. Valencienne firmly resists Camille's charms and urges him to turn his attention to Hanna instead. But Camille persists and eventually manages to persuade

Valencienne to join him in the summerhouse, where they are discovered by Zeta himself, peering through the keyhole. But before the door can be opened, Njegus manages to substitute Hanna for Valencienne. When Camille and Hanna emerge, Hanna explains events by announcing their engagement. Danilo is disgusted and rushes out; Hanna is sure now that he loves her.

ACT III To appeal to the pleasure-loving Danilo, Hanna has arranged her house to look like a nightclub and the girls from Maxim's perform a can-can. Danilo tells Hanna that she must not marry Camille and she reassures him that she never intended to. The two of them can no longer hide their love for each other and look forward to their happiness together.

Music and Background

The Viennese operetta to end them all, *Die Lustige Witwe* stands as a benchmark for the genre, full of deathless tunes, heart-lifting waltzes and uncommonly inventive orchestrations which periodically suggest that Lehár knew his Debussy as well as his Strauss.

Highlights

Everybody knows Hanna's song of the wood-maid, 'Vilja', in Act II, and ought to know the 'Lippen schweigen' waltz in Act III. Hanna and Danilo both have strikingly characterful entrance arias in Act I.

Did You Know?

Die Lustige Witwe was Hitler's favourite operetta, but Lehár was nonetheless forced to spend the war years in quiet retirement. His wife was Jewish.

Recommended Recording

Elisabeth Schwarzkopf, Eberhard Waechter, Nicolai Gedda, Philharmonia Orchestra/ Lovro von Matačič. EMI CDS7 47178-8. Schwarzkopf in her prime, recorded under the direction of her husband Walter Legge with a buoyant sense of theatre.

Ruggero Leoncavallo

(1857–1919)

I Pagliacci (1892)
La Bohème (1896)
Zazà (1900)

Born in Naples into a comfortably-off legal family, Leoncavallo's professional life began as a librettist assisting Puccini on the text for *Manon Lescaut*. But his ambition was to compose and he devoted much of his early life to plans for a grand Wagnerian trilogy on the Italian Renaissance which was to be an Italian answer to Wagner's Ring. It never happened. In the meantime another Italian composer, Mascagni, had scored a popular hit with the verismo, or realist, opera *Cavalleria Rusticana*, and Leoncavallo produced his *I Pagliacci* as a direct response to it, cashing in on what he (rightly) took to be a ready market. From the time in 1893 when the Metropolitan Opera, New York combined the two operas as a double bill, they have been virtually inseparable. *I Pagliacci* made Leoncavallo's name but thereafter his fortunes were sporadic, and he settled into a routine of writing lightweight operettas. One definite commercial success was the song 'Mattinata', written specifically for Caruso to record, accompanied by the composer, in 1904.

I Pagliacci
(The Clowns, The Strolling Players)

FORM: Opera in a Prologue and two acts; in Italian
COMPOSER: Ruggero Leoncavallo (1857–1919)
LIBRETTO: Ruggero Leoncavallo
FIRST PERFORMANCE: Milan, 21 May 1892

Principal Characters

Canio, leader of the players ∾ Tenor
Nedda, his wife ∾ Soprano
Tonio, a clown ∾ Baritone
Silvio, a villager ∾ Baritone

Synopsis of the Plot

Setting: A village in Calabria; about 1870

PROLOGUE Tonio tells the audience that the drama they are to see is a real one, about real people.

ACT I Canio and his colourful troupe arrive in the village and immediately start promoting their forthcoming performance. Canio is annoyed when Tonio helps Nedda and hits him; Tonio says he will get his own back on Canio, who goes off for a drink and is teased by the villagers about his wife's fidelity. Canio assures them that anyone who compromises Nedda will suffer for it. Meanwhile, Nedda finds herself alone with Tonio, who declares his love for her, but she becomes increasingly annoyed with him and slashes him across the face with a whip. He runs off. Silvio then enters and it is clear that he and Nedda are lovers; Silvio begs Nedda to run away with him that evening and she agrees. Tonio has crept back unseen, however, and is listening; he fetches Canio who challenges his wife, but not before Silvio has time to escape. Canio demands to know the name of his wife's lover, but Nedda refuses to tell him. Tonio reassures Canio, saying that he is sure to be in the audience that night and the lovers will give themselves away by a look or a gesture.

ACT II Nedda, in her Columbine costume, is collecting ticket money. She sees Silvio and warns him to be careful. The performance begins. In a play-within-a-play, a story of love and betrayal is acted out, but fantasy becomes reality as Nedda, in her role as Columbine, realises that Canio (in his role as Pagliaccio), is no longer acting as he repeatedly demands her lover's name. Finally, Canio stabs Nedda and strikes Silvio dead as he comes to her rescue; turning to the terrified audience Canio declares 'The comedy is over'.

Music and Background

I Pagliacci runs for only one hour, but it comes in two acts which play with an almost Wagnerian continuity despite the existence of numbers which stop and start in definite places (making it clear where the audience should applaud). The naturalistic presentation of life in the raw, with heightened sentiments and a shocking death, helped fix the tone of what was called verismo opera for the coming years – even if the 'reality' of *I Pagliacci's* storyline comes closer to melodrama than anything else. Along with its running partner *Cavalleria Rusticana* it has some claim to being the world's most frequently performed opera.

Highlights

Canio's tearful show-must-go-on aria 'Vesti la giubba' is a classic of the lyric tenor recipe, written to be sung with sobs and the sole reason why the opera comes in two acts (to allow the audience to recover their composure). Canio's final outburst of jealousy, 'Non, pagliaccio non son', is a cherishable moment of theatre-drama.

Did You Know?

🔸 The famous last words of the opera, 'La commedia è finita', were originally given to Tonio – appropriately, since he has the Prologue too. But in performance they are almost always stolen by Canio, claiming tenor's rights of precedence.

🔸 Leoncavallo is said to have taken the idea for the opera from a real court case tried by his magistrate father.

Recommended Recording

Carlo Bergonzi, Joan Carlyle, La Scala Milan/Herbert von Karajan. DG 419 257-2. A strong but refined performance of a score that needs all the refinement it can get.

Heinrich August Marschner

(1795–1861)

Der Vampyr (1828)
Der Templer und die Jüdin (1829)
Hans Heiling (1832)

After abortive law studies in Leipzig, Heinrich Marschner settled in Dresden and took employment at the city's opera house under the German Romantic composer Weber, whose *Der Freischütz* had set the tone for nationalist stage works of the time. Marschner proved to be Weber's natural creative heir and his first stage success, *Der Vampyr*, was very much in the spirit of *Der Freischütz*, with a supernatural story and the format of what Germans called a *Singspiel*, linking sung numbers with spoken dialogue. But Marschner's importance was that he extended the *Singspiel* style – dramatically (with psychologically developed characters), musically (with more advanced orchestral and harmonic techniques) and structurally (enlarging the musical numbers to the point where singing seems to flow almost continuously). In all these respects he became a sort of middle-man between Weber and Wagner, whose Romantic opera *Der Fliegende Holländer* couldn't have been written without the precedent of Marschner's scores. Besides *Der Vampyr*, two other operas achieved success in his lifetime, and *Hans Heiling*, a grand central European nature myth, seemed at the time to be his masterwork. But only *Der Vampyr* survives in repertory and even so, it does not often play outside the German-speaking countries.

Der Vampyr
(The Vampire)

FORM: Opera in two acts; in German
COMPOSER: Heinrich August Marschner (1795–1861)
LIBRETTO: W.A. Wohlbrück; after Polidori and Byron
FIRST PERFORMANCE: Leipzig, 29 March 1828

Principal Characters

Lord Ruthven, Earl of Marsden, the vampire ∾ **Baritone**
Sir John Berkley ∾ **Bass**
Janthe, his daughter ∾ **Soprano**
Sir Humphrey Davenaut ∾ **Bass**
Malwina, his daughter ∾ **Soprano**
Edgar Aubry ∾ **Tenor**
Emmy Perth, engaged to George Dibdin ∾ **Soprano**
George Dibdin, Davenaut's servant ∾ **Tenor**
The Vampire Master ∾ **Spoken role**

Synopsis of the Plot

Setting: Sir Humphrey Davenaut's castle and grounds, Scotland; 18th century

ACT I The Vampire Master, surrounded by witches and hobgoblins, introduces his newest recruit, Lord Ruthven. Ruthven has asked for another year on earth, and the Vampire Master agrees, providing Ruthven sacrifices three young girls by the following midnight. His first victim is Janthe, Sir John Berkley's daughter. But Ruthven himself is caught and stabbed by Sir John, who leaves him for dead. Edgar Aubry, knowing nothing of these events, comes across Ruthven's body on his way home and, on Ruthven's request, takes him to an open space so that he can be healed by the rays of the moon. Aubry gradually realises the truth about Ruthven, but Ruthven once saved Aubry's life and, when he swears him to secrecy, Aubry cannot refuse. As Ruthven revives, Aubry runs away in terror, arriving at the home of his sweetheart, Malwina Davenaut, who comes out to meet him. Sir Humphrey, her father, unaware of his daughter's love for Aubry, tells her she is to marry the Earl of Marsden, who is expected at the castle imminently. When Marsden arrives, Aubry is horrified to recognise Ruthven, but, sworn to secrecy, he says nothing.

ACT II Ruthven appears at the wedding celebrations of Emmy Perth and George Dibdin and immediately begins to seduce the bride. Aubry tries to persuade Ruthven not to hurt her, but he fails, and resigns himself to despair as Ruthven leads the girl away to become his second victim. Meanwhile, at the Davenaut castle, it is almost midnight and Malwina and Ruthven are about to be married. Malwina has submitted to her father's plans, but she has no idea that Ruthven is a vampire. Aubry, unable to keep silent any longer, and prepared to take the consequences, denounces Ruthven. Immediately Ruthven is surrounded by fiends and dragged down to hell to the sound of mocking laughter, and Malwina and Aubry are united in marriage.

Music and Background

A Hammer House of Horror opera with a vengeance, *Der Vampyr* sets out to chill the soul and does so with every trick in the 19th-century composer's book, including melodrama – the setting of spoken words against an undercurrent of music. One interesting feature is the central character, who comes across with the deliberate duality of a terrorising monster who commands some sympathy. The action is fast-moving with stage business and music tightly integrated – despite the fact that the score calls for a large orchestra with thunder machine and serpent (the S-shaped wind instrument popular in 19th-century military bands)!

Highlights

Ruthven's opening aria 'Ha! welche Lust!' is a blood-draining introduction to the anti-hero's nocturnal activities, rich in sinister chromatics. Emmy's Act II musing on the existence of vampires, 'Sieh Mutter, dort den bleichen Mann', is engaging and exactly the sort of number Weber gives Ännchen in *Der Freischütz*.

Did You Know?

❧ Many people feel that Marschner's modernity and psychological insight ought to have won him a more esteemed place in the enduring hierarchy of opera composers. If only the *music* were stronger.

Recommended Recording

None currently available, although a raunchy English-language adaptation was made for BBC TV in 1992 with Omar Ebrahim in the title role and selected extracts on Virgin Classics 79592942.

Pietro Mascagni

(1863–1945)

Cavalleria Rusticana (1889)
L'Amico Fritz (1891)
Iris (1898)
Parisina (1913)
Il Piccolo Marat (1919)

Mascagni was a one-opera composer who struck lucky with *Cavalleria Rusticana* when he was still young and, despite a long life, never managed to follow it up with anything of equal stature. Son of a Livorno baker, he studied music in Milan against his parents' wishes and became the first of the verismo school of composers to find fame when *Cavalleria Rusticana* won first prize in a publisher's competition for one-act operas. As a result, the piece was premiered in Rome in 1890, and its instant success proved inspirational to Leoncavallo, Cilea and the other *veristi* – or 'realists' – whose uniting quality was the depiction of real (usually low) life situations as sensationally as possible. In later life, still living off the reputation of *Cavalleria Rusticana*, Mascagni toed the fascist party line and re-established himself as a keeper of the flame of true Italian writing. In other words, an extreme conservative. When the fortunes of the totalitarian system sank, so did his.

Cavalleria Rusticana
(Rustic Chivalry)

FORM: Opera in one act; in Italian
COMPOSER: Pietro Mascagni (1863–1945)
LIBRETTO: G. Menasci and G. Targioni-Tozzetti; after Verga
FIRST PERFORMANCE: Rome, 17 May 1890

Principal Characters

Turiddu, a young soldier ❧ **Tenor**
Alfio, the village carter ❧ **Baritone**
Lola, his wife ❧ **Mezzo-soprano**
Mamma Lucia, Turiddu's mother and innkeeper ❧ **Contralto**
Santuzza, a village girl ❧ **Soprano**

Synopsis of the Plot

Setting: A Sicilian village; Easter Sunday

As the church bells ring out, Santuzza, searching for her lover, Turiddu, comes to see Mamma Lucia to ask where he is. Lucia tells her that Turiddu is away buying wine, but Santuzza knows this is not true, as she has seen him that morning. Alfio confirms her suspicion, saying he noticed Turiddu near his own cottage earlier on. When he leaves, the pregnant Santuzza tells Lucia of her seduction and betrayal by Turiddu. He has now rejected her in favour of his former love, Lola, who, tired of waiting for Turiddu to return from the army, married Alfio. When Turiddu enters, Santuzza begs him to stay with her, but he knocks her down and follows the mocking Lola into church. Alfio enters and Santuzza tells him of his wife's betrayal; he is furious and challenges Turiddu to a duel, during which Turiddu is killed and Santuzza collapses.

Music and Background

Cavalleria Rusticana packs a lot of passion into its hour-and-a-quarter running time, with music full of punch and impact (if not much subtlety), big scenes and tumultuous emotional crises. The scoring is more lurid than rich, and the groundplan of the piece unoriginal: playing most of the action against the background of the Easter service is much the same idea Bizet used in the final act of *Carmen*, where an intense personal drama plays against the public spectacle of the bullfight. But no matter, *Cavalleria Rusticana* speaks from the heart and to the heart, unsparingly melodious and dramatically effective.

Highlights

The big number is the Easter Hymn, 'Ineggiamo, il Signore non è morto', which makes a grand ensemble for Santuzza and the chorus. The Intermezzo that follows Santuzza's spilling of the beans is one of opera's most famous examples of purely orchestral music. Turiddu's farewell to his mother before he goes to fight the duel, 'Mamma, quel vino è generoso', is mawkish but a good moment for the tenor.

Did You Know?

🐚 *Cavalleria Rusticana* almost always plays as one half of a double bill with Leoncavallo's *I Pagliacci*. Known collectively as 'Cav and Pag', they are probably the most popular operas in the entire repertory.

🐚 The immediate success enjoyed by the opera haunted the composer all his life: 'It was a pity I wrote *Cavalleria* first,' he said, 'I was crowned before I was King.'

🐚 The famous Intermezzo was used in the films *Jean de Florette* (1986) and *The Godfather III* (1990), as well as in advertisements for Baci chocolates and Stella Artois lager.

Recommended Recording

Plácido Domingo, Renata Scotto, National Philharmonic Orchestra/ James Levine. RCA RD 83091. Domingo as good as you'll ever hear him, resounding with strength and glamour.

Jules Massenet

(1842–1912)

Le Roi de Lahore (1876)
Hérodiade (1881)
Manon (1882)
Le Cid (1884)
Werther (1887)
Esclarmonde (1888)
Thaïs (1893)
Cendrillon (1895)
Chérubin (1903)
Don Quichotte (1909)

The leading French composer for the stage in the last half of the
19th century, Massenet was the archetype of the true professional
composer: prolific, technically proficient, able to tackle any subject in
any style, and with a strong commercial instinct that ensured he gave his
audiences what they wanted – including (as fellow-composer Vincent
d'Indy described it) 'discreetly pseudo-religious eroticism'. Massenet
himself said, 'I don't believe in all this creeping Jesus business, but the
public likes it.' And the public also liked his fondness for stories of
young fallen women in need of reclamation. With a high sugar content,
most of Massenet's operas only occasionally surface outside France, but
he scored two enduring hits with the tragedies *Manon* and *Werther*.
Another deathless item is the violin solo 'Meditation' from *Thaïs* which,
needless to add, symbolises the stirring conscience and ultimate
conversion of an ancient Egyptian whore!

Manon

FORM: Opera in five acts; in French
COMPOSER: Jules Massenet (1842–1912)
LIBRETTO: H. Meilhac and P. Gille; after Abbé Prévost
FIRST PERFORMANCE: Paris, 19 January 1884

Principal Characters

Manon Lescaut ∼ Soprano
Lescaut, her cousin and soldier ∼ Baritone
Chevalier des Grieux ∼ Tenor
Count des Grieux, his father ∼ Bass
Guillot de Morfontaine, a government minister and womaniser
∼ Tenor
De Brétigny, a nobleman ∼ Baritone

Synopsis of the Plot

Setting: Amiens, Paris, near Le Havre; 1721

ACT I Lescaut is waiting at an inn for the arrival of his young cousin, Manon, whom he is to escort to a convent. When she arrives, Lescaut leaves her while he goes to find her luggage, and she is approached by Guillot, who is also at the inn, together with de Brétigny and three 'actresses'. Guillot, impressed by Manon's beauty, immediately offers to elope with her, but is sent away by Lescaut on his return. Left alone again when her cousin goes away to play cards, Manon is seen by des Grieux, who is instantly enchanted by her. Within minutes Manon is in love with him, and they leave together in the coach Guillot had ordered for his own use.

ACT II Now living with Manon in Paris, des Grieux writes to his father in the hope of obtaining his permission to marry Manon. They are visited by Lescaut and a soldier friend (actually de Brétigny in disguise). While des Grieux is assuring Lescaut that he hopes to marry Manon, de Brétigny, whom Manon has recognized, warns her that the Count des Grieux has arranged to have his son abducted by force that evening, and he offers her the opportunity of becoming his mistress. Manon is attracted by this prospect and, when the expected knock on the door is heard that evening, she fails to warn her lover and he is taken.

ACT III Manon, now de Brétigny's mistress, is enjoying her new-found wealth, when she learns from des Grieux's father (who does not realise who she is) that des Grieux is about to become a priest, as a result of an unhappy love affair. She goes to the seminary to see him and their reunion rekindles their love for each other. Once more they leave together.

ACT IV Manon has persuaded des Grieux to try his luck at an illegal gambling den, against his better judgement. His consistent wins provoke Guillot to accuse him of cheating, and des Grieux and Manon are arrested and taken away.

ACT V The charges against des Grieux are dropped, but Manon is to be deported as a prostitute and is en route for embarkation at Le Havre. Lescaut manages to bribe the guards to let him take her away for a while, and he leaves her and des Grieux alone together. Des Grieux tries to encourage Manon to escape with him, but she is too weak and ill and she dies in his arms.

Music and Background

Massenet's most popular stage score, *Manon* is an *opéra comique* – which is to say, it incorporates speech alongside and sometimes over music. It is a long score with too much stock business of the kind that 19th-century Paris audiences expected to see: this doesn't exactly make riveting theatre, and modern performances usually introduce substantial cuts. But its saving grace is charm, especially in the touches of 18th-century period pastiche that Massenet sprinkles through the writing, and although the title role is under-characterised, Manon manages to hold attention as one of opera's more effective representatives of the Eternal Feminine.

Highlights

Mostly Manon's showcase arias, from the opening 'Je suis encore tout étourdie' and 'Voyons, Manon' as she's off to the convent, to the sentimental 'Adieu, notre petite table' in Act II and 'N'est-ce plus ma main' which leads into the love duet at the close of Act III. The other love duets, 'Nous vivrons à Paris' in Act I and the terminal 'Ah! je sens une flamme' in Act V, are purple with passion. Des Grieux's 'En fermant les yeux' (Act II) and 'Manon, sphinx étonnant' (Act IV) are his big solo moments.

Did You Know?

Massenet was so taken with his own creation here that he composed a sequel, *Le Portrait de Manon* (1893) – but not before Puccini had stepped in with his own version of the original story, *Manon Lescaut* (1892).

Recommended Recording

Ileana Cotrubas, Alfredo Kraus, José van Dam, Capitole de Toulouse Orchestra/Michel Plasson. EMI CDS7 49610-2. All the style and charm the score demands from a well-balanced cast and idiomatic conductor.

Werther

FORM: Opera in four acts; in French
COMPOSER: Jules Massenet (1842–1912)
LIBRETTO: Blau, Milliet and Hartmann; after Goethe
FIRST PERFORMANCE: Vienna, 16 February 1892

Principal Characters

Werther, a young man ❧ **Tenor**
The Bailli, a magistrate ❧ **Bass**
Charlotte, his eldest daughter ❧ **Mezzo-soprano**
Sophie, her sister ❧ **Soprano**
Albert, engaged to Charlotte ❧ **Baritone**

Synopsis of the Plot

Setting: Near Frankfurt; 1780s

ACT I July: Werther arrives at the Bailli's home and is immediately attracted by the peaceful serenity of the house and garden. He watches as Charlotte, who has assumed the place of her dead mother in the family, occupies herself with taking care of the younger children. The Bailli introduces them and they spend much of the evening together; it is clear that they are falling in love. But the announcement of the arrival of Charlotte's fiancé, Albert, recalls her to her senses and she tells the despairing Werther that she must fulfil her promise to her dead mother to marry Albert.

ACT II September: Charlotte and Albert, married for three months, arrive for church. The tormented Werther curses his fate and is consoled by Albert. Werther assures him that he no longer thinks of Charlotte, but it is clear he is lying. He decides to go away, and Charlotte agrees, asking him to return, as a friend, at Christmas. Werther, in despair, contemplates suicide and leaves.

ACT III Christmas Eve: Charlotte is sadly reading Werther's letters and thinking about her love for him, when Werther himself quietly enters. They cannot hide their feelings for each other but, torn by guilt, Charlotte runs from the room. Albert's suspicions are aroused by his wife's distraught state, but he hardly has time to question her when a note arrives from Werther, asking Albert to lend him his pistols as he, Werther, is going on a long journey. The pistols are taken to him and, as soon as Albert leaves, Charlotte rushes out, praying she can reach Werther before he shoots himself.

ACT IV Christmas Night: Charlotte, arriving too late, finds the dying Werther and takes him in her arms. They confess, for the first time, that they love each other and he asks her to forgive him. As he dies, Werther hears children singing a carol, and he takes this as a sign of divine forgiveness.

Music and Background

The story is a set-piece of high-Romanticism but delicately and intimately told here, with no chorus and a close-in focus on the central characters, who are portrayed with considerable insight despite the fact that Werther himself (one of the few male characters to dominate a Massenet opera) only just escapes dismissal as a wimpish bore. Much of the music comes in low-key conversational style, and the energies of the piece take a while to build, but the orchestration is exquisite, with a generally dark tone appropriate to tragic narrative and the use of quasi-Wagnerian recurring themes effectively if simplistically done.

Highlights

In Act I the Music-box Waltz that gathers momentum into a big orchestral melody, and will return later; Werther's tunefully despairing Act II 'J'aurais sur ma poitrine'; and in Act III the whole of Charlotte's Letter Scene and succeeding duet with Sophie, followed by Werther's benchmark lyric-tenor number 'Pourquoi me réveiller' and almost-Love Scene, 'Ah! ce premier baiser'.

Did You Know?

 Goethe's novel is based on the true story of a young lawyer, Karl Jerusalem, who shot himself because of an unhappy love affair. Jerusalem borrowed pistols from a friend of Goethe, who knew the whole story, and the text in the note Werther sends to Albert in the opera is the same as in the note Jerusalem sent to Goethe's friend.
 Even in a genre where drawn-out deaths are *de rigueur*, Werther's Death Scene is exceptional in stretching across twenty minutes.

Recommended Recording

Plácido Domingo, Elena Obraztsova, Arleen Augér, Cologne Radio Symphony Orchestra/Riccardo Chailly. DG 413 304-2. Subtly conducted, sympathetically sung by Domingo.

Gian Carlo Menotti
(1911–)

The Medium (1945)
The Telephone (1946)
The Consul (1950)
Amahl and the Night Visitors (1951)
The Saint of Bleeker Street (1954)
Goya (1986)

Menotti's star has waned in recent years, but during the 1940s and '50s he was the big name in American opera and responsible for a string of successful works which were designed to play in Broadway theatres rather than conventional opera houses. His work had the wide-ranging appeal of Puccinian tunefulness (some would say sentimentality) allied to sharp-edged modern themes and a strong sense of theatre. Born in Italy, Menotti arrived in America as a young man to study at the newly opened Curtis Institute. There he met another young composer, Samuel Barber, who became his lover, and together they moved in the most glittering New York circles until – many years later – the relationship ended and Menotti came to live in Scotland in a Robert Adam mansion whose grandeur signalled just how successful he had been. A true musical polymath, Menotti has not only composed music but written libretti, directed for the stage, run opera houses, and devoted much of his energies to the organisation of his own festivals at Spoleto, Italy and Charleston, South Carolina.

Amahl and the Night Visitors

FORM: Television opera in one act; in English
COMPOSER: Gian Carlo Menotti (1911–)
LIBRETTO: Gian Carlo Menotti
FIRST PERFORMANCE: NBC, New York, 24 December 1951

Principal Characters

Amahl ∾ Treble
His mother ∾ Soprano
King Kaspar ∾ Tenor
King Melchior ∾ Baritone
King Balthazar ∾ Bass
The Page ∾ Baritone

Synopsis of the Plot

Setting: A poor shepherd's hut in the hills

Amahl, a young crippled boy, is sitting outside his home gazing at the starry sky. He is reluctant to go in when his mother calls him, and when he does, he tries to persuade her to look at a particularly bright star, which has a tail. She refuses to believe him, saying this is one of his 'stories'. As they sleep, Amahl is wakened by the voices of the approaching kings. Amahl's mother is sceptical when he reports that three kings are at the front door, but they are eventually allowed in. The kings show Amahl and his mother the gifts they have brought, and speak of the child they are searching for, led by the star. Amahl is sent to fetch the local shepherds, who arrive with baskets of fruit and vegetables for the kings, and stay to entertain their noble visitors. The shepherds leave and the rest settle down for the night. Towards dawn, Amahl's mother, resenting the riches that are to be presented to an unknown child while her own child is practically starving, attempts to steal some gold. She is caught by the Page, who is himself roundly attacked by Amahl with his crutch for laying hands on the boy's mother. The kings are angry at first, but Melchior forgives her and tells her she may keep the gold; she refuses, however, saying that, if she were not so poor, she would send a gift herself. Amahl then offers the kings his crutch for the child and, as he lifts it, takes a step unaided! A miracle has happened and they all give thanks. Amahl begs to be allowed to accompany the kings, and his request is granted.

Music and Background

This opera is to the American Christmas much as the Queen's Speech is in Britain: an annual rite. It was the first opera specifically written for television and gets broadcast every year – along with countless amateur performances in schools and colleges throughout the English-speaking world. Menotti's inspiration was the Hieronymous Bosch painting of *The Adoration of the Magi*, but the story is the composer's own, and it unfolds in simple tunes, conventionally harmonised and easily remembered. With a small orchestra and much charm, it tends to attract the contempt of the radical-minded but the undying affection of anyone exposed to it as a child.

Highlights

The ensemble for the mother and the kings 'Do you know a child?'; the shepherds' welcome to the kings; the stealing of the gold; and the sweetly poignant farewell duet 'I shall miss you very much'.

Recommended Recording

James Rainbird, Lorna Haywood, Royal Opera Covent Garden/David Syrus. That's Entertainment CDTER 1124. Touchingly done and not too sugar-coated.

The Consul

FORM: Opera in three acts; in English
COMPOSER: Gian Carlo Menotti (1911–)
LIBRETTO: Gian Carlo Menotti
FIRST PERFORMANCE: Philadelphia, 1 March 1950

Principal Characters

John Sorel, a political dissident 🔊 **Baritone**
Magda Sorel, his wife 🔊 **Soprano**
Sorel's mother 🔊 **Mezzo-soprano**
The Secretary 🔊 **Mezzo-soprano**
Assan, the Sorels' friend 🔊 **Baritone**

Synopsis of the Plot

Setting: The Sorels' flat, the consulate waiting room in a European city; after 1945

ACT I John Sorel has evaded capture but has been wounded by the secret police, and hides in the flat while the police search it. He tells Magda that he must go abroad, and Magda must get an exit visa for herself, their child and his mother, so that they can join him. Magda goes to the consulate where she joins a group of people, all coming daily with the apparently hopeless aim of obtaining an exit visa.

ACT II A month has passed and Magda is no nearer getting her visa. She learns that John is hiding in the mountains, refusing to leave the country until he knows that Magda will be able to join him. Magda tells Assan, their friend, to tell John she has the visa and will join him; this is not true, but she knows that it is the only way his life will be saved. When Assan leaves, Sorel's mother gently tells Magda that her little, half-starved baby has died. Back in the waiting room, Magda begs the others to allow her to go ahead of them and they agree. Refused access to the consul yet again, Magda bursts out in fury, denouncing the system that condemns men and women to live in this way. Astonishingly, the Secretary announces that Magda can see the consul, as soon as his visitor has left. But when Magda sees that the visitor is the secret police agent, she passes out.

ACT III Magda is still waiting at the consulate when Assan tells her that John has heard of the deaths of his mother and of the child; he intends to come back and fetch his wife, with or without a visa. Magda knows she must prevent this, and writes a note for Assan to give to her husband, refusing to say what she has written. She leaves and, just as the Secretary is closing up the office, John himself bursts in, in search of Magda. He is closely following by the secret police agent and arrested; the Secretary promises him to inform Magda. But it is too late; Magda has gassed herself and the telephone rings on in the silent flat.

Music and Background

Menotti's first full-length opera, *The Consul* is also his most compellingly dramatic and forward-looking score, with a toughness that captures the anxieties and frustrations of the plot and keeps the climaxes coming with the relentlessness of a TV thriller. Laced with moments of Puccinian sentiment and what would latterly be called 'magic realism', it was enormously successful when it first appeared and continues, albeit intermittently, to hold the stage.

Highlights

Magda's searing 'To this we've come' in Act II, and her hallucinating Dance of Death Scene, just before she kills herself in Act III.

Did You Know?

๛ *The Consul* is mid-20th-century verismo, complete with musical literalisms: notice the high-pitched dissonance in the orchestra when Magda turns on the gas.

Recommended Recording

There is no recording currently available.

Giacomo Meyerbeer
(1791–1864)

Robert le Diable (1831)
Les Huguenots (1836)
Le Prophète (1849)
L'Africaine (1864)

Meyerbeer was *the* exponent of French grand opera in the mid-19th century, with an all-conquering success in Paris (the Holy Mecca of the opera world at the time) that attracted the envy and resentment of other composers, including Wagner. Born in Germany into a wealthy Jewish family (something else for Wagner to object to), Meyerbeer learned his craft in Italy and had his first operas staged there. But from *Robert le Diable* onward he made Paris his centre of activity, and began a significant collaboration with the writer Eugène Scribe who went on to provide most of his libretti. Meyerbeer's taste was for spectacle, exotica, and dramas spiced with incidental shock-tactics, like the chorus of dancing nuns in *Robert le Diable* which created (as intended) a delectable Parisian scandal – always good for box office. His critics accused him of opportunism and artistic compromise, but he certainly left his mark on opera for years to come through the scale, complexity and unprecedented vocal demands of his work.

Les Huguenots

FORM: Opera in five acts; in French
COMPOSER: Giacomo Meyerbeer (1791–1864)
LIBRETTO: Eugène Scribe; after Deschamps
FIRST PERFORMANCE: Paris, 29 February 1836

Principal Characters

Raoul de Nangis, a Huguenot gentleman ⁊ **Tenor**
Marcel, his servant ⁊ **Bass**
Marguerite de Valois, engaged to Henry of Navarre ⁊ **Soprano**
Urbain, her page ⁊ **Mezzo-soprano**
Comte de Saint-Bris, a Catholic nobleman ⁊ **Bass**

Valentine, his daughter, engaged to de Nevers ✒ **Soprano**
Comte de Nevers, a Catholic nobleman ✒ **Baritone**

Synopsis of the Plot

Setting: Touraine and Paris; August 1572

ACT I De Nevers has invited the Huguenot, Raoul de Nangis, to a banquet at his house in recognition of a recently-signed peace treaty between the two factions, Catholic and Protestant. When the subject turns to love, Raoul is urged to reveal the name of his own sweetheart; but he cannot, because he has fallen in love with an unknown lady whom he saved from molestation by a group of students. Just then a message arrives for de Nevers that a lady has come to speak to him privately, and is waiting in the garden. When de Nevers goes out, the men rush to the window to see who it is and Raoul is distraught to recognise her as the same woman he rescued. He concludes that there must be an illicit relationship between the count and the lady, and sadly decides that he can no longer love her. Raoul has little time to reflect, however, as he himself suddenly receives a mysterious message, brought to him by Urbain, Queen Marguerite's page, asking Raoul to meet her secretly. Bewildered, Raoul leaves de Nevers' house for the rendezvous.

ACT II Queen Marguerite has decided that Raoul and Valentine should marry, thereby uniting two great families, Protestant and Catholic. She has already sent Valentine to her fiancé, de Nevers, to break off their engagement and, at the secret meeting, tells Raoul of the plan. But when he meets Valentine he is shocked to discover that she is the woman he saw in de Nevers' garden, and, knowing nothing of why she went there, remains deeply suspicious of her motives and rejects her. Tempers rise and old hatreds resurface; only the queen's intervention prevents bloodshed.

ACT III De Nevers and Valentine are to be married but Raoul interrupts the proceedings by challenging Saint-Bris, Valentine's father, to a duel. Valentine overhears a plan to ambush Raoul before the fight and tells Marcel, Raoul's servant, to warn his master to come heavily guarded. As a result the duel threatens to become a violent street brawl, only prevented by the timely arrival of Marguerite. Raoul then discovers the real reason for Valentine's secret meeting with de Nevers, and realises that he has lost her; she is now married to the count.

ACT IV Raoul, braving considerable danger, goes to see Valentine, but is forced to hide when men's voices are heard outside the room. The men discuss plans to massacre the entire Protestant population of Paris that night. De Nevers refuses to take part, is denounced as a traitor and led away in chains. After they leave, Raoul comes out of his hiding place and, in spite of Valentine's heartfelt pleas to him not to leave her, rushes out to help his fellow Protestants.

ACT V Raoul and Marcel are taking refuge in a churchyard, where they are found by Valentine, who pleads with Raoul to become a Catholic, telling him

218

that de Nevers is now dead and she is free to marry. But Raoul refuses to compromise his beliefs in this way, to which Valentine responds that she will become a Huguenot and die with him. The churchyard is stormed by Catholics but the three escape, although Raoul is seriously wounded. In the street they are challenged by Saint-Bris and his men and summarily shot. Only then does Saint-Bris realise he has killed his own daughter.

Music and Background

Meyerbeer knew – as no one before or since – how to use large forces, and in *Les Huguenots* he doesn't hold back. An enormous, epic work, its large cast and other requirements – not least an onstage military band – put it beyond the reach of any but the biggest opera houses and, for good reasons, it usually appears with cuts. The miracle is that its unwieldy structure works as well as it does – a mark of Meyerbeer's instinctive sense of theatre – and that subtleties of orchestration register alongside blockbusting effects.

Highlights

The Act IV Consecration of the Daggers by the Catholic conspirators, and the love duet that follows on, 'O ciel! où courez-vous?', are arguably the most effective music Meyerbeer ever wrote, and they form the unquestionable climax of this score. Raoul's Act I 'Plus blanche que la blanche hermine', in which he tells the story of the unknown lady, and his Act II 'Beauté divine' are fine numbers for a high, light-headed but heroic tenor.

Did You Know?

∞ The opera is known as the 'Night of the Seven Stars' because of the seven great voices which it demands in the leading roles.
∞ *Les Huguenots* was the piece that opened the present Covent Garden opera house in 1842.
∞ George Bernard Shaw attended a performance of *Les Huguenots* in 1889, in which Marguerite de Valois appeared in Act III riding a beautiful white horse. Unfortunately, the moment the queen began to sing, the horse began to waltz, resulting in the rapid removal of the royal rider and her steed's swift return to the circus from where it came.

Recommended Recording

Joan Sutherland, Martina Arroyo, Anastasios Vrenios, New Philharmonia Orchestra/Richard Bonynge. Decca 430 549-2. Worth it for Sutherland's Marguerite, if nothing else.

Claudio Monteverdi

(1567–1643)

La Favola d'Orfeo (1607)
Arianna (1608)
Il Combattimento di Tancredi et Clorinda (1624)
Il Ritorno d'Ulisse in Patria (1640)
L'Incoronazione di Poppea (1643)

Claudio Monteverdi was responsible for the first operas to survive to modern times in regular performance, and for the first operas that present real, developed human characters on stage – as opposed to mythological cartoon creations. Born in Cremona, he joined the musically-active court of the Duke of Mantua as a viol-player and singer; and it was probably on a tour of duty with the duke that he encountered the Florentine Camerata, a group of poets, musicians and aristocratic patrons who were experimenting with sung drama in the Renaissance capital. Armed with this discovery, Monteverdi returned to Mantua and wrote *La Favola d'Orfeo*, followed by *Arianna* (the score of which, except for the celebrated Lament of the central character, was subsequently lost, like most of Monteverdi's operatic music). In 1613 he moved to Venice to be music director at St Mark's, and spent the next few years concentrating on religious music. He also took holy orders. But the opening of the first public opera house in Venice (1637) renewed his interest in the stage, resulting in the late masterpieces *Il Ritorno d'Ulisse in Patria* and *L'Incoronazione di Poppea*. The surviving manuscripts of the Monteverdi operas are a scholastic minefield, with the result that stage performances vary greatly in terms of the musical forces they use.

La Favola d'Orfeo
(The Fable of Orpheus)

FORM: Opera in a Prologue and five acts; in Italian
COMPOSER: Claudio Monteverdi (1567–1643)
LIBRETTO: Alessandro Striggio; after Ovid, Virgil and Dante
FIRST PERFORMANCE: Mantua, 24 February 1607

Principal Characters

La Musica, the Prologue ❧ **Soprano**
Orpheus, a poet and musician ❧ **Soprano/Tenor**
Eurydice, his wife ❧ **Soprano**
Sylvia, the Messenger ❧ **Soprano**
Charon, the Ferryman ❧ **Bass**
Proserpine, Queen of the Underworld ❧ **Soprano**
Pluto, King of the Underworld ❧ **Bass**
Apollo ❧ **Tenor**
Four Shepherds ❧ **Three tenors/One Bass**
Hope ❧ **Soprano**

Synopsis of the Plot

Setting: Mythological Greece

PROLOGUE La Musica, the impersonation of music, sings of her power over humankind and introduces us to Orpheus, the singer whose voice can soothe wild beasts.

ACT I Nymphs and shepherds are joyfully anticipating the wedding of Orpheus and Eurydice. The two lovers pledge each other their undying love and everyone prays that they will be blessed with good fortune.

ACT II Orpheus and the shepherds are celebrating his new-found happiness when they are interrupted by Sylvia, who brings the dreadful news of Eurydice's sudden death. She tells how, while gathering flowers for a garland, Eurydice was bitten by a snake; despite frantic efforts to revive her Eurydice died, with Orpheus' name the last word on her lips. Orpheus determines to bring her back from the Underworld.

ACT III Guided by Hope, Orpheus enters the Underworld, where he is confronted by Charon, the Ferryman, who takes the dead across the river Styx, the only way into Pluto's domain. But Charon refuses to take Orpheus across the river and, in desperation, Orpheus uses all his musical powers to try and persuade him to change his mind. Still Charon remains obdurate, until Orpheus' sweet lyre music lulls him to sleep. Seizing his chance Orpheus takes the boat.

ACT IV Proserpine has been profoundly moved by Orpheus' singing and persuades Pluto, her husband, to allow Orpheus to take Eurydice back. But there is one condition: he must not look at her until they have left the Underworld behind. Orpheus, overjoyed, begins to lead his wife out of the Underworld but, gradually, his mood changes and he begins to doubt that she is, in fact, actually following him. He resists the temptation to look behind him until he suddenly hears an unexpected noise. Thinking that the Furies are carrying her away, Orpheus turns round and sees Eurydice for a single moment before she vanishes. Orpheus tries to follow her, but he is drawn irresistibly back to the upper world.

ACT V Orpheus is now a wanderer, forever grieving over the loss of Eurydice. Apollo, his father, takes pity on him, makes him a god and takes him to the heavens, from where he can see Eurydice's likeness in the stars.

Music and Background

Opera as we know it effectively begins with this work, although it owes much to a slightly earlier Florentine Camerata score, *Euridice* by Jacopo Peri, and to the way madrigals were written in 16th-century Italy. Monteverdi's innovation was to bring a new kind of expressivity and dramatic elaboration to these established techniques. Originally performed in quite intimate circumstances for the entertainment of the Mantuan court, it was probably done with an orchestra of about fifteen strings, brass and wind, plus a separate, smaller bass accompaniment to solo singing.

Highlights

The opening Toccata, a sort of instrumental fanfare, makes a rousing start to the score. The central vocal item comes in Act III with Orpheus' vividly ornamented attempt to charm Charon the boatman, 'Possente spirto'.

Did You Know?

🪕 In the original performance it is likely that all the female roles were sung by male castrati.

🪕 The ending given in the plot synopsis is not the original Classical ending, in which Orpheus was torn to pieces at a Bacchanalian orgy by women who were incensed at his constant longing for the lost Eurydice.

Recommended Recording

John Mark Ainsley, Julia Gooding, Catherine Bott, New London Consort/ Philip Pickett. Oiseau-Lyre 433 545-2. A thoroughly-researched but 'living' period performance, especially recommended for Catherine Bott.

L'Incoronazione di Poppea
(Poppea's Coronation)

FORM: Opera in a Prologue and three acts; in Italian
COMPOSER: Claudio Monteverdi (1567–1643)
LIBRETTO: G.F. Busenello; after Tacitus
FIRST PERFORMANCE: Venice, autumn 1642

Principal Characters

Fortuna, Goddess of Fortune ⁓ **Soprano**
Virtu, Goddess of Virtue ⁓ **Soprano**
Amore, Goddess of Love ⁓ **Soprano**
Poppea ⁓ **Soprano**
Arnalta, her old nurse ⁓ **Contralto**
Nero, Emperor of Rome ⁓ **Soprano**
Octavia, his wife ⁓ **Mezzo-soprano**
Ottone, Poppea's former lover ⁓ **Mezzo-soprano**
Drusilla, Octavia's lady-in-waiting ⁓ **Soprano**
Seneca, a philosopher ⁓ **Bass**

Synopsis of the Plot

Setting: Rome; c.AD 65

PROLOGUE The three goddesses dispute which of them has most power over the affairs of men. Amore offers the story of Nero and Poppea as final proof that love is the greatest power of all.

ACT I Ottone returns to Rome but is dismayed to discover Nero's soldiers guarding Poppea's house, at once realising that he has been displaced by the emperor in her affections. After Nero leaves, Poppea's old nurse, Arnalta, warns her of the danger she is getting into, but Poppea pays her no attention. At the palace, Nero's wife is deeply humiliated by her husband's behaviour, but Seneca advises restraint. Seneca is also consulted by Nero, who tells the philosopher of his intention to replace his current wife, Octavia, with Poppea; Seneca again urges caution, but his arguments annoy and anger Nero. Poppea is determined that Seneca shall not interfere with her plans to become empress and she persuades Nero to make sure that the philosopher dies very soon. She is later confronted with her infidelity by Ottone, but she dismisses him, and he turns to Drusilla, who loves him, although it is clear that his heart is still with Poppea.

ACT II Seneca has been told that he is about to die and he accepts his fate with resignation. Meanwhile, Octavia has forced Ottone, invoking an unpaid debt owed to her ancestors, to agree to kill Poppea. He disguises himself as Drusilla and enters Poppea's bedroom while she is asleep. But before he can act, Amore (or perhaps his own feelings) prevents him from carrying out the deed, and he runs away.

ACT III Drusilla has been arrested and threatened with torture and death for the attempt on Poppea's life. Ottone then confesses and implicates Octavia; his punishment is banishment, and Drusilla chooses to go with him into exile. Octavia's fate is to be cast adrift in a boat. The emperor and Poppea celebrate their love and she is crowned Empress of Rome. Amore has indeed triumphed.

Music and Background

The manuscript history of this opera is complicated and it's generally accepted that some of the music is not by Monteverdi at all, including the opening orchestral Sinfonia. But it remains the crowning achievement of Monteverdi's creative life, with a mixture of high drama, tragedy, comedy and love interest that looks forward to the style and taste of Baroque opera half a century on. It is also the first known opera to be based on real characters from history, and their scheming personalities are fully fleshed out in a way that was rare for the time. One consequence is that the score lasts even longer than *Il Ritorno d'Ulisse in Patria*.

Highlights

In Act III, Octavia's famous lament, 'Addio Roma', and the final love duet for Nero and Poppea, 'Pur ti miro'.

Did You Know?

It is hard to know what sort of voices originally sang the roles here, but Nero and Ottone were almost certainly castrati.

Recommended Recording

Arleen Augér, Della Jones, Linda Hirst, James Bowman, City of London Sinfonia/Richard Hickox. Virgin Classics VCT7 90775-2. Uses a spare-textured authentic-style performing edition but it is sung with ravishing warmth by Augér.

Il Ritorno d'Ulisse in Patria
(Ulysses' Return Home)

FORM: Opera in a Prologue and five (sometimes three) acts;
in Italian
COMPOSER: Claudio Monteverdi (1567–1643)
LIBRETTO: Giacomo Badoaro; after Homer
FIRST PERFORMANCE: Venice, February 1641

Principal Characters

Human Frailty ⮑ Soprano
Time ⮑ Bass
Fortune ⮑ Soprano
Cupid ⮑ Soprano
Ulysses ⮑ Tenor
Penelope, his wife ⮑ Mezzo-soprano
Telemachus, their son ⮑ Mezzo-soprano
Minerva, Goddess of Wisdom ⮑ Soprano
Eumaeus, Ulysses' former servant ⮑ Tenor
Penelope's suitors ⮑ Two Tenors/One Bass

Synopsis of the Plot

Setting: Mythical Ithaca

PROLOGUE Human Frailty is mocked by Time, Fortune and Cupid, who claim the power to control man's fate.

ACT I Faithful Penelope still grieves over Ulysses' long absence, and remains uninterested in the various suitors who have come to offer themselves as replacement husbands. Meanwhile, the sleeping Ulysses has been left on the shore of his own country by the Phaeacians, against the express wishes of Neptune, God of the Sea, who retaliates by turning their ship into a rock. Ulysses wakes and is confronted by Minerva, who tells him he is in Ithaca, his homeland; but she also tells him that his wife is surrounded by men who have already taken up residence in the palace, and advises him to disguise himself as a beggar, so that he can see exactly what the situation is before making himself known. Minerva leaves for Sparta to bring Ulysses' son, Telemachus, home to help him.

ACT II Ulysses has found his old servant, Eumaeus, who has been banished from court. Eumaeus does not recognise his master, but is overjoyed when Minerva arrives with Telemachus in her chariot. Telemachus sends Eumaeus to Penelope, to tell her of his arrival. Once he has gone, Ulysses makes himself known to his son and, after a joyful reunion, sends him to his mother, promising to come himself very soon.

ACT III At the palace, Penelope is surrounded by her suitors, but rejects each one of them. When Eumaeus comes in with the news of Telemachus' arrival, Penelope is sceptical, saying that hope only increases her unhappiness. The suitors, however, decide to kill Telemachus when he arrives, and redouble their efforts to win Penelope.

ACT IV Telemachus is now reunited with his mother and he tells her of his adventures in Sparta. The suitors are vainly trying to win the queen with lavish presents, observed by Ulysses, who has arrived unnoticed in his beggar's disguise. Finally, Penelope says she will marry the one who can string Ulysses' bow. They all attempt and fail, of course, until the 'beggar' steps forward and asks permission to try. Ulysses strings the bow and, suddenly releasing his pent-up fury, attacks and kills the suitors.

ACT V Penelope is still reluctant to believe that Ulysses has really come back to her, even when Eumaeus, Telemachus and Ulysses himself urge her to accept the truth. Finally, however, she allows herself to believe it and releases all the love and longing she has held in check for so long.

Music and Background

Written when Monteverdi was seventy-three (but not sounding like the work of an old man), *Il Ritorno d'Ulisse in Patria* represents a considerable advance on his music for *La Favola d'Orfeo*, composed more than thirty years earlier. The divisions between recitatives, arias and ensembles are freer, looser, and it consciously sets out to woo its audience with a more popular style – for this was Monteverdi's first 'commercial' opera, intended for performance in the new Venetian public theatre. In the effort to give paying customers their money's worth, it is also twice the length of *La Favola d'Orfeo*.

Highlights

The Recognition Scene in Act II as Ulysses is reunited with Telemachus: 'O padre sospirato' and the parallel scene in Act V where Penelope finally accepts that the beggar is her husband: 'Sospirato mio sole'.

Recommended Recording

Christoph Prégardien, Bernada Fink, Lorraine Hunt, Concerto Vocale/ René Jacobs. Harmonia Mundi HMU 90 1427/9. Characterful singing under a conductor who is a singer himself and allows the voices to blossom.

Wolfgang Amadeus Mozart

(1756–91)

Mitridate, Re di Ponto (1770)
Idomeneo (1781)
Die Entführung aus dem Serail (1782)
Le Nozze di Figaro (1786)
Don Giovanni (1787)
Così fan Tutte (1789)
Die Zauberflöte (1791)
La Clemenza di Tito (1791)

The astonishing amount of music Mozart produced in his short life – including forty-one numbered symphonies, twenty-seven piano concertos, twenty-three string quartets – must make him the hardest-working composer in history; and seven mature full-scale operas is no mean achievement either, although it took him comparatively longer to get into his stride with theatre music. His first operas (three by the age of twelve!) were written in Salzburg where, as a boy and young man, he served the court of the prince-archbishop. But Salzburg had no state theatre, and it was only on trips abroad that he managed to get commissions for professional performance, the first major one being *Mitridate, Re di Ponto* for Milan. With *Idomeneo* for Munich he produced his first opera score of real stature; and it was shortly afterwards that he left the prince-archbishop (stormily) and moved to Vienna, where things were different and commissions plentiful. *Die Entführung aus dem Serail* was the immediate result. Then, in collaboration with the librettist Da Ponte, he produced three supreme masterpieces in succession – *Le Nozze di Figaro*, *Don Giovanni* and *Così fan Tutte* – which can truly be said to have changed the course of opera history. Frantic work in the last year of his life brought about two more opera scores, utterly unalike in tone and subject: *Die Zauberflöte* and *La Clemenza di Tito*. Mozart's broad achievement was the instinctive humanisation of operatic characters: they live, breathe, and demand your love. Even the villains. And the music he wrote for the stage proved radiantly influential on his orchestral scores, especially the piano concertos of the mid-1780s.

La Clemenza di Tito
(The Clemency of Titus)

FORM: Opera in two acts; in Italian
COMPOSER: Wolfgang Amadeus Mozart (1756–91)
LIBRETTO: Pietro Metastasio and Caterino Mazzolà
FIRST PERFORMANCE: Prague, 6 September 1791

Principal Characters

Titus, the Roman Emperor ⁓ Tenor
Sextus, Titus' friend, in love with Vitellia ⁓ Contralto/Mezzo-soprano
Vitellia, daughter of the former emperor ⁓ Soprano
Annius, Sextus' friend, in love with Servilia
⁓ Soprano/Mezzo-soprano
Servilia, Sextus' sister, in love with Annius ⁓ Soprano
Publius, commander of the guard ⁓ Bass

Synopsis of the Plot

Setting: Rome; during Titus' reign, AD 79–81

ACT I Vitellia, whose father has been deposed by Titus, is furious to find
that she is to be displaced as Titus' future wife and empress of Rome by a
foreign princess. She urges Sextus, who loves her deeply, to join a plot to kill
Titus. However, Titus changes his mind and announces that, after all, he will
marry a Roman – but it is to be Servilia, not Vitellia. Servilia confesses to
Titus that she loves Annius, but she is prepared to give him up if the emperor
commands her to. Titus, acknowledging her honesty, at once withdraws his
claim over her. Vitellia, meanwhile, is enraged at being passed over again and
promises Sextus that she will marry him as soon as he kills Titus. As Sextus
leaves, Vitellia is joined by Publius and Annius, who bring her the news she
has longed for: she is to be Titus' new wife and the next empress. Vitellia's
consequent hysterics (for she has just arranged for the emperor's death) are
taken to be the effects of having received such unexpected, if joyful, news.
Meanwhile, Sextus has arrived at the Capitol and is in agonies of indecision
– how can he murder his friend, a good, just man, for Vitellia, who does not
even love him? Just then he sees that the Capitol is on fire; the conspirators
have struck already and Sextus hears the people mourning their dead
emperor.

ACT II Annius tells Sextus that Titus has survived, and advises him to ask
the emperor for mercy. Vitellia tells him his part in the conspiracy has been
discovered and he should escape while he can, but it is already too late and
Sextus is arrested. At the trial, Titus cannot believe his friend should have

wanted to betray him, but Publius advises him not to judge everyone else by his own high standards. Sextus confesses but refuses to implicate Vitellia; he is sentenced to be thrown to the animals. In desperation Annius and Servilia beg Vitellia to admit her part in the plot and, knowing she could not become empress with such a guilty secret, Vitellia confesses to Titus that her jealousy and ambition were the cause of Sextus' actions. Titus, deciding that magnanimity would serve him more effectively than revenge, forgives them all.

Music and Background

Given that it came at the end of his life, after the freewheeling exhilaration of the Da Ponte pieces, *La Clemenza di Tito* is a surprisingly sombre, straight-laced score that resurrects the grand formalities of old-time opera seria: the sort of thing Handel was doing sixty years before. Why? Because it was written (hurriedly) to an old libretto for a grand state occasion that required diplomacy, dignity, and conservatism. The scoring is spare by comparison with Mozart's other mature operas, but with a prominent part for basset-horn (a kind of clarinet) written for his friend Anton Stadler. Vitellia gets the best of the piece, with a role that demands tempestuous, fiery emotions and an awesome vocal range.

Highlights

Vitellia's Act II aria of sacrificial resolve, 'Non più di fiori' (with basset-horn accompaniment) is the big number. Otherwise the Act I finale (offstage chorus against onstage quintet) is strikingly effective; and 'Ah perdona', the stately expression of Annio and Servilia's hopeless love in Act I, is a memorable tune.

Did You Know?

So tight were the deadlines for finishing the score that Mozart subcontracted out the simple recitatives to his pupil Sussmayr (who also completed the unfinished Requiem).

Recommended Recording

Anthony Rolfe Johnson, Julia Varady, Anne Sofie von Otter, English Baroque Soloists/John Eliot Gardiner. DG 431 806-2. Taken from live performances and uncommonly dramatic.

Così fan Tutte
(Women Are Like That)

FORM: Opera in two acts; in Italian
COMPOSER: Wolfgang Amadeus Mozart (1756–91)
LIBRETTO: Lorenzo da Ponte
FIRST PERFORMANCE: Vienna, 26 January 1790

Principal Characters

Fiordiligi ~ Soprano
Dorabella, her sister ~ Soprano
Guglielmo, Fiordiligi's fiancé ~ Bass
Ferrando, Dorabella's fiancé ~ Tenor
Don Alfonso ~ Baritone
Despina, the sisters' maid ~ Soprano

Synopsis of the Plot

Setting: A village near Naples

ACT I Guglielmo and Ferrando are locked in an argument with Don Alfonso concerning the female capacity for faithfulness; Guglielmo and Ferrando stoutly maintain their unshakeable belief in the absolute fidelity of their sweethearts, Fiordiligi and Dorabella, but Alfonso is altogether more cynical. Finally, a bet is made: Alfonso will prove to the young men that their trust is unfounded, on condition that they do exactly as he says. Guglielmo and Ferrando, certain of the outcome, discuss what to do with their winnings. Alfonso then goes to see the sisters and tells them that their fiancés have been ordered away by their regiment and must leave immediately. A tearful farewell follows, accompanied by Alfonso's mocking laughter. Some time later Alfonso introduces two of his 'foreign friends' to Fiordiligi and Dorabella, actually Guglielmo and Ferrando in disguise. The 'Albanians' attempt to charm the sisters, but are roundly rejected, to which their response is to take poison and collapse at their feet. Despina, who has been prevailed upon by Alfonso, disguises herself as a doctor and rushes in with a giant magnet (as prescribed by the great Dr Mesmer) which miraculously restores the 'Albanians' to life. Pretending to believe they are in heaven, the two beg for a kiss – but are, once again, rejected.

ACT II Despina persuades the sisters to indulge in a little mild flirting with these attentive young foreigners. Dorabella admits she is drawn to the disguised Guglielmo, while Fiordiligi finds the disguised Ferrando more attractive (thus reversing their original partners). The seduction then begins, with Dorabella's resistance crumbling first, even to the extent of giving her new admirer the locket containing Ferrando's portrait; Fiordiligi struggles longer with her conscience, but eventually capitulates. The men are furious, but Alfonso shrugs and consoles them with the thought that 'women are all like that'. The sisters are giving a party to celebrate their betrothal to the 'Albanians', when news arrives that Ferrando and Guglielmo are on their way back from the war. The 'Albanians', terrified, rush off, to be replaced by Ferrando and Guglielmo. On discovering the marriage contract they run out to find the 'Albanians' before returning as themselves, carrying their disguises. The truth is revealed; Alfonso has his winnings; the sisters are forgiven and all ends happily.

Music and Background

Attitudes to this opera have changed with time. Until quite recently the wafer-thin plot with its mixture of farce, romance and the manipulation of emotions was held to scorn or deplored as immoral; and even today the idea of the piece – not to mention its title – offends all notions of political correctness. But Così fan Tutte has been redeemed by the beauty of its score and the consequent efforts of Mozart-lovers to find psychological truth behind the surface values of the text. There is a purity about the music of Così fan Tutte which is arguably unmatched by any other Mozart opera; and although there is also an element of self-parody in some of the numbers – Mozart making fun of the standard forms of 18th-century opera within which he himself worked – they also stand as wonderful examples of those forms. Notice the symmetry with which the music works, balancing the two male lovers against the two female, and listen in the Overture for the five emphatic chords that will later become the five syllables of the sung title, Co-sì-fan-tut-te.

Highlights

The supremely golden moments are the Farewell quintet and following trio, 'Soave sia il vento', in Act I : Mozart wrote nothing lovelier. Fiordiligi has two big display arias of such exaggerated range and technical requirement that they suggest parody: 'Come scoglio' in Act I and 'Per pietà' in Act II. The two seduction numbers ('Il core vi dono', Guglielmo, Act II, and 'Vogli a me pietoso', Ferrando, Act II) are especially beautiful.

Did You Know?

- Latterday stage directors are never so sure that the two couples *do* get together again at the end – at least, not in their original pairings.
- Regarded as immoral and frivolous by the Victorians, the opera was not much performed in the 19th century.
- Fernando's Act III aria 'Un'aura amorosa' featured in the 1989 film *My Left Foot*.

Don Giovanni

FORM: Opera in two acts; in Italian
COMPOSER: Wolfgang Amadeus Mozart (1756–91)
LIBRETTO: Lorenzo da Ponte
FIRST PERFORMANCE: Prague, 29 October 1787

Principal Characters

Don Giovanni, a young nobleman and womanizer **Baritone**
Leporello, his servant **Bass**
Don Ottavio, his friend **Tenor**
Donna Anna, Ottavio's fiancée **Soprano**
The Commendatore, her father **Bass**
Donna Elvira, deserted by Giovanni **Soprano**
Masetto, a peasant **Bass**
Zerlina, his fiancée **Soprano**

Synopsis of the Plot

Setting: Seville; 17th century

ACT I The heavily-disguised Giovanni has attacked and attempted to seduce Donna Anna; she cries out and her father, the Commendatore, comes to her assistance. In the ensuing fight the Commendatore is killed, and Giovanni escapes. Ottavio swears to avenge his death. In the street, Giovanni and Leporello meet a disguised woman who is bewailing the faithlessness of her lover. Giovanni decides to 'console' her, but runs off when he recognises his deserted lover, Donna Elvira, leaving Leporello to run through a list of his master's conquests, much to her horror; Elvira too decides on revenge. Meanwhile, Masetto and Zerlina are about to be married; Giovanni, instantly attracted to the pretty girl, arranges that Leporello should take the rest of the guests to his own palace for a party, leaving her behind. He is in the process of exerting his charms over her and she, indeed, is on the point of submitting, when Elvira sees them and takes Zerlina away for her own protection. The infuriated Giovanni is then approached by Anna and Ottavio, who have come to ask for his help in finding her father's murderer. They are interrupted by Elvira, who upbraids

Giovanni for his behaviour; he dismisses her words as the ravings of a madwoman and drags her off the stage, but not before Anna recognises his voice as that of her attacker. The wedding celebrations for Masetto and Zerlina are underway at Giovanni's palace, although Masetto is keeping a close eye on Giovanni and his fiancée. Elvira, Anna and Ottavio, masked, join the party to try and trap Giovanni. Under cover of the lively dancing, Giovanni makes another attempt to seduce Zerlina, but her piercing scream alerts the revellers. Ottavio, Anna and Elvira unmask and denounce Giovanni, who escapes before he can be caught.

ACT II Giovanni has a new quarry in his sights, Elvira's maid. He arranges to exchange cloaks with Leporello, who, as Giovanni, will lure Elvira away while he pursues the maid. The plan appears to work until, in the middle of a serenade outside the girl's window, Giovanni is confronted by Masetto and a group of armed men. Giovanni, in Leporello's cloak, pretends to be his servant, and sends the men in various directions to search for 'Giovanni'. Left alone with Masetto, Giovanni beats him soundly and runs off, leaving Zerlina to console him. Leporello, meanwhile, still disguised as Giovanni, has been forced to reveal his true identity to avoid capture; he manages to escape when Ottavio goes in search of a warrant for Giovanni's arrest. Reunited again, Leporello and Giovanni see a statue of the Commendatore in a cemetery; the statue speaks to them, much to Leporello's terror, but Giovanni audaciously invites it to dinner. Later, Giovanni is dining cheerfully at the palace when the statue appears; defiant to the last, Giovanni takes the Commendatore's proffered hand and, refusing to repent, is dragged down to the fires of hell.

Music and Background

Mozart called *Don Giovanni* a *dramma giocoso* – a jovial drama – which sums up the schizophrenic qualities of the piece: on the one hand a dark and deadly-serious moral tale of murder, sexual exploitation and betrayal; on the other, a fast-moving comedy with knockabout leanings. The divide is seen within the cast of characters. Anna and Ottavio are solemn creatures out of old-time opera seria. Leporello and the peasantry are comic. Elvira is somewhere in between: a *mezzo carattere*. And Giovanni himself is an ambiguous mystery: part-demon, part-hero, and without a proper aria to call his own. Only a couple of seduction songlets and the brief, brazen, hardly revealing party song 'Fin ch'han dal vino'. Note the sombre use of trombones to chill the spine in the Graveyard Scene, and the quotes from other operas (including his own *Le Nozze di Figaro*) which 18th-century audiences would have immediately picked up in the Supper Scene. There was a time when the final scene used to be cut, on the grounds that its jollity was inappropriate to the mood of awesome retribution at the end, but these days it tends to be accepted as in keeping with the dual nature of the piece. If Act II feels like a log-jam of arias, it's because Mozart made changes to the score when it moved from Prague to Vienna, squeezing in extra numbers. In some cases they were substitutes for what was already there, but modern audiences love the old *and* new items and expect to hear them together.

Highlights

Act I: Leporello's Catalogue Aria, 'Madamina', in which he torments Elvira with a list of Don Giovanni's other conquests (1003 in Spain alone!); Giovanni's seduction of Zerlina 'Là ci darem'; Anna's majestic 'Or sai chi l'onore (with its fourteen top As); Ottavio's classically mellifluous response 'Dalla sua pace'; Giovanni's frantic 'Fin ch'han dal vino'; the three conflicting dances going on at the same time in the party scene. Act II: Giovanni's serenade 'Deh vieni alla finestra; Ottavio's Comfort Aria 'Il mio tesoro'; Elvira's formidable 'Mi tradì'; Anna's 'Non mi dir'; the statue's arrival for supper, and Giovanni's descent to hell.

Did You Know?

🎵 Mozart wrote the title role for a singer who was only twenty-one at the time of the Prague premiere, which may acount for the fact that Giovanni has no heavy arias.

Recommended Recording

Thomas Allen, Carol Vaness, Maria Ewing, London Philharmonic Orchestra/Bernard Haitink. EMI CDS7 470 37-8. The record of a memorable Glyndebourne production, with Thomas Allen in his prime and in his best role.

Die Entführung aus dem Serail
(The Abduction from the Harem)

FORM: Opera in three acts; in German
COMPOSER: Wolfgang Amadeus Mozart (1756–91)
LIBRETTO: Gottlieb Stephanie; after C.F. Bretzner
FIRST PERFORMANCE: Vienna, 16 July 1782

Principal Characters

Belmonte, a Spanish nobleman 🎵 **Tenor**
Pedrillo, his servant 🎵 **Tenor**

The Bassa (Pasha) Selim ❧ **Speaking role**
Osmin, his servant ❧ **Bass**
Konstanze, a Spanish noblewoman ❧ **Soprano**
Blonde, Konstanze's maid ❧ **Soprano**

Synopsis of the Plot

Setting: Turkey; mid-16th century

ACT I Belmonte is searching for his beloved Konstanze, who has been kidnapped by pirates, together with her maid, Blonde, and Belmonte's servant, Pedrillo. Arriving outside a grand palace, Belmonte questions Osmin about its occupants, but learns little, except that Osmin has a lively hatred for the gardener, Pedrillo, none other than Belmonte's own servant. Belmonte is overjoyed to discover from Pedrillo that Konstanze is alive and well, and although she is a prisoner of the Pasha, who has tried hard to win her, she has remained faithful to him. Belmonte decides to pose as an eminent visiting architect, offering his services to Selim, so that he can gain access to the palace.

ACT II Osmin is attempting to seduce Blonde, but to no avail; Selim, also, is making little progress with the aptly-named Konstanze, and, in exasperation, threatens her with torture if she does not comply with his wishes. Blonde is delighted to hear from Pedrillo that she and her mistress are to escape that very night. Pedrillo effectively removes the main obstacle, Osmin, by getting him extremely drunk, and Konstanze and Belmonte are joyfully united.

ACT III At the last minute the escape plan goes wrong; Konstanze, Belmonte, Blonde and Pedrillo are all captured and brought before Osmin, who is triumphant at this turn of events. Selim, on hearing Belmonte's true identity, reveals that Belmonte's father is one of his greatest enemies, a man who has grievously wronged him; in revenge, all four will be tortured. But before they are taken away, Selim decides that it would degrade him to act in the same way as his enemy, so he releases them and allows them to go, to their great joy.

Music and Background

This was Mozart's first big work after his move from Salzburg to Vienna, written for a state occasion and in the national style of *Singspiel*: a mixture of speech and song in vernacular German as opposed to the grander form of all-sung Italian (although the piece is also known by the Italian name of *Il Seraglio*). The plot is frivolously silly but with noble moments which are filled out by the beauty of Mozart's score. It creates an odd unevenness among the cast that the important role of Selim is spoken and usually turns out rather dull – especially against the vocal fireworks required of Konstanze. Notice the splashy, percussion-dominated janissary (Turkish) music which colours the orchestral writing and was an exotic fashion of the time.

235

Highlights

Act I: Osmin's doleful gardening song, 'Wer ein Liebchen hat gefunden' with its trallalera refrain. Act II: Konstanze's magnificent, death-defying set-piece 'Martern aller Arten', which is one of the great vocal spectacles of the whole Mozart repertoire. Act III: Belmonte's opening aria 'Ich baue ganz' and the big subsequent love duet with Konstanze that starts with 'Welch ein Geschick!'; the closing vaudeville with its endlessly repeating tune that bounces around the characters.

Did You Know?

❧ The Emperor Joseph II famously remarked of *Die Entführung aus dem Serail* that it had too many notes, to which Mozart replied: 'Exactly the number necessary, Your Majesty'.

Recommended Recording

Yvonne Kenny, Lilian Watson, Peter Schreier, Zürich Opera/Nickolaus Harnoncourt. Warner 2292 42643-2. Invigorating, rough-edged and decidedly individual reading from a period-specialist conductor.

Idomeneo

FORM: Opera in three acts; in Italian
COMPOSER: Wolfgang Amadeus Mozart (1756–91)
LIBRETTO: Giambattista Varesco; after Danchet
FIRST PERFORMANCE: Munich, 29 January 1781

Principal Characters

Idomeneo, King of Crete ❧ **Tenor**
Idamante, his son ❧ **Soprano/Tenor**
Ilia, a Trojan princess ❧ **Soprano**
Elettra, a Greek princess ❧ **Soprano**
Arbace, Idamante's friend ❧ **Tenor**

Synopsis of the Plot

Setting: Ancient Crete

ACT I Ilia has been captured and imprisoned by the Cretans, but her hatred for them is tempered by her love for Idamante, the king's son. Elettra, a Greek princess living as a refugee in Crete, also loves Idamante and is jealous of Ilia's influence over him. These rivalries are temporarily forgotten when the dreadful news arrives that Idomeneo's fleet, returning home after many years' absence, has been shipwrecked and the king has been drowned. On the seashore, the people plead with the gods to spare the Cretans and their prayers appear to have been answered when Idomeneo himself steps ashore. But the king's life has been bought at a price: he vowed to Neptune, God of the Sea, that he would sacrifice the first person he met, if Neptune spared his life. And the first person he meets is his own son, Idamante.

ACT II Idomeneo consults Idamante's friend, Arbace, and they decide to send Idamante away for safety; he will accompany Elettra back to Greece. Elettra is delighted at the prospect of a long journey with Idamante and rushes down to the harbour. Neptune, however, is angry at being thwarted and sends a violent storm and a sea monster to punish the Cretans. The people run away in terror as Idomeneo begs the god to punish him alone.

ACT III Idamante vows to Ilia that he will kill the monster or die in the attempt, and they sing of their undying love for each other. Arbace warns Idomeneo that the sea monster has attacked the city, many of his people lie dead and the survivors are demanding action. Finally, Idomeneo confesses to the people that he has brought these disasters on them by not fulfilling his vow, and the people call on him to honour it. At that moment a great cry is heard; Idamante has killed the monster but, in spite of this, he offers himself as a willing sacrifice to allow his father's vow to be fulfilled. Idomeneo raises his sword but before he can strike, Ilia runs in and begs to be sacrificed instead of her beloved. Such nobility and selflessness melts the heart of the great Neptune and he decrees that Idamante and Ilia shall live and reign in Crete as king and queen.

Music and Background

Idomeneo was Mozart's first big commission – received at the age of twenty-four – and his first operatic masterpiece. Essentially the music looks to the past, setting a story of gods, kings and noble sacrifice in the old manner of Baroque opera seria; but Mozart brings new ideas to the form, breaking down some of the divisions between set-piece numbers with long, lyrical skeins of accompanied recitative that make the music feel continuous. The orchestration is probably richer than in any other Mozart opera – because it was designed to show off the famous Mannheim orchestra, brought to Munich by the musical Elector Karl Theodore and much admired by Mozart. The elaborate orchestration was also designed to camouflage the fact that the Idomeneo and Idamante of the original production weren't up to much, forcing Mozart to modify what he would otherwise have given them to sing. The Idamante was a castrato role, subsequently adapted by Mozart for a tenor.

Highlights

Act II: Ilia's 'Se il padre perdei' is one of Mozart's loveliest soprano arias, memorably accompanied by a wind quartet; Idomeneo's 'Fuor del mar' is a tumultuous challenge to Neptune; the amiable embarkation chorus 'Placido è il mar' and farewell trio 'Pria di partir' are classically fine ensembles. Act III: 'Andrò, ramingo e solo' is a quartet of true stature; Elettra's rage aria 'D'Oreste, d'Ajace' is a dazzling piece of virtuosic venom.

Did You Know?

Elettra is arguably the toughest female role in any Mozart opera, and Arbace arguably the dullest male role – which is why his arias are often cut in modern performances.

Recommended Recording

Anthony Rolfe Johnson, Anne Sofie von Otter, Sylvia McNair, Monteverdi Choir/John Eliot Gardiner. DG 431 674-2. A full, deliberately raw-edged version on old instruments with unbeatable soloists.

Le Nozze di Figaro
(The Marriage of Figaro, Figaro's Wedding)

FORM: Opera in four acts; in Italian
COMPOSER: Wolfgang Amadeus Mozart (1756–91)
LIBRETTO: Lorenzo da Ponte; after Beaumarchais
FIRST PERFORMANCE: Vienna, 1 May 1786

Principal Characters

Count Almaviva ⁓ Baritone
Countess Almaviva ⁓ Soprano
Figaro, the Count's servant ⁓ Baritone
Cherubino, the Count's page ⁓ Soprano/Mezzo-soprano
Susanna, the Countess' maid ⁓ Soprano
Dr Bartolo ⁓ Bass
Marcellina, his former housekeeper ⁓ Soprano

Don Basilio, a music teacher ✒ **Tenor**
Antonio, the gardener ✒ **Bass**

Synopsis of the Plot

Setting: A country house near Seville; mid-18th century

ACT I Susanna and Figaro are soon to be married, although their happiness is marred by Almaviva, who has recently been making advances to Susanna, much to Figaro's anger, and he vows revenge. But Figaro himself is also the target of revenge: firstly from Marcellina, who wishes to punish him for not choosing her as a wife by forcing him to marry her or pay back the money he owes; and secondly from Dr Bartolo, who has not forgiven Figaro for helping his ward to elope with the Count. Cherubino comes to see Susanna to ask her to intercede with the Count for him (he has been dismissed), but they are interrupted by Almaviva himself, and Cherubino hides behind the armchair. The Count flirts with Susanna, but when they hear the music teacher, Basilio, outside the door he, too, hides behind the armchair, a spot just vacated by Cherubino, who is now hiding on the chair, concealed by a dress. Basilio begins to make insinuations about Cherubino's relationship with the Countess, at which the enraged Count springs up and castigates Cherubino. Susanna defends him but the Count relates how, the day before, he found Cherubino hiding under a table in a young girl's room (he does not say what he, the Count, was doing there in the first place!). The Count, to demonstrate how he lifted up the tablecloth, raises the dress on the chair to reveal – Cherubino! The wedding is postponed and Cherubino ordered to join the Count's regiment immediately.

ACT II The Countess and Susanna have decided to trick the Count by pretending to arrange an assignation between him and Susanna, and actually sending Cherubino in her place, dressed as a girl. However, they are just getting him ready when they are interrupted by the Count himself – which sends both Susanna and Cherubino into different hiding places. The Count, hearing noises from an inner room, orders his wife to open the door and, on her refusal, takes her away with him to fetch a hammer to break it down. While they are away, Susanna releases Cherubino from the room, he jumps out of the window and Susanna takes his place. The Count (and Countess!) are astonished when not Cherubino but Susanna emerges demurely from the room, and the Count is forced to apologise to his wife. Figaro joins them, announcing that it is time for the wedding, but is soon followed by the aggrieved gardener, Antonio, complaining loudly that the plants under the Countess' window have been destroyed. Figaro claims to be responsible, at which Antonio returns to him papers found beneath the window. The Count snatches them from him and asks the baffled Figaro what they are; surreptitiously assisted by Susanna and the Countess, he explains that they are his army commission papers (they are, of course, Cherubino's papers), but the Count is not convinced. At this point, Marcellina, Bartolo and Basilio arrive to urge the Count to take action in Marcellina's case against Figaro.

ACT III Figaro's defence against marrying Marcellina lies in his claim that he is of noble birth and therefore must have his parents' permission. In proof he shows them a curious mark on his arm – at which Marcellina recognises him as her long-lost son and, even more astonishing, Bartolo is his father. Susanna, coming in to find Figaro in Marcellina's embrace, slaps his face, but all is then explained to her satisfaction. The Countess, meanwhile, is still unhappy with her wayward husband and determined to trap him in his infidelities. She and Susanna plan to slip him a note arranging a secret assignation; the Count will arrive expecting Susanna, but will find his own wife. The note is passed to him during the wedding celebrations.

ACT IV Figaro has learnt of his new wife's intended assignation with the Count and, with witnesses, hides in the garden to trap her. The Countess and Susanna arrive, each in the guise of the other. A complicated series of mistaken identities, deceptions and flirtations follows in the dark garden, culminating in Figaro passionately embracing the 'Countess'. The Count, furious at his wife's behaviour, calls on all present to witness her disgrace: he pulls away her cloak to reveal, of course, Susanna! At last the Count is humbled and shamed; his wife forgives him and everyone is happy.

Music and Background

Fast-moving, funny, touching and alive, *Le Nozze di Figaro* has to be one of the supremely great works ever written for the stage in any medium, but in its time it was also highly subversive. The play on which the piece was based had been banned from performance in Vienna: the idea of servants claiming moral victory over their masters was just too uncomfortable for an aristocratic 18th-century society. How Da Ponte persuaded the emperor to permit a sung setting we will never really know, and although his adaptation toned down the revolutionary elements, it retained Figaro's menacing 'Se vuol ballare' as a challenge to all feudal power-brokers everywhere. The joy of *Le Nozze di Figaro* is its characters: probably the most *human* beings to be found on the opera stage. The plot moves swiftly – it all happens on a single, crazy day, unfolding from morning to night – with a lot of minor intrigues that can be confusing, especially in Act IV. But the detail all gets swept into accumulating formal structures that override the old, traditional distinctions between aria and recitative and build into great finales which count among the most impressive music Mozart ever wrote.

Highlights

Act I: the Overture; Figaro's challenge, 'Se vuol ballare'; Cherubino's tenderly amorous 'Non so più'; Figaro's mock-martial 'Non più andrai'. Act II: the Countess' melancholic 'Porgi, Amor'; Cherubino's endearingly seductive 'Voi che sapete'; the whole of the finale. Act III: the Countess' deeply moving 'Dove sono'. Act IV: the final scene of pardon.

Did You Know?

- The first-ever *Le Nozze di Figaro* had an English soprano, Nancy Storace, as Susanna, an Irish tenor, Michael Kelly, as Basilio and a twelve-year-old girl as Barbarina.
- Hector Berlioz considered *Le Nozze di Figaro* to be 'fit only for fairs and carnivals'.

Recommended Recording

Samuel Ramey, Lucia Popp, Thomas Allen, Kiri Te Kanawa, Frederica von Stade, London Philharmonic Orchestra/Georg Solti. Decca 410 150-2. Allen and Te Kanawa in roles that have been central to their careers, superbly sung.

Die Zauberflöte
(The Magic Flute)

FORM: Opera in two acts; in German
COMPOSER: Wolfgang Amadeus Mozart (1756–91)
LIBRETTO: Emanuel Schikaneder
FIRST PERFORMANCE: Vienna, 30 September 1791

Principal Characters

Tamino, a prince ~ Tenor
Papageno, a bird-catcher ~ Baritone
The Queen of the Night ~ Soprano
Pamina, her daughter ~ Soprano
The Queen's ladies-in-waiting
~ Two Sopranos/One Mezzo-soprano
Sarastro, High Priest of Isis and Osiris ~ Bass
Monostatos, a Moor and Sarastro's servant ~ Tenor
Three Boys ~ Two Sopranos/One Mezzo-soprano

Synopsis of the Plot

Setting: Ancient Egypt

ACT I Tamino is pursued by a huge snake and faints in terror. The snake is killed by the Queen of the Night's ladies-in-waiting but, when Tamino awakes, the feathered bird-catcher, Pagageno, claims the brave deed was his. The three ladies reappear, padlock Papageno's mouth as a punishment, and present Tamino with a portrait of the Queen's daughter, Pamina. Tamino instantly falls in love with her and, at the urging of the Queen herself, sets out with Papageno (now released from his padlock) to rescue her from the priest, Sarastro, who is holding her captive. The ladies supply them with a magic flute and a set of magic pipes, to help them in their task, and three boys to show them the way. Papageno is the first to find Pamina – in the process of being importunately wooed by Monostatos. But when the Moor sees the feathered man he runs away and Papageno assures Pamina that Tamino will soon come for her. Meanwhile, Tamino has wandered into a temple where he learns that Sarastro is no tyrant, as the Queen had maintained, but a man of wisdom. Disturbed by this conflicting information, Tamino plays the flute, and, on hearing Papageno's pipes in answer, he rushes off to find him. Papageno and Pamina have been caught trying to escape by Monostatos and his slaves, but Papageno plays his pipes and they all dance away. Sarastro comes upon the scene and Pamina confesses that she was running away from Monostatos, to which Sarastro replies that the only reason he is holding her captive is to free her from her mother's malign influence. And when Monostatos returns, dragging Tamino with him and expecting a reward, Sarastro sentences him to a sound beating for attacking Tamino.

ACT II The gods have decreed that Pamina and Tamino can marry, but they must first undergo trials. The Queen of the Night is determined to thwart these plans and sends the three ladies to tempt Tamino and Papageno, but they resist. She then gives Pamina a knife and instructs her to kill Sarastro. Monostatos overhears her and attempts to blackmail Pamina, but he, in turn, is overheard by Sarastro, who dismisses him. In the next trial, Papageno is confronted by an old woman who declares she is his lover, Papagena, much to his incredulous amusement. But Tamino, ordered to keep silent, causes the innocent Pamina much misery when he refuses to speak to her. Sarastro orders Pamina and Tamino to part forever and Pamina is on the point of committing suicide, when the three boys reassure her that Tamino's love is true. In the meantime, Papageno has received another visit from the old woman and, under threat of permanent imprisonment, has agreed to be faithful to her. At that moment she reveals herself to be the woman of his dreams, young, lovely – and feathered! Unfortunately she is hurried away by a priest before he can act. Tamino, about to undergo the final ordeal, by fire and water, is joined by Pamina and, guided by the magic flute, they pass through safely. Papageno, having failed to find Papagena, is about to hang himself but, advised by the three boys, he plays his pipes and she reappears, to their mutual joy. A final attempt to undermine Sarastro by the Queen of the Night is foiled and the forces of good celebrate their triumph.

Music and Background

At one level *Die Zauberflöte* is an enchanting pantomime which reflects the circumstances in which it was written – hurriedly, for a suburban, rough-and-ready theatre company run by a travelling showman called Emanuel

Schikaneder. The style is popular, knockabout, and given voice in the vernacular German mixture of speech and song known as *Singspiel*, which Mozart had used earlier in his career for *Die Entführung aus dem Serail*. But it does seem to carry deeper implications, through the ideals of love and brotherhood and the barely-concealed masonic symbolism that runs through the piece. Mozart and Schikaneder were both freemasons, and it may well be that the whole plot of the *Die Zauberflöte* was meant to read as some kind of socio-religious allegory. The certain thing is that the story is clumsily constructed and riddled with inconsistencies, while the spoken text can be tedious. It is saved by Mozart's music, which comes with a simple directness unmatched by any of his previous operas. Partly that was a matter of keeping the score within the capabilities of performers who wouldn't have been so sophisticated as the ones available to him at court (the obvious exception being the Queen of the Night, whose music is peculiarly demanding and at very high altitude). But it was also indicative of the way his mature writing had begun to pare down its means to the absolute essential – a common enough phenomenon in the late works of composers, although Mozart was only in middle age at the time and didn't know that this would *be* a late work.

Highlights

Act I: the Overture (with its three masonic chords); Papageno's bird-catching song, 'Der Vogelfänger bin ich ja'; the Queen of the Night's athletic first aria, 'Zum Leiden bin ich auserkoren'; the adorable Papageno/Pamina duet 'Bei Männern'; the mesmerising tune with which Tamino charms the animals; the grand final chorus 'Es lebe Sarastro'. Act II: Sarastro's classic, deep-down bass aria 'O Isis und Osiris'; the Queen of the Night's show-stopping second aria, 'Der Hölle Rache'; Pamina's 'Ach, ich fühl's' and outburst of joy 'Tamino mein!'; Papageno's feather-flying duet with Papagena 'Pa-Pa-Pa'.

Did You Know?

Mozart and his librettist were keen freemasons at a time when it was officially discouraged in Austria. The setting of the opera in Egypt (where freemasonry was thought to have originated), the trials which Tamino and Papageno undergo and some of the words of the libretto relate to the brotherhood. The Queen of the Night appears to represent Empress Maria Theresa, strongly pro-Catholic and very hostile to freemasonry.

Recommended Recording

Kiri Te Kanawa, Cheryl Studer, Francisco Araiza, Olaf Baer, Academy of St Martin's in the Field/Neville Marriner. Philips 426 276-2. Nicely characterised, with a light touch.

Modest Musorgsky

(1839–81)

Boris Godunov (1872)
Sorochintsy Fair (1877)
Khovanshchina (1880)

*M*usorgsky was the most tragically (though, in the judgement of history, interestingly) maverick figure of the group of mid-19th-century Russian composers based in St Petersburg and known as 'The Mighty Handful'. Essentially self-taught semi-professionals, earning their living by means other than music, they formed a mutual support group, collaborating on large-scale projects and sorting out each others' scores. And with Musorgsky there was plenty of sorting out to do. A civil servant as well as a musician, he drank heavily, died young (at forty-two) and finished little. Of his six opera projects, only one was actually completed – *Boris Godunov* – and that had a messy history, appearing in successive and conflicting versions. Rimsky-Korsakov, the most fluent of the 'Handful' composers, devoted much of his energies to tidying up Musorgsky's scores, in the belief that they were scarred by 'absurd, disconnected harmony, ugly part-writing, sometimes strikingly illogical modulation, sometimes a depressing lack of it'; and that would have been a common view at the time. But in recent years the raw, earthy, often awkward immediacy of Musorgsky's work has come to be valued as original and potent; and new performing editions endeavour to unravel Musorgsky's own intentions from the 'improvements' of later hands.

Boris Godunov

FORM: Opera in a Prologue and four acts; in Russian
COMPOSER: Modest Musorgsky (1839–81)
LIBRETTO: Modest Musorgsky; after Pushkin
FIRST PERFORMANCE: St Petersburg, 8 February 1874

Principal Characters

Boris Godunov, Tsar of Russia ～ **Bass-baritone**
Pimen, an old monk ～ **Bass**

Grigori (later Dmitri), a monk; later the usurper ⁊ **Tenor**
Fyodor, Boris' son ⁊ **Mezzo-soprano**
Princess Marina, a Pole, Grigori's sweetheart ⁊ **Mezzo-soprano**
Prince Shuisky ⁊ **Tenor**
The Simpleton ⁊ **Tenor**

Synopsis of the Plot

Setting: Russia and Poland; 1598–1605

PROLOGUE Outside a monastery, the people have been ordered to say prayers and appeal to Boris to accept the vacant throne of the tsar. Next day they appear outside the Kremlin, as instructed, to cheer dutifully as Boris emerges from his coronation.

ACT I The young monk, Grigori, tells Pimen of a recurrent nightmare in which he falls to his death from a great height. Pimen tells Grigori how, many years ago, he saw the body of the dead prince, Dmitri, the late tsar's son, who is believed to have been killed on the orders of the usurper, Boris Godunov. Pimen comments that Dmitri would now have been the same age as Grigori. The story inspires Grigori and he leaves the monastery, intending to impersonate Dmitri and raise an army against Boris. Making for the Lithuanian border, he just manages to escape as Boris' police arrive to arrest him.

ACT II In the Kremlin, Boris is troubled by thoughts of the murdered Dmitri and the sufferings of his country. Prince Shuisky brings him news of a Pretender, going by the name of Dmitri, who has raised an army against him with the support of the King of Poland. Boris, greatly disturbed, asks Shuisky to confirm that Dmitri was indeed killed. Left alone, his imagination overcomes him and he sinks to the ground.

ACT III In Poland, Princess Marina and Grigori (now Dmitri) have fallen in love, and she dreams of being Empress of Russia. She is persuaded that it is her duty to convert Dmitri (and thus Russia) to the Catholic Church, and convinces Dmitri to take a Catholic spiritual adviser with him.

ACT IV The Council of Boyars is meeting in the Kremlin and Shuisky is in the process of reporting on Boris' fragile mental state, when the tsar himself staggers in. Shuisky brings in Pimen, who tells of a miracle that took place at the murdered Dmitri's tomb, and Boris collapses. Knowing he is dying, Boris sends for his son, Fyodor, and urges him to uphold the true values of the nation. Meanwhile, a group of Dmitri's followers have gathered in a forest, where they are tormenting a captured supporter of the tsar and preparing to lynch two priests. But when Grigori arrives, he orders them to release the man and the priests and calls on the people to follow him to Moscow. They all go, leaving behind only the Simpleton, whose mournful song foretells the unhappy times ahead for Russia.

Music and Background

More a grand historical pageant than an attempt to tell a coherent, flowing story, *Boris Godunov* is best approached as a sequence of free-standing scenes with not much more than the theme of the central character's guilt to connect them. Musorgsky's music is big-boned, strong, undecorative but scaling up to magnificent statements like the sound of the Russian bells in the Coronation Scene. And although the chorus is in many ways the star of the show, his writing for individual voices is uniquely expressive, incorporating techniques that now seem way ahead of their time. Modern performances come basically in one of two forms: with Musorgsky's bare orchestration or with Rimsky-Korsakov's more sumptuous additions. One other variable is a scene outside St Basil's Cathedral which Musorgsky replaced with the Polish scenes (inserted to provide a proper female role). Although they were meant as alternatives, some productions still play them side by side.

Highlights

The whole Coronation Scene in the Prologue; Boris' vision of Dmitri in Act II (terror against a ticking clock); the Dmitri/Marina love duet at the end of Act III; Boris' death and the arrival of the new tsar in Act IV.

Recommended Recording

Anatoly Kotscherga, Sergei Larin, Marjana Lipovsek, Samuel Ramey, Berlin Philharmonic Orchestra/Claudio Abbado. Sony S3K 58977. A recent issue that comes as close as possible to an understanding of Musorgsky's intentions (although it does, for the sake of completeness, include the dropped St Basil's Scene). For something less scrupulous, more old-fashioned but with the exemplary Boris Christoff as not just Boris but Pimen and Varlaam as well, try EMI's historic (mono) reissue CHS5 65192-2.

Khovanshchina
(The Khovansky Rising)

FORM: Opera in five acts; in Russian
COMPOSER: Modest Musorgsky (1839–81)
LIBRETTO: Modest Musorgsky and Vladimir Stasov
FIRST PERFORMANCE: St Petersburg, 21 February 1886

Principal Characters

Prince Ivan Khovansky, leader of the Streltsy ∾ **Bass**
Prince Andrei Khovansky, his son ∾ **Tenor**
Prince Vasily Golitsin ∾ **Tenor**
The Boyar Shaklovity ∾ **Baritone**
Dosifei, leader of the Old Believers ∾ **Bass**
Marfa, a young widow ∾ **Mezzo-soprano**
Emma, a young German girl ∾ **Soprano**
A Scrivener ∾ **Tenor**

Synopsis of the Plot

Setting: In and around Moscow; 1680s

ACT I Red Square at dawn. A Scrivener sets up his table and is engaged by the Boyar Shaklovity to write an anonymous letter to the tsar, warning him of Khovansky's plots. But the Scrivener quickly disappears into the crowd when Khovansky himself arrives, and assures the people that his sole interest is to destroy the tsar's enemies. Khovansky soon enlists the people's support and they agree that his men, the Streltsy (musketeers), can patrol the city. The crowds disperse and Emma runs in, followed by Andrei Khovansky who tries to kiss her, in spite of her obvious reluctance. Marfa intercedes to protect the girl, and Andrei threatens her with a knife. Further violence is prevented by the arrival of Khovansky and Dosifei, who arrange for Marfa to take care of Emma.

ACT II Prince Golitsin sends for Marfa to read his fortune, but he is disturbed at her predictions of disgrace and poverty and, after she leaves, orders his servants to drown her. His next visitor is Ivan Khovansky, who angrily complains that Golitsin has too much influence at court, but the two men are reconciled by Dosifei, who urges them to join him in restoring the old ways and customs which Peter has discarded. They are interrupted, however, by the sudden return of a furious Marfa, who accuses Golitsin's servants of trying to kill her; she was only saved by the unexpected arrival of the tsar's bodyguard. The three men are perturbed by this news but, before they can act, Shaklovity announces that Khovansky has been denounced in a letter to the tsar as a traitor (although he does not mention that the denunciation came from himself).

ACT III In the Streltsy area, Marfa sings wistfully of her lost love and is comforted by the sympathetic Dosifei. The Streltsy themselves straggle in, singing a drinking song, and urging each other to repay old scores with death and destruction. They are joined by their womenfolk, who upbraid them for their drinking, but the ensuing uproar is quickly silenced by the arrival of the Scrivener, who reports seeing mercenary soldiers attacking unarmed people on the edge of their district. The Streltsy appeal to their leader, Khovansky, but he refuses to retaliate against Peter's forces.

ACT IV Prince Khovansky is being entertained at home by the singing of his servant girls and the dancing of his Persian slaves. Shaklovity arrives with a summons from Prince Golitsin: Khovansky is to go to a meeting with Sophia, the tsar's half-sister. But as Khovansky leaves the room, Shaklovity stabs him in the back. Golitsin has been sent into exile. Dosifei, the last one left, is much saddened by the fall of the two great nobles, his fellow sympathisers. Andrei Khovansky is rescued by Marfa and taken to a secret hiding place as the crowd demands the death of all the Streltsy. But Peter has decided to be merciful and he sends word that he has pardoned them.

ACT V Deep in a forest, the Old Believers, led by Dosifei, recognise that their cause is lost, and decide to kill themselves rather than surrender their religious principles. A pyre is built and they proceed into the flames with Marfa and Andrei, to the horror of the tsar's soldiers, come to arrest them.

Music and Background

Musorgsky's big problem with this opera – apart from it being unfinished – was that he was not allowed by the Russian imperial censors to portray any member of the Romanov family on stage – and the Romanovs ought to be the central characters. The result is another sequence of epic tableaux, not so much telling a story as creating a cumulative picture of great history unfolding. Saturated with grandeur and gloom – an endless bewailing of the tragic fortunes of Mother Russia – it can be heavy going; and the demands for a huge number of people on stage make it a rare feature of opera repertory outside Eastern Europe. However, the sheer spectacle of the score can be enthralling. Musorgsky left no orchestrations at all, and various composers since have tried their hand at it, including Rimsky-Korsakov, Ravel and Stravinsky. Shostakovich's version is the one which is currently in favour.

Highlights

Act I: the solemn hymn in which the chorus lament the troubles of their country, and the subsequent chorus song of praise for Khovansky. Act III: Boyar Shaklovity's patriotic song and the uproar that precedes the Scrivener's arrival. Act IV: the March of the Streltsy, prepared for death.

Did You Know?

🐁 As a matter of history, the Streltsy were never pardoned by the tsar but suffered terrible deaths.

Recommended Recording

Bulat Minjelkiev, Vladimir Galusin, Olga Borodina, Kirov Opera/Valery Gergiev. Philips 432 147-2. Less sophisticated but bolder than some of its rivals, this version uses the Shostakovich orchestration very effectively.

Otto Nicolai

(1810–49)

Die Lustigen Weiber von Windsor (1849)

Otto Nicolai is one of the intriguing what-ifs of opera history, and the question is: what might have happened if he hadn't died at thirty-eight, just as he seemed to have found his metier in the one work – *Die Lustigen Weiber von Windsor* – for which he is remembered? Until then he had been a German composer seduced into Italian ways after living in Rome, and writing bel canto operas in the manner of Bellini. With *Die Lustigen Weiber von Windsor* he ventured into the very different territory of German light opera, and with a success he never lived to see because he died from a stroke just two months after the premiere. His Italian operas are now completely forgotten, as are his symphonies and piano concerto.

Die Lustigen Weiber von Windsor
(The Merry Wives of Windsor)

FORM: Opera in three acts; in German
COMPOSER: Otto Nicolai (1810–49)
LIBRETTO: Hermann Salomon Mosenthal; after Shakespeare
FIRST PERFORMANCE: Berlin, 9 March 1849

Principal Characters

Sir John Falstaff ⮕ Bass
Frau Fluth ⮕ Soprano
Herr Fluth, her husband ⮕ Baritone
Frau Reich ⮕ Mezzo-soprano
Herr Reich, her husband ⮕ Bass
Anna Reich, their daughter ⮕ Soprano
Spärlich, suitor to Anna ⮕ Tenor
Fenton, suitor to Anna ⮕ Tenor
Dr Caius, suitor to Anna ⮕ Bass

Synopsis of the Plot

Setting: Windsor; 15th century

ACT I Frau Fluth and Frau Reich discover, much to their indignation, that Sir John Falstaff has sent identical love letters to each of them, and they decide to teach him a lesson. Meanwhile, Herr Reich has a different problem to solve: which of her three suitors (Spärlich, Caius and Fenton) will make the most suitable husband for his daughter, Anna? After some thought, Herr Reich rejects Fenton, who is desperately in love with Anna, in favour of the wealthy Spärlich. Frau Fluth and Frau Reich put their plan to punish Falstaff into action; they arrange for him to visit Frau Fluth at home and then, as he begins his seduction routine, Frau Reich bursts in to warn them that Herr Fluth, alerted by a secret message (actually from his wife) is on his way home. The bulky Falstaff is unceremoniously bundled into a laundry basket and deposited in the river, as Fluth orders the house to be searched and his wife upbraids him for his suspicions.

ACT II Falstaff is enjoying himself at the Garter Inn when Fluth, still dogged by suspicions, comes in disguise to question Falstaff about his relationship with Frau Fluth. Falstaff's boasting horrifies Fluth, who only manages to maintain his disguise and his dignity with great difficulty. Meanwhile, Anna is serenaded in her garden by the three prospective suitors and, much to the fury of Caius and Spärlich, she pledges herself to Fenton. There are high emotions in the house, too: the enraged Fluth has returned from the inn and warns his wife that he will definitely trap her lover this time. They are interrupted by the arrival of Spärlich, Caius and Herr Reich at the door, and, in the general commotion, Falstaff (who was in the house when Fluth came home) is disguised as an old, deaf woman and smuggled safely out. Fluth instigates another fruitless search of the house and his wife again derides his jealousy.

ACT III Frau Reich and Frau Fluth explain the situation to their husbands and, together, they concoct a plan which will finally put an end to Falstaff's amorous adventures. The question of Anna Reich's husband is also now settled: her mother tells her it is to be Dr Caius and her father tells her it is to be Spärlich! Anna, naturally, has already decided it is to be Fenton and determines to outwit her parents. Later that night Fluth, Reich and their neighbours (dressed as elves and fairies) gather in moonlit Windsor Forest to wait for Falstaff who, when he arrives, is tormented and teased mercilessly by the 'elves' and 'fairies' until he is quite distracted. Meanwhile, Anna and Fenton take the opportunity of slipping away to get married. Finally, everything is resolved and the opera ends happily with a general reconciliation.

Music and Background

This piece is a musical hybrid, combining the Germanic qualities of a *Singspiel*, speech-and-song format with the easy, decorative lyricism of Italian vocal style. The strength of the orchestral writing is definitely in the German tradition, but even so, it comes with a lightness and grace that few of Nicolai's countrymen of the time could have equalled. Ultimately the score suffers invidious comparison with Verdi's treatment of the same subject. It survives through its charm.

Highlights

Falstaff's comic duet with Ford in Act II 'O! Ihr beschämt mich' and Fenton's Act II romance 'Horch, die Lerche singt im Hain!', with its accompanying bird-like trills from piccolo and flute.

Recommended Recording

Karl Ridderbusch, Wolfgang Brendel, Helen Donath, Bavarian Radio Symphony Orchestra/Rafael Kubelík. Decca 443 669-2. A fun recording from the 1970s, with nothing in the way of available rivals.

Carl Nielsen
(1865–1931)

Saul og David (1901)
Maskarade (1906)

Denmark's one, true, great composer, Carl Nielsen, was also one of the great symphonists of modern times and will always be remembered principally for the six works he wrote in that genre. Their collective stature bears comparison with the symphonies of Sibelius, his Finnish contemporary. He also had a natural instinct for vocal music, developed out of the vernacular folk songs he learned as a child in poor, rural circumstances on the island of Funen. As a young man Nielsen played in the pit orchestra of the Copenhagen Royal Theatre, graduating to the position of conductor for some years. His two operas present a complete contrast in outlook: one a darkly serious score, the other an entirely frivolous comedy. Their currency outside Scandinavia has always been limited by the language (both were written in Danish) and by the fact that the full score to *Maskarade* only existed in a form riddled with inconsistencies and errors. A new performing edition, financed by the Danish government, may well change that.

Maskarade

FORM: Opera in three acts; in Danish
COMPOSER: Carl Nielsen (1865–1931)
LIBRETTO: Vilhelm Andersen; after Holberg
FIRST PERFORMANCE: Copenhagen, 11 November 1906

Principal Characters

Jeronimus, a citizen of Copenhagen ∾ **Bass**
Magdelone, his wife ∾ **Mezzo-soprano**
Leander, their son ∾ **Tenor**
Henrik, his valet ∾ **Baritone**
Mr Leonard, a citizen of Copenhagen ∾ **Tenor/Baritone**
Leonora, his daughter ∾ **Soprano**
Pernille, her maid ∾ **Soprano**
Arv, Jeronimus' servant ∾ **Tenor**

Synopsis of the Plot

Setting: Copenhagen; 1723

ACT I Leander and his valet, Henrik, are recovering from the previous night's revelry at the masked ball, where Leander fell in love with an unknown lady. Henrik reminds his master that, long ago, Jeronimus promised him as husband to the unknown daughter of a Mr Leonard. They are interrupted by Magdelone, Leander's mother, who is most intrigued by the masquerade and intimates that she, too, would like to go. But any ideas of this frivolous nature are firmly dismissed by Jeronimus, whose arrival is followed shortly by that of Mr Leonard, who has come to say that his daughter has fallen in love with an unknown man at the masquerade. Jeronimus lectures his son severely on his duties and responsibilities, but the spirited Leander refuses to make promises he cannot keep.

ACT II Jeronimus has posted the slow-witted Arv as nightwatchman, to prevent Leander from leaving the house. Pretending to be a ghost, Henrik terrifies the servant into confessing his 'crimes' and then blackmails him into letting Leander go by. The whole of Copenhagen, it seems, is going to the second night of the ball, including Jeronimus, who, having discovered the absence of Leander and Henrik, goes with Arv to buy a disguise and search for them at the ball, and Magdelone and Mr Leonard who meet, unaware of each other's real identity, and indulge in some mild flirting.

ACT III Leander is ecstatically reunited with his unknown lady and they pledge undying love to each other. Henrik, recognising Jeronimus behind his Bacchus mask, contrives to get him drunk and the upright Jeronimus even forgets himself so far as to join in a lively dance and flirt, unsuccessfully, with one of the dancers. The hour for unmasking arrives and, to their great joy, the unknown lady is revealed as Leonora, Mr Leonard's daughter, and therefore Leander's betrothed. The befuddled Jeronimus is rather slow to grasp this fact but a rousing dance sweeps all his confusion away, as Henrik turns to the audience and begs their approval.

Music and Background

This is effectively the Danish national opera: steeped affectionately in local dance and folk styles but with a debt to Mozart too, which gives the piece the feeling of a cross between *The Bartered Bride* and *Le Nozze di Figaro* (Holberg's Henrik was, in literary terms, a milder-mannered precedent for Beaumarchais' wilful servant). The musical invention is uneven, but at its best it speaks warmly from the heart, with touching solos, spirited duets, and an infectious bonhomie throughout.

Highlights

The Overture; the prelude to Act II and ensuing love duet between Leander and Leonora; the dance of the cockerels and magically tender unmasking scene in Act III.

Did You Know?

～ Nielsen was partly motivated to write this opera by his experiences in the Copenhagen opera pit, sitting through tedious local fodder. He was sure he could do better, and he did.

Recommended Recording

Ib Hansen, Tonny Landy, Mogens Schmidt Johansen, Danish Radio Symphony Orchestra/John Frandsen. Unicorn DKPCD 9073/4. Modestly accomplished singing that will have to do until something better comes along, but well conducted with a sense of pace.

Jacques Offenbach
(1819–80)

Orphée aux Enfers (1858)
La Belle Hélène (1864)
La Vie Parisienne (1866)
La Grande-Duchesse de Gérolstein (1867)
La Périchole (1868)
Les Contes d'Hoffmann (1880)

J acques Offenbach was a Francophile German who went to study in
Paris, stayed there, and more or less single-handedly created French
operetta with *Orphée aux Enfers*: a huge success that made him the
Andrew Lloyd Webber of Parisian theatre music in the mid-19th
century and influential on other composers who achieved fame in
similar genres, including Arthur Sullivan. The son of a Jewish cantor in
Cologne, Offenbach first attracted attention as a cellist, but was
diverted into composition of small-scale satirical one-acters for the
Bouffes-Parisiens, a modest theatre off the Champs-Élysées. With
Orphée aux Enfers he upgraded the scale of the enterprise, and carried
on writing in the same vein until public tastes changed in the 1870s. His
one serious opera, *Les Contes d'Hoffmann*, came at the very end of his
life. Left incomplete at his death, it was finished by another composer,
Ernest Guiraud.

La Belle Hélène
(Beautiful Helen)

FORM: Operetta in three acts; in French
COMPOSER: Jacques Offenbach (1819–80)
LIBRETTO: Henri Meilhac and Ludovic Halévy;
after classical mythology
FIRST PERFORMANCE: Paris, 17 December 1864

Principal Characters

Paris, son of King Priam ⟞ **Tenor**
Menelaus, King of Sparta ⟞ **Tenor**
Helen, Queen of Sparta ⟞ **Mezzo-soprano**
Agamemnon, King of Argos ⟞ **Baritone**
Achilles, King of Phthiotis ⟞ **Tenor**
Ajax 1, King of Salamis ⟞ **Tenor**
Ajax 2, King of Locris ⟞ **Baritone**
Calchas, High Priest of Jupiter ⟞ **Bass**

Synopsis of the Plot

Setting: Classical Greece

ACT I The goddess Venus has won the golden apple from Paris and, in return, has promised him the most beautiful woman in the world. This puts Helen, wife of King Menelaus, in a rather exciting, if delicate, situation for, as she knows full well, she herself is the most beautiful woman in the world. Paris arrives, disguised as a shepherd, and immediately makes a favourable impression on Helen, who is bored with her rather dull husband. But they hardly have time to exchange more than a few words when the four Greek kings (the two Ajaxes, Agamemnon and Achilles) arrive with Menelaus to arrange a game of charades. Paris joins in, wins and, much to her consternation, reveals his true identity to Helen. Calchas, the high priest, announces an unexpected decree from Jupiter, which obliges Menelaus to go immediately to Crete – although it does not specify the reason why.

ACT II A month has passed and Helen is still retaining her virtue, albeit tenuously. Paris, meanwhile, is becoming increasingly impatient to claim the prize sanctioned by Venus and hides in Helen's bedroom as she sleeps. Helen, dreaming of love, mistakes Paris' lovemaking for a dream and happily cooperates until they are interrupted by the sudden return of Menelaus, who is shocked at what he sees. Paris makes a hasty departure as Helen turns on Menelaus, blaming him for the fracas by returning from Crete without letting her know first.

ACT III The whole court has retired to the beach at Nauplia for the summer season. The Greek kings bemoan the recent moral decline of the people and blame Menelaus, saying the new sexual licence is Venus' revenge for having her wishes thwarted. Menelaus sends for one of Venus' Cytherean priests, a vivid young man who arrives yodelling a happy song. The priest tells the king that he must allow him to take Helen, alone, to Cytherea for a special sacrifice to placate the goddess. Helen, after some persuasion, agrees to go and, once on board, the priest throws off his disguise to be revealed, of course, as Paris! The outraged Greek kings are left impotently behind on the shore as the ship sets sail with the happy lovers on board.

Music and Background

A calculated successor to *Orphée aux Enfers*, the score of *La Belle Hélène* is as riotously silly as the story it sets, with parodies of Rossini, Wagner and almost everything sacred to music of the time, but it also introduces a new note of Romanticism, designed to flatter the voice and personality of Hortense Schneider, the celebrated soprano for whom the title role was conceived. The equally celebrated overture was arranged not by Offenbach but by an unknown assistant.

Highlights

Helen's opening air 'Amours divins!'; Paris' 'Au mont Ida' – one of Offenbach's best-known tunes; Helen's sharply witty lament for her fatal beauty, 'Dis-moi Venus'; the love duet 'Oui, c'est un rêve'.

Did You Know?

✍ This whole piece is a thinly-disguised satire on French Second Empire society. Contemporary audiences would have recognised in the game of charades a reference to Napoleon III and his wife Eugénie who were notoriously obsessed with party games.

Recommended Recording

Jessye Norman, John Aler, Capitole de Toulouse Orchestra/Michel Plasson. EMI CDS7 47157-8. Ms Norman being not as grand as you'd expect, and John Aler nicely idiomatic.

Les Contes d'Hoffmann
(The Tales of Hoffmann)

FORM: Opera in a Prologue, three acts and an Epilogue; in French
COMPOSER: Jacques Offenbach (1819–80)
LIBRETTO: Jules Barbier and Michel Carré; after Hoffmann
FIRST PERFORMANCE: Paris, 10 February 1881

Principal Characters

Hoffmann, a poet ～ Tenor
Nicklausse, his friend ～ Mezzo-soprano
Lindorf ～ Baritone
Spalanzani, an inventor ～ Tenor
Dr Coppelius ～ Baritone
Olympia, Spalanzani's 'daughter' ～ Soprano
Antonia ～ Soprano
Crespel, her father, a councillor ～ Baritone
Dr Miracle ～ Baritone
A voice, Antonia's mother ～ Mezzo-soprano
Giulietta, a courtesan ～ Soprano
Schlemil, her admirer ～ Bass
Pittichinaccio, her admirer ～ Tenor
Dapertutto, a magician ～ Baritone
Stella, an opera singer ～ Soprano

Note: The roles of Olympia, Antonia, Giulietta and Stella are often played by the same singer, as are the roles of Lindorf, Dr Coppelius, Dr Miracle and Dapertutto.

Synopsis of the Plot

Setting: The Prologue and Epilogue are set in Nuremberg,
the three acts in Paris, Munich and Venice respectively

PROLOGUE Hoffmann, the poet, joins a lively crowd of students in a beer-cellar close by the opera house, where his beloved, Stella, is performing. The sight of Lindorf, Hoffmann's rival for Stella's affections, turns Hoffmann's thoughts to his past loves, all of which were thwarted by different manifestations of Lindorf, the embodiment of evil.

ACT I Hoffmann is in love with Olympia, 'daughter' of the inventor Spalanzani, in spite of warnings from his friend, Nicklausse, that Spalanzani is obsessed with making lifelike dolls. Dr Coppelius, Spalanzani's rival inventor and the maker of Olympia's eyes, sells Hoffmann a pair of spectacles which make her appear human, and Hoffmann is even more enchanted with her. Spalanzani is very proud of Olympia and arranges a splendid social gathering to introduce her to the public. He dismisses Coppelius' claims for a share of the profits he will make by giving him a cheque which he knows will not be honoured. Olympia is led out to the admiration of all present, especially the love-struck Hoffmann. She sings and plays the harp exquisitely – although she has a tendency to slow down in the middle of a performance, followed by the sound of Spalanzani energetically cranking up a mechanism! But Hoffmann, still besotted, hardly seems to notice and, later, he declares his love for her. They dance together, whirling faster and faster, until Spalanzani stops Olympia with a tap on the shoulder. Hoffmann, dizzy, falls to the ground, smashing his spectacles. Coppelius returns and, in revenge for the worthless cheque, destroys the doll. Hoffmann, appalled, is deluded no longer.

ACT II Hoffmann is in love with Antonia, the frail young daughter of councillor Crespel. Crespel has forbidden Antonia to sing, for singing aggravates her illness and he is afraid she will die of tuberculosis, like her mother. In spite of this, Hoffmann and Antonia are together, singing a love duet, when they hear Crespel approaching and Hoffmann quickly hides. The evil Dr Miracle is announced and, in spite of Crespel's insistence that he leave without treating Antonia, he proves almost impossible to eject – coming back through a wall after leaving by the door. Finally he is forced out, Hoffmann emerges from his hiding place and leaves Antonia, asking her to promise him never to sing again. Instantly Dr Miracle reappears and tells Antonia that she has a wonderful future ahead of her as a singer. Bewildered, she turns to her mother's portrait for comfort, whereupon Miracle brings the painting to life. The portrait urges her to sing and Miracle encourages her by producing a violin which he plays wildly, increasing her excitement until she collapses, dying, when Miracle vanishes.

ACT III Hoffmann is now in love with Giulietta, but she has other admirers, especially Schlemil and Pittichinaccio. Nicklausse warns his friend not to fall for her, but Hoffmann takes no notice and is determined to pursue her. He is observed by the shadowy figure of the evil Dapertutto, who offers Giulietta a large diamond if she will help him take Hoffmann's soul by capturing his reflection in a mirror. Giulietta agrees and tricks Hoffmann into looking in the mirror, after which she leaves him. Hoffmann, confronted with his rival, Schlemil, tries to take the key of Giulietta's room away from him; they fight and Schlemil is killed. Hoffmann retrieves the key and rushes off to Giulietta's room – only to find that she has abandoned him and is floating away in a gondola with Pittichinaccio.

EPILOGUE Hoffmann's tales have come to an end and he is sunk in a gloomy misery, which he attempts to relieve by becoming increasingly drunk. The opera next door is over and Stella appears – on Lindorf's arm. The dejected Hoffmann decides he would do better to devote his life to poetry, rather than to love.

Music and Background

Here, for once, Offenbach was not preoccupied with parodies of other composers but being himself, and the effort taxed him. The score remained unfinished at his death, and although it was completed more or less immediately by a colleague, Ernest Guiraud, the lack of 'authority' has left the score easy prey to adaptation ever since. Try as scholars may, there can be no definitive version – some come with changes of order in the scenes, some with spoken dialogue, some with everything sung – and the different episodes in the story can be hard to hold together in performance. One solution is to have all Hoffmann's loves sung by the same soprano and all his adversaries sung by the same bass. That way you at least get a stronger sense of the piece as a coherent, more directed narrative of the central character's decline and fall.

Highlights

Act I: 'Ah! vivre deux', Hoffmann's song of love for the doll; 'Les oiseaux dans la charmille', Olympia's brilliantly mechanical response. Act II: the celebrated barcarolle, 'Belle nuit, ô nuit d'amour', one of the best-known melodies in all opera; 'Scintille, diamant', Dappertutto's Diamond Aria; 'O Dieu! de quelle ivresse', Hoffmann's declaration of love for Giulietta. Act III: Antonia's 'Elle a fui, la tourterelle'; the duet 'C'est une chanson d'amour'; the trio between Antonia, the ghost and Dr Miracle, 'Chère enfant!'

Did You Know?

🙝 *The Tales of Hoffmann* is Offenbach's only serious opera (he wrote nearly one hundred operettas). He did not live to see it performed.
🙝 The music for 'Scintille, diamant' was lifted from a previous operetta and slotted into a dark moment here. That it fits so well suggests that Offenbach's style in this serious score wasn't so far removed from that of his frivolous ones.
🙝 The barcarolle has been used in advertisements for Bailey's Irish Cream Liqueur.

Recommended Recording

Plácido Domingo, Joan Sutherland, Gabriel Bacquier, Suisse Romande Orchestra/Richard Bonynge. Decca 417 363-2. An award-winning version, beautifully done – with spoken dialogue and a change to the normal order of scenes but still easily the best around.

Orphée aux Enfers
(Orpheus in the Underworld)

FORM: Operetta in four (originally two) acts; in French
COMPOSER: Jacques Offenbach (1819–80)
LIBRETTO: Hector Crémieux and Ludovic Halévy;
after classical mythology
FIRST PERFORMANCE: Paris, 21 October 1858;
revised version Paris, 7 February 1874

Principal Characters

Orpheus, a violinist ❧ Tenor
Eurydice, his wife ❧ Soprano
Public Opinion ❧ Mezzo-soprano
Jupiter, King of the Gods ❧ Baritone
Pluto, God of the Underworld/Aristaeus ❧ Tenor
John Styx, Pluto's servant ❧ Tenor

Synopsis of the Plot

Setting: Classical Greece

ACT I The married Orpheus and Eurydice have reached a stage of mutual
indifference and boredom with each other. Eurydice has gone so far as to
take a lover, Aristaeus, and when Orpheus challenges her, they quarrel.
Eurydice insults her husband's musical ability by saying she has always
loathed his violin playing, and Orpheus responds by announcing he will play
her his new one-and-a-half-hour violin concerto. In addition, he says, he has
filled the cornfield that her lover must cross with poisonous snakes. In trying
to warn the approaching Aristaeus, Eurydice herself is bitten, whereupon
Aristaeus reveals himself to be Pluto, God of the Underworld, and sets off to
his domain with a delighted Eurydice (who thoughtfully leaves an
explanatory note behind for her husband). Orpheus is overjoyed to find she
has gone but is soundly admonished by Public Opinion, who insists he goes
down to Hades to try and get Eurydice back.

ACT II On Mount Olympus, the gods are becoming dissatisfied with
Jupiter's high-handed and hypocritical ways. Pluto arrives, having been
summoned by Jupiter to explain his abduction of a mortal woman. In
defending himself, Pluto is supported by the other gods, whose rebellious
thoughts are now expressed openly. Just then Public Opinion arrives,
bringing Orpheus, who reluctantly requests Eurydice's return. Jupiter orders
Pluto to free her and, to make sure his instructions are carried out, the entire
company of gods decide to descend to Hades themselves.

ACT III Eurydice, guarded by the slow-witted John Styx, is becoming very bored with Hades. When Jupiter arrives, he finds himself quite fascinated by her and turns himself into a fly, so that he can pass through the keyhole. Eurydice plays with the fly and Jupiter allows himself to be caught, whereupon he resumes his god-like form and suggests Eurydice should, under cover of Pluto's forthcoming party, escape with him to Olympus.

ACT IV The party is in full swing but when Jupiter tries to slip away with Eurydice, he is stopped by Pluto, who points out that Orpheus, with Public Opinion, has just arrived in Hades. Jupiter tells Orpheus he can take Eurydice back to the upper world with him on one condition: that she follows behind him and on no account does he look round. Orpheus agrees and they set off; but cunning Jupiter hurls a thunderbolt behind him which shocks Orpheus into turning round. Eurydice stays with the gods, much to everyone's delight – except for the censorious Public Opinion – and they all join in a spirited version of the famous cancan.

Music

This was Offenbach's first full-length operetta, taking advantage of a change to the licence of the Bouffes-Parisiens theatre to allow for larger productions. The objective of its satire was the solemn classicism of the Second Empire Comédie-Française, which took itself and its productions very seriously. The score includes a notorious spoof on 'Che faro senza Euridice', the most famous number in Gluck's *Orfeo*, and an equally notorious moment when a sedate minuet transforms into a wild *galop infernal* – aka the cancan.

Highlights

Act I: 'La femme dont le coeur rêve', Eurydice's song about her new lover, and Orphée's 'Libre! ô bonheur', when he hears his wife is dead. Act II: Mercury's 'Eh hop! Eh hop!', and the exhilarating ensemble of the gods 'Gloire, gloire à Jupiter'. Act III: Eurydice's complaint 'Personne encore!', and the Policemen's Chorus. Act IV: Eurydice's invocation to the God of Wine 'J'ai vu le Dieu Bacchus', and the cancan number 'Ce bal est original'.

Did You Know?

- The famous overture to *Orphée aux Enfers* isn't by Offenbach at all, but cobbled together by one Carl Binder.
- 'Cancan' by Bad Manners was a Top Ten hit in July 1981.

Recommended Recording

Michel Sénéchal, Mady Mesplé, Capitole de Toulouse Orchestra/Michel Plasson. EMI CDS7 49647-2. The full four acts, done with zest.

La Vie Parisienne
(Parisian Life)

FORM: Operetta in five acts (Act IV is frequently omitted); in French
COMPOSER: Jacques Offenbach (1819–80)
LIBRETTO: Henri Meilhac and Ludovic Halévy
FIRST PERFORMANCE: Paris, 31 October 1866

Principal Characters

Raoul de Gardefeu ⁓ Tenor
Bobinet ⁓ Baritone
Métella ⁓ Mezzo-soprano
Joseph, Raoul's former servant ⁓ Spoken role
Baron de Gondremarck, a Swedish tourist ⁓ Baritone
Baroness de Gondremarck, his wife ⁓ Soprano
Brazilian tourist ⁓ Tenor/Baritone?
Gabrielle, a glovemaker ⁓ Soprano
Frick, a bootmaker ⁓ Baritone
Pauline, a chambermaid ⁓ Soprano
Madame de Quimper-Karadec, Bobinet's aunt ⁓ Mezzo-soprano
Madame de Folle-Verdure, her niece ⁓ Soprano

Synopsis of the Plot

Setting: Paris; 1868

ACT I The two young gentlemen-about-town, Raoul and Bobinet, are waiting at the station for the arrival of Métella, a young lady of doubtful reputation for whose affections they are rivals. But when she steps from the train, Métella is escorted by yet another young man and pretends not to know them. Then Raoul sees his former servant, Joseph, who tells them he is now working as a hotel guide and is at the station to meet an aristocratic Swedish couple. Out of curiosity the two young men wait until the tourist train arrives. As soon as he sees the Baroness, Raoul is struck by her beauty, and persuades Joseph to let him take his place as guide.

ACT II The Baron and Baroness are installed in Raoul's own house, which he pretends is a hotel, and the Baron, determined to enjoy himself in Paris, hardly seems to notice Raoul's energetic efforts to be alone with his wife. On their first evening, Raoul throws a party for his guests at which Gabrielle, the glovemaker, masquerades as a colonel's widow and Frick, the bootmaker, as an army major.

ACT III For the second evening of their stay Raoul has arranged a grand party for his guests. Bobinet, in the role of a Swiss admiral, hosts the party at the home of his absent aunt. Pauline, the maid, is delegated to seduce the Baron, leaving Raoul plenty of opportunity to consolidate his efforts to seduce the Baron's wife, whom he plans to entertain, alone, at his own house. Fuelled by copious quantities of alcohol, the party becomes more and more frantic, culminating in a wild cancan.

ACT IV Raoul and the Baroness are enjoying an intimate supper at his home when they are interrupted by Bobinet's aunt who, having returned unexpectedly to Paris, has found her own house apparently taken over by a disreputable crowd. Her niece, Madame de Folle-Verdure, has advised her aunt to stay that night at the 'hotel' where her friend, the Swedish Baroness, is currently staying. Raoul has no choice but to give Madame de Quimper-Karadec the Baron's room – with predictable consequences when he returns, very merry, from the party.

ACT V A rich Brazilian tourist is throwing a splendid masked ball at the Hôtel Anglais to which, it seems, the entire Parisian demi-monde has been invited. Total confusion reigns for most of the evening but, eventually, Métella is reunited with Raoul, the Baron with the Baroness and the Brazilian millionaire finds true love in the arms of Gabrielle, the glovemaker, much to her delight.

Music and Background

This was written as a contemporary farce, to coincide with prospective excitement about the World Exhibition which was to open in Paris the year after the premiere. Musically it's not so modern and falls back on familiar routines, although with a generally plainer vocal style forced on Offenbach by the fact that his original cast were actors rather than singers. The best music tends to come in the dance tunes.

Highlights

Bobinet's party in Act III, with its riotous conclusion 'Soupons, soupons, c'est le moment'. The Brazilian's party in the final act, with its concluding resolution 'Célébrons Paris'.

Did You Know?

The two party scenes were influential on Johann Strauss' later *Die Fledermaus*.

Recommended Recording

Régine Crespin, Mady Mesplé, Capitole de Toulouse Orchestra/Michel Plasson. EMI CDS7 47154-8. Classic casting, brilliant fizz.

Francis Poulenc
(1899–1963)

Les Mamelles de Tirésias (1944)
Les Dialogues des Carmélites (1953)
La Voix Humaine (1959)

One of the group of French composers known as 'Les Six', Poulenc had a privileged background (thanks to the family company Rhône-Poulenc) and led a largely charmed life as part of the inter-war salon circuit of Paris. Much of his music, especially the songs (of which there are many), could be described as salon chic: possessed of a sophisticated elegance that some listeners find an alternative to substance. But personal tragedy (the horrific death of a close friend) and the experience of wartime Occupation left deep marks on the composer and his work, resulting in a rediscovery of faith and a considerable output of religious music. *Les Mamelles de Tirésias* (*The Breasts of Tiresias*) is at face value a surreal farce, but embracing an undercurrent of patriotism and despair at the fall of France to the Germans. *Les Dialogues des Carmélites* is a profound examination of human weakness which, despite its historical setting at the time of the French Revolution, speaks for more recent events and with autobiographical authority.

Les Dialogues des Carmélites
(Dialogues of the Carmelites)

FORM: Opera in three acts; in French
COMPOSER: Francis Poulenc (1899–1963)
LIBRETTO: Francis Poulenc; after Georges Bernanos
FIRST PERFORMANCE: Milan, 26 January 1957 (in Italian)

Principal Characters

Blanche de la Force, an aristocrat ∞ **Soprano**
The Chevalier de la Force, her brother ∞ **Tenor**
Madame de Croissy, the prioress ∞ **Contralto**
Mother Marie of the Incarnation of God, assistant prioress
∞ **Mezzo-soprano**
Sister Constance, a young nun ∞ **Soprano**
Father Confessor ∞ **Tenor**

Synopsis of the Plot

Setting: Carmelite convents in Compiègne and Paris
during the French Revolution, 1789–94

ACT I The Revolution has started and the atmosphere is one of tension and anxiety for the future of France. Blanche de la Force, who is nervous and easily frightened, resolves to become a Carmelite nun. She is accepted into the convent as a novice, but the prioress warns her that the convent is not an escape from the world outside – indeed it depends on its members to protect it from danger. Soon after she is admitted, Blanche is unnerved by Sister Constance, who tells her of a vision she had in which she saw herself and Blanche dying young together. A further shock comes with the death of the ageing prioress, who approaches her end in some anguish, seeing visions of desecration and ruin.

ACT II Blanche is left alone with the prioress' body, but she is suddenly assailed by nameless fears and runs out of the room, to be restrained by Mother Marie. Later, taking flowers to the grave, Blanche discusses the manner of the prioress' death with Constance: perhaps, she suggests, we die not for ourselves but for others; the prioress may have got the 'wrong' death, the death of a 'bad' person instead of her own death as a 'good person' – much as we may be given someone else's cloakroom ticket by mistake. By now the Revolution has entered the period of the Terror, especially dangerous for an aristocrat and nun such as Blanche. The priesthood has been proscribed and the nuns are ordered to leave the convent.

ACT III The convent has been destroyed. Mother Marie gathers the nuns together and suggests that they take a secret vote, to commit themselves to a vow of martyrdom. Blanche is the only nun to vote against, but she is saved from humiliation by Constance, who declares that the vote was hers, and she has now changed her mind. Preparations are made for each nun to make her vow, but Blanche, unable to accept the consequences of the decision, runs away. Later, living as a servant in her ruined home, her father guillotined, Blanche receives a visit from Mother Marie who tells her that she may have saved her life, but not her soul. When Blanche learns that the Carmelites have been imprisoned and are to be executed, she goes to Paris and mingles with the spectators round the guillotine. As the nuns calmly file past, one by one, Blanche emerges from the crowd and takes her place beside Constance, serenely accepting her death.

Music and Background

In a sense this is an opera in celebration of opera, with music that consciously looks back to precedents in Debussy, Monteverdi, Verdi and Musorgsky: four composers who are all named as dedicatees on the score. With such an overwhelmingly female cast there was a risk that the singing roles wouldn't provide enough variety to the ear, but Poulenc invents for each soloist a distinctive musical character and pitch-range so the audience can tell one nun from another without too much trouble. It is also a profoundly religious opera about the spiritual conquest of fear, with Renaissance church music never far from the parameters of the score, and taking centre-stage finally as the nuns process with a serene determination to their deaths singing the 'Salve Regina'.

Highlights

The opening, with its jagged and recurring motif, and the uncomfortably veristic Death Scene of the old prioress at the end of Act I. The procession to the scaffold at the end of Act III – one of the most bizarrely affecting conclusions in all opera, as the music is repeatedly punctuated by the thud of the guillotine-blade and the nuns go, one by one, to their deaths.

Did You Know?

~ The title *Les Dialogues des Carmélites* is a product of the complicated pre-history of this opera. At one stage, the material that became Poulenc's libretto was worked into a film-script, then a play.

~ The story of the Compiègne Carmelite nuns was told by Mother Marie of the Incarnation of God, who survived the Terror and the Revolution; her testimony led to the beatification of the nuns in 1906.

Recommended Recording

Catherine Dubosc, Rita Gorr, Rachel Yakar, José van Dam, Lyon Opera/ Kent Nagano. Virgin VCD7 59227-2. The first on the market for a long while, and vividly dramatic.

La Voix Humaine
(The Human Voice)

FORM: Opera in one act; in French
COMPOSER: Francis Poulenc (1899–1963)

LIBRETTO: Jean Cocteau
FIRST PERFORMANCE: Paris, 6 February, 1959

Principal Character
The Woman ～ Soprano

Synopsis of the Plot
Setting: The present

The Woman lies on a bed; she rises and goes to the door, but the telephone rings and she turns back. It is a wrong number, but soon the telephone rings again and this time it is her former lover, who has rejected her. For the following forty minutes we witness her conversation – punctuated by the crossed lines, interruptions, breakdowns and wrong numbers of an embryonic telephone system (Cocteau's play, on which he based the libretto, was written in 1928). These mechanical problems of communication are echoed in the monologue, in which the Woman reveals her desperate longings, frustrations, fears, hopes and jealousies. She is by turns self-pitying, sentimental, accusatory and wheedling, but the real truth, that the affair is over and she can no longer communicate with her lover in any meaningful way, is too devastating for her to accept. Finally, inevitably, the conversation is over; the line is dead. The Woman winds the telephone cord around her neck and lies on the bed, holding the receiver close to her and whispering 'I love you'.

Music and Background

Although the one and only character here – identified as 'Elle' – is female, there is a strong element of autobiography at work. The despair and panic-driven self-degradation of unrequited love was something Poulenc knew from personal experience, and he described the piece as 'a sort of musical confession' in which the protagonist was 'more or less myself'. Lasting only forty minutes and scored for full orchestra against the solo voice, it's an extravagant conception but justified by a soprano of dramatic virtuosity, able to project charisma out of pathos.

Did You Know?

～ At the time of writing people joked that Poulenc had written *La Voix Humaine* for the tempestuous Maria Callas so she wouldn't have to share the stage with anyone. It wasn't true.

Recommended Recording

Carole Farley, Adelaide Symphony Orchestra/José Serebrier. Chandos 8331. An American singer but with good French and a sense of theatre.

Sergei Prokofiev
(1891–1953)

Maddelena (1911)
The Gambler (1917)
The Love for Three Oranges (1919)
The Fiery Angel (1923)
Semyon Kotko (1939)
Betrothal in a Monastery (1941)
War and Peace (1943)
The Story of a Real Man (1948)

Prokofiev was one of the supreme all-round composers of the 20th century, with a huge output that embraced symphonies (seven), piano concertos (five), chamber music (especially for his own instrument: he was a virtuoso pianist), choral works, film scores and ballets. In almost every genre he produced a masterpiece, and reached vast audiences with scores like *Peter and the Wolf* and *Lieutenant Kijé*, which count among the most approachable of modern classics. But the operas have had a harder time establishing themselves. They were always a priority in his output – he is known to have worked on five (!) while he was still studying in St Petersburg – but nothing was actually completed until *The Gambler*, which didn't reach the stage until years later. Leaving Russia in 1918, he went to America where he wrote *The Love for Three Oranges* (a success, albeit with a delayed premiere) and *The Fiery Angel* (never staged in his lifetime). Returning home in the mid-1930s with an over-optimistic idealism about what he would find there under the Soviet system, he encountered new problems. *Semyon Kotko*, an attempt at popular patriotism, failed; *War and Peace* was never staged in his lifetime; and *The Story of a Real Man* was proscribed by the Soviet authorities after only one performance. By grim coincidence Prokofiev died on the same day as Stalin.

The Fiery Angel

FORM: Opera in five acts; in Russian
COMPOSER: Sergei Prokofiev (1891–1953)
LIBRETTO: Sergei Prokofiev; after Bryusov
FIRST PERFORMANCE: (Concert) Paris, 25 November 1954;
(Stage) Venice, 14 September 1955.

Principal Characters

Ruprecht, a knight ↷ **Baritone**
Renata ↷ **Soprano**
The Landlady ↷ **Mezzo-soprano**
Agrippa von Nettesheim, a philosopher ↷ **Tenor**
Mephistopheles ↷ **Tenor**
Faust ↷ **Baritone**
The Inquisitor ↷ **Bass**
Count Heinrich, Renata's former lover ↷ **Silent role**

Synopsis of the Plot

Setting: Germany; 16th century

ACT I Ruprecht is staying at an inn and has gone to his room for the night, when he is suddenly startled by hysterical and disturbing noises from the next room. He forces the door and sees Renata who, distraught and terrified, begs him to defend her from an unseen attacker. When her fear subsides, Renata tells Ruprecht of Madiel, the beautiful angel, surrounded by flames, who appeared to her constantly as she was growing up. Just as she was reaching the age of sexual maturity, however, the angel left her, after promising to return to her in human form. For a year she lived happily with Count Heinrich, the lover she believed to be a human incarnation of Madiel, but he left her and she is now trying to find him. At this point the landlady, disturbed by the commotion, interrupts them, telling Renata she is a witch and a troublemaker and ordering her to leave the inn. Ruprecht, immensely attracted to the lovely woman, leaves with her.

ACT II Renata and Ruprecht are in Cologne, obsessively searching for Heinrich, but they have found nothing. In despair they turn to magic, reading books and casting spells, but even Ruprecht's visit to the greatest proponent of the black arts, the philosopher Agrippa, produces nothing.

ACT III While Ruprecht is consulting Agrippa, Renata has found Heinrich, but he has rejected her, claiming she is possessed by the devil. On Ruprecht's return, Renata asserts that she was altogether mistaken about Heinrich, he was never the incarnation of Madiel; she persuades Ruprecht that she now loves only him and that he should avenge her by duelling with

Heinrich and killing him. Ruprecht, who is besotted with her, agrees to her demands, but when Renata sees the two men at a window, Heinrich is once more transformed into the fiery angel in her eyes and she orders Ruprecht not to harm him. The duel takes place, Ruprecht is badly injured and, overwhelmed by remorse, Renata promises to take care of him.

ACT IV Renata and Ruprecht, by now much recovered from his wounds, are in a garden beside an inn. Renata tells Ruprecht that she has decided to enter a convent and when Ruprecht protests, she threatens suicide, turning to attack him when he intervenes. They are observed by Faust and Mephistopheles, who befriend Ruprecht and arrange to meet him the next day.

ACT V Renata is now a nun, but she has disturbed the convent with her feverish visions and obsessions, unleashing a pervasive feeling of evil. She is questioned by the Inquisitor in an atmosphere of increasing hysteria which eventually rises to frenzied delirium. The Inquisitor tries to exorcise the evil but fails and, as Ruprecht and Mephistopheles look triumphantly on the scene, denounces Renata as a heretic and sentences her to torture and death.

Music and Background

The writing of this opera was a protracted and difficult process tied to premieres that were planned but didn't materialise. It was never staged in the composer's lifetime. In the original text it is not clear whether Renata's visions are genuine or hallucinatory. In the opera everything is seen through her eyes, so doubt is eliminated. The central role is formidable in the demands it makes for persistent hysterical display at high volume. Opinions of the opera's musical stature vary: it isn't comfortable listening, but it certainly has impact, and a vividly coloured orchestral score.

Highlights

The Act III duet between Renata and Ruprecht is an attractive and richly-textured piece of writing; and the recurring theme associated with Renata and Madiel has a soaring memorability.

Did You Know?

After failing to obtain a performance for *The Fiery Angel*, Prokofiev reworked some of the music into his Third Symphony.

Recommended Recording

Galina Gorchakova, Sergei Leiferkus, Kirov Opera/Valery Gergiev. Philips 446 078-2PH2. A highly-charged performance, captured live and kicking at the Kirov.

The Love for Three Oranges

FORM: Opera in a Prologue and four acts; in Russian
COMPOSER: Sergei Prokofiev (1891–1953)
LIBRETTO: Sergei Prokofiev; after Gozzi
FIRST PERFORMANCE: Chicago, 30 December 1921 (in French)

Principal Characters

King of Clubs ∼ Bass
The Prince ∼ Tenor
Clarissa ∼ Contralto
Leander, Prime Minister and King of Spades ∼ Baritone
Truffaldino, the jester ∼ Tenor
Pantaloon, the King of Clubs' adviser ∼ Baritone
Tchelio, a wizard and the King of Clubs' protector ∼ Bass
Fata Morgana, a witch and Leander's protector ∼ Soprano
Princess Linetta ∼ Contralto
Princess Nicoletta ∼ Mezzo-soprano
Princess Ninetta ∼ Soprano
Farfarello, a devil ∼ Bass
Smeraldina, a black slave girl ∼ Mezzo-soprano

Synopsis of the Plot

Setting: An imaginary kingdom in which the inhabitants
are dressed as playing cards

PROLOGUE The advocates of various forms of theatre – tragedy, comedy and lyric drama – are arguing about the relative merits of their favourite form, when they are interrupted by the Chorus who announce the beginning of the performance.

ACT I The King of Clubs fears that his son, the Prince, will die unless he can be made to laugh, and the throne will be inherited by the king's niece, the much-disliked Clarissa. The king orders Leander to organise an elaborate programme of parties and comedy shows, but Leander is secretly plotting to secure the throne for himself and Clarissa, and is determined that the Prince will not recover. The scene changes to a symbolic card game in which Fata Morgana, the protector of Leander (as King of Spades) plays against Tchelio, the King of Clubs' protector. To the dismay of the Chorus, Tchelio loses all three games. Meanwhile, Leander and Clarissa are discussing ways to increase the Prince's depression, and Leander decides that filling the Prince with tragic verse will produce the best results.

ACT II Truffaldino, the jester, tries to make the Prince laugh, but instead he vomits the tragic verse fed to him by Leander. Persuaded to attend the comic entertainments provided for him, the Prince remains unamused until Fata Morgana, who is observing the proceedings disguised as an old woman, falls over with her legs in the air. The Prince roars with laughter, but the enraged witch puts a curse on him, condemning him to fall in love with three oranges which he will follow to the ends of the earth. The curse works instantly; the Prince and Truffaldino set off together, propelled on their way by a blast of air from the devil Farfarello's enormous bellows.

ACT III Tchelio intervenes to help the Prince and persuades Farfarello to blow the two wanderers into the kitchen of the witch Creonta, where they will find the oranges. He gives the Prince a magic ribbon to distract the cook and warns him that the oranges must only be opened near water. The Prince and Truffaldino secure the oranges, but they soon grow to an enormous size. Exhausted with carrying them, the two men lie down in the desert to rest. But Truffaldino is too thirsty to sleep; he cuts open one of the oranges and the beautiful Princess Linetta steps out, calling for water. Hoping to find juice, Truffaldino cuts open the second orange; the lovely Nicoletta emerges, again calling for water. The princesses collapse and Truffaldino runs away. The Prince now wakes, sees the dead bodies (which are conveniently taken away for burial by some passing soldiers) and, equally regardless of Tchelio's warning, cuts open the third orange. Out steps Ninetta and the two fall in love. She is about to share the fate of her predecessors when the Chorus intervene with a welcome bucket of water. The Prince leaves Ninetta to arrange for her reception at the palace. But Fata Morgana is not so easily beaten: bringing Smeraldina with her, she transforms Ninetta into a rat and Smeraldina takes her place. The Prince and the court return and, much to the Prince's dismay, Smeraldina proclaims herself the princess and the king insists that the Prince marries her.

ACT IV Tchelio and Fata Morgana are quarrelling and each accuses the other of cheating. The Chorus decide to take action and push Fata Morgana off the stage and lock her up. The King and his court arrive back at the palace to find a large rat sitting on the throne. The soldiers fire at it but Tchelio, realizing that it is Ninetta, manages to stop them and return her to her normal form. The Prince is overjoyed; Leander, Clarissa and Smeraldina are sentenced to hang but Fata Morgana reappears and opens a trapdoor down which all four of them disappear. The court celebrates the new prince and princess.

Music and Background

The Love for Three Oranges is a parody of traditional 'quest' fairy-stories taken to deliberately unrealistic extremes – and in the process positioning itself in the front line of modernism. The way the squabbling chorus break into the action, exposing it as nothing more than artifice, prefigures the experimental techniques of much later dramatists. Otherwise, the opera's humour is a mixture of traditional Italian commedia dell'arte (Carlo Gozzi,

273

the originator of the story, was an 18th-century Venetian playwright) and Russian absurdism in the spirit of Gogol. The vocal style is declamatory with not much to linger in the mind, but the orchestral writing is superb – which is why the most celebrated sections of the score, organised by Prokofiev into a free-standing concert suite, are sections where nobody sings. This is entirely appropriate for an opera the tone of which is all ironic detachment.

Highlights

Act I: the card game between Tchelio and Fata Morgana. Act II: the famous orchestral march. Act III: the entr'acte Scherzo which plays as Truffaldino and the Prince are blown on their continuing journey, and the discovery of the princesses in the desert.

Recommended Recording

Gabriel Bacquier, Jean-Luc Viala, Lyon Opera/Kent Nagano. Virgin VCD 791084-2. Sung in French, with no real stars but a genuine sense of company effort – which is the right approach to this piece.

War and Peace

FORM: Opera in two parts, comprising an Epigraph
and thirteen scenes; in Russian
COMPOSER: Sergei Prokofiev (1891–1953)
LIBRETTO: Sergei Prokofiev and Mira Mendelson-Prokofieva;
after Tolstoy
FIRST PERFORMANCE: Leningrad, 12 June 1946 (first 8 scenes only);
Moscow, 8 November 1957 (13 scenes)

Principal Characters

Prince Andrei Bolkonsky ❧ Baritone
Natalya (Natasha) Rostova ❧ Soprano
Sonya, her cousin ❧ Mezzo-soprano
Hélène Bezukhova ❧ Mezzo-soprano
Prince Anatol Kuragin, her brother ❧ Tenor
Dolokhov, an officer and Kuragin's friend ❧ Baritone
Count Pyotr Bezukhov ❧ Tenor
Field Marshal Prince Mikhail Kutuzov ❧ Bass
Napoleon Bonaparte ❧ Baritone

Synopsis of the Plot

Setting: Russia; 1809–12

PART ONE Peace

EPIGRAPH The Russian people reassert their determination to repel invaders and defeat their enemies.

SCENE 1 Spring 1809. Prince Andrei Bolkonsky, recently widowed, is visiting his friends, the Rostovs, at their country home. He overhears Natasha singing of the beauty of the spring and finds his spirits much lifted by her optimism.

SCENE 2 New Year's Eve 1810. Andrei meets Natasha Rostov again at a grand ball in Moscow. They talk and dance together and begin to fall in love, but Natasha has also caught the eye of the dissolute Anatol Kuragin.

SCENE 3 February 1812. Andrei and Natasha wish to become engaged, but old Prince Bolkonsky refuses to allow it, saying that Natasha's social standing is unacceptably low for his son. He forces Andrei to spend a year away in the army.

SCENE 4 May 1812. Natasha and her cousin, Sonya, are attending a fashionable ball, given by Hélène Bezukhova, Anatol Kuragin's sister. Hélène contrives to leave Natasha alone with Anatol, who declares that he is passionately in love with her. Natasha is clearly flattered by his attention, although she is warned by Sonya that he is not a man to be trusted.

SCENE 5 June 1812. Anatol has persuaded Natasha to elope with him and is about to leave home for their assignation. His friend, Dolokhov, warns him of the risk he is taking (Anatol is already married), but he ignores his friend and, picking up the fur coat he had previously given to his mistress, leaves for Natasha's house.

SCENE 6 Sonya has betrayed Natasha and the whole household lies in wait for Anatol to arrive. But he grasps the situation immediately and escapes before he can be caught. Natasha, told that he is already married, collapses in tears and appeals to Count Bezukhov, Anatol's brother-in-law, to beg Andrei to forgive her.

SCENE 7 The count goes home and, disgusted with Anatol's behaviour, orders him to hand over any letters he has received from Natasha and leave Moscow immediately. News arrives that Napoleon and his army have crossed the border into Russian territory.

PART TWO War

SCENE 8 August 1812. Andrei is at the battlefront, hoping to forget Natasha. He rejects Field Marshal Kutuzov's suggestion that he join his staff at headquarters, preferring to stay and fight. A shot is fired and the Battle of Borodino begins.

SCENE 9 In the French camp, Napoleon is disturbed by news of the Russian army's courage and resilience.

SCENE 10 Two days have passed and the Russians have lost at Borodino. The Russian generals meet for a council of war: should they defend Moscow and risk the entire army, or retreat and regroup to fight again? Kutuzov decides that they will abandon Moscow to the French.

SCENE 11 The French march into Moscow to find that much of it has been set on fire by its residents, most of whom have disappeared into the countryside. Bezukhov joins a small group of Muscovites complaining about French looting, and he learns that Natasha and her family have escaped, taking with them some wounded prisoners, including Andrei (as yet unrecognised by Natasha).

SCENE 12 Andrei lies on a bed in a peasant's hut, sick with fever and longing to see Natasha again. She comes to him, begs his forgiveness and they reaffirm their love for each other before Andrei dies.

SCENE 13 November 1812. The Russian winter has defeated the French and a small number of troops, with their prisoners, are straggling away from Moscow in a blizzard. They are attacked by partisans and the prisoners released, among whom is Bezukhov. Field Marshal Kutuzov congratulates the Russians and the people reassert their belief in their sovereignty.

Music and Background

By any measure this is epic opera and stands in the tradition of the great historic-tableaux works of Glinka and Musorgsky. It deliberately inflates the personal drama at the heart of Tolstoy's novel with heroic-patriotic scenes of heart-on-sleeve emotion, designed to give the opera popular appeal and win over the Soviet authorities. In that respect it failed, but it remains one of the great operas of the 20th century. With big tunes, spirited dances and grand chorus numbers, it follows the hard act of its literary original in ways that balance the straightforwardness of 'people's opera' against the subtlety and sophistication of high art.

Highlights

Natasha's waltz theme, first heard as she dances with Andrei in Scene 2. Kutuzov's great hymn to Moscow in Scene 10. The intense Scene 12 where the sound of the blood pounding in Andrei's ears is supplied by an offstage chorus singing 'piti-piti-piti'.

Recommended Recording

Lajos Miller, Galina Vishnevskaya, Nikola Ghuiselev, French National Orchestra/Mstislav Rostropovich. Erato 2292 45331-2. High-impact performances from all concerned.

Giacomo Puccini
(1858–1924)

Le Villi (1883)
Edgar (1888)
Manon Lescaut (1892)
La Bohème (1895)
Tosca (1899)
Madama Butterfly (1903)
La Fanciulla del West (1910)
La Rondine (1916)
Il Trittico (1918)
Turandot (1924)

The greatest composer of Italian opera after Rossini and Verdi, Puccini is also (arguably) the most popular opera composer of all time – although the features of his work that *make* him popular haven't always won him critical esteem. Never quite achieving the 'respectability' of his predecessors, his music gets condemned for its sensationalism and his theatre for its opportunism: a cynical manipulation of the audience's emotions. But few composers could rival his understanding of what works on stage, and fewer still could match his gift for melody. Born in Lucca, he was raised on church music but began dabbling in opera as a student in Milan. After two early scores that can effectively be discounted as juvenilia – *Le Villi* and *Edgar* – he found his feet with *Manon Lescaut*, which was the first in a series of highly successful collaborations with the librettist partnership Luigi Illica and Giuseppe Giacosa. *La Bohème*, *Tosca* and *Madama Butterfly* followed in regular but not especially rapid succession (Puccini liked to enjoy himself as well as work), and they shared not only librettists but a fondness for saturating the plot and, to some extent, the music in the atmospheric colours of a specific location. *La Fanciulla del West* used different librettists but still opted for local colour, in a tale of singing cowboys that probably counts as the original spaghetti western. Puccini's problem, though, was that his work didn't develop. Essentially conservative, it showed signs of growing stale in *La Rondine*, an Italian take on Viennese operetta, and the three one-act operas – *Il Tabarro*, *Suor Angelica* and *Gianni Schicchi* – known collectively as *Il Trittico*. When he died – ironically, of throat cancer – in 1924, *Turandot* was left unfinished.

La Bohème
(The Bohemian Life)

FORM: Opera in four acts; in Italian
COMPOSER: Giacomo Puccini (1858–1924)
LIBRETTO: Giuseppe Giacosa and Luigi Illica; after Murger
FIRST PERFORMANCE: Turin, 1 February 1896

Principal Characters

Rodolfo, a poet ~ **Tenor**
Marcello, a painter ~ **Baritone**
Colline, a philosopher ~ **Bass**
Schaunard, a musician ~ **Baritone**
Mimì, a seamstress ~ **Soprano**
Musetta, a young woman ~ **Soprano**
Alcindoro, Musetta's rich admirer ~ **Bass**

Synopsis of the Plot
Setting: Paris; 1830s

ACT I It is Christmas Eve and the young artists decide to leave their freezing garret and go out to the nearby Café Momus to celebrate, leaving Rodolfo behind to finish an article he is writing. As he is working, Mimì, his young neighbour, timidly knocks at the door and asks for a light for her candle, which has gone out on the stairs. Rodolfo is instantly taken with her and does all he can to prolong her stay, telling her about his hopes and dreams, to which Mimì responds with her own story. They are interrupted by Rodolfo's friends, impatiently calling him from the street. Standing by the window, Mimì is caught in the moonlight and Rodolfo is completely overcome by her fragile beauty. Together they make their way downstairs.

ACT II The street outside is full of the hustle and bustle of Christmas time. Rodolfo buys Mimì a bonnet and they join the others at the café. The arrival of the vibrant Musetta, Marcello's former lover, on the arm of her rich admirer, Alcindoro, causes a sensation. Marcello pretends to ignore Musetta but when she sends Alcindoro away on an errand, the two fall into each other's arms. The party is still in full swing when the bill arrives – but Musetta decides that Alcindoro shall pay and the young Bohemians disappear into the crowd.

ACT III On a bleak February day Mimì, wracked by a terrible, consumptive cough, comes to find Marcello at the inn where he is living with Musetta. Marcello encourages her to come in, but she refuses, as she knows Rodolfo is there. Mimì tells Marcello she is tormented by Rodolfo's unreasonable jealousy and there is no future for them. When Rodolfo himself comes out, Mimì hides, and hears him tell Marcello that Mimì is a flirt and they would be better off apart. But then he admits that he is very worried about her failing health which is not helped by their life in the garret. An attack of tearful coughing gives Mimì's presence away and, as Marcello rushes back to the inn to stop Musetta flirting, Rodolfo and Mimì sing sadly of their love and agree to stay together until the spring.

ACT IV Some time has passed and the young artists are indulging in a bout of friendly horseplay when Musetta arrives at the garret to tell them that Mimì is desperately ill and dying; she is waiting outside and asks that she be allowed to return to the place where she was once so happy. They all do what they can to make her comfortable, even pawning their belongings, including Colline's overcoat, to buy medicine and a muff. It is not long, however, before she peacefully drifts away from them, leaving Rodolfo inconsolable.

Music and Background

One of the most frequently performed of all operas, *La Bohème* is a more sophisticated example of the everyday verismo theatre-formula established by *Cavalleria Rusticana* and *I Pagliacci*: sentimental, but with a lightness of touch that keeps the music moving, buoyant and bright. The melodies may be long but the pace is generally fast, leaving the sense of something busily compact and flowing seamlessly to its conclusion. All four acts are over and done with in under two hours; and to understand how deftly Puccini deals with the story, such as it is, you only have to compare the treatment of exactly the same subject that Leoncavallo was working on at the same time. Leoncavallo, in fact, claimed to have originated the idea and litigation ensued. But his version, which reached the stage a year after Puccini's, was clumsier, bulkier, and never made it into repertory.

Highlights

In Act I: the sequence of Rodolfo's 'Che gelida manina' ('Your tiny hand is frozen'), Mimì's 'Mi chiamano Mimì' and their combined 'O soave fanciulla' makes probably the most celebrated love scene in all opera. Musetta's waltz in the Café Momus is the great set-piece of Act II. And the entire Act IV Death Scene is disarmingly effective, with Rodolfo's final cries of 'Mimì, Mimì' guaranteed to be accompanied by stifled sobs from the auditorium in any half-decent performance.

Recommended Recording

Mirella Freni, Luciano Pavarotti, Elizabeth Harwood, Berlin Philharmonic Orchestra/Herbert von Karajan. Decca 421 049-2. Superb performances given time to make their point by Karajan and unbeatable by any other version except EMI's with Beecham and de los Angeles – but that was made in 1956 and is only available on mono discs.

La Fanciulla del West
(The Girl of the Golden West)

FORM: Opera in three acts; in Italian
COMPOSER: Giacomo Puccini (1858–1924)
LIBRETTO: Guelfo Civinini and Carlo Zangarini; after Belasco
FIRST PERFORMANCE: New York, 10 December 1910

Principal Characters

Minnie, owner of the Polka Bar ❧ **Soprano**
Dick Johnson/Ramerrez, a bandit ❧ **Tenor**
Sid, a miner ❧ **Baritone**
Jack Rance, the sheriff ❧ **Baritone**
Ashby, the Wells Fargo agent ❧ **Bass**

Synopsis of the Plot

Setting: A Californian mining camp in the gold rush of 1849–50

ACT I The miners are enjoying an evening at the Polka Bar, playing cards and drinking. Sid, caught cheating, is swiftly ejected and Ashby, the Wells Fargo agent, tells the men about Ramerrez, the bandit for whose capture his company has offered a $5,000 reward. All heads turn on the entrance of Minnie and the men quieten down and listen as she reads to them from the Bible. Jack Rance declares his love for Minnie, but he is already married and Minnie rejects him, saying she hopes to find the kind of true love her parents knew. When a stranger, calling himself Dick Johnson, arrives, Minnie and he recognise each other from the past. As the men go out to look for Ramerrez, the two are left alone and it soon becomes clear that they are falling in love with each other.

ACT II Minnie is in her cabin, excitedly waiting for Dick to arrive. They eat supper, talk together of Minnie's life in the mountains and Dick is completely enchanted with her, kissing her passionately. But as he goes to leave they discover that a heavy snowfall has trapped them and Minnie agrees to let him stay the night. As Dick goes to the bedroom, Rance bursts in, telling Minnie that Johnson is, in fact, the bandit Ramerrez. After he goes, Minnie confronts Dick with the accusation, which he does not deny, and she orders him to leave. Moments after the door closes behind him shots ring out and, unable to stop herself, Minnie opens the door and helps the wounded Dick back inside the cabin. She tends his wounds and hides him in the loft. Rance returns, searching for Dick, whose hiding place is revealed by drops of blood falling on Rance's hand. In desperation, Minnie urges Rance to play poker with her: if she wins, Dick goes free; if she loses, Rance wins both Dick and Minnie. Rance agrees; they play and Minnie wins, her cheating unnoticed by Rance.

ACT III Dick has been caught in the forest and the miners are about to hang him. Minnie rushes in and begs for his life, citing all the kindnesses she has done for the miners in the past. Finally they capitulate and Minnie and Dick leave for a new life.

Music and Background

The original spaghetti western, *La Fanciulla del West* is another of Puccini's voyages to what, for a European in the early years of this century, would have been an exotic world. Creakily melodramatic in places and awkward to stage, it nonetheless has a spectacular potential that you hear as well as see. Without heavy reliance on Americanisms (beyond fragments of Camptown Races and saloon bar dialogue that always sounds absurd when sung by non-Italians in Italian accents), the music has a Big Country grandeur that could almost have come out of a Hollywood studio, had such things existed at the time. Harmonically and colouristically, it is one of Puccini's more adventurous scores and makes use of special effects – notably the wind machine that whips into action when the weather invades the plot.

Highlights

Act I: the impressively falling orchestral figure that accompanies Minnie's entrance – a grand moment in a good production – and Minnie's waltz, which grows from an accordion tune into a full-scale show-stopper. Act III: Johnson's big aria, 'Ch'ella mi creda' and the final ensemble 'Et tu mio trin'.

Did You Know?

🕭 The show-stopping qualities of Minnie's waltz were not lost on Andrew Lloyd Webber, whose big tune from *The Phantom of the Opera* accordingly sounds very familiar.
🕭 This is perhaps the only opera in which the composer stipulates a horse on stage!

Recommended Recording

Renata Tebaldi, Mario del Monaco, St Cecilia Academy/Franco Capuana. Decca 421 595-2. An oldie, from 1958, but beautifully remastered and with sumptuous voices.

Madama Butterfly

FORM: Opera in three acts; in Italian
COMPOSER: Giacomo Puccini (1858–1924)
LIBRETTO: Giuseppe Giacosa and Luigi Illica; after Belasco
FIRST PERFORMANCE: Milan, 17 February 1904

Principal Characters

Cio-Cio San (Butterfly) ✧ Soprano
F.B. Pinkerton, lieutenant in the US Navy ✧ Tenor
Suzuki, Butterfly's servant ✧ Mezzo-soprano
Sharpless, US consul in Nagasaki ✧ Baritone
Goro, a marriage broker ✧ Tenor
Kate Pinkerton, Pinkerton's American wife ✧ Mezzo-soprano

Synopsis of the Plot

Setting: Nagasaki; early 1900s

ACT I Pinkerton has arranged with Goro to go through a spurious marriage ceremony with a fifteen-year-old geisha, Butterfly, and has leased a house for them overlooking Nagasaki. Sharpless, who knows Pinkerton's motives to be purely those of self-interest, attempts to dissuade his friend from going ahead with the marriage, but fails. Butterfly, on the other hand, is very much in love with Pinkerton, and has even renounced her religion to be with him, an act which alienates her from her family. The ceremony over, the couple celebrate their love.

ACT II It is three years later. Pinkerton has long since sailed away and Butterfly is the mother of his son, Trouble. Butterfly and Suzuki live in extreme poverty and are virtually friendless, but Butterfly still believes that Pinkerton will return to her. This confidence seems to be well founded when Sharpless returns one day to tell her that Pinkerton's arrival is imminent. But what he cannot bring himself to tell her is that Pinkerton is accompanied by his American wife. Butterfly and Suzuki joyfully decorate the house and wait all night for Pinkerton's arrival.

ACT III The next morning Pinkerton arrives with Kate. Overcome with shame and remorse, he quickly departs, leaving Kate to deal with the situation. Butterfly, shocked and demoralised, is persuaded to allow Trouble to return to America with Pinkerton and Kate, on condition that Pinkerton collects the boy himself. She hides and watches as the man she still loves takes away their son, then stabs herself to death.

Music and Background

This is an opera where East meets West, and not entirely comfortably. Puccini's idea of orientalism was appropriate to its time but seems, in retrospect, not far removed from that of Gilbert and Sullivan in *The Mikado*. Modern-day directors have their work cut out accommodating the aspects of the piece to new political sensitivities; and modern Butterflys have trouble persuading their audience that the heroine amounts to more than a sad case of self-delusion. Add the perpetual difficulty of casting a role that demands the appearance of a schoolgirl plus the vocal stamina of an industrial pile-driver, and you have what ought to be a problem-piece that opera companies shy away from. But they don't, because the audience loves it. And the sheer emotional charge of the last Act is undeniably hard to resist. The waiting, the disappointment, the betrayal of an innocent, are all part of Puccini's stock-in-trade – it's calculating but it works. The only pity is that Pinkerton and Sharpless are so swept into the margins: minor characters, when they ought to be more of a counterbalance to Cio-Cio-San. Puccini attempted several versions of the piece, some of which compress Acts II and III into a single, though subdivided entity.

Highlights

Act I: Butterfly's ascent of the hill 'Ah! Quanto cielo', and the very long love duet – some twenty minutes' worth – that closes the Act. Act II: Butterfly's 'Un bel dì' and the Humming Song as she waits. Act III: her farewell to her son, and to her life, 'Lascialo giocar'.

Did You Know?

ⓡ *Madama Butterfly* had a disastrous opening and only became a success after Puccini revised it.

ⓡ The plot of *Madama Butterfly* lives on, updated to the Vietnam War, in *Miss Saigon*.

ⓡ The music of *Madama Butterfly* has had several subsequent lives, not least in a 1980s pop version of 'Un bel dì' which reached No.13.

ⓡ The famous aria has also turned up in a Twinings tea advertisement and the 1987 film *Fatal Attraction*, starring Glenn Close, and the Humming Chorus has been used by Del Monte for its orange juice advertisements.

Recommended Recording

Mirella Freni, Luciano Pavarotti, Vienna Philharmonic Orchestra/Herbert von Karajan. Decca 417 577-2. Rich and spacious sound, with Freni at her youthful best.

Manon Lescaut

FORM: Opera in four acts; in Italian
COMPOSER: Giacomo Puccini (1858–1924)
LIBRETTO: Marco Praga, Domenico Oliva and Luigi Illica;
after Abbé Prévost
FIRST PERFORMANCE: Turin, 1 February 1893

Principal Characters

Manon Lescaut ✿ Soprano
Lescaut, her brother, a guardsman ✿ Baritone
The Chevalier des Grieux ✿ Tenor
Geronte de Revoir, the Treasurer General ✿ Bass
Edmondo, a student ✿ Tenor
The Captain ✿ Bass

Synopsis of the Plot

Setting: Amiens, Paris, Le Havre, Louisiana; 18th century

ACT I Des Grieux and Edmondo have joined a group of people enjoying the summer evening outside an inn in Amiens. A coach arrives, bringing Manon, her brother Lescaut, who is accompanying his young sister to a convent to complete her education, and the rich old roué, Geronte, who has already cast a lascivious eye on the lovely Manon. The two men go into the inn to arrange accommodation, leaving Manon alone outside. Des Grieux and Manon meet and are instantly attracted to each other. Meanwhile, Edmondo overhears Geronte discussing his plans to abduct Manon and take her to Paris, with her brother's blessing. Edmondo warns des Grieux, who persuades Manon to run away with him and they escape in the coach Geronte has ordered for himself. The furious Geronte is consoled by Lescaut, who assures him that he will get her back easily enough when she has spent all des Grieux's money.

ACT II Lescaut's prophecy has indeed come to pass and Manon is installed in luxury as Geronte's mistress. Des Grieux comes to visit her and reproaches her for her faithlessness, but he cannot resist her for long and when Geronte unexpectedly returns, it is to find them in each other's arms. Manon unwisely taunts Geronte with his unattractiveness, and, muttering threats, Geronte leaves them. Des Grieux urges Manon to run away with him, but she is reluctant to leave her life of luxury and delays too long. Lescaut rushes in to tell them Geronte is bringing the police, and Manon gathers up as many precious things as she can. The guards enter and Manon is arrested for theft and prostitution.

ACT III Manon has been sentenced to deportation and is waiting at Le Havre to embark. Des Grieux's plan to rescue her fails and one by one the prisoners are paraded before the crowds as they are taken to the ship, bound for North America. Des Grieux, in frantic desperation, throws himself at the captain's feet and begs to be allowed to go with Manon. The captain, moved by his pleas, allows him to go on board and the ship sails.

ACT IV Once in America, des Grieux manages to help Manon escape, but it means a life of permanent flight. Outside New Orleans, in a vast desert, Manon can go no further and faints with exhaustion. Des Grieux goes to find water but when he returns Manon is past all help; dying, she reassures him of her eternal love, and he collapses beside her.

Music and Background

This was Puccini's first real success, although it was achieved with much struggle and many revisions and substitutions that leave no definitive form to the score. One initial problem was that Massenet had produced an opera on the same subject only a decade earlier, so Puccini's version had to assert a strong, clear individuality to avoid the charge of plagiarism. The result of all the changes is a poor libretto (which passed through numerous hands) and a selection of scenes from Prévost's novel with nothing to link them into something like a continuous narrative. As story-telling, it's an utter failure, but Puccini's dramatic instinct works miracles within the scenes themselves, and turns at least the first three of the four acts into viable, self-contained theatre. The music is youthful, ardent, and obviously indebted to Verdi and Wagner, but at the same time building a distinctive personality that no one with an ear for the composer's idiom could mistake for someone else's work.

Highlights

Act I: des Grieux's eulogy on Manon, 'Cortese damigella', and the ensuing duet. Act II: Manon's nostalgia for her former life, 'In quelle trine morbide', and the grand passion of the reunion duet, 'Tu, tu amore?' Act III: the inventive choral writing in the prisoners' Roll-call Scene. Act IV: the finale – 'Non voglio' – to what is effectively one long duet.

Did You Know?

Puccini's response to criticism that the story had been set too often was cavalier: 'A woman like Manon can accommodate more than one lover.'

Recommended Recording

Mirella Freni, Plácido Domingo, Philharmonia Orchestra/Giuseppe Sinopoli. DG 413 893-2. Freni sounding younger than her years and with more eloquent companionship from Domingo than she gets from Pavarotti in her later Decca recording under James Levine.

Tosca

FORM: Opera in three acts; in Italian
COMPOSER: Giacomo Puccini (1858–1924)
LIBRETTO: Giuseppe Giacosa and Luigi Illica; after Sardou
FIRST PERFORMANCE: Rome, 14 January 1900

Principal Characters

Angelotti, a political prisoner ⁓ **Bass**
Mario Cavaradossi, a painter ⁓ **Tenor**
Floria Tosca, a singer ⁓ **Soprano**
Baron Scarpia, the police chief ⁓ **Baritone**
Spoletta, a police agent ⁓ **Tenor**

Synopsis of the Plot

Setting: Rome; June 1800

ACT I Angelotti, an escaped political prisoner, takes refuge in the church of Sant'Andrea della Valle where he recognises an old friend, Cavaradossi, who has been engaged to paint a Madonna. Cavaradossi promises his friend to help him safely out of the city, and when they hear Tosca's voice outside, Cavaradossi quickly gives his friend his own basket of food and tells him to hide. But Tosca has heard their whispering and suspects Cavaradossi of having had an assignation with another woman. Cavaradossi reassures her and they part, having arranged to meet that evening. The sound of a distant cannon means that Angelotti's escape has been discovered and the two men quickly leave the church. It is not long before Scarpia, the police chief, and his agent, Spoletta, track Angelotti to the church and they order it to be thoroughly searched. The food basket is found and Scarpia suspects Cavaradossi of being involved. When Tosca returns, Scarpia, who is greatly attracted to her, tries to make her jealous and suspicious of Cavaradossi, hoping thereby that she will lead them first to Cavaradossi and thus to Angelotti. Tosca's temper is quickly aroused and she leaves, followed, unseen, by Spoletta.

ACT II Scarpia, alone in his rooms at the Palazzo Farnese, contemplates his desire for Tosca which, he hopes, is shortly to be satisfied. Spoletta announces that Cavaradossi has been arrested, although Angelotti has not yet been found. Scarpia is interrogating Cavaradossi when Tosca is admitted and Cavaradossi is dragged away to the next room. Tosca refuses to answer Scarpia's questions and he orders Cavaradossi to be tortured within earshot. His cries of pain weaken her resolve and Tosca tells Scarpia where Angelotti is hiding. Suddenly news arrives that Napoleon has won the battle of Marengo, and Cavaradossi is jubilant. Scarpia's response is to order his immediate execution. Left alone with Tosca, Scarpia promises to arrange a mock execution and provide a safe conduct for Cavaradossi and Tosca, if she will submit to him. Tosca agrees but, when he is writing, takes up a knife; as he turns to her she stabs him to death. Quickly snatching up the safe conduct, Tosca pauses to place candles round Scarpia's body and a crucifix on his lips, before leaving the room.

ACT III It is dawn and Cavaradossi is brought to the battlements of the Castel Sant'Angelo where he is to be executed. Tosca comes to tell him that she has killed Scarpia, but not before arranging the mock execution and the safe conduct. He must, she says, fall down when he is shot – although the bullets will not be real – and they can then go away together. The execution goes ahead. Cavaradossi falls to the ground but, to Tosca's horror, he does not rise; Scarpia has tricked her. As Spoletta comes to arrest her for Scarpia's murder, Tosca, defiant, throws herself over the parapet to her death.

Music and Background

Puccini drew a contrast between *La Bohème* (all poetry, no action) and *Tosca* (all action, no poetry); and from the opening chords, which proclaim the dark power of Scarpia, the score asserts itself as urgent, fierce, attention-grabbing – with a nice line in sensationalism (not to say, sadism) which caused American musicologist Joseph Kerman to describe it (deathlessly) as a 'shabby little shocker'. In truth, *Tosca* is a masterpiece of theatrical planning. The three acts follow the (imagined) course of a specific day in history through three actual Roman locations, and Puccini uses this structural foundation brilliantly, with a sure sense of how to shape the emotional contours of each scene: when to relax the tension, when to tighten it, and when to squeeze the trigger.

Highlights

Act I: the 'black eyes' jealous-love duet, 'Qual'occhio', is Puccini at his most engaging; Scarpia's 'Va, Tosca!', sung against the gathering ecclesiastical procession, is Puccini at his most menacing. Act II: the Torture Scene is unbearable but gripping; Tosca's 'Vissi d'arte' – invariably sung with the soprano in a crumpled heap on the floor – ranks among opera's greatest set-piece arias. Act III: the opening dawn music for offstage shepherd boy and bells is magical; and Cavaradossi gets a classically impassioned solo – his big moment – in 'E lucevan le stelle'.

Did You Know?

🙟 Callas' last stage appearance was in a production of *Tosca* at Covent Garden in 1965, when she wore a purple dress and tiara – later to become iconic symbols of the role. At the time of writing, Covent Garden Toscas still perform in them and resurrect her memory.

Il Trittico
(The Triptych)

FORM: A series of three one-act operas; in Italian
COMPOSER: Giacomo Puccini (1858–1924)
LIBRETTO: *Il Tabarro*: Giuseppe Adami; after Gold. *Suor Angelica*:
Giovacchino Forzano. *Gianni Schicchi*: Giovacchino Forzano;
after Dante
FIRST PERFORMANCE: New York, 14 December 1918

Note: The three operas were originally intended to be shown together, but today it is more usual to find two of the three performed in a single evening.

Il Tabarro
(The Cloak)

Principal Characters

Michele, a middle-aged bargemaster ◆ **Baritone**
Giorgetta, his young wife ◆ **Soprano**
Luigi, a young bargeman ◆ **Tenor**
Il Tinca, a middle-aged bargeman ◆ **Bass**

Synopsis of the Plot
Setting: Paris

Michele and Giorgetta are at home on their barge on the Seine; the sun is setting, the day's work is almost over. Giorgetta offers the men a glass of wine and, when a wandering organ-grinder comes by, she dances first with Il Tinca and then with Luigi. But soon the others drift away, she is left alone with Luigi and it becomes clear that they are lovers. Giorgetta, fearful of discovery by Michele, tells Luigi to go, arranging an assignation for later that evening when she will signal, by a light, that it is safe for them to meet. That evening she behaves coldly towards Michele and he torments himself with the thought that Giorgetta is unfaithful; he decides to sit on deck and wait for her lover, wrapping himself in his coat and lighting his pipe. Luigi, mistaking the light for the signal, runs on to the barge. Michele overpowers him and, after forcing a confession from him, strangles him. As he hears Giorgetta returning, Michele grasps the body and holds it under his cloak. When his wife comes close to him he opens the cloak and lets her lover's body fall at her feet.

Music and Background

This is life-in-the-raw verismo with a vengeance: darkly atmospheric, sharply characterised, and packing an extraordinary amount of natural (not to say, macabre) detail into its less-than-an-hour duration. Puccini called it Grand Guignol, and the ending certainly packs a grim punch. But at the same time, the orchestration and harmonic colouring are innovative (for an otherwise conservative composer), almost Debussy-like, and some commentators regard it as his most sophisticated score. Note the street-singer's passing reference to *La Bohème*.

Highlights

The Giorgetta/Luigi duet 'Ma chi lascia' supplies the chief musical interest, followed by the exchange between Michele and Giorgetta, 'Erano sere come queste'.

Did You Know?

~ Puccini originally intended *Il Tabarro* to accompany his first and, at that time, unperformed opera *Le Villi*; but the First World War intervened and his plans were never realised.

~ Puccini was so anxious to capture the atmosphere of contemporary Parisian city life that he specifically wrote a motor horn into the score.

Recommended Recording

Tito Gobbi, Margaret Mas, Giancinto Prandelli, Rome Opera/Vincenzo Bellezza. EMI CMS7 64165-2. An old mono classic of unsurpassed atmospheric strength, packaged with the other *Il Trittico* scores.

Suor Angelica
(Sister Angelica)

Principal Characters

Sister Angelica, a nun ❧ **Soprano**
Sister Genevieve, a nun ❧ **Soprano**
The Princess, Angelica's aunt ❧ **Mezzo-soprano**

Synopsis of the Plot

Setting: A convent; late 17th century

The nuns have finished their evening devotions and, as the sun sets, some of the sisters talk about life in the convent. Genevieve admits that, as a former shepherdess, she misses the touch and sight of the lambs. Angelica denies that there is anything that she misses, but the nuns, knowing she has heard nothing from her family for seven years, are aware that this is not the truth. The sisters are sympathetic towards Angelica and, when the the arrival of a mysterious visitor in a grand carriage is announced, they all hope it means good news for her. The visitor, it transpires, has indeed come for Angelica; it is her aunt, the Princess, a cold, austere woman, bringing a contract for Angelica to sign, in which she relinquishes any claim she might have over the family's estate. The Princess reminds her of the disgrace she has brought on the family by bearing an illegitimate child. Angelica assures her aunt of her profound repentance but asserts that she can never forget her child. The Princess calmly responds that he died two years ago. Once more alone, the weeping Angelica longs only to die herself, so that she can be united with her son. Emotionally distraught and in a state of religious ecstasy, she mixes a poisonous potion and drinks it, joyfully anticipating the peace to come. But suddenly she realises, with horror, that by killing herself she is condemned to eternal damnation and will never be united with her son. In anguish she implores divine forgiveness for her act. Angels' voices are heard and a vision of the Virgin Mary, with a small child, appears; the child steps towards her and the dying Angelica falls to the ground.

Music and Background

This is the least-often performed of the *Il Trittico* operas and the one usually dropped when directors feel compelled – for reasons of running time – to play just two of the three pieces as a double- rather than a triple-bill. That the cast is entirely female isn't of itself a problem (Poulenc's convent opera *Les Dialogues des Carmélites* thrives with mostly women) but Puccini could have done more to create variety of voice-types. And he could certainly have done more to reduce the sugar-content of the story. This is a sickly, sentimental piece, saved only by strong performances of the Princess-Aunt, and by directors who make an effort to underplay the vision of the Blessed Virgin and kill off the resurrected child.

Highlights

Angelica's 'Senza mamma, o bimbo' is the big set piece, rivalled only by the magic of the bell motif that opens the score.

Gianni Schicchi

Principal Characters

Gianni Schicchi ~ **Baritone**
Lauretta, his daughter ~ **Soprano**
Rinuccio ~ **Tenor**
A Notary ~ **Baritone**

Synopsis of the Plot

Setting: Florence; late 13th century

Buoso Donati's family are gathered round his deathbed, mourning extravagantly, when a rumour that the old man has left all his money to a monastery sends them searching frantically for his will. Rinuccio finds it first, but before he reads it, he asks the family if, now they are rich, they will agree to his marrying his sweetheart, Lauretta, Gianni Schicchi's daughter. They impatiently agree and the will is opened – only to find, to their dismay and anger, that Buoso has indeed left his money to the monks. Each one tries to think of a way of circumventing the old man's wishes but to no avail. It is left to Rinuccio to suggest approaching Gianni Schicchi for his help; he is, asserts Rinuccio, renowned for his cunning and although the relatives deplore his lowly social status (and the fact that he is not a Florentine), they finally, if reluctantly, agree. Schicchi's plan involves hiding Buoso's body (no one else knows of his death) and impersonating the dead man himself – at least for long enough to make a new will. The plan is unanimously approved, but then the relatives fall to arguing violently over the division of the spoils, each bribing Schicchi to act in his or her favour. The notary and the witnesses arrive and Schicchi begins to dictate his will – leaving almost the whole of Buoso's fortune to himself! Once the notary has gone, the relatives fall upon Schicchi, but he beats them off with a stick and drives them away. Rinuccio and Lauretta can now be married and, Schicchi asks the audience, could Buoso's money have been used in any better way?

Music and Background

By common consent, this is the best – and certainly best-loved – panel of the triptych: a brilliant little comedy that moves at lightning speed and makes you wonder why Puccini never managed to achieve something like it on a larger scale. (The comic elements in his full-length works are usually laboured.) A true and worthy successor to Verdi's *Falstaff*, *Gianni Schicchi* manages to contain memorably larger-than-life characters, a great deal of action, and some ravishingly poignant melodies within its fifty-five minutes. Nothing else in opera quite compares with its vitality and sense of timing.

Highlights

Everything, from start to finish: but especially Lauretta's famous aria 'O mio babbino caro' and Schicchi's ruse to deceive the notary, 'Il testa la cappellina'.

Did You Know?

Lauretta's aria had a new lease of life as the theme to Merchant Ivory's film *A Room with a View*.

Recommended Recording

Tito Gobbi, Victoria de los Angeles, Rome Opera/Gabriele Santini. EMI CMS7 64165-2. The only stereo recording in EMI's classic 1950s package of all three *Il Trittico* operas, and incomparably done by singers who turn out to have a real (sometimes unexpected) gift for comedy.

Turandot

FORM: Opera in three acts; in Italian
COMPOSER: Giacomo Puccini (1858–1924)
LIBRETTO: Giuseppe Adami and Renato Simoni; after Gozzi
FIRST PERFORMANCE: Milan, 25 April 1926

Principal Characters

Princess Turandot ∼ Soprano
The Emperor Altoum, her father ∼ Tenor
The Unknown Prince (Calaf) ∼ Tenor
Timur, his father ∼ Bass

Liù, a slave girl ∽ **Soprano**
Ping, Pang and Pong, the emperor's ministers
∽ **Baritone and two Tenors**
A mandarin ∽ **Bass**
The Prince of Persia ∽ **Tenor**

Synopsis of the Plot

Setting: Peking; legendary times

ACT I A mandarin reads out a decree to the people: the Princess Turandot will only marry a prince of the royal blood and he must solve her three riddles. If any suitor fails to answer correctly, he will be executed. And, in fact, an execution is about to take place, that of the Prince of Persia, who has failed the test. The crowd surges forward in anticipation and in the crush an old blind man is knocked down. His companion, a slave girl, Liù, calls for help and a young man, Calaf, rushes forward – only to recognise Timur, his own father and a secret refugee, like himself, from their homeland, which has been taken over by a usurper. Meanwhile, the execution proceeds and Turandot herself appears on a balcony. Calaf is instantly bedazzled and resolves to win her, in spite of attempts by Timur, Liù and even the emperor's ministers, Ping, Pang and Pong, to dissuade him. He strikes three times on the ceremonial gong, committing himself to the contest.

ACT II Ping, Pang and Pong reflect on the happier days before Turandot's bloody reign and long for the princess to find love and peace. But the familiar sounds of the gathering crowds and the preparations for another contest bring them back to reality. The aged emperor tries to persuade Calaf to renounce his challenge, but he is insistent. Turandot herself appears and explains the reasons for her brutal behaviour, saying that she does it in revenge for the rape of one of her ancestors, and that she has vowed to keep herself pure. Turandot gives Calaf one final opportunity to withdraw, but he refuses to do so. One by one she asks her riddles and, one by one, Calaf responds correctly. Turandot, shocked and dismayed, begs her father to release her from her own decree, but he refuses. Turandot, turning to Calaf, asks him if he wants to take her by force; he demurs and offers her the chance of escape: if she can discover his name by the next morning, he will allow himself to be executed; if not, she must be his.

ACT III The princess has ordered Ping, Pang and Pong to discover Calaf's name – failure will mean death – and they try in various ways to tempt him to tell them. Then Timur and Liù are dragged in (Calaf has been seen talking to them). Liù courageously says that she alone knows the prince's name and she is taken away to suffer cruel tortures. However, she refuses to give way. When Turandot asks her what gives her the strength to resist such agony, she replies that her love for the prince gives her the power to endure the suffering. The tortures are renewed and finally Liù seizes a dagger from one of the soldiers and stabs herself, predicting, as she dies, that her sacrifice will awaken Turandot's own love for Calaf. Calaf and Turandot are left alone and Calaf kisses her passionately, awakening in her the first feelings of love for him. Turandot, ashamed, begs him to leave her but instead he tells her his name, thereby placing his life in her hands. As dawn breaks, Turandot announces to the crowd that she has discovered the prince's name – 'His name is Love'.

Music and Background

In this score Puccini returned to the orientalism of *Madama Butterfly* but with a richer, more truly exotic palette of orchestral colours. It is an odd hybrid of a piece that doesn't comfortably fit the composer's image as a verismo composer: in essence a comic fairy tale, with Ping, Pang and Pong bouncing in and out of the action as thinly-disguised envoys from the Italian commedia dell'arte tradition. But the death of Liù somehow raises the stakes of the narrative. She is the one truly sympathetic character here, and however decorously her Torture Scene is done on stage, it remains one of the most gratuitous examples of what Puccini called his 'neronic' tendency: a sadistic streak that specialised in the dramatic potential of suffering. It also risks the possibility that Liù will upstage Turandot, which is why her death is conveniently forgotten at the end. A tough role, usually sung by sopranos with chain-saw voices, Turandot *has* to keep the focus of attention; and the whole piece ultimately hangs on how successfully she manages to communicate a vulnerable heart behind the ice-cold glamour.

Highlights

Act I: Liù's touching plea to Calaf 'Signore, ascolta'. Act II: the introduction to the riddles, starting with Turandot's historical summary, 'In questa reggia', and climaxing in what becomes a duet with Calaf, 'Mai nessun m'avra!'. Act III: Calaf's 'Nessun dorma!', elevated by international football to the most famous tenor aria in existence, and Liù's pre-mortem number, 'Tanto amore segreto'. Act IV: the concluding, if corny, choral reprise of 'Nessun dorma'.

Did You Know?

🎵 Puccini died before completion of the final duet, which had to be filled out by a younger composer, Franco Alfano, from surviving sketches.

🎵 'Nessun dorma' was used by the BBC for its 1990 World Cup theme tune and, in its recording by Luciano Pavarotti, went to No. 1 in the charts.

Recommended Recording

Birgit Nilsson, Franco Correlli, Renata Scotto, Rome Opera/Francesco Molinari-Pradelli. EMI CMS7 69327-2. Nilsson's second recording of the title role, done with terrifying immediacy.

Henry Purcell
(c.1659–95)

Dido and Aeneas (1689)
Dioclesian (1690)
King Arthur (1691)
The Fairy Queen (1692)
The Indian Queen (1695)

Purcell is widely considered the first great composer of opera in England, with a genius for English word-setting which passed without equal until modern times. But in his short life (he died at thirty-six) he actually produced just one piece which can properly be called an opera: *Dido and Aeneas*. The rest of his stage works were hybrid scores known as 'semi-operas' – in other words, spoken dramas with musical interludes which were sung or danced. And even these semi-operas were a sort of afterthought, crowded into what turned out to be the last years of his life. Until then, he had been preoccupied with writing choral and instrumental music for the court. Born and raised in London, he served under four monarchs – Charles II, James II, William and Mary – and produced quantities of ceremonial music with an emotional power which transcended its 'official' function: not least, his music for Queen Mary's funeral. In complete contrast, he also produced much incidental theatre music and bawdily knockabout street ballads.

Dido and Aeneas

FORM: Opera in three acts; in English
COMPOSER: Henry Purcell (c.1659–95)
LIBRETTO: Nahum Tate; after Virgil
FIRST PERFORMANCE: London, December 1689

Principal Characters

Dido, Queen of Carthage ∙ **Soprano**
Aeneas, a Trojan prince ∙ **Tenor**
A Sorceress ∙ **Mezzo-soprano**
Two witches ∙ **Two Sopranos**

Synopsis of the Plot

Setting: Mythological Carthage

ACT I Prince Aeneas has escaped from the destruction of Troy and, blown off course on his way to Rome to found a new empire, has been welcomed by Dido, the widowed Queen of Carthage. Dido and the handsome hero soon fall in love, and Dido's advisers encourage her to consider marrying him, thus uniting two great dynasties. The two lovers acknowledge their passionate feelings for each other before leaving on a hunting expedition to the country.

ACT II In a cave a sorceress gathers her witches about her and they cast a spell to hurt Dido, whom they hate. They resolve to part the queen and Aeneas by reminding him of his destiny, to found a new empire in Rome. In the meantime they conjure up a storm to ruin the hunt, which indeed it does, sending everyone hurrying back to the city, except Aeneas. Alone, he sees a false vision of the god Mercury, urging him to leave Dido immediately and set off for Rome. Sorrowfully the prince accepts that he has no choice: he must leave Dido and Carthage.

ACT III Aeneas' men have gathered at the harbour and are preparing to set sail, watched gleefully by the sorceress and her coven of witches. But Dido is heartbroken and bitterly accuses Aeneas of betraying her. Aeneas at first offers to stay with her after all but changes his mind again, and they part forever. Dido, inconsolable, cannot live without him and dies.

Music and Background

The circumstances surrounding the first performance of this first great English opera are obscure, but it seems to have been written for amateur performance by the girls of a Chelsea boarding school. It is short (one hour) and compact in the way it tells the story, but with immaculately detailed attention to the words, deep emotion, and prominent dance elements (probably incorporated because the owner of the girls' school was also a dancing master). Despite the suggested equality of the title, Dido is a far more prominent role than Aeneas, who barely figures.

Highlights

Dido's Lament, 'When I am laid in earth', is a supremely dignified example of its kind, with the text sung over a 'ground' bass that repeats ten times, and a cumulative intensity that builds into one of the truly memorable moments of Baroque opera. Otherwise, the Act III sequence of sailors' dance, chorus and witches' brew claim most attention.

Did You Know?

~. Purcell's Dido is the first appearance in opera of the 'abandoned woman', the model for the heroines of later works such as *Madama Butterfly* and *La Traviata*.

> ✍ It is a mark of the cavalier 17th-century attitude to text that not long after Purcell's death his opera was adapted for insertion into performances of Shakespeare's *Measure for Measure*.
> ✍ George Bernard Shaw attended a performance of *Dido and Aeneas* in 1889 and wrote of Purcell's 'spirit, his freshness, his dramatic expression and his unapproached art of setting English speech to music'.

Recommended Recording

Janet Baker, Raimond Herincx, English Chamber Orchestra/Anthony Lewis. Decca 425 720-2. A 1960s classic, with Janet Baker in the role that brought her stardom.

The Fairy Queen

FORM: Semi-opera in five acts; in English
COMPOSER: Henry Purcell (c.1659–95)
LIBRETTO: Anonymous; after Shakespeare
FIRST PERFORMANCE: London, 2 May 1692

Principal Characters

Duke Theseus ✍ Spoken role
Hermia, in love with Lysander ✍ Spoken role
Lysander, in love with Hermia ✍ Spoken role
Demetrius, in love with Hermia ✍ Spoken role
Helena, in love with Demetrius ✍ Spoken role
Titania, Queen of the Fairies ✍ Spoken role
Oberon, King of the Fairies ✍ Spoken role
Puck, a fairy ✍ Spoken role
Nick Bottom, a weaver ✍ Spoken role
Drunken Poet ✍ Bass-baritone
Mystery ✍ Soprano
Secrecy ✍ Countertenor
Night ✍ Soprano
Juno ✍ Soprano

Synopsis of the Plot

Setting: Theseus' palace in Athens, a nearby wood and gardens

ACT I Hermia is in love with Lysander but her father (supported by Athenian law and backed by the Duke) insists that she shall marry Demetrius. Demetrius is happy to marry Hermia, with whom he is in love, but in turn is loved by Helena. The four Athenians leave the city and wander in the nearby woods, where, in another part, a group of craftsmen, led by Bottom, are rehearsing a play to entertain the guests at Hermia's forthcoming wedding. Titania has also come to the woods to avoid her jealous husband, Oberon. Her fairy attendants, seeing a drunken poet wandering nearby, tease and torment him mercilessly.

ACT II Titania asks for music to help her to sleep and is soothed by the singing of Night, Mystery and Secrecy. When she is finally asleep, Puck enters and, on the instructions of Oberon, administers a love potion to her: this will make her fall in love with the first person she sees on waking. Oberon has also instructed Puck to administer the potion to Demetrius, so that he will fall in love with Helena, leaving Hermia free to marry Lysander. The four Athenians are now lost in the forest and decide to stay there for the night.

ACT III Puck has given the potion to Lysander instead of Demetrius. Lysander wakes, sees Helena, and instantly falls in love with her, unceremoniously abandoning Hermia. The weaver, Bottom, unconsciously now sports an ass' head, imposed upon him by Puck. Titania, waking, sees him and is smitten by him.

ACT IV Oberon resolves the confusion between the mortal lovers, relieves Bottom of his ass' head and releases Titania from the spell. Oberon and Titania are reconciled. The Athenian lovers tell the Duke of their experiences in the forest, but he refuses to believe them until Oberon and Titania come to the palace to convince him that they are telling the truth, invoking the blessing of the great goddess Juno. The goddess herself enters in a carriage drawn by peacocks, and a magnificent Chinese masque is performed in celebration of love and marriage.

Music and Background

This is an example of a semi-opera, where the story (an oddly distorted version of the familiar Shakespeare) is told in speech and the music comes in the form of self-contained, symbolic masques which are more decorative than essential. It follows that the main roles are for actors rather than singers, and the piece is difficult to bring off in performance. However, the score remains a masterpiece, incorporating some of Purcell's finest melodies as well as instances of his earthier humour.

Highlights

Act II: the Masque of Sleep. Act III: the chorus 'If love's a sweet passion' and the slapstick duet for Corydon and Mopsa 'Now the maids and the men'. Act V: the countertenor air with trumpet, 'Thus, the gloomy world'.

> ### Did You Know?
>
> 🎵 Purcell devised the work for the United Company of the Theatre Royal and it cost an astonishing £3,000 to stage; in Act IV alone, the composer specified a twelve-foot fountain on the stage and the entry of Phoebus in a chariot drawn by four horses!

Recommended Recording

Nancy Argenta, Lynne Dawson, Les Arts Florissants/William Christie. Harmonia Mundi HMC 90 1308/9. A lively, vigorous period-conscious recording where the soloists join forces to become their own chorus.

King Arthur, or The British Worthy

FORM: Semi-opera in five acts; in English
COMPOSER: Henry Purcell (c.1659–95)
LIBRETTO: John Dryden; after Arthurian legend
FIRST PERFORMANCE: London, May/June 1691

Principal Characters

King Arthur 🎵 **Spoken role**
Emmeline, his fiancée 🎵 **Spoken role**
Grimbald, an evil spirit 🎵 **Baritone**
Philidel, a good spirit 🎵 **Soprano**
Oswald, leader of the Saxons 🎵 **Spoken role**
Osmond, the Saxon magician 🎵 **Spoken role**
Cold Genius 🎵 **Bass**

Synopsis of the Plot

Setting: Arthurian Britain

ACT I King Arthur and the Britons have been waging war on the Saxons, and are about to launch their final attack. Oswald, the Saxon leader, offers a sacrifice to the gods then, taunted by the Britons, they join in battle.

ACT II The Saxons have been defeated and are running away, closely pursued by the Britons. The evil spirit, Grimbald, attempts to lure the Britons into dangerous areas, but he is countered by the good spirit, Philidel, who tries to guide them on to safer land. The Saxons resort to further treachery by kidnapping the blind Emmeline, daughter of the Duke of Cornwall and engaged to Arthur.

ACT III Emmeline, now Oswald's prisoner, has her sight restored by Philidel and, much to her consternation, becomes an object of desire for Osmond, the Saxon magician. Emmeline rejects his advances, whereupon he shows her the extent of his powers by conjuring up a vision of winter, a frozen landscape dominated by the Cold Genius.

ACT IV With the help of Philidel, Arthur tries to rescue Emmeline, but is challenged at every turn by new demonstrations of Saxon magic.

ACT V Arthur has overcome the power of Saxon magic, defeats Oswald in single combat and is reunited with Emmeline. He magnanimously forgives the Saxons, and the work ends with a masque extolling the glories of Britain.

Music and Background

Another semi-opera where the major roles speak and only the minor ones have anything to sing (with Philadel and Grimbald as in-betweens who do both). But this time the music and the story are more closely bound together, and the text (by the distinguished poet John Dryden) is superior to most of the libretti Purcell worked with. Rarely has patriotism been so elegantly, touchingly and acceptably portrayed on the stage, and the pity is that the practical problems of staging semi-opera stop it from being seen more often.

Highlights

The golden moment is the song that crowns the Act V masque, 'Fairest Isle'. Many consider it the most perfect of all Purcell's theatre music. Otherwise, there is startling originality (not to say comedy) in the Act II alternative chorus 'Hither this way'; and a bizarre modernity in the icy shimmer of the Frost Scene in Act III.

Did You Know?

❧ 'Fairest Isle' found new celebrity in 1995 as the rallying call for the BBC's year-long celebration of British music – in honour of Purcell's tercentenary.

Recommended Recording

Jennifer Smith, Gillian Fischer, Stephen Varcoe, English Baroque Soloists/John Eliot Gardiner. Erato 2292 45211-2. Period sound, with spirited speeds and fresh conviction.

Maurice Ravel
(1875–1937)

L'Heure Espagnole (1909)
L'Enfant et les Sortilèges (1925)

A small fastidious Parisian whose great loves seem to have been his mother and a collection of clockwork automata that filled his house, Ravel has acquired the reputation of a 'petit maître': the author of decorative, exquisite music with more charm than depth of feeling. But that's too easy a description of a composer who had a highly complex creative mind. His output was certainly small and mostly salon-scale: piano music, songs, chamber scores. It also tends to wear a mask of formality, with a nostalgic regard for old French styles and dance-forms. But behind the mask you glimpse a passionate and sometimes dark heart, and the division in his character may well reflect his family origins – a Swiss father and a Basque mother. Both his operas are small-scale one-acters.

L'Enfant et les Sortilèges
(The Child and the Spells)

FORM: Opera in one act; in French
COMPOSER: Maurice Ravel (1875–1937)
LIBRETTO: Colette
FIRST PERFORMANCE: Monte Carlo, 21 March 1925

Principal Characters
The Child ⁊ Mezzo-soprano
Mother ⁊ Contralto
The Armchair ⁊ Bass
The Grandfather Clock ⁊ Baritone
The Teapot ⁊ Tenor
The Fire/Fairy Princess ⁊ Soprano

The Little Old Man ~ **Tenor**
The Black Cat ~ **Baritone**
The White Cat ~ **Mezzo-soprano**

Synopsis of the Plot

Setting: An old country house and garden in Normandy

SCENE 1 The Child is struggling with his homework and, bored and irritated, sticks his tongue out at his mother when she tries to encourage him. Confined to his room as a result, the Child releases his frustration in an orgy of destruction – from pulling off strips of wallpaper, smashing crockery and furniture and pulling the cat's tail, to swinging on the grandfather clock pendulum and breaking it. Finally, with a shout of triumph, he tears up all his books. Exhausted by his efforts, the Child is about to sink into the Armchair when it hobbles away from him, complaining about its treatment at his hands. Other abused and broken objects join in, including the Grandfather Clock, the Fire (on which the Child poured water) and the Teapot. The Fairy Princess rises from the torn storybook, but the Child has destroyed the final pages of her story, and she sinks through the floor as he tries to hold her back. Searching through the scattered pages on the floor, the Child finds his arithmetic book; out of it springs a Little Old Man and a crowd of Numbers; they torment the Child with a quick-fire volley of nonsensical pseudo-mathematical questions until he collapses. It is now evening, the moon is out and the Black Cat in the room serenades his mate, the White Cat, in the garden. Soon the Black Cat joins his mate, the walls fall away and the Child finds himself in the garden.

SCENE 2 Now it is the turn of the trees, animals, birds and insects that the Child has hurt and damaged to vent their anger against him. Suddenly the Child feels very isolated and afraid, and he cries out the one word 'Maman'. Immediately the atmosphere changes and there is menace in the air. The animals turn on the Child and push him roughly between them until, in their excitement, they turn on each other. The Child is thrust aside and joined by a little wounded squirrel. Gently he takes the animal's paw and binds it with a ribbon, watched, in incredulous amazement, by the other animals. This act of kindness transforms their attitude towards him and, trying to imitate his shout of 'Maman' to help him, they guide him back to the house.

Music and Background

The enclosed, magic world of this opera contains some of the most poignantly beautiful sounds Ravel ever imagined, although it also encompasses brash, revue-style jazz elements, including a foxtrot for the animated Teapot and Teacup. The pot sings in nonsense English, the cup in cod Chinese. The idea for *L'Enfant et les Sortilèges* came from the novelist Colette, who had to bully the composer into taking it on. His reluctance is surprising, given how closely the world of the libretto mirrored his own preoccupation with childhood fantasy and (not less) his mother, who had recently died.

Highlights

The Child's lament for the Fairy Princess 'Toi, le coeur de la rose' and the hushed, concluding chorus of forgiveness 'Il est bon, l'enfant'.

Recommended Recording

Susan Davenny Wyner, Arleen Augér, Philip Langridge, London Symphony Orchestra/André Previn. EMI CD-EMX 224. Strong dramatic appeal in a recording that was withdrawn but which has returned to the catalogue at mid-price.

L'Heure Espagnole
(The Spanish Hour)

FORM: Opera in one act; in French
COMPOSER: Maurice Ravel (1875–1937)
LIBRETTO: Franc-Nohain (Maurice Legrand)
FIRST PERFORMANCE: Paris, 19 May 1911

Principal Characters

Torquemada, a clock-maker ๛ **Tenor**
Concepción, his wife ๛ **Soprano**
Ramiro, a muleteer ๛ **Baritone**
Gonzalve, a poet ๛ **Tenor**
Don Inigo, a banker ๛ **Bass**

Synopsis of the Plot

Setting: A clock-maker's shop in Toledo; 18th century

Torquemada sits at his workbench mending a watch given to him by the muleteer, Ramiro. Concepción, Torquemada's wife, reminds her husband that it is Thursday, the day when he spends an hour going round the town winding up all the public clocks. Torquemada leaves, asking Ramiro to wait for him in the shop, much to his wife's annoyance, as she keeps this one hour of freedom each week especially to enjoy her love affairs. Concepción decides to get Ramiro out of the shop by asking him to take a heavy grandfather clock upstairs to her bedroom. While Ramiro is occupied with this task, the first of Concepción's admirers, Gonzalve, arrives. But before Concepción can take any useful advantage of Ramiro's absence, he is back downstairs again. The quick-thinking Concepción tells him that she asked him to move the wrong clock;

303

could he bring it down and take a different one up? The obliging muleteer disappears upstairs and Concepción hides Gonzalve in the second clock Ramiro is about to move to her room. Meanwhile, Inigo, her second lover arrives, and Concepción explains to Ramiro, who is now ready to take the second clock upstairs, that Inigo is a removal man. Concepción follows Ramiro upstairs and Inigo, deciding that this is his best chance of being alone with Concepción, inserts himself, with difficulty, into another clock. Ramiro, having completed the second removal, is now waiting in the shop. But he is soon rejoined by Concepción, who, dissatisfied with Gonzalve's poetic flights of fancy, tells Ramiro the clock upstairs is broken and should be exchanged with the one containing Inigo. Again Ramiro obliges. But Inigo turns out to be no more satisfying than Gonzalve and soon he rejoins Gonzalve back in the shop, still in his clock. Concepción, determined not to be thwarted, invites the strong, handsome Ramiro upstairs instead. When Torquemada returns he finds the two rejected lovers still in the clocks and, being a practical man, he accepts the situation and even takes the opportunity of selling them a clock each!

Music and Background

This delicate, sophisticated little opera makes a neat precis of the two sides to Ravel's character: Latin passions controlled into elegant formality. Throughout the score you hear the mechanistic whirring of the clock-shop. But it's a *Spanish* clock-shop, which provides an excuse for habanera rhythms and dreamy melodies that exactly reflect the tone of suppressed sexuality in the libretto. Full of musical as well as verbal double-entendres, *L'Heure Espagnole* was thought risqué when it premiered. Today it just seems utterly endearing.

Highlights

Ramiro's two dream fantasies stand out; but at a total duration of only fifty minutes, the entire score counts as one long highlight.

Did You Know?

✎ The orchestral introduction features the ticking of clocks at different speeds, coinciding every fifteen seconds, pointing to the tension between order and disorder which underlies the comedy.

Recommended Recording

Jane Berbié, Michel Sénéchal, Gabriel Bacquier, Paris Opera/Lorin Maazel. DG 423 719-2. A 1960s recording, chic but tender.

Nikolai Rimsky-Korsakov
(1844–1908)

The Maid of Pskov (1872)
May Night (1879)
Mlada (1890)
Christmas Eve (1894)
Sadko (1896)
***The Legend of the Invisible City of Kitezh* (1905)**
***The Golden Cockerel* (1907)**

Rimsky-Korsakov was, in his own lifetime, the most celebrated member of the group of St Petersburg-based nationalist composers known as 'The Mighty Handful'. He was also the one notoriously responsible for 'cleaning up' the work of the others, devoting much of his energy to editions, compilations and completions of the Musorgsky operas for which history has judged him ill – although he did it selflessly, attempting only to ensure the music a future life. Rimsky's own (fifteen) operas are notable for their brilliant orchestration and love of fantasy, tending towards exotic myths and comic folk-tales rather than the epic realism of Musorgsky. They don't often get staged outside Russia, but recent recordings and tours by the Kirov Opera under Valery Gergiev have encouraged new interest in the West.

The Golden Cockerel

FORM: Opera in a Prologue, three acts and an Epilogue; in Russian
COMPOSER: Nikolai Rimsky-Korsakov (1844–1908)
LIBRETTO: Vladimir Bel'sky; after Pushkin
FIRST PERFORMANCE: Moscow, 7 October 1909

Principal Characters

Tsar Dodon ❧ Bass
Prince Gvidon, his elder son ❧ Tenor
Prince Afron, his younger son ❧ Baritone
General Polkan ❧ Bass
Queen of Shemakha ❧ Soprano
Golden Cockerel ❧ Soprano
Astrologer ❧ Tenor

Synopsis of the Plot

Setting: Legendary Russia

PROLOGUE The Astrologer tells the audience that the story has a moral.

ACT I The ageing Dodon has called the Council of State together to ask advice on what he should do about an imminent invasion of his country. His two sons each make futile suggestions, which are nevertheless received with extravagant admiration and approval by everyone, with the exception of General Polkan. Failing to reach agreement, they call on the services of the Astrologer, who offers the Tsar a Golden Cockerel; the bird will raise the alarm when danger threatens and turn to face the direction from which it comes. Dodon is delighted and offers the Astrologer anything he wishes; the Astrologer is grateful but declines to accept any reward for the present. Dodon, happy to have found a solution to his problems, climbs into bed and falls asleep. His dreams of a beautiful woman are twice interrupted by the Golden Cockerel's alarm call; the first time Dodon orders his sons to go and fight the enemy, but the second time he is forced to lead the army into battle himself, to the resounding cheers of his people.

ACT II High in the mountains, the Tsar mourns Gvidon and Afron, who lie dead among the remnants of their army, but his desire for revenge is thwarted by the fact that no one knows where the enemy is. Suddenly, the early morning mist clears to reveal a magnificent tent, from which a beautiful woman emerges, telling Dodon that she is the Queen of Shemakha. Dodon is instantly infatuated with her and she skilfully sets about seducing him until the besotted king does everything she asks – even making himself look ridiculous by singing and dancing at her behest. Finally, Dodon asks her to marry him, she accepts, and they return to his kingdom.

ACT III The spectacular procession which celebrates Dodon's return is interrupted by the Astrologer, who comes to claim his reward – the Queen of Shemakha. Dodon, after desperately offering him alternatives, strikes the Astrologer on the head, killing him instantly. Suddenly the Golden Cockerel crows loudly, flies down from its perch and attacks and fatally wounds the Tsar. A loud crack of thunder is followed by the Queen's laughter as darkness descends. When it clears, the Queen and the Golden Cockerel have vanished and the people mourn their dead king.

EPILOGUE The Astrologer returns to reassure the audience: only he and the Queen were real, the rest were just illusions, figments of the imagination.

Music and Background

This was the culmination of Rimsky's operatic achievement: a compact but highly-wrought score that relies on an elaborate system of motifs associated with the different characters. You hear a summary of the most important ones in the opening prologue, including the trumpet figure that represents the cockerel itself; and as they progress through the score, they function in something like the leitmotifs in Wagner, revealing information above and beyond the letter of the libretto. In keeping with the cartoon-like satire of the piece, Rimsky's score is full of musical jokes, including the parodies of folk style and an improbably high-tenor range for the Astrologer.

Highlights

Act II: the Queen of Shemakha's Hymn to the Sun, accompanied by solo clarinet, is one of Rimsky's best-known vocal compositions. Act III: the sustained top E (!) required of the Astrologer when he declares his intention to marry.

Did You Know?

🔊 Rimsky had spent the earlier years of his life in the navy, and he clearly wrote *The Golden Cockerel* as a satire on the military incompetence of Nicholas II's court (which had just lost the Russo-Japanese War). Unsurprisingly, it ran into censorship problems, which delayed the premiere until after Rimsky's death.

Recommended Recording

At the time of writing no version of the complete score is available: only a DG recording (447 084-2) of the orchestral suite from the opera by the Russian National Orchestra under Mikhail Pletnev.

The Legend of the Invisible City of Kitezh

FORM: Opera in four acts; in Russian
COMPOSER: Nikolai Rimsky-Korsakov (1844–1908)
LIBRETTO: Vladimir Bel'sky; after Mel'nikov, Meledin
and other traditional sources
FIRST PERFORMANCE: St Petersburg, 20 February 1907

Principal Characters

Prince Yury, ruler of Kitezh   **Bass**
Prince Vsevolod, his son   **Tenor**
Fevroniya   **Soprano**
Grishka   **Tenor**

Synopsis of the Plot

Setting: Legendary Russia

ACT I Fevroniya lives in the forest with her woodsman brother. One day, while she is wandering among the trees, she meets a huntsman who has lost his way and the two fall in love. Hearing the sound of his companions approaching, the young man leaves, after promising to send representatives to her brother to ask for her hand in marriage. When the hunting party arrives, searching for the young man, Fevroniya learns that he is Prince Vsevolod, Prince Yury's son.

ACT II Fevroniya is on her way to the city of Greater Kitezh to be married. As her procession passes through the town of Lesser Kitezh, the people turn out to greet and entertain her. But there is some dissatisfaction among a certain group, who deride the bride's low-born status and encourage the drunken Grishka to mock and humiliate her. Suddenly, the town is attacked by Tartars and Fevroniya and Grishka are taken hostage; Grishka is forced to guide the Tartars to Greater Kitezh and Fevroniya prays that the city will become invisible to the enemy.

ACT III In Greater Kitezh, preparations are being made to defend the city from the Tartars and Prince Yury appoints his son to lead the attack. As the soldiers march away, a golden mist envelops the city and it vanishes. Meanwhile, Grishka has taken the Tartars to a hilltop, from where they should be able to see the city. Seeing nothing but a golden mist, the Tartars accuse Grishka of treachery and threaten to torture him. Soon Vsevolod is killed, his army routed and the Tartars set to dividing the spoils of war. That night, Grishka, beset by guilt and shame, begs Fevroniya to untie him; once released he runs to the lake to drown himself, but the rays of the rising sun reveal the reflection of Kitezh in the water. The terrified Grishka runs away, taking Fevroniya with him.

ACT IV Grishka and Fevroniya are struggling through the forest. By now Grishka's mind is almost completely unbalanced, and, beset by visions and illusions, he runs off, howling, into the darkness. Fevroniya, alone, falls asleep and the forest around her is transformed – candles and exotic flowers appear and strange birds sing. The spirit of Vsevolod appears and leads her to the Invisible City, where the interrupted wedding celebrations are joyfully resumed.

Music and Background

Arguably the most alluring of all Rimsky's operas, this colourful collage of Christian mysticism, pantheism and folklore is sometimes called the Russian *Parsifal*: a lofty comparison but not without justification. Wagner was certainly a model, and Rimsky must have had him firmly in mind when he was writing the miracle music of Acts III and IV, and the transcendent chorale-like theme of the final scene. But *Kitezh* remains rooted in Russian tradition: a thing of grand spectacle, awkward structure, ravishing orchestral sounds, and with a collective rather than an individual focus – which means (as always with Rimsky) that the characterisation is not strong.

Highlights

The opening scene (often compared to the Forest Murmurs Scene in Wagner's *Siegfried*), and the symphonic music linking the two scenes of Act IV: a breathtaking example of Russian scenery in sound, as the bells chime and Fevroniya's soul passes to the Invisible City.

Did You Know?

🞜 Rimsky taught Stravinsky at the St Petersburg Conservatoire, and his fantasy operas had enormous influence on Stravinsky's own early stage works.

Recommended Recording

There is no recording currently available.

Gioacchino Rossini

(1792–1868)

Tancredi (1813)
L'Italiana in Algeri (1813)
Il Turco in Italia (1814)
Il Barbiere di Siviglia (1816)
La Cenerentola (1817)
La Gazza Ladra (1817)
Mosè in Egitto (1817)
Ermione (1819)
Semiramide (1823)
Il Viaggio a Reims (1825)
Le Comte Ory (1828)
Guillaume Tell (1829)

Rossini was by any standards a phenomenon. At the age of thirty he had written thirty-nine operas and was the most famous stage composer in Europe. The energy, pace, wit and all-round brilliance of his writing had set the world standard for opera in the early 19th century and effectively fixed its rules as well. The strategic planning with which he organised his work had been taken up and copied by just about everyone around him. The theatres of Italy, France, Austria and Germany were his for the asking. He was envied by Beethoven and Schubert. Then, suddenly, he retired. He lived on for nearly another forty years but produced very little and not a single opera. Why? Partly because he had moved his base from Naples to Paris where, in 1830, a political revolution destabilised his relationship with the Opéra. Partly because he felt that public tastes were moving on and leaving him behind. Partly because of ill health. But mostly, it seems, because he was burnt out. His creative drive had gone and he was rich enough for new income to be irrelevant, so he stopped. In his retirement years he stayed in Paris, where his *Samedi soirs* ('Saturday evenings') were legendary.

Il Barbiere di Siviglia
(The Barber of Seville)

FORM: Opera in two acts; in Italian
COMPOSER: Gioacchino Rossini (1792–1868)
LIBRETTO: Cesare Sterbini; after Beaumarchais
FIRST PERFORMANCE: Rome, 20 February 1816

Principal Characters

Count Almaviva, a young nobleman ✍ Tenor
Figaro, a barber ✍ Baritone
Dr Bartolo ✍ Bass
Rosina, his rich ward ✍ Mezzo-soprano
Don Basilio, a singing teacher ✍ Bass

Synopsis of the Plot

Setting: Seville; 18th century

ACT I Almaviva, in love with Rosina, romantically serenades her beneath her window, but there is no response. He is still morosely waiting outside the house when Figaro comes along and the two men recognise each other. Figaro offers to help Almaviva in his attempts to win Rosina but he also warns the Count that Dr Bartolo aims to marry Rosina himself. At that moment a note flutters down from Rosina's window and Almaviva retrieves it; in it, Rosina asks for the name of her unknown admirer. Almaviva responds with a song in which he tells her he is Lindoro, a poor student, as he does not wish his true identity as a wealthy aristocrat to influence her feelings for him. Now Almaviva is more desperate than ever to win Rosina and begs Figaro to think of a plan, pressing money in his hand to encourage him. The two men part and the scene changes to Dr Bartolo's house. The doctor has heard rumours of the Count's arrival in the city and, anxious to make sure his rich ward becomes his wife, resolves to marry her that very day. As the doctor and Don Basilio go out to draft the contract, Figaro arrives for his appointment to shave Dr Bartolo. In the doctor's absence he takes the opportunity of telling Rosina that his 'cousin', Lindoro, is desperately in love with her. Rosina feigns modest surprise, but in fact has already written a letter to him, which she hands to Figaro. At that moment Bartolo returns and, after accusing Rosina of writing secret notes to a lover, threatens to lock her up. The quarrel is interrupted by the entry of Almaviva, disguised as a drunken soldier, and waving an order billeting him at Bartolo's house. The doctor protests, Almaviva insists and the ensuing row attracts the attention of the city watch. Almaviva is arrested, but when the Count quietly reveals his true identity, he is promptly released and, moreover, saluted! The company is momentarily stunned into silence by this inexplicable development, but soon falls again to wrangling and confusion.

ACT II Dr Bartolo is reflecting on the day's events when the Count, newly disguised, is ushered in; he has come, he says, for Rosina's music lesson, deputising for Don Basilio who is ill. Bartolo fetches Rosina and the 'music lesson' begins, allowing the two lovers a longed-for opportunity to express their feelings for each other. Then Figaro arrives, once more, to shave Bartolo, followed unexpectedly by Don Basilio, who, encouraged by a purse of gold from Almaviva, decides he really is ill, after all, and goes home. The lovers plan their elopement but are overheard by Bartolo, who summarily ejects Figaro and Almaviva from his house, resolving to marry Rosina immediately. That evening, Almaviva and Figaro climb up to Rosina's balcony, but she refuses to leave until she is told the whole truth about Almaviva's identity; by that time, however, the ladder has disappeared. Basilio arrives with the notary, ready to formalise the betrothal of Bartolo and Rosina, but is persuaded, instead, to join together Almaviva and Rosina with Basilio (bribed by a valuable gift) as witness. Bartolo arrives, but too late, and the opera ends in general reconciliation.

Music and Background

Rossini's masterpiece and arguably the greatest of all comic operas, *Il Barbiere di Siviglia* plays like a text-book demonstration of all the vital ingredients in Rossini opera put to perfect use. The combination of energy, elegance and ironic wit is matchless. The finesse of the orchestral writing is superlative. And there's no better example of the 'Rossini crescendo' (a short phrase endlessly repeated with ever-growing accompaniment) than the explosive accumulating force of Basilio's Calumny Aria. The story is effectively a prequel to the situation in Mozart's *Le Nozze di Figaro*, taken from the same Beaumarchais source. 'Lindoro' and Rosina are the younger selves of Mozart's Count and Countess, although Rossini assigns them to different voices. In modern performances, however, Rosina's role is often transposed up and sung (as in Mozart) by a soprano.

Highlights

The Overture (borrowed from an earlier Rossini opera but still very effective). Act I: Figaro's famous opening cavatina 'Largo al factotum'; 'Lindoro's' serenade 'Se il mio nome'; Rosina's spectacular showpiece 'Una voce poco fa'; Basilio's show-stopping 'La calunnia'; the grand finale of confusion 'Fredda ed immobile'. Act II: the whole Music Lesson Scene and the elopement trio 'Ah! Qual colpo inaspettato'.

Did You Know?

Il Barbiere di Siviglia is supposed to have been written in under a fortnight.

312

~ Adelina Patti sang the role of Rosina many times, and in response to the usual demands for an encore in the Music Lesson Scene, she always offered 'Home, Sweet Home', which eventually became her signature tune. ~ Berlioz recounted how, on a visit to Italy, he noticed that the overtures to *Il Barbiere di Siviglia* and *La Cenerentola* had become particular favourites of church organists, 'which gave an unusual flavour to divine service'.

Recommended Recording

Cecilia Bartoli, Leo Nucci, Paata Burchuladze, Teatro Comunale di Bologna/Giuseppe Patanè. Decca 425 520-2. An early Bartoli recording that reveals her at her youthful best: a rich but brilliant mezzo making more impact on disc than it ever would in a theatre.

La Cenerentola
(*Cinderella*)

FORM: Opera in two acts; in Italian
COMPOSER: Gioacchino Rossini (1792–1868)
LIBRETTO: Jacopo Ferretti; after Charles Perrault
FIRST PERFORMANCE: Rome, 25 January 1817

Principal Characters

Don Magnifico, an impoverished nobleman ~ **Bass**
Clorinda, his daughter, half-sister to Cinderella ~ **Soprano**
Tisbe, his daughter, half-sister to Cinderella ~ **Mezzo-soprano**
Angelina, known as Cinderella, Don Magnifico's step-daughter
~ **Mezzo-soprano**
Ramiro, Prince of Salerno ~ **Tenor**
Alidoro, his tutor ~ **Bass**
Dandini, the prince's valet ~ **Baritone**

Synopsis of the Plot

Setting: Don Magnifico's house and the palace

ACT I At home, Cinderella goes about her household tasks while her half-sisters spend their time preening in front of the mirror. Alidoro arrives, disguised as a beggar, and Cinderella gives him some food, much to her sisters' annoyance. But their irritation is soon forgotten when news arrives that Prince Ramiro is to throw a magnificent ball, at which he will choose his future wife; indeed, an invitation will be delivered to their household by the Prince himself! Clorinda and Tisbe redouble their efforts before the mirror and the 'beggar' leaves, but not before telling Cinderella that she will soon be happy. Meanwhile, Alidoro has reported back to the Prince, who decides to investigate Don Magnifico's household for himself. He disguises himself as his servant, Dandini, and arrives at the Don's house where he falls instantly in love with Cinderella, and she with him. Dandini, masquerading as Ramiro, soon follows him and issues the invitation to the ball. Cinderella begs her father to take her, with her sisters, but he refuses and tells her to stay at home. Alidoro then returns (as himself), bringing a list of all the unmarried women in the region; he asks Don Magnifico the whereabouts of his third daughter. The Don, confused, replies that she is dead. When they are alone together, Alidoro tells an incredulous Cinderella that she shall indeed go to the ball – and he will take her. At the ball, Clorinda and Tisbe are being mercilessly teased by the Prince and Dandini, each still disguised as the other. A mysterious lady arrives and, when she removes her veil, her beauty and her strange resemblance to Cinderella cause great astonishment.

ACT II Dandini, as Ramiro, has fallen in love with Cinderella, but she tells him she loves his 'valet' (the real prince). Before leaving, she gives the 'valet' a bracelet and says he will find her wearing its companion; if he loves her, he will search for her and she will be his. The ball over, the sisters and Don Magnifico return home to find Cinderella in front of the fire. Suddenly, the Prince himself arrives (Alidoro had arranged for his coach to 'break down' outside their home); he recognises Cinderella and takes her away to the palace. Clorinda and Tisbe are forgiven and Cinderella celebrates her wonderful change of fortune.

Music and Background

The comedy of *La Cenerentola* doesn't fizz in quite the same way as *Il Barbiere di Siviglia*, *L'Italiana in Algeri* and the other Rossini comedies: it is subtler, more affectionate, and with a touching pathos in the presentation of the central character. Cinderella is another of Rossini's low-flying, mezzo coloraturas (which means she has to be capable of florid singing), but her role comes with a repeating theme tune as simple, gentle and unfussy as a folk song. The whole opera was conceived and written in under a month (over a Christmas too!), and in the haste of it all Rossini borrowed a pre-existing overture and hired an assistant to help with some of the music. The assistant's numbers were later replaced by Rossini himself, but much of the surviving recitative remains the work of other hands.

Highlights

The Overture (albeit borrowed). Act I: Cinderella's wistful ballad 'Una volta c'era un rè'; the Ramiro/Cinderella duet 'Un soave non so che'; the comic ensemble 'Come un'ape'; Cinderella's touching request to go to the ball, 'Signor, una parola'; the grand finale, starting with 'Zitto, zitto' and culminating in a big 'Rossini crescendo' number 'Mi par d'essere sognando'. Act II: the duet for two basses – Dandini and the father – 'Un segreto d'importanza'; the intricate sextet 'Siete voi?'

Did You Know?

∾ The substitution of a bracelet for the glass slipper in the story was almost certainly to placate the Roman censors who wouldn't have cared for the spectacle of a naked foot in their local theatres.

Recommended Recording

Cecilia Bartoli, William Matteuzzi, Alessando Corbelli, Teatro Comunale di Bologna/Riccardo Chailly. Decca 436 902-2. One of the best Rossini issues of recent years, with Bartoli positively relishing her own accomplishment in the title role.

Guillaume Tell
(William Tell)

FORM: Opera in four acts; in French
COMPOSER: Gioacchino Rossini (1792–1868)
LIBRETTO: Étienne de Jouy, H-L-F. Bis and Armand Marrast;
after Schiller
FIRST PERFORMANCE: Paris, 3 August 1829

Principal Characters

William Tell ∾ Baritone
Jemmy, his son ∾ Soprano
Arnold, in love with Mathilde ∾ Tenor
Melcthal, Arnold's father ∾ Bass
Gesler, the Austrian governor ∾ Bass
Mathilde, an Austrian princess ∾ Soprano
Leuthold, a shepherd ∾ Bass

315

Synopsis of the Plot

Setting: Switzerland; 14th century

ACT I The villagers gather beside Lake Lucerne to celebrate an ancient festival, during which the village patriarch, Melcthal, blesses young lovers. But this peaceful and happy occasion is set against an increasingly threatening political situation and the Swiss are becoming more and more vulnerable in the face of Austrian aggression. Indeed, before the day is over, the celebrations are interrupted by the sudden arrival of Leuthold, a shepherd who, having killed an Austrian soldier to prevent him from raping his daughter, is now being hunted by the enemy. Leuthold begs someone to take him across the lake to safety and William Tell immediately volunteers. As soon as they leave, Austrian soldiers arrive; angry at being cheated of their quarry, they take Melcthal prisoner and loot the village.

ACT II Arnold, Melcthal's son, and his beloved, the Austrian princess, Mathilde, meet and reaffirm their love for each other. But when she sees Tell approaching, she runs away, promising to meet Arnold the next day. Tell relates the sad news that Melcthal has been executed and Arnold swears to avenge his death. They are joined by representatives from other cantons who have travelled from far and near to swear an oath of allegiance and fight against the Austrian oppressors.

ACT III Gesler, the Austrian commander, has put his hat on top of a pole in the town of Altdorf and, to celebrate one hundred years of Austrian rule, compels all the Swiss townspeople to salute it. Tell and his son, Jemmy, refuse to do so and, as he is also recognised as the man who saved Leuthold, Tell is arrested. Gesler announces that Tell can save himself by shooting an apple from his son's head and this Tell does, announcing that a second arrow he had concealed would have been for Gesler, had he harmed Jemmy. This prompts Gesler to rearrest Tell and send him to the notorious dungeons at Küssnecht Castle.

ACT IV On learning that Tell is a prisoner, Arnold takes over his role as leader of the patriots and reveals the secret cache of arms hidden by Melcthal and Tell. Mathilde has rescued Jemmy and offers herself to the patriots as a hostage for the release of Tell. As Gesler, Tell and the guards board the boat to cross the lake, Jemmy lights the beacon that signals the beginning of the insurrection. Out on the lake, the boat is threatened by a violent storm and Tell's hands are freed so that he can guide the boat ashore. Once there, however, Tell leaps ashore and manages to propel the boat, and its passengers, out on the stormy lake again. He takes his bow and shoots Gesler. Altdorf is freed from Austrian rule and the Swiss celebrate as the skies clear to reveal the magnificent mountain landscape.

Music and Background

Rossini is essentially remembered today as a comedian, but most of his work was serious, and his years in Naples were dominated by a large output of romantic-historical scores which prepared the ground for *Guillaume Tell* –

by far the grandest and weightiest of his theatre works. *Guillaume Tell* was his final opera, written after his move to Paris and addressing the specific expectations of French audiences in the mid-19th century. It is grand opera with a vengeance: long, imposing, richly scored with ballet sequences, considerable spectacle and massive choruses. In fact, the chorus largely carries the plot, through epic scenes of patriotic fervour. In contrast to the lightning facility with which Rossini seems to have worked in the past, *Guillaume Tell* had a tortuous birth; and the problems may well have been another factor in his decision to write nothing more for the stage.

Highlights

The Overture (positively infamous). Act I: Arnold's 'Ah, Mathilde'. Act II: Mathilde's 'Sombres forêts'; the oath-taking trio for Arnold, Tell and Walter leading to the grand assembly of the Cantons. Act III: Tell's 'Sois immobile' before the Trial Shot. Act IV: Arnold's 'Asile hereditaire', sung as he revisits his birthplace.

Did You Know?

🔊 While working on the score of *Guillaume Tell* Rossini obtained from the French government a lifetime annuity in recognition of his services to opera.
🔊 Gilbert-Louis Duprez (1806–90) was reputedly the first tenor to sing top C as a chest note in the 1831 Italian premiere of *Guillaume Tell*. Rossini likened it to the 'squawk of a chicken having its throat cut'.

Recommended Recording

Gabriel Bacquier, Montserrat Caballé, Nicolai Gedda, Royal Philharmonic Orchestra/Lamberto Gardelli. EMI CMS7 69951-2. Sung in French, with sensitivity, and generally preferable to the rival Italian version with Pavarotti and Freni on Decca.

L'Italiana in Algeri
(*The Italian Girl in Algiers*)

FORM: Opera in two acts; in Italian
COMPOSER: Gioacchino Rossini (1792–1868)
LIBRETTO: Angelo Anelli
FIRST PERFORMANCE: Venice, 22 May 1813

Principal Characters

Mustafà, the Bey of Algiers ❧ **Bass**
Elvira, his wife ❧ **Soprano**
Haly, Captain of the Guard ❧ **Bass**
Isabella ❧ **Contralto**
Lindoro, her beloved ❧ **Tenor**
Taddeo, her elderly admirer ❧ **Bass**

Synopsis of the Plot

Setting: Algiers; early 1800s

ACT I Mustafà, the Bey of Algiers, is bored with his wife, Elvira, and orders Haly to go to Italy to find him a new one, much to Elvira's dismay. Haly does not need to go very far, however, for before he leaves, a ship is wrecked off the Algerian coast carrying the Italian, Isabella, and her ageing admirer, Taddeo. The pair have been travelling the seas searching for Isabella's sweetheart, Lindoro, now a servant of the Bey. News of the capture of a beautiful Italian girl quickly reaches the palace and Mustafà promises Lindoro his freedom (and money) if he will return to Italy and take Elvira with him, leaving the Bey free to marry the Italian girl. Isabella is brought in and Mustafà is instantly captivated (although Isabella is considerably less taken with his unprepossessing appearance). When Lindoro and Elvira come to take their leave before embarking for Italy, the two lovers recognise each other. Isabella, with great presence of mind, disconcerts the ardent Mustafà by saying she could never marry a man who treated his wife in such a way; in addition, Mustafà should allow Lindoro, as an Italian like herself, to remain with her in Algiers.

ACT II Isabella and Lindoro plan an escape, as the lovelorn Mustafà becomes increasingly desperate to be alone with his lovely potential bride, who always manages to evade him. Mustafà's patience is wearing thin (and there is always the threat of impalement in the background), when Isabella announces, to his immense delight, that she has planned a special ceremony to bestow on Mustafà the noble Italian order of the Pappataci, in which members undertake to 'eat and be silent' (the characteristics of a perfect, complaisant husband). The ceremony begins with trials to test Mustafà's commitment to the noble order, including the sight of Lindoro and Isabella indulging in a display of mutual passion in front of him. Mustafà fails this test. The next test involves Isabella and Lindoro embarking on a ship (crewed by the Bey's Italian servants), which then sails away. Taddeo, who has by now been made Grand Kamaikan of Algeria by the Bey, alerts his master to the escape. But Mustafà quickly reconciles himself to the fact that he has been duped, and acknowledges that Italian girls are much too clever for him. He turns again to the faithful Elvira, who willingly forgives him.

Music and Background

L'Italiana in Algeri is either a masterpiece of comic invention or a silly romp, depending on your point of view and the vitality of the staging, but the discipline of the writing is undeniable, and an extraordinary feat of control for a composer who was only twenty-one when he wrote it. This was in fact his first enduring comic hit, and although it is effectively driven by farce, there are moments of poignancy that substantiate the writing. The patriotism in the piece is also semi-serious and considered in its time as politically subversive: a rallying call for the unification of a still-divided Italy.

Highlights

The Overture – one of Rossini's very best. Act I: Lindoro's touching cavatina 'Languir per una bella'; the Isabella/Taddeo ruse duet 'Ai capricci della sorte'; the nonsensical finale of confusion 'Va sossopra il mio cervello'. Act II: the 'Pappataci' trio; Isabella's patriotic song 'Pensa alla patria'; the finale 'La bella Italiana'.

Did You Know?

In the year preceding this opera, Rossini had written no fewer than six others. *L'Italiana in Algeri* was allegedly completed in twenty-seven days.

Recommended Recording

Agnes Baltsa, Ruggero Raimondi, Vienna Philharmonic Orchestra/Claudio Abbado. DG 427 331-2. Award-winning discs taken from a Vienna State Opera production with a fiery but elegant cast.

Camille Saint-Saëns

(1835–1921)

Samson et Dalila (1877)
Henry VIII (1883)

*B*orn in Paris, Saint-Saëns pursued a broad range of musical interests as a pianist, organist, conductor and scholar through a long life. He died in Algiers at the age of eighty-six. Only one of his thirteen operas, *Samson et Dalila*, proved successful in his lifetime, and it remains the only one in the repertory today. Otherwise, he was known for his orchestral works, including five symphonies (two of them withdrawn), and sacred choral music. A regular visitor to Britain, where he was much admired, he wrote a march for the coronation of Edward VII in 1902. Saint-Saëns is generally thought of as a craftsman rather than as an inspired man of the theatre, responsible for solid, workmanlike scores with a strong sense of form but limited emotional appeal. This is partly true. But it is also true that he was indebted to the great Romantic, Liszt, and through the formal clarity of his writing he was capable of touching hearts, as *Samson et Dalila* shows.

Samson et Dalila
(Samson and Delilah)

FORM: Opera in three acts; in French
COMPOSER: Camille Saint-Saëns (1835–1921)
LIBRETTO: Ferdinand Lemaire; after the Bible (Old Testament)
FIRST PERFORMANCE: Weimar, 2 December 1877 (in German)

Principal Characters

Samson, Hebrew warrior ✒ **Tenor**
Delilah, Philistine beauty ✒ **Mezzo-soprano**
High Priest of Dagon ✒ **Baritone**
Abimelech, Philistine Satrap of Gaza ✒ **Bass**

Synopsis of the Plot

Setting: Biblical Gaza

ACT I The Jews have gathered together by the Temple of Dagon to bemoan their domination by the Philistines. Samson speaks out, saying that God has told him that they will soon be free. The crowd's enthusiasm attracts the attention of Abimelech, who mocks the Jews and their God. As he goes to attack Samson, Samson seizes Abimelech's sword and kills him. This act precipitates a large-scale and successful uprising of the Jews across the country. When Delilah and several other Philistine women arrive, supposedly to celebrate the Jews' victory, Samson is overcome by her overwhelming beauty and asks God to help him resist her; but it is no use, he is spellbound.

ACT II Outside her house, Delilah contemplates how her love for Samson has now turned to hatred and, encouraged by the High Priest, considers how she can use her power over him to destroy him. When she is joined by Samson, Delilah tells him how much she loves him and, as a thunderstorm gathers overhead, begs him to tell her the secret of his strength. Unable to resist her, Samson gives way; when he is asleep, Delilah cuts off his hair, the source of his strength, and he is led away by Philistine soldiers.

ACT III Samson, blinded and manacled, turns the millwheel in the prison, suffering the reproaches of his fellow Jews. At the instigation of the High Priest, he is taken to the Temple of Dagon where celebrations are under way. Mocked and derided, Samson is led to the central pillars of the temple where, calling on God to give him back his strength once more, he pushes away the supports and brings down the temple, destroying himself as well as his enemies.

Music and Background

Saint-Saëns originally planned this piece as an oratorio, and some indications of its origin remain in the way the old oratorio precedents colour the writing for the opposing choral groups. The Hebrews sing in the style of Bach, the Philistines tend towards Handel. That apart, the model here is Meyerbeerian grand opera, programmed for spectacle but scaled down for taste. Delilah gets the best of the score, with three varied arias that build into a powerfully three-dimensional portrait of one of opera's most alluring *femmes fatales*.

Highlights

Act I: Samson's opening scene, 'Arrêtez, ô mes frères', and call to liberty 'Israël! romps ta chaîne'. Delilah's ensnarement aria 'Printemps qui commence'. Act II: Delilah's steely 'Amour! viens aider ma faiblesse' and seductive 'Mon coeur s'ouvre à ta voix' – the opera's most celebrated number. Act III: Samson's 'Vois ma misère', and the Bacchanale in the temple.

Did You Know?

✎ *Samson et Dalila*'s Biblical subject matter and sometimes symphonic style took a long while to find favour in France, where there was no staging until thirteen years after the score was completed. Thereafter, it became an instant hit, its tunes much-loved by street musicians.

✎ Objections to the plot also kept the opera from London until 1909, when, after personal intervention by Edward VII to lift the Lord Chamberlain's ban, it was finally performed.

✎ Between 1890 and 1920, the opera achieved great success, being performed over five hundred times worldwide in those thirty years.

Recommended Recording

Plácido Domingo, Waltraud Meier, Bastille Opera/Myung-Whun Chung. EMI CDS7 54470-2. Domingo's second recording of this opera for EMI and arguably the better of the two: intelligent, heroic, with Meier providing in excitement what she lacks in pure beauty.

Aulis Sallinen

(1935–)

The Horseman (1975)
The Red Line (1978)
The King Goes Forth to France (1984)
Kullervo (1988)
The Palace (1993)

A remarkable phenomenon of recent years is the emergence of Finland from nowhere as a centre for new opera, and the composer most obviously responsible is Aulis Sallinen, who came to prominence in the 1970s with the first of a striking series of scores which have mostly premiered in Finland's famous Savonlinna Opera Festival. To most ears he counts as a conservative figure, writing in lyrical reaction against the twelve-tone procedures that governed his earliest works, and there are unarguable traces of Sibelius and Bartók in his music, as well as a biting strain of Shostakovich which shows up in the grim, sardonic humour and surreal whimsy of *The King Goes Forth to France* or *The Palace*. But there is also an uncompromising toughness, heard most obviously in *Kullervo*: a brutal Finnish epic set in searing, hard-edged sounds.

The Red Line

FORM: Opera in two acts; in Finnish
COMPOSER: Aulis Sallinen (1935–)
LIBRETTO: Aulis Sallinen; after Kianto
FIRST PERFORMANCE: Helsinki, 30 November 1978

Principal Characters

Topi, a peasant ~ Baritone
Riika, his wife ~ Soprano
Simana Arhippaini, a pedlar ~ Bass
Puntarpää, a political agitator ~ Baritone
A vicar ~ Tenor
A young priest ~ Baritone
Kunilla, the cobbler's wife ~ Spoken role

Synopsis of the Plot

Setting: Finland, 1907, at the time of the first election
under universal suffrage

ACT I The peasant, Topi, and his wife, Riika, are living lives of abject
poverty and misery, barely surviving the cold and hardships of winter. Topi's
discovery of a sheep savaged to death by the great bear plunges him into new
depression. Even sleep can bring him no comfort, for he dreams that his last
desperate efforts to get poor relief from the church are doomed – although
the vicar offers him a bargain price for the burial of his three little children,
since they will all fit into one coffin! Simana, a travelling pedlar, passes by
and asks for shelter for the night; he tells them of growing unrest in the
country and, later, after a visit to the village, Topi himself excitedly brings
news of speeches he has heard announcing a 'new order' to come and even
an election where the poor will have the power to vote for what they want.
Topi and Riika attend a political meeting at which the professional agitator,
Puntarpää, whips up the poorly-educated, politically-unsophisticated
villagers into a frenzy of anti-clerical feeling and class hatred. Finally, he
exhorts his largely illiterate audience each to draw a red line in the 'right'
place on the voting papers to bring in the glorious new age of liberty, equality
and fraternity.

ACT II As the election approaches, Topi and his neighbours discuss the
best ways of making their mark, the red line, on the ballot paper as the dogs
howl outside at the restless turning of the great bear in his winter sleep. Topi
and his wife proudly cast their votes on polling day, ignoring the priest's
prophecy of forthcoming strife. Later, Riika is waiting miserably at home for
Topi's return from the logging camp where he has work. Their children have,

324

one by one, succumbed to malnutrition and illness and, when Topi at last returns home, it is to discover that all his children have died. As he goes out to arrange the funeral, he recollects his dream – maybe, he thinks, the vicar will give him a cut-price deal as they will all fit into one coffin. News arrives that the election has been won and Kunilla, the cobbler's wife, joyfully anticipates a golden future for them all. But for Topi it is too late; hearing the terrified lowing of his last cow and the frenzied barking of the dogs, he knows that the bear has woken and is on the prowl. Rushing outside he tackles the animal but he is no match for it. Distraught, Riika finds her husband dead in the snow, a red line of blood seeping from his throat.

Music and Background

This is a prime example of post-Sibelius Finnish nationalism, with contrasting choruses that represent the old traditions of folk life and the new revolutionary stirrings for political freedom (Finland was a vassal state of Russia until 1917). But it is also a realistic portrayal of human beings, with sympathy and depth and an underlying lyricism that survives a story as bleak and desperate as anything in Thomas Hardy. *The Red Line* sets out to shock, but does so with compassion. It is certainly one of the most effectively theatrical operas to have been written in the second half of the 20th century.

Highlights

It's not that sort of a score.

Did You Know?

The Finnish elections of 1907 were the first in Europe in which women were allowed to vote.

Recommended Recording

Jorma Hynninen, Taru Valjakka, Finnish National Opera/Okko Kamu. FACD 102. Outstanding for the lead role of the Finnish baritone Hynninen but, in any event, the only recording.

Arnold Schoenberg

(1874–1951)

Erwartung (1909)
Die Glückliche Hand (1913)
Moses und Aron (1932, unfinished)

Born in Vienna, Arnold Schoenberg was largely self-taught as a musician but became *the* great music teacher of modern times, devising in the mid-1920s a system known as Serialism which revolutionised 20th-century composition and came to dominate the production of new works over the next forty years. Essentially it was a development of his highly chromatic (and highly neurotic) late-Romantic/Expressionist scores of the 1900s, which include the two short psychodramas *Erwartung* and *Die Glückliche Hand*. With ever more tortuous harmonic schemes, they had been moving gradually away from the traditional expectations of music written in a specific key signature. 'Serial' music marked the ultimate abandonment of keys. Instead, the music was constructed out of 'tone rows': series of all twelve semitones of the chromatic scale, with no one note enjoying dominance over any of the others. Schoenberg's *Moses und Aron* is an example, one of the very few twelve-tone operas to survive in something like repertory, even though it was never finished. Schoenberg was Jewish and in 1933 he was forced to flee Europe; he settled in California and died there in 1951.

Moses und Aron
(Moses and Aaron)

FORM: Opera in three acts; in German
COMPOSER: Arnold Schoenberg (1874–1951)
LIBRETTO: Arnold Schoenberg, after the Bible (Old Testament)
FIRST PERFORMANCE: Zürich, 6 June 1957

Principal Characters

Moses ⁓ Bass speaking role
Voice from the Burning Bush (God) ⁓ Semi-chorus of six singers
Aaron, Moses' brother ⁓ Tenor

Synopsis of the Plot

Setting: Biblical Egypt at the time of the Israelites' captivity

ACT I Moses, at prayer, hears the Voice from the Burning Bush and receives the call from God to lead the captive Israelites to the Promised Land. Moses' response is to plead his lack of eloquence in the face of such a task, but the Voice tells him that his brother, Aaron, will be his mouthpiece. When Moses meets Aaron in the Wasteland, Aaron already knows what is expected of him, but the two men have different approaches to their task. To Moses, God is unknowable and unimaginable, pure thought in fact; but the pragmatic Aaron believes that images and miracles are more likely to persuade the Israelites of the power of God and thus to follow Moses out of Egypt. These contrasting attitudes to God are reflected in the messages Moses and Aaron bring to the people, who are sceptical of Moses' concept of an infinite, invisible God, but much more inclined to be convinced when Aaron turns Moses' staff into a snake, the first of three miracles which persuade the people to put their faith in God and to set out on the long march through the desert to freedom.

ACT II Some time has passed and Moses has been away on the Mount of Revelation for forty days, receiving the new Law. The people have become restless and mutinous and they demand a return to their former beliefs and gods. Aaron tells them to bring him gold and he will make them an image of their new God, something tangible that they can see and worship. The Golden Calf is made and the people rejoice in a wild orgy of sacrifice (human and animal), slaughter, fighting, drunkenness, rape and sexual excess. As the orgy finally subsides into exhaustion, a lone voice announces Moses' return from the mountain, bringing with him the tablets of the Law. The Golden Calf falls to pieces and the people run away. Moses and Aaron argue and Aaron again maintains that the people need something concrete, something comprehensible which will represent their faith; indeed, he points out, the tablets of the Law that Moses has brought back are images in just the same way as the Golden Calf. Moses' response to this is to smash the tablets and pray to God to relieve him of his burden. Behind them, the Israelites have resumed their march to the desert and are seen following another image, the pillar of fire; Aaron joins them and Moses is left alone, in despair at his inability to convince the people of the true nature of God.

ACT III Aaron is brought to Moses in chains and, in an extended discussion, they restate their different approaches to the idea of God. Aaron's defence of his actions proves inadequate but nevertheless Moses orders his chains to be struck off. At the moment of his release, Aaron falls dead.

Music and Background

No one could pretend that this is easy listening. Entirely constructed from a single twelve-note row, the score is complex, tough, and demands careful attention, with vocal writing that implies but rarely delivers recognisable lyricism. The libretto hangs on a debate about revelation and communication which can read in drily academic terms. And there are two problems that prove unsurmountable: the allocation of speech rather than song to the central role, and the fact that there is no music for Act III (which productions accordingly either ignore or present as spoken theatre). The surprising thing about *Moses und Aron* is that it works as well as it does on stage: oratorio-like but with strong, dynamic choral writing and vividly imagined spectacle – not least the naked virgins and the orgy of self-destruction in Act II. *Moses und Aron* will never be popular, but it rewards effort.

Highlights

Act I: the music for the Voice of God out of the Burning Bush; the miracle sequence in the closing scene. Act II: the dance around the Golden Calf.

Did You Know?

≥. Schoenberg was obsessed by numerology, and deliberately misspelled 'Aaron' with only one 'a' because the title would otherwise have had thirteen letters.

Recommended Recording

Günther Reich, Richard Cassilly, BBC Symphony Orchestra/Pierre Boulez. Sony SM2K 48456. Abrasive but telling performances, under the iron hand of a master conductor.

Dmitri Shostakovich

(1909–75)

The Nose (1928)
Lady Macbeth of the Mtsensk District (1932)
The Gamblers (1942, unfinished)

*I*n Stalinist Russia it was generally safer to write abstract instrumental music than narrative stage works, and Shostakovich survived periods of extreme artistic repression by focusing his energies on orchestral and chamber writing. His fifteen symphonies and fifteen string quartets are among the finest of this century. However, *The Nose* was withdrawn, under attack as 'bourgeois decadence'. *Lady Macbeth* provoked a dangerously hostile article in *Pravda*, supposedly dictated by Stalin himself, and was similarly withdrawn. *The Gamblers* was abandoned when he realised that he would never be permitted to stage it. Crushed by the system all his life, Shostakovich developed an introverted way of writing, masking his emotions in burlesque and irony in terms influenced by Gustav Mahler.

Lady Macbeth of the Mtsensk District (Katerina Izmailova)

FORM: Opera in four acts; in Russian
COMPOSER: Dmitri Shostakovich (1905–75)
LIBRETTO: Dmitri Shostakovich and Alexandr Preis; after Leskov
FIRST PERFORMANCE: *Lady Macbeth*, Leningrad, 22 January 1934;
Katerina Izmailova, Moscow, 26 December 1962

Principal Characters

Katerina Izmailova ～ **Soprano**
Boris Izmailov, her father-in-law ～ **High baritone**
Zinovy Izmailov, her husband ～ **Tenor**
Sergei, a workman ～ **Tenor**
Aksinya, the cook ～ **Soprano**
Priest ～ **Baritone**
Chief of Police ～ **Baritone**
Policeman ～ **Baritone**
Sonyetka ～ **Contralto**

Synopsis of the Plot

Setting: In and around a Russian millhouse
and a Siberian prison camp; 19th century

ACT I Katerina has been married for five years and is bored and frustrated by life at the mill. Zinovy, her husband, is called away to the country but before he goes, he takes on a new workman, Sergei. Sergei quickly arouses Katerina's anger by taking the lead in cruelly baiting the cook, Aksinya; Katerina threatens him with a thrashing, but instead she allows herself to be tempted into a wrestling match with him and they are both on the ground when Boris unexpectedly returns. The sexual implications of their action are clear and Boris threatens to tell Zinovy of Katerina's scandalous behaviour. Katerina goes to bed but it is not long before Sergei comes knocking at her door and, without much resistance, she allows herself to be seduced.

ACT II Boris is walking outside Katerina's window when he realises what has been happening. He catches Sergei when he tries to leave and personally whips him, before having him locked in the storeroom and sending a messenger to bring Zinovy home. Katerina, apparently repentant, brings Boris a dish of mushrooms, but they are laced with rat-poison. As Boris collapses, Katerina retrieves the storeroom key from his belt. A priest arrives just in time to hear Boris accuse Katerina of poisoning him, but no one takes any notice of his words. Later, Katerina and Sergei are in bed together when they hear Zinovy's arrival home. Sergei quickly hides, but the furious Zinovy sees his belt in Katerina's room and whips his wife with it. Sergei emerges from his hiding-place and, assisted by Katerina, beats Zinovy to death before pushing his body into the cellar.

ACT III Some time has passed and Katerina and Sergei are to be married. One of those present, a drunken peasant, breaks into the cellar in search of more alcohol. He is horrified to discover Zinovy's decaying corpse and runs off to report his discovery to the police. The policemen, insulted at not being invited to the wedding, are only too pleased to be able to interrupt the celebrations by arresting the bride and groom.

ACT IV Sergei and Katerina are among a group of convicts en route to a new prison. The men and women are separated, but Katerina bribes a guard to allow her to see Sergei. However, Sergei has tired of her and he rejects her, preferring the younger Sonyetka. Sonyetka demands that he bring her some stockings and Sergei tricks Katerina into giving him her own, which he then presents to Sonyetka. The furious Katerina, mocked and humiliated by the other prisoners, pushes her rival into the river and then throws herself in after her. No one attempts to rescue them and the prisoners are ordered to march away.

Music and Background

A stark, sometimes shocking piece with a truly symphonic role for the orchestra, *Lady Macbeth* is conservative but individual in its style and proved popular with Russian audiences until Stalin saw it and objected. It was immediately withdrawn, forcing Shostakovich to do penance for his next symphony: No. 5, entitled 'A Soviet artist's reply to just criticism'. Some years later the opera was reworked (i.e. toned down) and re-presented as *Katerina Izmailova*; but latter-day productions generally prefer the original. Like Britten's *Peter Grimes*, the scenes of *Lady Macbeth* are held together by orchestral interludes, including a tension-building passacaglia (a repeating tune with accompanimental variations).

Highlights

Act I: Katerina's song of loneliness and the ensuing Love Scene. Act II: the devastating battery of brass chords that close the Death Scene, and the following passacaglia for orchestra. Act IV: Katerina's lament after Sergei rejects her.

Did You Know?

🐚 Shostakovich planned a trilogy of operas about Russian women but, after the official reception of this one, dropped the idea.

Recommended Recording

Galina Vishnevskaya, Nicolai Gedda, London Philharmonic/Mstislav Rostropovich. EMI CDS7 49955-2. The husband-and-wife team of Vishnevskaya and Rostropovich make a happier relationship than the couple in the opera: searing drama, balancing the brutalism and the beauty of the score.

Bedřich Smetana

(1824–84)

The Brandenburgers in Bohemia (1863)
The Bartered Bride (1866)
Dalibor (1867)
The Devil's Wall (1882)

*B*orn in Bohemia and spending most of his life in Prague, Smetana is remembered as the archetypal Czech national composer of the 19th century – although in his time he was considered a Wagner-disciple – and the content of his operas looks back through Mozart to the lighter vocalism of Italian writing. It was fortuitous that he emerged as a composer at exactly the time when Prague opened its first Czech-language theatre (performances were otherwise in German), and it was there that his career was based, as a conductor as well as a composer. Deafness dogged the last decade of his life, forcing him to stop conducting; and his consequent feelings of frustration and bitterness were agonisingly portrayed in his First String Quartet, which reproduces the effect of tinnitus with a sustained, high-level, whistling dissonance.

The Bartered Bride

FORM: Opera in three acts; in Czech
COMPOSER: Bedřich Smetana (1824–84)
LIBRETTO: Karel Sabina
FIRST PERFORMANCE: Prague, 30 May 1866

Principal Characters

Mícha, a landlord ᴥ **Bass**
Jeník, his long-lost son by his first wife ᴥ **Tenor**
Vašek, his son by his second wife ᴥ **Tenor**
Háta, Mícha's second wife ᴥ **Mezzo-soprano**
Kecal, a marriage broker ᴥ **Bass**
Krušina, a peasant ᴥ **Baritone**
Ludmila, his wife ᴥ **Soprano**
Mařenka, their daughter ᴥ **Soprano**

Synopsis of the Plot

Setting: A Bohemian village on its saint's day; early 19th century

ACT I Mařenka, alone among the joyful festivities, is sadly contemplating her future as the wife of Vašek, Mícha's slow-witted son – a marriage arranged for her by her parents through Kecal, the marriage broker. She is further annoyed that Jeník, her sweetheart, does not seem to show much interest or concern for her situation. Jeník, however, reassures her of his love and they leave happily together.

ACT II In the inn, the young people are singing and enjoying themselves. Mařenka meets up with the hapless Vašek and, without revealing her identity, tries to put him off his bride, warning him that she will bring him to an early death. She succeeds in making Vašek promise not to marry Mařenka, and runs off with the young man in hot pursuit. Meanwhile, Kecal persuades Jeník to renounce Mařenka for 300 crowns, to the disgust of everyone present. But when the contract is drawn up, Jeník insists on inserting a clause to the effect that Mařenka will marry only Mícha's eldest son.

ACT III Alone on the village green, Vašek encounters a troupe of strolling players, is instantly smitten by Esmeralda, the Spanish dancer, and easily persuaded to take the part of a dancing bear in their next performance. Meanwhile, Kecal produces the marriage contract but Mařenka is reluctant to sign and asks for time to think. Finally, out of bitter resentment against Jeník, she agrees to do so and is congratulated by everyone. However, when Vašek's parents, Háta and Mícha, next see Jeník they are taken aback when he greets Mícha as his father (Jeník is, of course, Mícha's eldest son, who left home many years ago, when his father married Háta; this, of course explains the clause added to the contract). Jeník has outwitted them and Mařenka finds herself engaged to Jeník, not Vašek, much to Háta's fury, which is exacerbated when Vašek himself erupts onto the scene in his role as a dancing bear.

Music and Background

Smetana's second opera, *The Bartered Bride*, comes with a brilliant lightness of touch that suggests operetta, although the composer always resented that comparison and insisted on Mozart's *Le Nozze di Figaro* as his true precedent. He had a point, but in its original form, with spoken dialogue, the piece must certainly have seemed like popular German *Singspiel*; and it was only later revisions, enlarging the score and introducing the famous dances, that really tipped the balance towards opera proper. Dance rhythms, especially the fast double-time of the polka, permeate the score and are largely responsible for its Czech national character. The melodies seem folk-like, but there's little here that isn't original music.

Highlights

The Overture. Act I: the Mařenka/Jeník love duet. Act II: the Drinking Chorus; Jeník's self-congratulatory song after the barter. Act III: Mařenka's song of disbelief that Jeník could abandon her, and the lovers' angry duet.

Did You Know?

🐀 Consider the plot and you'll find there *is* a definite parallel with *Le Nozze di Figaro*: two pairs of lovers, a long-lost son, and general reconciliation at the end.

Recommended Recording

Gabriela Beňačkova, Peter Dvorský, Czech Philharmonic Orchestra/ Zdeněk Košler. Supraphon 10 3511-2. As authentically Czech as these things come, with two distinguished international voices in the leads.

Johann Strauss II
(1825–99)

Die Fledermaus (1874)
Eine Nacht in Venedig (1883)
Der Zigeunerbaron (1885)

Johann Strauss was born into the 19th-century Viennese tradition of popular dance music. His father, Johann Strauss I, was a celebrated waltz composer and conductor, and he followed suit, making his name with deathless tunes that travelled around the world. His interest in operetta came later, stirred by the success (in Vienna, Strauss' home territory!) of imported scores by Offenbach. He began to produce theatre works in the late 1860s and completed some eighteen scores. Only a handful of them survive in repertory, but they survive with panache and, in the case of *Die Fledermaus*, have attracted sufficient critical esteem to transcend the category of 'operetta' and count among the classic works of opera at its grandest.

Die Fledermaus
(The Bat)

FORM: Operetta in three acts; in German
COMPOSER: Johann Strauss II (1825–99)
LIBRETTO: Carl Haffner and Richard Genée;
after Meilhac and Halévy
FIRST PERFORMANCE: Vienna, 5 April 1874

Principal Characters

Gabriel von Eisenstein ~ Tenor
Rosalinde, his wife ~ Soprano
Alfred, an opera singer ~ Tenor
Dr Blind, a lawyer ~ Tenor
Dr Falke, Eisenstein's friend ~ Baritone
Colonel Frank, a prison governor ~ Baritone
Prince Orlovsky, a wealthy Russian ~ Mezzo-soprano/Tenor

Synopsis of the Plot

Setting: Vienna; 19th century

ACT I Rosalinde's former admirer, Alfred, is attempting to gain her attention by serenading her, but her concern is more for her husband, Eisenstein, who is about to go to jail for several days as punishment for a minor misdemeanour. Eisenstein himself enters, accompanied by his lawyer, Dr Blind, whom he accuses of gross ineptitude – even managing to get his incarceration increased from five days to eight! Eisenstein is to begin his sentence that same evening and Rosalinde goes to find some old clothes for her husband to wear. When she has gone, Eisenstein's friend, Dr Falke, arrives and persuades Eisenstein to go instead to Prince Orlovsky's masked ball, assuring him that he is quite safe so long as he reports to the prison by six o'clock the next day. Rosalinde, though rather surprised that her husband is setting off to prison in full evening dress, says a tearful goodbye. Once he has gone, however, Alfred reappears and they settle down to a cosy evening together. The sudden arrival of Colonel Frank, the prison governor, puts Rosalinde into a very delicate position; the only way she can protect her reputation is by pretending Alfred is her husband – so her hapless lover is duly escorted to prison.

ACT II Eisenstein, disguised, is thoroughly enjoying himself at Orlovsky's grand ball. He meets a mysterious Hungarian countess (whom he fails to recognise as his wife) and immediately starts to flirt with her, playfully pretending to time her heartbeat with his watch. But the 'countess' is not so easily won over and, equally playfully, sweeps off, taking his watch with her. Dr Falke tells the company of how, years ago, his friend Eisenstein contrived to make him walk home from just such a ball dressed as a bat, much to the amusement of passers-by. The prince suggests a toast to champagne and Eisenstein and Colonel Frank raise their glasses to each other. The chiming of six o'clock brings Eisenstein and Falke to their senses and they hurry out.

ACT III Alfred sits in jail, trying to keep his spirits up by singing. Eisenstein, still masked, arrives and is astonished to see Colonel Frank, his new friend from the ball. He is even more astonished to learn that Frank himself arrested 'Eisenstein' the previous evening. Determined to discover who was at home with his wife, Eisenstein persuades Blind, who has come to see his supposedly jailed client, to lend him his cloak, wig and spectacles. He then questions Alfred and, shortly, Rosalinde who arrives to try and arrange Alfred's release. Furious at her deception, Eisenstein throws off his disguise and accuses them – only to be confronted by his own wife's 'Hungarian' accent and his watch in her hand! Faced with this irrefutable evidence of his own hypocrisy, Eisenstein can do little else than forgive and forget, and they all drink to the magical properties of champagne.

Music and Background

This is essentially a French farce softened by Viennese charm and the sentimental realisation of a way of life that was vanishing even as Strauss transcribed it into song. As a vehicle for hit tunes it has no obvious equal: they flow with a relentless elegance that compensates for lack of depth, and although the structure of the piece is far from perfect, the momentum (in a good production) rarely flags. In other words, *Die Fledermaus* is a brilliant exercise in camouflage, hiding its weaknesses behind a bold front. The only weakness it fails to hide is the spoken comic monologue for Frosch the jailer: an indulgence that modern productions tend to cut or otherwise circumnavigate.

Highlights

The Overture. Act I: 'So muss allein ich bleiben' – Rosalinde's farewell to Eisenstein, which enlarges into an ensemble of pretended grief; Rosalinde's show-stopping 'Mein Herr, was dächten Sie von mir'. Act II: Orlovsky's 'Ich lade gern mir Gäste ein'; Adele's celebrated laughing song 'Mein Herr Marquis'; Rosalinde's mock-Hungarian 'Klänge der Heimat'; the Champagne Song 'Im Feuerstrom der Reben'; Eisenstein's schmaltzy 'Bruderlein' song, which leads into the Fledermaus waltz. Act III: the culmination of the Eisenstein/Alfred/Rosalinde trio 'Ja, ich bin's den Ihr belogen', and the grand finale.

Did You Know?

 Die Fledermaus is a favourite Viennese entertainment for New Year's Eve, when the Ball Scene usually features surprise guests.

Recommended Recording

Kiri Te Kanawa, Edita Gruberová, Wolfgang Brendel, Richard Leech, Vienna Philharmonic Orchestra/André Previn. Philips 432 157-2. Glorious singing, lots of atmosphere, and held together with surprising exuberance by Previn.

Der Zigeunerbaron
(The Gypsy Baron)

FORM: Opera in three acts; in German
COMPOSER: Johann Strauss II (1825–99)
LIBRETTO: Ignaz Schnitzer; after Jókai
FIRST PERFORMANCE: Vienna, 24 October 1885

Principal Characters

Sándor Barinkay ⌘ Tenor
Kálmán Zsupán, a pig farmer ⌘ Baritone
Arsena, his daughter ⌘ Soprano
Ottokar, her sweetheart ⌘ Tenor
Czipra, a gypsy leader ⌘ Mezzo-soprano
Sáffi, her daughter ⌘ Soprano
Conte Carnero, a government commissioner ⌘ Baritone
Count Peter Homonay, the provincial governor ⌘ Baritone

Synopsis of the Plot

Setting: Hungary; 18th century

ACT I Sándor Barinkay, accompanied by Conte Carnero, the government commissioner, has returned to his family estate after many years of exile. Carnero, who is responsible for the official return of the estate, tries to persuade the gypsy, Czipra, to witness the deed, but she is illiterate and says she will read their palms instead. Czipra predicts a faithful wife for Barinkay, who will lead him to hidden treasure. Another witness is Zsupán, the wealthy but equally illiterate pigfarmer, who is displeased at Barinkay's return as he has been freely using the estate lands for his own purposes for many years. To avoid any ill-feeling, Barinkay suggests that he takes Zsupán's daughter, Arsena, as his bride. Zsupán agrees, but when she joins them Arsena refuses Barinkay's offer of marriage, saying that his lowly social status is beneath her – she can only consider marrying a baron. (Arsena is, in fact, in love with Ottokar, and he with her, and she has no intention of marrying anyone else.) Barinkay, offended at her rejection, is attracted by the singing of Sáffi, Czipra's daughter, which somehow reminds him of his childhood days. He goes with the gypsies for supper and when Czipra tells her band that he is the rightful owner of the castle and lands, they make him their leader, the 'gypsy baron'. Barinkay again asks Arsena to marry him, now that he is a 'baron', but again she rebuffs him. Barinkay then turns to Sáffi and the two agree to marry, much to Zsupán's fury.

ACT II Czipra, who has spent the night in the ruins of the castle with Sáffi and Barinkay, tells them of a dream she had in which she discovered the

338

location of the legendary buried treasure on Barinkay's land. The treasure is quickly located and the three return to the gypsy camp, where they find themselves confronted by Zsupán who, determined to cause trouble, has brought along Carnero to make an official complaint about the immoral relationship between Barinkay and Sáffi. Carnero is unimpressed by Barinkay's assurance that they were married according to gypsy law, but before he can take action they are interrupted by the arrival of Count Homonay, the provincial governor, who has come to recruit men for the war against Spain. Zsupán and Ottokar are drafted, and when Czipra tells Barinkay that Sáffi is not really her daughter but a Turkish pasha's child, Barinkay feels he is too far below her in social status and has no alternative but to leave her and go away to the war himself.

ACT III The war is over and there are great celebrations in Vienna. Ottokar is reunited with Arsena, and Barinkay, rewarded with a baronetcy, wastes no time in claiming his beloved Sáffi.

Music and Background

This is the only Strauss operetta to approach the quality of *Die Fledermaus*, and its Hungarian local colour – richer, more exotic than the champagne sparkle of the purely Viennese shows – won it an instantly admiring audience. Hanslick, the German critic who was the scourge of Wagner, praised its mastery of form and 'finer, more characteristic handling of the drama'. The romantic music is slightly soupy but evocative.

Highlights

Act I: Barinkay's waltz-song 'Ja, das alles auf Ehr', Zsupán's 'Ja, das Schreiben' and Sáffi's 'So elend und so treu'. Act II: the waltz 'Ha! Seht es winkt', the lovers' duet 'Wer uns getraut?' and the recruiting song 'Her die Hand'.

Did You Know?

- In Act II, the gypsies sing while working at their forge – a clear reference to the Anvil Chorus in Verdi's *Il Trovatore*.
- The duet 'Wer uns getraut?' was later turned by Hollywood into the popular song 'One day when we were young'.

Recommended Recording

Elisabeth Schwarzkopf, Nicolai Gedda, Hermann Prey, Philharmonia Orchestra/Otto Ackermann. EMI CDH7 69526-2. An old, 1950s recording but unsurpassed in style or elegance by modern rivals.

Richard Strauss
(1864–1949)

Feuersnot (1901)
Salome (1905)
Elektra (1908)
Der Rosenkavalier (1910)
Ariadne auf Naxos (1916)
Die Frau ohne Schatten (1917)
Intermezzo (1923)
Die Aegyptische Helena (1927)
Arabella (1932)
Die Schweigsame Frau (1935)
Capriccio (1941)

The leading composer of German opera after Wagner, Strauss was born in Munich and first made his name in the 1880s and '90s with a succession of tone poems – *Till Eulenspiegel, Also Sprach Zarathustra, Don Quixote* among them – which established his mastery of large-scale orchestral forces. At the same time he was conducting operas and beginning to write his own. But it wasn't until the early 1900s that he found real fame in the theatre, with two scores designed to shock: the divinely decadent *Salome* and the scorchingly modernist *Elektra. Elektra* began a twenty-five-year collaboration with the librettist Hugo von Hofmannsthal which became one of the most productive partnerships in the history of opera. Their greatest achievement was *Der Rosenkavalier*, a softer, more conservative heir to what had gone before. After *Arabella*, when Hofmannsthal died, Strauss turned to Stefan Zweig as his new partner. But Zweig was Jewish, and their relationship was cut short by the Third Reich. During the Second World War Strauss kept his head down and retreated into the escapism of works like *Capriccio*, an exquisite 'conversation piece' opera in which 18th-century aristocrats discuss the relationship between words and music. As with so many of his other fourteen stage works, it was primarily a vehicle for the female voice, an obsession Strauss carried through to his valedictory *Four Last Songs*.

Arabella

FORM: Opera in three acts; in German
COMPOSER: Richard Strauss (1864–1949)
LIBRETTO: Hugo von Hofmannsthal
FIRST PERFORMANCE: Dresden, 1 July 1933

Principal Characters

Arabella ☙ Soprano
Zdenka, her sister ☙ Soprano
Count Waldner, their father, a retired cavalry officer ☙ Bass
Adelaide, their mother ☙ Mezzo-soprano
Count Mandryka, a Croatian landowner ☙ Baritone
Matteo, a young officer ☙ Tenor
Count Elemer, Arabella's suitor ☙ Tenor
A fortune-teller ☙ Soprano

Synopsis of the Plot

Setting: Venice; 1860, on Carnival Day (Shrove Tuesday)

ACT I Count Waldner and his family live in a hotel in Venice. A retired cavalry officer, the count spends most of his days gambling (and losing) heavily, and the family fortunes are inexorably slipping away. As Zdenka (who has been brought up as a boy, Zdenko, on grounds of economy – the family cannot afford to introduce two daughters into society at the same time!) fends off creditors at the door, her mother consults a fortune-teller and her father plans a marriage for Arabella that will save the family from financial ruin. Fortunately, Arabella is already pursued by three noble suitors, plus the young officer, Matteo, but she is much more intrigued by a mysterious stranger who has been watching her in the street. Zdenka, on the other hand, is secretly in love with the lovelorn Matteo, and worries that he may become suicidal at Arabella's constant rejection. As the two sisters leave for a sleigh ride with Count Elemer, one of Arabella's suitors, Count Waldner receives a visit from the nephew of a wealthy ex-army friend, Count Mandryka, to whom he had sent Arabella's photograph in the hope of exciting a romantic response. But the old count is now dead, this young, attractive man has inherited his title and fortune – and has come to woo the lady in the photograph. Count Waldner is dazzled and foresees his imminent financial salvation.

ACT II At the Coachmen's Ball that evening Arabella is introduced to Count Mandryka, whom she recognises as her mysterious stranger. The two promise their love to each other and agree to marry. Then Arabella asks the count's permission to say her final goodbyes to everyone and enjoy her last evening of young, free girlhood. The count agrees happily but he is horrified, later, when he overhears Zdenka talking to Matteo and giving him a letter, supposedly from Arabella and containing the key of her room (actually Zdenka's room). Mandryka cannot believe the deception, but when he receives a letter from Arabella excusing herself for the rest of the evening, he is convinced and proceeds to get drunk, flirt outrageously and insult the Waldners.

ACT III Later, at the Waldners' hotel, Matteo is descending the stairs as Arabella comes in through the front door, happily musing on her future with Mandryka. Matteo goes to her but his ardent behaviour annoys her and he, for his part, cannot understand her coldness after what has so recently passed between them. As they argue, they are joined by Mandryka and the Waldners, who burst in making accusations and demanding explanations. Suddenly Zdenka, in her nightdress, hurls herself from her room and down the stairs, on her way to drown herself in the Danube. Explanations follow and misunderstandings are resolved; Count Waldner accepts Matteo as a husband for Zdenka and, after some hesitation, Arabella finds it in her heart to forgive Mandryka for his lack of faith.

Music and Background

Arabella revisits the waltzing Viennese world of *Der Rosenkavalier* but with less wit, more romance, and a far simpler story of love at first sight. The style is light, transparent, close to operetta, and that's exactly what it could be, but for the substance with which the two central characters are conceived. Hofmannsthal's death prevented the process of revision he and Strauss invariably undertook before declaring a piece complete, and some commentators sense a consequent lack of fine-tuning. Nevertheless, it is an enchanting excuse for fine singing.

Highlights

Act I: Arabella's 'Aber der Richtige' and her later 'Mein Elemer!' – the pivotal aria in the score. Act II: the Arabella/Mandryka duet 'Der Richtige – so hab'ich still zu mir gesagt'. Act III: Mandryka's 'Sie gibt mir keinen Blick'.

Did You Know?

~ Hofmannsthal's death came in peculiarly tragic circumstances. He had just finished the libretto when his son committed suicide. He then suffered a stroke on the day of the funeral, and never recovered.

Recommended Recording

Kiri Te Kanawa, Franz Grundheber, Royal Opera, Covent Garden/Jeffrey Tate. Decca 417 623-2. Some questionable casting in the smaller roles, but worth it for the radiant sound of Te Kanawa at her very best.

Ariadne auf Naxos
(Ariadne on Naxos)

FORM: Opera in a Prologue and one act; in German
COMPOSER: Richard Strauss (1864–1949)
LIBRETTO: Hugo von Hofmannsthal
FIRST PERFORMANCE: Stuttgart, 25 October 1912;
revised version Vienna, 4 October 1916

Principal Characters

The Major-Domo ✍ Spoken role
The Music Master ✍ Baritone
The Dancing Master ✍ Tenor
The Composer ✍ Soprano
The Tenor/Bacchus ✍ Tenor
The Prima Donna/Ariadne ✍ Soprano
Naiad, a nymph ✍ Soprano
Dryad, a nymph ✍ Contralto
Echo, a nymph ✍ Soprano
Zerbinetta, an actress ✍ Soprano

Synopsis of the Plot

Setting: A private theatre in a grand Viennese house; early 18th century

PROLOGUE The 'richest man in Vienna' is giving a sumptuous banquet and has arranged for both a serious opera and a comedy to be performed to entertain his guests. The Composer, distraught at the idea of his opera being followed by a 'vulgar' comedy, is truly horrified when the Major-Domo announces that his master, their patron, has decided that the two entertainments must take place simultaneously so that they can meet the deadline of nine o'clock for the fireworks display. Insult is added to injury when the Dancing Master suggests that the Composer should cut some of his music so that his dances can be retained, a suggestion which, predictably, causes uproar, especially as the Tenor and the Prima Donna each demand cuts in the other's role. The Music Master attempts to reassure everyone and a measure of calm is restored, during which Zerbinetta, an actress with the comedy troupe, learns the story of the opera, *Ariadne*, and is highly amused and not a little cynical at the idea of a woman pining away for the love of a man. The Composer, much attracted by Zerbinetta, tries to explain the power of idealistic love, but she is not convinced.

ACT I On stage, the story of Ariadne, who saved Theseus from the Minotaur's labyrinth and was then abandoned by him on Naxos, is about to unfold. The three nymphs, Dryad, Naiad and Echo, watch over the sleeping

Ariadne and tell of her perpetual weeping and longing for death. The actors, observing from the sidelines, comment on this and when Ariadne awakes, only to sing of the joyful prospect of death, they try to lift her spirits with singing and dancing. But nothing seems to help; even when Zerbinetta tries to encourage her by saying that the best cure for a broken heart is to take another lover as soon as possible, Ariadne retreats, pointedly, to her cave, leaving the actress to reflect alone on her own, more colourful, love life. The actors then perform their own entertainment, which revolves around Zerbinetta and the four men who are courting her. They are replaced by the nymphs who excitedly announce the arrival of the god, Bacchus. Ariadne emerges from her cave, but only because she mistakes Bacchus for Hermes, the god of death. Alone together the two find they respond passionately to each other and Ariadne's desire for death is transformed into a desire for love. The final words are those of the wordly-wise Zerbinetta, who considers that her point has been well made.

Music and Background

This has always been an awkward shotgun wedding of a piece, with problems that arise from the messy circumstances through which it came into being. The original idea was for a novel combination of speech and song: the first half spoken drama (an adaptation of Molière's *Le Bourgeois Gentilhomme*), the second half pure singing (Hofmannsthal's idea of the entertainment the *Bourgeois Gentilhomme* characters might expect to see after dinner). When it reached the stage it lasted six hours and was clearly impracticable. Jettisoning the play and replacing it with a shorter, sung prologue about preparations for the entertainment was the solution. But it still leaves two halves of a piece that don't comfortably make a whole. The consolation is that the score contains some of Strauss' finest music; and with three wonderfully contrasted soprano leads (the Composer is sung by a mezzo-soprano dressed as a man) it provided another excuse for Strauss to indulge his love of the female voice.

Highlights

Prologue: the touching Composer/Zerbinetta duet 'Ein Augenblick ist wenig'. Opera: the opening trio leading into Ariadne's ravishing 'Wo war ich?'; the song-and-dance routine 'Die Dame gibt mit truben Sinn'; Zerbinetta's 'Noch glaub ich dem', building into a display of virtuoso high coloratura; the Ariadne/Bacchus duet climaxing on 'Gibt es kein Hinuber?'

Did You Know?

Strauss usually demands enormous orchestras, but here the scoring is for just thirty-six players – and *still* he manages to make an opulent sound in the second half.

Strauss' *Ariadne* demands three types of soprano: lyric (the Composer), dramatic (Ariadne) and coloratura (Zerbinetta).

Capriccio

FORM: Opera in one act; in German
COMPOSER: Richard Strauss (1864–1949)
LIBRETTO: Richard Strauss and Clemens Krauss
FIRST PERFORMANCE: Munich, 28 October 1942

Principal Characters

Countess Madeleine, a young widow ❧ **Soprano**
The Count, her brother ❧ **Baritone**
Flamand, a composer ❧ **Tenor**
Olivier, a poet ❧ **Baritone**
La Roche, a theatre director ❧ **Bass**
Clairon, an actress ❧ **Contralto**
Italian singer ❧ **Soprano**
Italian singer ❧ **Tenor**

Synopsis of the Plot

Setting: A château near Paris; about 1775

The Countess is shortly to celebrate her birthday and Flamand, the musician, has written a string sextet in her honour. Accompanied by his rival, the poet Olivier, who has written a play for the Countess, Flamand watches anxiously as she and her brother listen next door to the first performance of his music. (The third man in the room, the theatre director, La Roche, has already made his comment on the music by falling asleep!) The two artists, the man of music and the man of letters, argue the merits of their respective artistic fields, a discussion which is next taken up by the Countess and her brother, the former inclining to music and the latter to poetry. The Count's predilection is hardly surprising, however, as he is in love with the famous actress, Clairon, formerly Olivier's mistress, whose arrival is expected imminently as she has agreed to play the lead in Olivier's play. The actress duly appears and rehearsals begin. Olivier composes a sonnet for the Countess which effectively declares his love for her, and Flamand promptly sets it to music – thus provoking an argument about whose work it now is. Olivier is summoned by La Roche to attend the rehearsal of his play and Flamand declares his love to the Countess; she promises to let him know her answer the next morning and he leaves her. The Countess orders refreshments and entertainment for the company, which includes a ballet and an operatic duet, sung floridly by the two Italians, and which encourages more extensive debate on the fundamental nature of art: music or words? La Roche then announces his absurdly extravagant plans for the Countess' birthday celebrations, which are received with much sarcasm and general laughter. Attacked by both Olivier and Flamand, La Roche passionately defends his own role as director; he serves the essential needs of the theatre itself, he alone can present human life in all its comic and tragic variety, he is the guardian of art. The Countess suggests that Olivier and Flamand should collaborate on an opera to be directed by La Roche, but with the ending to be decided upon by herself. This is agreed and the guests leave for Paris. Later, in pensive mood, the Countess enters alone, musing on the possible ending of the opera, on whether she is more moved by words or music, Olivier or Flamand. Is there, she ponders, any possible ending that is not just trivial? She goes in to supper, leaving the question unanswered.

Music and Background

This was Strauss' last opera, and valedictory in mood and content. It looks back over issues – above all, the relationship between words and music – which preoccupied Strauss throughout his life, revisiting the Prologue to *Ariadne auf Naxos* and the Levee Scene in *Der Rosenkavalier*; its supremely civilised drawing-room discussion manner is extraordinary for something written in Nazi Germany at the height of the Second World War. For Strauss, *Capriccio* was clearly an exercise in escapism: withdrawal into an inner, saner world than he otherwise found himself forced to deal with. The music comes mostly in the flowing, conversationally melodic recitative that characterises his later work, with technically remarkable ensembles and orchestral writing of exquisite delicacy. It works like lieder writ large. The Countess is one of his most alluring female characters; and her final, twenty-minute scena is the most perfect farewell to the stage any composer could hope to make.

Highlights

The opening instrumental sextet; the servant's commentary; the parody music for the Italian singers; the Countess' closing scene.

Did You Know?

The first performances played to packed houses in the middle of the Munich air raids.

Elektra

FORM: Opera in one act; in German
COMPOSER: Richard Strauss (1864–1949)
LIBRETTO: Hugo von Hofmannsthal; after Sophocles
FIRST PERFORMANCE: Dresden, 25 January 1909

Principal Characters

Elektra Soprano
Chrysothemis, her sister Soprano
Orestes, her brother Baritone
Clytemnestra, her mother Mezzo-soprano
Aegisthus, Clytemnestra's lover Tenor

Synopsis of the Plot

Setting: Mythological Mycenae

In the palace courtyard the servants are talking about Elektra, Queen Clytemnestra's daughter, who now lives a strange, wild life, full of obsessions and hatreds. Elektra, who has overheard the servants from her hiding place, emerges when they have gone and recalls the death of her father, Agamemnon, at the hands of Clytemnestra, who now lives with her lover, Aegisthus, in the palace. Elektra calls on her dead father's spirit to help her and prophesies vengeance and bloodshed, after which she will dance for joy. She is interrupted by her sister, Chrysothemis, who warns her that Clytemnestra and Aegisthus plan to imprison her, and the two sisters hurriedly part as the queen is heard approaching. Clytemnestra, showily dressed and bedecked with jewels and ornaments, sweeps in and, seeing her daughter, tells her of her terrible nightmares, asking her what she can do to prevent them. Elektra replies that only a ritual sacrifice will be enough – Clytemnestra's own death – and she will be put to death by her own son, Elektra's brother, Orestes, who has disappeared. Clytemnestra is clearly shaken at Elektra's words, but when a servant delivers a whispered message to her, her confidence is restored and she returns triumphantly to the palace. Chrysothemis then returns to tell her sister that news has arrived of Orestes' death – this is the news that had pleased Clytemnestra so much. Elektra's response is to try and persuade her sister to join her in destroying their mother, but Chrysothemis is afraid of her and runs away. Elektra then decides that she must act alone and begins frantically to dig for the axe which her mother used to murder her father and which she herself buried. Just then a stranger enters and, although she does not recognise him at first, Elektra is overjoyed to discover that it is Orestes. Orestes goes into the palace and avenges Agamemnon's death by killing both Clytemnestra and Aegisthus. Elektra's exultation is unconfined and she dances a wild, hysterical dance, as she had promised, before collapsing lifeless.

Music and Background

This is Strauss at his toughest and most abrasive: a shocker of a score, designed to purge the audience's ears, just as the original Greek drama was meant to purge their souls. The orchestra is huge (eight clarinets, eight horns, a big percussion section, extra strings) and it takes capacious voices to be heard above its dissonant attack. But there are also moments of beguiling lyricism to be found among the battery of noise, including waltz music that might have been more at home in *Der Rosenkavalier*; and it is important to remember that the sound world of the opera is largely derived from women's voices. No male voice of any significance appears until three-quarters of the way through. And however shrill and power-driven the writing for Elektra and Clytemnestra, the music for Chrysothemis is soft and warm. The single act is long but runs without a break.

Highlights

The orchestra's opening flourish, which rhythmically spells the name 'Agamemnon'; Elektra's first monologue, beginning 'Allein! Weh, ganz allein'; Chrysothemis' yearning 'Ich kann nicht sitzen'; Elektra's appeal to her sister, 'Von jetz an will ich deine Schwester'; the Elektra/Orestes duet 'Lass zittern diesen Leib'; and the closing moments.

Did You Know?

In some performances the front desks of the violas change instruments to become a fourth section of violins – adding to the already dense orchestral texture.

Recommended Recording

Birgit Nilsson, Regina Resnik, Marie Collier, Vienna Philharmonic Orchestra/Georg Solti. Decca 417 345-2. A truly violent response to the score, with Solti stabbing home the rhythms.

Intermezzo

FORM: Opera in two acts; in German
COMPOSER: Richard Strauss (1864–1949)
LIBRETTO: Richard Strauss
FIRST PERFORMANCE: Dresden, 4 November 1924

Principal Characters

Robert Storch, a conductor ‧ **Baritone**
Christine, his wife ‧ **Soprano**
Franz, their son ‧ **Spoken role**
Baron Lummer ‧ **Tenor**
Resi, his girlfriend ‧ **Soprano**
Stroh, a conductor ‧ **Tenor**
A notary ‧ **Baritone**

Synopsis of the Plot

Setting: Grundlsee and Vienna; 1920s

ACT I Storch is packing for an engagement in Vienna while his wife, Christine, fusses about him, arguing and complaining. After he has gone she receives an invitation to go out, which cheers her up, and she is soon happily tobogganing down the snowy slopes – at least until she collides with the aristocratic skier, Baron Lummer. Impressed by his status and concerned for his welfare, Christine arranges to meet him and they go to a dance at the inn. Discovering that he is in Grundlsee for his health, Christine proceeds to 'mother' him; she finds him a clean and respectable room with the notary and is much concerned about his recurrent migraines. Later, Christine is writing to her husband and telling him about her new acquaintance, when she is joined by the Baron himself. He tells her that his father wants him to study law, while he prefers natural history, but does not have the means to follow his preference without his family's agreement. Subtle and not-so-subtle hints are dropped and Christine enthusiastically promises him her husband's generous support on his return. Back in his room the impatient Baron wonders how much longer he can continue to humour Christine and wait for the promised money. His girlfriend, Resi, comes to visit him, but he quickly sends her away before the landlady can see her and tell Christine. This event convinces him it is time to act and he writes a note to Christine in which he asks outright for a loan of 1,000 marks. The next day he visits her, as usual, and is subjected to her outraged indignation at his shameless request. In the middle of her harangue, however, she receives a note, addressed to her husband from a certain Mitzi Meier, in which the writer asks her 'sweetheart' to let her have two tickets for the opera and promises to meet him in the bar afterwards. Christine's response is to send the Baron away, dispatch a telegram to Storch announcing she is leaving him, order the maid to pack everything into suitcases and melodramatically tell their young son of his father's betrayal.

ACT II In Vienna, Storch's colleagues and friends are playing cards and discussing how very much they prefer Storch to his irascible wife. When they are joined by the conductor himself they tease him gently about Christine, and Storch responds that he finds her volatile temperament stimulating, exactly what he needs. But when Christine's telegram is delivered, her husband is truly dumbfounded and he hurries out. Meanwhile, Christine has gone straight to the notary in Grundlsee to arrange a divorce, but flounces out of his office when he refuses to act for her until he has seen Storch, whom he respects. Back in Vienna, Storch is relieved to find that Mitzi Meier is Stroh's friend – but she confused their names and sent the note to the wrong person – and he insists that Stroh goes to Grundlsee himself to tell Christine of the mistake. First Stroh explains what happened, then Storch himself arrives to reassure his wife, only to be met with demands that he apologise for causing her such distress. Finally, however, Christine is mollified, and husband and wife are happily reunited.

Music and Background

Strauss called it a 'bourgeois comedy', but *Intermezzo* is actually a bizarrely candid piece of autobiography, based on an incident in his marriage to the formidable (and, as it turned out, fiercely jealous) soprano Pauline de Ahna. Self-exposure of this kind is not necessarily in the best taste, and Pauline certainly didn't appreciate it. But the music is engaging, in Strauss' accustomed manner of continuously flowing conversational recitative, and the sheer domesticity of the concept, setting the minutiae of ordinary life to music was, in its time, quietly radical. As the chatter goes on, the orchestral accompaniment provides Wagner-like clues to the real, underlying feelings of the characters. Twelve orchestral interludes link the scenes.

Highlights

Act I: the waltz interlude and following scene at Grundlsee; the interlude that introduces the scene in the Baron's room. Act II: the final reconciliation.

Recommended Recording

Lucia Popp, Dietrich Fischer-Dieskau, Bavarian Radio Symphony Orchestra/Wolfgang Sawallisch. EMI CDS7 49337-2. Nicely judged, with Lucia Popp in radiant form.

Der Rosenkavalier
(The Knight of the Rose)

FORM: Opera in three acts; in German
COMPOSER: Richard Strauss (1864–1949)
LIBRETTO: Hugo von Hofmannsthal
FIRST PERFORMANCE: Dresden, 26 January 1911

Principal Characters

The Marschallin ⚬ Soprano
Octavian, her young lover ⚬ Soprano
Baron Ochs auf Lerchenau, her cousin ⚬ Bass
Valzacchi, an Italian intriguer ⚬ Tenor
Annina, his partner ⚬ Mezzo-soprano
Herr von Faninal, a wealthy entrepreneur ⚬ Baritone
Sophie, his daughter ⚬ Soprano
Commissioner of Police ⚬ Bass

Synopsis of the Plot

Setting: Vienna; mid-18th century

ACT I It is early morning and the Marschallin and her young lover, Octavian, are together in her room. Baron Ochs, the Marschallin's cousin, unexpectedly arrives and Octavian disguises himself as the Marschallin's maid, Mariandel. The Baron asks the Marschallin to recommend a young nobleman to take the traditional silver rose to his fiancée, Sophie von Faninal, but his eye is constantly drawn to the attractive 'Mariandel' and he flirts outrageously with 'her'. By now it is time for the Marschallin's morning reception and her room is soon filled with servants, petitioners, tradesmen and the two Italian 'hangers-on', Valzacchi and Annina. The reception over, the Marschallin, alone, thinks about the young girl who is about to marry her coarse and vulgar cousin, and reflects on her own similarly arranged marriage. Her thoughts then turn to Octavian, who she knows will eventually leave her for a younger woman. When Octavian joins her he is hurt by her apparent mistrust of his feelings and leaves her. Only when he has gone does the Marschallin realise she has not kissed him goodbye. Sadly, she gives her page, Mahomet, the casket with the silver rose and tells him to take it to Octavian.

ACT II Octavian, the Rosenkavalier, arrives in splendour at Sophie's home and the two are immediately attracted to one another. As they are talking together, Ochs himself arrives and proceeds to behave in a gross and insulting way towards his young bride-to-be. Eventually Octavian challenges the Baron to a duel, during which the Baron receives a superficial scratch.

351

He collapses as if he were dying and the household rushes in; Sophie's father sends Octavian away and threatens his daughter with a convent if she refuses Ochs. Ochs, meanwhile, is slowly recovering his customary bombast and, when Annina brings him a note from 'Mariandel' arranging an assignation, his recovery is complete.

ACT III Octavian has arranged for Ochs' assignation with 'Mariandel' to take place in a special room at a shabby inn on the outskirts of Vienna. The room is special because it is supplied with secret trapdoors, windows and other devices which Octavian intends to use to the full. Ochs arrives and settles down to supper with 'Mariandel'; he tries his best to seduce the girl but makes little progress. Indeed, each time he desperately tries to get close to her, ghostly faces appear at the windows or pop up through trapdoors. 'Mariandel' pretends not to see them, but Ochs is terrified. He is even more disconcerted when Annina bursts in, impersonating a deserted wife, followed by four children who address him as 'papa', then come the landlord of the inn and his staff. The police are called and Ochs claims that 'Mariandel' is Sophie Faninal, his fiancée. But Octavian has sent Valzacchi to fetch Faninal and Sophie and their arrival refutes his story. The police restore some measure of order and 'Mariandel' disappears behind a screen to emerge as Octavian. The Marschallin has been sent for and she placates the police commissioner by saying the whole affair was just a masquerade. She advises Ochs to leave – which he does, pursued by 'wife', 'children', assorted creditors and the staff of the inn. Observing Octavian and Sophie together, the Marschallin realises that they are in love with each other, and she movingly renounces any claim she has over Octavian before leaving with Faninal.

Music and Background

This sweetly Viennese confection of romance, nostalgia and farce is Strauss' best-known and best-loved opera score: always in repertory, despite the fact that it is a massive undertaking which demands large forces and a long running-time. The concept is Neoclassical, revisiting the 18th-century world of Mozart's *Le Nozze di Figaro*, with its bedroom escapades and cross-dressed Cherubino figure. However, the music is of a different world altogether: a post-Wagnerian medley of heavily-orchestrated leitmotifs that recur and interweave, and – above all – a glorious collection of Viennese waltzes, the like of which could never have existed in the 18th century. The music focuses – as elsewhere in Strauss' operas – on three contrasted sopranos who come together in the final scene for a trio which provides arguably the most ravishingly beautiful moment in modern opera. The character of the Marschallin is certainly one of the great and supremely sophisticated creations for the lyric stage.

Highlights

The Overture and orchestral lead-in (with birdsong) to the first scene; the Italian tenor's song in the levee; the poignant closing scene between the Marschallin and Octavian, beginning 'Ach! Du bist wieder da?' Act II: the Presentation of the Rose; Baron Och's waltz tune 'Mit mir'; the Duel Scene and close. Act III: the seduction duet 'Nein, nein'; the Marschallin/Octavian duet 'Heut' oder morgen'; the great trio 'Hab' mir's gelobt'; the final Octavian/Sophie duet 'Spur' nur dich'.

Did You Know?

∾ So immediately successful was *Der Rosenkavalier* that special 'Rosenkavalier' trains were organised to bring audiences from all over Germany to the performances.
∾ In America in the 1920s Strauss conducted excerpts from the score in department stores.

Recommended Recording

Elisabeth Schwarzkopf, Christa Ludwig, Otto Edelman, Teresa Stich-Randall, Nicolai Gedda, Philharmonia Orchestra/Herbert von Karajan. EMI CDS7 49354-8. An all-round classic: one of the great opera recordings of all time.

Salome

FORM: Opera in one act; in German
COMPOSER: Richard Strauss (1864–1949)
LIBRETTO: Hedwig Lachmann; after Wilde
FIRST PERFORMANCE: Dresden, 9 December 1905

Principal Characters

Salome ∾ Soprano
Herodias, her mother and Herod's wife ∾ Mezzo-soprano
Herod, the king, her stepfather ∾ Tenor
Jokanaan (John the Baptist) ∾ Baritone
Narraboth, captain of the royal guard ∾ Tenor
A page ∾ Contralto

Synopsis of the Plot

Setting: King Herod's palace; Biblical times

Narraboth, captain of the guard, stands on a terrace above the cistern where Jokanaan has been imprisoned for denouncing Herod's marriage to his dead brother's wife. But Narraboth is more concerned with watching the lovely Salome in the banqueting hall than with his prisoner, despite the page's warnings that he has strong forebodings of doom associated with her. Salome herself then joins them; she is irritated by her stepfather's lewd behaviour towards her and bored by the constant religious arguments between the Jews, Egyptians and Romans at the feast. Hearing Jokanaan's voice, she coaxes Narraboth into allowing her to meet the prisoner, strictly against her stepfather's orders. Jokanaan emerges, vilifying Herod and all his acts, and Salome is instantly fascinated by him. Although he is dirty and unkempt after his confinement, she is strongly sexually attracted by him and declares her desire to kiss and touch him. Jokanaan repels her, much to her fury, but her desire for him becomes even more urgent. Narraboth, horrified at her behaviour, stabs himself to death and falls between them. Herod, accompanied by Herodias, comes on to the terrace, looking for Salome. He offers her wine and fruit, but she behaves coldly towards him. Jokanaan's voice is again heard and Herodias urges her husband to give him to the Jews or have him killed. But Herod is afraid of the prophet and refuses. As he observes his stepdaughter, Herod is overwhelmed by the force of his desire for her and orders her to dance for him. But she refuses, and continues to do so until, in desperation, the king promises her anything she wants. Salome's performance is her most seductive, the Dance of the Seven Veils, and she duly claims her reward – Jokanaan's head. Herod is aghast but she insists that he keeps his promise. The head is brought to her and, as Herod moves away, she ecstatically kisses the dead lips. Looking back, the king is sickened at the sight and orders his men to kill her.

Music and Background

Salome was Strauss' first operatic success, achieved through calculated notoriety. Steeped in *fin-de-siècle* decadence, lurid sexuality, and a steamily atmospheric score, the like of which had never been heard on an opera stage, it caused immediate scandal and was banned from production in London, Vienna and New York on the grounds of depravity. Even today it registers a certain shock value – not least from the impact of a huge orchestra which is inventively deployed but tends to overwhelm the voices. Salome herself is a near-impossible role to cast. She should be able to portray an adolescent girl in the grip of a perverse erotic obsession, but carry the vocal power of a Valkyrie. Not many sopranos are capable of doing both.

Highlights

The orchestral music accompanying Jokanaan's entrance from the cistern; Salome's attempted seduction of Jokanaan, climaxing on 'Ich will deinen Mund küssen'; Salome's Dance of the Seven Veils; the offstage execution of Jokanaan; Salome's ecstatic scene with the severed head.

Did You Know?

✎ The first singer to play Salome refused to perform the Dance of the Seven Veils on the grounds that she was a 'respectable woman', so a dancer was provided as a stand-in for her.

✎ The opera evoked strong protests, particularly from the Church, and in Berlin the Kaiser allowed performances only if the Star of Bethlehem appeared in the sky – even though the action takes place about thirty years after the birth of Christ.

✎ The Kaiser said of Strauss, 'I like the fellow, but *Salome* will do him damage.' Strauss later replied, 'The damage helped me build my house in Garmisch.'

Recommended Recording

Cheryl Studer, Bryn Terfel, Leonie Rysanek, Deutsche Oper, Berlin/ Giuseppe Sinopoli. DG 431 810-2. Studer doing gloriously on disc what no one would want to see her do on stage. With a truly awesome prophet from Terfel.

Igor Stravinsky

(1882–1971)

Le Rossignol (1914)
Mavra (1922)
Oedipus Rex (1927)
The Rake's Progress (1951)

One of the dominating forces in 20th-century music, Stravinsky was a truly international figure: born in Russia, living in France, Switzerland and America, and dying in Venice. A student of Rimsky-Korsakov, he came to public notice through ballet scores for Diaghilev: notoriously *The Rite of Spring* in 1913, which proved a landmark on the road to all things modern. Before that time he was still writing in the Russian fantasy manner of his old teacher, and his first opera, *Le Rossignol*, followed suit. But from the 1920s and *Mavra* he turned to Neoclassicism, reinventing the music of the past with an emotional detachment that makes *Oedipus Rex* a chilly, if glamorous, score and gives a stiff Mozartian conventionality to *The Rake's Progress* (written after his move to America during the Second World War). His later American work became increasingly austere and took up the twelve-note technique of his great rival for the hearts and minds of modern musicians, Schoenberg.

Oedipus Rex
(King Oedipus)

FORM: Opera in two acts; in Latin
COMPOSER: Igor Stravinsky (1882–1971)
LIBRETTO: Jean Cocteau; after Sophocles.
Translated into Latin by J. Daniélou
FIRST PERFORMANCE: Paris, 30 May 1927 (as oratorio);
Vienna, 23 February 1928 (stage production)

Principal Characters

Oedipus, King of Thebes ❧ Tenor
Jocasta, his wife ❧ Mezzo-soprano
Creon, Jocasta's brother ❧ Bass-baritone
Tiresias, a wise man ❧ Bass
The Messenger ❧ Bass-baritone
The Shepherd ❧ Tenor
Narrator ❧ Spoken role

Synopsis of the Plot

Note: The Narrator introduces each scene and outlines the events we are to see.

Setting: Classical Thebes

ACT I The Thebans come to Oedipus, begging him to save their city from the plague. Oedipus replies that he has already sent Creon, his brother-in-law, to ask the oracle of Apollo what must be done. Creon returns and gives the people the god's response: Thebes will only be released from its misery if the people find the murderer of their former king, Laius, and drive him away. Oedipus assures the people that he will spare no effort in finding him and consults Tiresias, who refuses to help him until, exasperated, the king accuses the wise man himself of being the murderer. Tiresias responds with the words 'The king's murderer is a king', at which Oedipus turns furiously on him, believing Tiresias to be in a conspiracy with Creon to depose him.

ACT II Jocasta, Oedipus' wife, upbraids Creon and Oedipus for quarrelling in a city blighted by plague, and she advises Oedipus not to put his trust in oracles. She knows they can lie, she says, because they foretold that her son would kill his father, her former husband, Laius, whereas he was actually murdered by a thief at a crossroads. Oedipus becomes uneasy – he remembers once killing an old man at a crossroads – but he believes himself to be the son of Polybus, King of Corinth. Disturbed, Oedipus determines to find out the truth. At that moment a Messenger arrives to announce the death of Polybus and to confirm that he, the Messenger, had found Oedipus, as a baby, exposed on a mountainside and had taken him to Polybus, where he was raised as the king's son. A shepherd confirms the story and Oedipus finally realises the horrifying truth: he is the son of Jocasta and Laius and has murdered his father and married his mother. Jocasta hangs herself and, after blinding himself with her golden brooch, Oedipus, broken and mutilated, leaves the city.

Music and Background

Oedipus Rex is an experiment in theatre: half-opera, half-oratorio, and intended to be staged with ceremonial formality with the singers standing statue-like in rigid tableaux. The sung Latin text is emotionally distancing, and although the spoken narrations are intended to be given in the language of the audience, they are clipped and dry and don't give away that much information. A knowledge of Sophocles is assumed. Musically, Stravinsky's models are the oratorios of Handel and, to some extent, the operas of Verdi. Everything comes in set numbers: rugged, muscular, austerely living out Stravinsky's notion of heroic tragedy.

Highlights

Act I: the closing chorus of welcome for Jocasta, 'Gloria'. Act II: Jocasta's aria 'Non erubescite, reges'; the final section, as Oedipus is expelled from Thebes.

Did You Know?

∾ *Oedipus Rex* was famously performed at London's Festival Hall in the 1950s with Stravinsky conducting and Cocteau reading the narrations.

Recommended Recording

Vinson Cole, Anne Sofie von Otter, Swedish Radio Symphony Orchestra/ Esa-Pekka Salonen. Sony SK48057. A fresh, modern recording with high-impact performances.

The Rake's Progress

FORM: Opera in three acts; in English
COMPOSER: Igor Stravinsky (1882–1971)
LIBRETTO: W.H. Auden and Chester Kallmann; after Hogarth
FIRST PERFORMANCE: Venice, 11 September 1951

Principal Characters

Trulove, a country gentleman ∿ Bass
Anne, his daughter ∿ Soprano
Tom Rakewell ∿ Tenor
Nick Shadow ∿ Baritone
Mother Goose, a brothel owner ∿ Mezzo-soprano
Baba the Turk ∿ Mezzo-soprano

Synopsis of the Plot

Setting: England; 18th century

ACT I Tom Rakewell is courting Anne in the garden of her country home. Although he is a gentleman he has no money, and Anne's father offers to help him find a job in London. But Tom is not very keen on this idea: he has higher hopes for himself and wishes to acquire a great deal of wealth as soon as possible. Suddenly Nick Shadow appears and tells him that he has been left a fortune by a rich relative – but he must go to London to claim it. Anne and her father are overjoyed and Tom, now employing Nick as his servant, leaves for London, promising to send for Anne and Trulove as soon as possible. However, ably assisted by Nick, Tom quickly succumbs to the temptations of the city and soon catches the eye of Mother Goose. Anne, meanwhile, is very worried by the lack of news from London and determines to set off, alone and unaided, to find Tom.

ACT II Tom is becoming bored with his life and is easily persuaded by Nick to marry the bizarre bearded lady, Baba the Turk. On the very evening of the wedding Anne arrives outside Tom's house and observes the bride's arrival, but when Anne sees what has become of Tom she sadly turns away and leaves. After an argument with Baba, during which he crams his wig on her head, Tom dreams of a wonderful machine which can turn stones into bread. On waking he finds that Nick has actually invented just such a machine and Tom decides to invest in it, envisaging a grand fortune for himself.

ACT III Tom is ruined and all his property, including Baba who is still under the wig, is to be auctioned. Anne, however, still loves him and is looking for him. Tom finds himself in a graveyard, with Nick, who is revealed as the Devil himself. Nick announces to Tom that it is now time that Tom paid him his reward for his past help and claims Tom's soul. However, he agrees to let the result depend on a game of cards; Tom wins, but as the Devil sinks into a grave, he curses Tom with madness. The Devil's curse cannot be withstood and Tom's final home is Bedlam, the insane asylum, where the faithful Anne manages to find him, just moments before he dies.

Music and Background

In one sense *The Rake's Progress* is the *ne plus ultra* of Neoclassicism: a perfectly-proportioned 18th-century pastiche inspired by Hogarth, complete with Mozartian orchestra and harpsichord continuo. But it's also a subtle and many-layered score which re-fashions the past into something unmistakably of our own times. W.H. Auden's libretto is one of the most distinguished contributions ever made to a largely undistinguished genre of literature: eloquent, concise, and perfectly attuned to Stravinsky's retrospective music. That the music doesn't always seem attuned to Auden's words – or at least, their natural pronunciation – is partly because Stravinksy had little previous experience of setting English, and partly because he didn't care. He treated words as nothing more than an excuse for music, to be used as the composer pleases. This is why he liked to set Latin – and why the text of *The Rake's Progress* can be hard to follow.

Highlights

Act I: Tom's brothel aria 'Love too easily betrayed'; Anne's closing scena and cabaletta 'I go to him' – the big number of the score, with an arresting and high-flying finish. Act II: Baba's wonderfully comic 'Come sweet, come. Why so glum?' Act III: the Auctioneer Scene; Anne's lullaby in Bedlam, 'Gently, little boat'.

Did You Know?

~ A complete set of the Hogarth illustrations from which this opera derives can be seen in the Sir John Soane Museum, London.

Recommended Recording

Alexander Young, Judith Raskin, John Reardon, Royal Philharmonic Orchestra/Igor Stravinsky. Sony M2K 46299. Recorded in London in 1964 and still the best, with a fine balance between precision and lyricism.

Arthur Sullivan

(1842–1900)

Cox and Box (1866)
Trial by Jury (1875)
The Sorcerer (1877)
HMS Pinafore (1878)
The Pirates of Penzance (1879)
Patience (1881)
Iolanthe (1882)
Princess Ida (1884)
The Mikado (1885)
Ruddigore (1887)
The Yeomen of the Guard (1888)
The Gondoliers (1889)
Ivanhoe (1891)
Utopia Limited (1893)

The son of a Sandhurst bandmaster, Arthur Sullivan studied in London and Leipzig, made headlines writing theatre music at the age of nineteen, and produced a number of youthful concert works which were well-received. Like Johann Strauss II in Vienna, he was seduced into operetta by the imported commercial success of Offenbach, which he sought to imitate with *Cox and Box*. Joining forces with the writer W.S. Gilbert, Sullivan produced his first hit, *Trial by Jury*, which launched the 1870s and '80s series of what came to be known as the Savoy Operas – after the Savoy Theatre which Richard D'Oyly Carte had built to house them. Sullivan also maintained his contact with the serious concert world, writing popular though now-forgotten oratorios. After a row with Gilbert during the composition of *The Gondoliers*, he abandoned operetta to write a serious opera, *Ivanhoe*, which was intended to run continuously like a West End play. When it flopped he returned to Gilbert for *Utopia Limited*. His music was largely a mixture of pastiche and pathos, carrying considerable debts to Handel, Verdi and Wagner. His most enduring piece beyond operetta is probably the hymn tune 'Onward Christian soldiers'.

The Gondoliers,
or The King of Barataria

FORM: Operetta in two acts; in English
COMPOSER: Arthur Sullivan (1842–1900)
LIBRETTO: W.S. Gilbert
FIRST PERFORMANCE: London, 7 December 1889

Principal Characters

Duke of Plaza-Toro ᴥ Baritone
Duchess of Plaza-Toro ᴥ Mezzo-soprano
Casilda, their daughter ᴥ Soprano
Luiz, their servant ᴥ Tenor
Marco Palmieri, a young gondolier ᴥ Tenor
Giuseppe Palmieri, a young gondolier ᴥ Baritone
Tessa, his bride ᴥ Mezzo-soprano
Gianetta, Marco's bride ᴥ Soprano
The Grand Inquisitor ᴥ Bass-baritone
Inez, Luiz's mother ᴥ Contralto

Synopsis of the Plot

Setting: Venice and the imaginary kingdom of Barataria; 1750s

ACT I The two Venetian gondoliers, Marco and Giuseppe, have chosen their brides, Gianetta and Tessa, but their celebrations are interrupted by the arrival of the Duke of Plaza-Toro, accompanied by his wife, his daughter Casilda, and his faithful retainer, Luiz, who is secretly in love with Casilda, and she with him. The duke's purpose is to find the future king of Barataria who, in infancy, was abducted by the Grand Inquisitor and taken to Venice, where he was lodged with a gondolier who brought him up as a brother to his own young son. The old king has now died and the duke has come to fetch his successor. But no one can remember which of the two young gondoliers is the king's son, so it is decided that they both will go to Barataria, where Luiz's mother, the baby's nurse, will surely be able to distinguish the rightful heir. The two gondoliers agree to leave together for Barataria, where they will reign jointly until a final decision is made.

ACT II Marco and Giuseppe are now joint rulers of Barataria and have remodelled the monarchy along more egalitarian principles, much to the disapproval of the Grand Inquisitor. But they miss their young brides and are overjoyed when the two young women arrive to join them. Their pleasure is quickly followed by consternation, however, when the Duke of Plaza-Toro reveals that Casilda was betrothed as a baby to the infant prince and is therefore the rightful queen, bride of the rightful king. The time has come for Inez, the baby's nurse, to choose between Marco and Giuseppe. To everyone's astonishment, however, she declares that, because of the dangerous political situation at the time, she substituted her own child for the royal prince, thus bringing up the prince as her own son, Luiz who, acclaimed as the new king, is joyfully united with Casilda.

Music and Background

A satire on democracy and its abuses, *The Gondoliers* is unusual in beginning with twenty minutes of uninterrupted music – a sop to Sullivan's sensitivities as a 'serious' composer. The score dabbles in Latin colouring appropriate to the location of the story.

Highlights

The Inquisitor's 'No possible doubt whatever'; Marco's 'Take a pair of sparkling eyes'; the finale Cachucha.

Did You Know?

➤ *The Gondoliers* proved to be one of the most popular of the Savoy operas and enjoyed an initial run of over 550 performances.

Recommended Recording

Richard Suart, Jill Pert, David Fieldsend, Alan Oke, D'Oyly Carte Opera/ John Pryce-Jones. That's Entertainment CD-TER2 1187. Modern, 1990s sound, done with spirit (but no spoken dialogue).

HMS Pinafore,
or The Lass That Loved a Sailor

FORM: Operetta in two acts; in English
COMPOSER: Arthur Sullivan (1842–1900)
LIBRETTO: W.S. Gilbert
FIRST PERFORMANCE: London, 25 May 1878

Principal Characters
Ralph Rackstraw ~ Tenor
Captain Corcoran ~ Baritone
Josephine, his daughter ~ **Soprano**
Sir Joseph Porter ~ Baritone
Dick Deadeye ~ Baritone
Mrs Cripps (Little Buttercup) ~ Mezzo-soprano
Hebe ~ Mezzo-soprano

Synopsis of the Plot
Setting: Portsmouth; 19th century

ACT I The happy ship, HMS *Pinafore*, is now anchored at Portsmouth, where Ralph, a humble sailor, hopes to pursue his courtship of Josephine, the captain's daughter, in spite of their differences in social status. But Josephine's father, Captain Corcoran, has his sights set on a much more exalted son-in-law, none other than the First Lord of the Admiralty, Sir Joseph Porter, in spite of Josephine's evident reluctance to consider him as a possible husband. When Sir Joseph arrives with an extensive entourage of relatives and supporters, he proudly recounts the history of his rise from humble office boy to cabinet minister. This does little to impress Josephine, who, finding she loves Ralph, is nevertheless much confused about whether she should commit herself to a man of so much lower birth. However, faced with Ralph's threat to commit suicide if she rejects him, she feels she must accept him. With the help of Ralph's shipmates, the two make plans to elope that night – only the wicked Dick Deadeye plots to thwart their intentions.

ACT II By the evening, however, Josephine has become concerned about the possible hardships that she will face as Ralph's wife. Sir Joseph, misinterpreting her evident disquiet as being caused by her consciousness of the social differences between her status and his own (and knowing nothing of her plans to elope), thinks to promote his own cause by telling her that love ignores all social rank and makes everyone equal. Josephine accepts these words as justification for her marriage with Ralph and the lovers are just about to slip away when, warned by Dick Deadeye, Captain Corcoran bars their way. Ralph speaks up proudly for his rights as a freeborn Englishman, but is taken off to the ship's jail anyway. Suddenly Mrs Cripps, the bumboat woman formerly known as Little Buttercup, makes a dramatic announcement: in a former career as a baby-farmer she mixed up two babies, Ralph and Corcoran, so, socially, Ralph is the captain and the captain only an ordinary seaman. The lovers can therefore be united, Corcoran marries Mrs Cripps and Sir Joseph proposes to his cousin Hebe instead.

Music and Background
Pseudo-patriotism and jibes at the class system in the Royal Navy made this the first of the Gilbert and Sullivan operettas to tackle direct political and social satire. Musically it goes for easy options – not least the reprise of tunes

that ends the score and the overuse of the Buttercup waltz, but at least the tunes are memorable.

Highlights

Act I: Mrs Cripps' 'I'm called Little Buttercup'; Captain Corcoran's 'What, never?'; Sir Joseph's 'When I was a lad'. Act II: Ralph's 'I am an Englishman'.

Did You Know?

Sir Joseph is reputedly based on the newspaper magnate, W.H. Smith, who rose from office boy to become First Lord of the Admiralty.

Recommended Recording

John Reed, Jeffrey Skitch, Thomas Round, New Symphony Orchestra/ Isidore Godfrey. Decca 414 283-2. A 1960 set, with dialogue.

Iolanthe,
or The Peer and the Peri

FORM: Operetta in two acts; in English
COMPOSER: Arthur Sullivan (1842–1900)
LIBRETTO: W.S. Gilbert
FIRST PERFORMANCE: London, 25 November 1882

Principal Characters

Iolanthe, a fairy **Mezzo-soprano**
Strephon, her son **Baritone**
Phyllis, his sweetheart and ward of the Lord Chancellor **Soprano**
The Lord Chancellor **Baritone**
Fairy Queen **Contralto**
Private Willis **Baritone**

Synopsis of the Plot

Setting: Arcadia and Westminster; 19th century

ACT I Strephon, son of a fairy mother, Iolanthe, and a mortal father, is in love with Phyllis, a ward of court, and hopes to marry her. He is encouraged by promises of help from the Fairy Queen, who has just pardoned Iolanthe and brought her back from exile, the punishment for her misalliance twenty-five years ago (although the usual one is death). But Phyllis' guardian is the Lord Chancellor, whose consent Strephon requires to marry a ward of court; the Lord Chancellor wishes to make Phyllis his own bride and refuses Strephon's petition. In desperation Strephon turns to his mother for help, but their meeting is observed by Phyllis, who takes the youthful-looking Iolanthe as a rival. Piqued, Phyllis decides to marry someone else and selects a peer or two from the range available to her in the House of Lords, each member of which is utterly smitten with love for her. The Fairy Queen, hearing of Strephon's problems and insulted by the Lord Chancellor, announces revenge. She arranges for Strephon to become a member of parliament, where his fairy powers will give him unparalleled opportunities to create political havoc.

ACT II Strephon is happily causing chaos in parliament, where his wishes on all issues are obeyed (including opening the peerage to competitive examination). The fairies are delighted at his achievements, but the Queen is disturbed at their tendency to fall in love with the peers. She points out the necessity of resisting this attraction to mortals, just as she herself resists her attraction to the young guardsman, Private Willis. Meanwhile, Phyllis and Strephon have removed the misunderstanding between them, but the Lord Chancellor is still adamant that Phyllis will be no one's bride but his alone. Then Iolanthe, seeing no other way to solve the problem, pleads her son's case to the Lord Chancellor and finally, in desperation, reveals that she is his long-lost wife. All obstacles to the union of Strephon and Phyllis are now removed and fairy law is changed so that it is a capital crime not to marry a mortal. The Queen saves herself by marrying Private Willis, the fairies marry the peers and they all fly away to Arcadia.

Music and Background

Iolanthe is a more structured piece than most of the Gilbert and Sullivan collaborations, with a coherent overture (as opposed to a mere run-through of the tunes you're about to hear), stronger characters than usual, and some eloquent love music. It was also the first of the collaborations written specifically for the new Savoy Theatre.

Highlights

Act I: the Peers' chorus 'Loudly let the trumpet bray'; the Lord Chancellor's 'The law is the true embodiment'. Act II: Mountararat's 'When Britain really ruled the waves'; the Fairy Queen's 'O foolish fay'; and the Lord Chancellor's 'When you're lying awake'.

Did You Know?

 The first production of *Iolanthe* presented the Fairy Queen as a parody of Wagner's Brünnhilde.

The Mikado,
or The Town of Titipu

FORM: Operetta in two acts; in English
COMPOSER: Arthur Sullivan (1842–1900)
LIBRETTO: W.S. Gilbert
FIRST PERFORMANCE: London, 14 March 1885

Principal Characters

The Mikado of Japan ∾ Bass
Nanki-Poo, his son ∾ Tenor
Ko-Ko ∾ Baritone
Yum-Yum, his ward ∾ Soprano
Pooh-Bah, his friend ∾ Bass-baritone
Pitti-Sing, his friend ∾ Mezzo-soprano
Katisha ∾ Mezzo-soprano

Synopsis of the Plot

Setting: The imaginary Japanese city of Titipu

ACT I Nanki-Poo, son of the Mikado of Japan, has fled his father's court to avoid the unwanted amorous attentions of the elderly Katisha. Disguised as a wandering minstrel, he has come to Titipu, where he has fallen in love with Yum-Yum, and hopes to marry her. He is dismayed, therefore, to learn that Yum-Yum is to marry Ko-Ko, her guardian, once a tailor condemned to death for flirting, but now elevated by the Mikado to the position of Lord High Executioner. His new job is not without its problems, however, for the Mikado has sent word that he is dissatisfied with the number of executions taking place under Ko-Ko's command (there have, in fact, been none). Nanki-Poo threatens suicide because he cannot have Yum-Yum and Ko-Ko takes advantage of this by arranging a compromise: Nanki-Poo can marry his beloved Yum-Yum immediately but he must agree to be beheaded after a month. Nanki-Poo is overjoyed – and even the dramatic appearance of the irritating Katisha, who has tracked him down, cannot spoil his happiness.

ACT II Yum-Yum and Nanki-Poo look forward to their coming wedding with happy anticipation, but all seems lost when Ko-Ko discovers a law which decrees that when a man is beheaded, his wife must be buried alive. Before they can decide what to do, the Mikado himself arrives to deal with the capital punishment problem, and Ko-Ko, Poo-Bah and Pitti-Sing attempt to win him over with spurious accounts of a 'recent execution'. But when the Mikado learns that the 'victim' was his own son, he sentences Ko-Ko and his friends to a lingering death. Panic-stricken they turn to Nanki-Poo for help, but he refuses to come 'back to life' and thus save his 'executioners' from their own fate unless Ko-Ko agrees to marry the annoying Katisha and thus stop her from pestering him. Ko-Ko has little choice but to agree. Nanki-Poo reappears, united with Yum-Yum, and the Mikado forgives them all.

Music and Background

The Japanese trappings of *The Mikado* sometimes distract attention from the true objective of its satire – which was English middle-class behaviour. Jonathan Miller's modern-classic production for English National Opera grasps that point very firmly, setting the action in an Edwardian grand hotel. Not all directors do. Apart from the quotation of a Japanese tune for the Mikado's entrance, the orientalism in the score is wafer-thin. Most commentators consider it Sullivan's masterpiece, and historically it has certainly been his most successful stage work.

Highlights

Act I: Nanki-Poo's 'A wandering minstrel'; Ko-Ko's Little List song; the 'Three Little Maids' trio; the chorus 'For she's going to marry Yum-Yum'. Act II: the mock madrigal 'Brightly dawns our wedding day'; the Mikado's 'My object all sublime'; the duet 'The flowers that bloom in the spring'; and Ko-Ko's mock lament 'Tit-willow'.

Did You Know?

The work was an immediate success and enjoyed an initial run of 672 performances. Phrases from the libretto such as 'Let the punishment fit the crime' have become an accepted part of everyday language.

Recommended Recording

Donald Adams, Anthony Rolfe-Johnson, Richard Suart, Felicity Palmer, Welsh National Opera/Charles Mackerras. Telarc CD 80284. Distinguished singers on a modern, award-winning issue.

Patience,
or Bunthorne's Bride

FORM: Operetta in two acts; in English
COMPOSER: Arthur Sullivan (1842–1900)
LIBRETTO: W.S. Gilbert
FIRST PERFORMANCE: London, 23 April 1881

Principal Characters

Reginald Bunthorne, a poet ✍ Baritone
Patience, a dairymaid ✍ Soprano
Archibald Grosvenor, a poet ✍ Baritone
Colonel Calverley ✍ Bass-baritone
Major Murgatroyd ✍ Baritone
Lieutenant the Duke of Dunstable ✍ Tenor

Synopsis of the Plot

Setting: England; 19th century

ACT I Reginald Bunthorne, a rather pretentious poet, is adored by many lovely maidens, but his heart yearns only for the village dairymaid, Patience, who has no time for him. The officers of the Dragoon Guards, who were formerly accustomed to enjoying the attentions of all the young ladies in the vicinity, are considerably annoyed by this turn of events, which they regard as a slight upon their collective manhood. Alone, however, Bunthorne admits he is no more than a poseur, exploiting his image simply to win admiration. Meanwhile, Patience's childhood sweetheart, Archibald Grosvenor, now a poet himself, unexpectedly returns, but Patience, having been told that true love is unselfish, feels duty bound to reject him, accepting instead the melancholic Bunthorne. The maidens return to the disgruntled guardsmen, but only temporarily, as the sight of the newcomer, Grosvenor, rekindles their passionate admiration of the artistic and they unhesitatingly abandon the officers once again.

ACT II Grosvenor, who loves Patience, is greatly irritated by the ardent attentions of the young ladies, while Bunthorne finds he is unhappy without them. The colonel, major and lieutenant, exasperated by this latest turn of events, dress themselves in what they suppose to be an artistic manner and attempt to strike impressive poses, in the hope of winning back the maidens' affections. Bunthorne discusses the situation with Grosvenor and the latter agrees to abandon his aesthetic style, become an ordinary man and marry his love, Patience. The field is once again clear for Bunthorne, but unfortunately for him the fickle maidens have been won over by the Dragoons at last and he is left quite alone.

Music and Background

A double satire on theatrical conventions and the aesthetic movement, led in Britain by the still-young Oscar Wilde, *Patience* has some enduringly attractive ensembles and calls for one of the principals, Lady Jane, to be able to play the cello – or at least pretend to.

Highlights

Act I: the 'Twenty lovesick maidens' chorus; Patience's 'I cannot tell what this love may be?'; and Bunthorne's 'If you're anxious for to shine'. Act II: Lady Jane's 'Silvered is the raven hair'; and the quintet 'If Saphir I choose to marry'.

Did You Know?

➤ The subtitle is meant to be ironic: Bunthorne never gets a bride.

Recommended Recording

Mary Sansom, John Reed, Gillian Knight, D'Oyly Carte Opera/Isidore Godfrey. Decca 425 193-2. Good on the military details.

The Pirates of Penzance,
or The Slave of Duty

FORM: Operetta in two acts; in English
COMPOSER: Arthur Sullivan (1842–1900)
LIBRETTO: W.S. Gilbert
FIRST PERFORMANCE: Paignton, 30 December 1879 (token staging for copyright purposes); New York, 31 December 1879

Principal Characters

Frederic ➤ Tenor
Ruth, his former nursemaid ➤ Mezzo-soprano
Pirate King ➤ Bass-baritone

Mabel ∿ Soprano
Major-General Stanley, her father ∿ **Baritone**
Sergeant of Police ∿ Bass

Synopsis of the Plot

Setting: Cornwall; 19th century

ACT I Frederic, apprenticed to the pirates as a boy, has now reached the age of twenty-one and is accepted as a full member of the crew. But he has decided, on moral grounds, to leave the pirate trade. Ruth, once Frederic's nursemaid and actually responsible for his pirate apprenticeship (she confused the word 'pirate' with 'pilot'), has also been working for the pirates, and her future plans include marrying Frederic. Frederic, having had little experience of female companionship, is fairly amenable to the idea until the day he unexpectedly comes across a party of young women on the beach; he immediately falls in love with all of them and begs one, any one, to take him as a husband. Kindly Mabel takes pity on him and accepts his offer. Frederic is joined by his fellow pirates who decide to carry all the young ladies off, but their hearts are softened by the Major-General, who arrives in the nick of time and persuades them not to rob him, an orphan, of the only family he has, his beloved daughters. After the pirates leave, the Major-General confides that, in fact, he lied – he is not an orphan at all.

ACT II The Major-General, tormented by his conscience, cannot sleep, while Frederic, encouraged by Mabel, has informed the police of his former comrades' whereabouts and a raid is planned. Confronted by the Pirate King and Ruth, Frederic is told that, by a curious turn of fate, his birthday was actually on 29 February, in a leap year, and he was apprenticed to the pirates until his twenty-first birthday, not until he was twenty-one years old. Since his twenty-first birthday will not arrive until well into the next century, he will be apprenticed to the pirates for many years to come! Frederic has no choice but to say a sad goodbye to Mabel and leave with the pirates. Later, the pirates discover that the Major-General lied to them about being an orphan and they determine to take their revenge. They attack and overpower the policemen who are waiting for them, but submit when asked to do so in the queen's name. The pirates are all revealed to be noblemen who have 'gone astray'; their crimes are forgiven and they are released, into the arms of the Major-General's daughters, for whom they are now suitable husbands. Mabel and Frederic are united and all ends happily.

Music and Background

The Pirates of Penzance is an obvious follow-up to *HMS Pinafore*: one aiming its humour at the navy, the other at the army. But *The Pirates of Penzance* has better music, and is probably funnier. It has special ties with America in that it effectively premiered in New York. A prior performance in Paignton was no more than a token run-through to protect the score's British copyright.

Highlights

Act I: Mabel's ballad 'Poor wand'ring one'; the interlocking chorus 'How beautifully blue the sky' and duet 'Did ever maiden wake'; Stanley's 'I am the very model of a modern Major-General'. Act II: The Mabel/Frederic duet 'Leave me not to pine alone'; the Sergeant's 'When a felon's not engaged in his employment'.

Did You Know?

🔊 The US connection probably explains how the tune for 'Come friends who plough the sea' became the American song 'Hail, hail, the gang's all here'.

Recommended Recording

John Reed, Donald Adams, Philip Potter, Valerie Masterson, Owen Brannigan, Royal Philharmonic Orchestra/Isidore Godfrey. A D'Oyly Carte enterprise with higher-grade performers than usual.

The Yeomen of the Guard,
or The Merryman and His Maid

FORM: Operetta in two acts; in English
COMPOSER: Arthur Sullivan (1842–1900)
LIBRETTO: W.S. Gilbert
FIRST PERFORMANCE: London, 3 October 1888

Principal Characters

Colonel Fairfax 🔊 Tenor
Sergeant Meryll, Yeoman of the Guard 🔊 Baritone
Phoebe, his daughter 🔊 Mezzo-soprano
Elsie Maynard, a wandering player 🔊 Soprano
Jack Point, a wandering player 🔊 Baritone

Wilfred Shadbolt, a jailer 〜 **Baritone**
Sir Richard Cholmondeley, Lieutenant of the Tower 〜 **Bass-baritone**

Synopsis of the Plot
Setting: London; 16th century

ACT I Colonel Fairfax, wrongfully imprisoned in the Tower of London, is much admired by Phoebe, daughter of Sergeant Meryll, a Yeoman of the Guard. Fairfax, condemned to death, asks Sir Richard Cholmondeley, Lieutenant of the Tower, to allow him to marry a blindfolded bride so that when he dies, his possessions will not come into the hands of his unscrupulous relatives. Sir Richard sympathises with his prisoner and, when he encounters the wandering players Elsie Maynard and Jack Point, he persuades Elsie to take the role of Fairfax's bride. Meanwhile, the sympathetic Sergeant Meryll and Phoebe have planned Fairfax's escape. Phoebe wheedles the key to his cell from the jailer, Shadbolt, who is in love with her, and Fairfax is disguised as Phoebe's brother, Leonard, due shortly to join the Yeomen, and spirited out of his cell. There is uproar when the executioners arrive to find their prisoner has vanished.

ACT II Jack Point, who is in love with Elsie, is anxious to restore his relationship with her, but she refuses his attentions as she is still married to Fairfax. Point persuades Shadbolt to say he shot Fairfax dead as he swam across the Thames. Elsie accepts this but, in the meantime, she has fallen in love with 'Leonard'. Point, given practical lessons by 'Leonard' on the art of courtship, is horrified when Elsie accepts 'Leonard's' proposal of marriage. Phoebe, annoyed, rouses Shadbolt's suspicions that 'Leonard' is not her brother and she is forced to promise to marry him as the price of his silence. News arrives that Fairfax has been reprieved so he can now resume his true identity. He claims Elsie for his own, whereupon the heartbroken Point collapses at her feet.

Music and Background
More 'serious' than the other Savoy Operas, and less topical in its wit, *The Yeomen of the Guard* even manages a sad ending, and tends generally towards pathos rather than comedy. The songs are strong and the overture is a musically coherent piece of writing rather than a medley.

Highlights
Act I: the Jack/Elsie duet 'I have a song to sing'. Act II: the famous Jester's Song and following duet 'Tell a tale of cock and bull'.

Recommended Recording

John Reed, Donald Adams, Philip Potter, Elizabeth Harwood, Royal Philharmonic Orchestra/Malcolm Sargent. Decca 417 358-4. Grand forces taking the piece very seriously indeed.

Pyotr Ilyich Tchaikovsky

(1840–93)

Cherevichki (Vakula the Smith) (1874)
Eugene Onegin (1878)
Mazeppa (1883)
The Queen of Spades (1890)
Iolanta (1891)

Born near Moscow and educated in St Petersburg, Tchaikovsky was never part of the Nationalist group of composers that existed in Russia during his time, and he is generally regarded as European in outlook. But that is to mistake technical sophistication for Western leanings. Tchaikovsky was as Russian as any of his contemporaries: he just expressed it with more eloquence than most. And never was he more eloquent than in his operas, which tend to be overshadowed by his achievements as a symphonist and writer of ballet music, but which were absolutely central to his creative life. Only two Tchaikovsky operas survive in regular repertory – *Eugene Onegin* and *The Queen of Spades* – but there were ten in total, six of them derived from Pushkin. The quality varies but the lyricism is consistent, as is the sense that these scores mattered deeply to the composer. *Eugene Onegin* incorporates an element of self-reference in that it was written at the time of Tchaikovsky's disastrous and abortive marriage to a young woman who had pursued him against his own inclinations. Much of his music reflects the turbulence of his inner life and emotions, the product of a naturally depressive temperament and the anxiety of someone forced to keep his homosexuality under wraps. His death remains a mystery but was very likely suicide – ordered by a kangaroo court which had 'tried' him for alleged homosexual involvement with a member of the Russian royal household.

Eugene Onegin

FORM: Opera in three acts; in Russian
COMPOSER: Pyotr Ilyich Tchaikovsky (1840–93)
LIBRETTO: Tchaikovsky and K.S. Shilovsky; after Pushkin
FIRST PERFORMANCE: Moscow, 29 March 1879

Principal Characters

Madame Larina, a landowner ❧ **Mezzo-soprano**
Tatyana, her daughter ❧ **Soprano**
Olga, her daughter ❧ **Contralto**
Vladimir Lensky, Olga's fiancé ❧ **Tenor**
Eugene Onegin, his friend ❧ **Baritone**
Filipyevna, the old nurse ❧ **Mezzo-soprano**
Prince Gremin, Tatyana's eventual husband ❧ **Bass**

Synopsis of the Plot

Setting: A Russian country estate outside St Petersburg; 1820s

ACT I Madame Larina and her daughters welcome Lensky, Olga's future husband, who introduces a new neighbour, Eugene Onegin. Tatyana, in particular, is much taken with the romantic, sophisticated Onegin and, that night, she writes him an impassioned letter, which she asks Filipyevna to send the next morning. When they next meet, however, Onegin is cold and distant; he makes it clear that love and marriage are not for him and Tatyana is crushed.

ACT II Madame Larina is holding a dance to celebrate Tatyana's birthday, and both Lensky and Onegin have come. Onegin, bored and annoyed by some gossip he has heard linking him with Tatyana, starts to flirt with Olga. When Lensky remonstrates with Olga she is so annoyed that she goes off to dance with Onegin once more, and this prompts Lensky to challenge Onegin to a duel. They fight the next morning and, to Onegin's horror, Lensky is killed.

ACT III Onegin has now returned to Russia, after several years abroad, and finds himself invited to a grand ball in St Petersburg. He is astonished to learn that his host, Prince Gremin, is married to Tatyana, to whom Onegin now feels himself strongly drawn. Later, just as the younger Tatyana had once written passionately to him, Onegin writes to Tatyana, ardently expressing his love for her. She agrees to see him and, in response to his declarations, finally admits that she does still love him. Onegin begs her to go away with him but, with difficulty, Tatyana reminds him of her duty to her husband and refuses. Onegin leaves, utterly defeated.

Music and Background

Tchaikovsky described *Eugene Onegin* as a sequence of 'lyric scenes', and that's exactly what it is. There are seven of them, charting the history of an abortive relationship, but self-contained, without the connective tissue of standard story-telling and making their point with a delicacy that caused Tchaikovsky to entrust the premiere to student singers rather than set-in-their-ways professionals. Although there are big theatre-moments with formal dancing, the heart of the score belongs to intimate exchanges between the principals and, especially, the Letter Scene which counts among the most engaging and endearing of monologues in all opera. It was the first part of the score to be written, inspired not only by Pushkin's text but by a bizarrely similar event in the composer's own life when a young, unknown woman sent him a declaration of love. Unlike Onegin, Tchaikovsky accepted and married his admirer – an attempt to stifle his homosexuality which ended in disaster and breakdown. Nonetheless, his depiction of Tatyana is enchanting; and her development from awkward ingénue into sophisticated woman is one of the dramatic pleasures of the piece, along with Onegin's progress from haughtiness to passion.

Highlights

Act I: Lensky's love song at the end of the first scene; Tatyana's Letter Scene in its entirety. Act II: the opening waltz, Monsieur Tricquet's song, the mazurka, and Lensky's farewell before the duel. Act III: the polonaise and écossaise dance numbers, Gremin's aria on the joys of married life, and Onegin's declaration of love (sung to the same melody Tatyana sang for *him* in Act I).

Did You Know?

∼ Pushkin's originating verse novel was not the thing of romantic passion Tchaikovsky turned it into but an exercise in literary irony, written in wryly detached terms. Early audiences criticised the opera as being no match for the sophistication of its source.

∼ Pushkin himself was killed in a duel six years after writing the novel upon which the opera is based.

Recommended Recording

Mirella Freni, Thomas Allen, Neil Shicoff, Dresden State Orchestra/James Levine. DG 423 959-2. A wonderfully detailed and refined performance by Tom Allen, coupled with singing from Freni that could *almost* be that of a young girl.

The Queen of Spades

FORM: Opera in three acts; in Russian
COMPOSER: Pyotr Ilyich Tchaikovsky (1840–93)
LIBRETTO: Modest and Pyotr Tchaikovsky; after Pushkin
FIRST PERFORMANCE: St Petersburg, 19 December 1890

Principal Characters

The Countess, an old woman ~ Mezzo-soprano
Lisa, her grand-daughter ~ Soprano
Prince Yeletsky, Lisa's fiancé ~ Baritone
Pauline, Lisa's friend ~ Contralto
Herman, a young officer ~ Tenor
Count Tomsky ~ Baritone

Synopsis of the Plot

Setting: St Petersburg; late 18th century

ACT I Herman reveals to his friends that he is tormented by his love for Lisa, a girl whom he has never met because of their differences in social status. Lisa is, in fact, already engaged – to Prince Yeletsky – but when she sees Herman's anguished face she is profoundly moved. Tomsky tells Herman that Lisa's grandmother, the Countess, is known as the Queen of Spades because, many years ago, she was given the secret of winning at cards in return for her sexual favours. Herman is fascinated by this story and determines to win Lisa. Later that evening, in a highly emotional and even disturbed state of mind, Herman climbs through the window of Lisa's bedroom and pours out his love for her. Eventually, Lisa confesses that she loves him too.

ACT II Lisa and Herman are both guests at a masked ball. Lisa sends him a note asking him to come and see her the following evening; she leaves him a key and says he can reach her room by way of the Countess' room. But Herman insists on coming to her that same evening and, determined also to gain the secret of winning at cards, hides in the Countess' room. He emerges from his hiding place when the old lady is alone and tries to persuade her to tell him the secret; but the Countess is terrified of him and cannot speak, and when he draws a pistol to threaten her she dies from shock. Lisa enters and, realising what he has done, angrily accuses Herman of killing her grandmother, before sending him away.

ACT III Lisa, thinking she may have unjustly blamed Herman for the Countess' death, asks him to meet her on the quayside. But before he sees Lisa, the Countess' ghost appears to Herman and gives him the secret – three, seven, ace. Herman meets Lisa as arranged but instead of passionate declarations of love, he urges her to go with him to the casino, now that he has the secret. She begs him not to go, but he pushes her away and, in despair, Lisa drowns herself. In the casino Herman, wild-eyed and obsessed, wins on the first two cards and stakes all his money on the last card. But the card in his hand is not the ace, as the ghost promised, but the queen of spades. The Queen of Spades herself, the Countess, appears to Herman, who has by now completely lost his senses, and he stabs himself to death.

Music and Background

An obsessive romantic fantasy, sometimes cited as the first example of musical surrealism, *The Queen of Spades* was written at speed and with a passion that shows in the furious, compacted energy of the score. Once again, it was an example of Tchaikovsky turning an ironically detached novel by Pushkin into full-blooded romantic tragedy. But the music also indulges the composer's fondness for 18th-century pastiche (in the Ballroom Scene), and its structure is generally tight, with driving rhythms and a galvanising use of recurring motto themes.

Highlights

Act I: Herman's two-part aria of love for the as yet unknown Lisa; the ensuing little vocal quintet; and Tomsky's old wives' tale of The Three Cards. Act II: Yeletsky's song of love addressed to Lisa; the Bedroom Scene – especially Herman's opening monologue (sung to a tense, insistent orchestral ostinato) and his confrontation with the Countess. Act III: Lisa's aria as she waits for Herman by the Neva.

Did You Know?

❥ Tchaikovsky identified closely with the character of Herman and confessed to having wept as he composed the Death Scene.

Recommended Recording

Gegam Grigorian, Vladimir Chernov, Maria Gulegina, Irina Arkhipova, Olga Borodina, Kirov Opera/Valery Gergiev. Philips 438 141-2. One of the more impressive issues in Gergiev's ongoing series of Russian operas, with idiomatic singing and strong orchestral attack.

Michael Tippett

(1905–)

The Midsummer Marriage (1952)
King Priam (1961)
The Knot Garden (1969)
New Year (1988)

ichael Tippett was born before Benjamin Britten but took so long to get into his stride as a composer that he feels like a later figure in the chronology of English music – a feeling reinforced by the fact that he has continued to produce major works in the final years of a very long life, well after Britten's death. Brought up in a freethinking and unorthodox family, partly in Suffolk, partly in France, he developed into a maverick figure writing lyrical music of passionate and visionary beauty but with complexities that caused many to dismiss his work as dilettante and impracticable. The awkwardness of his own libretti (for oratorios as well as operas) has attracted criticism. But no one doubts his seer-like stature as a great humanitarian; and from the oratorio *A Child of Our Time* onwards, he has made his music a vehicle for debate on issues such as peace and tolerance. A committed socialist and pacifist, his beliefs earned him a term of imprisonment during the Second World War; and in other respects, not least his homosexuality, he has always been an anti-establishment figure – although it didn't stop him receiving a knighthood in 1966. His operas mostly deal with themes that venture into the realms of the unconscious and relate back to an early interest in Jungian psychotherapy. Full of symbolism, they suggest a lifelong spiritual quest for wholeness and can be considered as ongoing reflections on a key phrase in Tippett's libretto for *A Child of Our Time* which asks to 'know my shadow and my light'.

King Priam

FORM: Opera in three acts; in English
COMPOSER: Michael Tippett (1905–)
LIBRETTO: Michael Tippett; after Homer
FIRST PERFORMANCE: Coventry, 29 May 1962

Principal Characters

Priam, King of Troy ❧ **Baritone**
Hecuba, his wife ❧ **Soprano**
Hector, their eldest son ❧ **Baritone**
Andromache, his wife ❧ **Soprano**
Paris, Priam's younger son ❧ **Tenor**
Helen, wife of King Menelaus of Sparta ❧ **Mezzo-soprano**
Achilles, a Greek hero ❧ **Tenor**
Patroclus, his friend ❧ **Baritone**
Nurse ❧ **Mezzo-soprano**
Old Man ❧ **Bass**
Young Guard ❧ **Tenor**
Hermes, Messenger of the Gods ❧ **Tenor**

Synopsis of the Plot

Setting: Legendary Troy and Sparta

ACT I Hecuba, King Priam's wife, has given birth to their son, Paris, but is greatly troubled by a dream she has had. The Old Man is sent for to interpret the dream and, to the consternation of Hecuba and Priam, announces that Paris will, in due course, bring about his father's death. Hecuba, hysterical, orders the baby's immediate death, but Priam, torn between his roles and responsibilities both as father and as king, hesitates before commanding that the unfortunate baby be murdered. The baby is taken away and the Nurse, Old Man and Young Guard (the chorus) approach the front of the stage and comment, directly to the audience, on the problems of choices and consequences raised by the action so far. Many years pass, and Priam and his son, Hector, are demonstrating their physical prowess when they are dazzled by the daring feats of an unknown young man. It is, of course, Paris, who had not been killed but given to a shepherd to bring up. Priam is momentarily stunned by the revelation, but quickly makes Paris welcome, relieved and happy that 'the gods' have reversed his long-ago decision. The chorus again reflect on these momentous events and bring the story up to date, before they are displaced by wedding guests who have come to celebrate the marriage of Hector and Andromache. The guests discuss the recent rift between Hector and Paris and Paris' subsequent decision to leave for Sparta. In Sparta, Paris and Helen, Menelaus' wife, have begun a passionate affair. Paris insists that Helen chooses between her husband and himself, although he knows full well that if he takes Menelaus' wife it will mean war. Helen decides to leave with Paris, plunging Troy and Sparta into conflict.

ACT II Troy is under siege and Hector and Paris are quarrelling. In the Spartan camp, Achilles, the Greek hero, has retreated to his tent because of a disagreement with his chief, Agamemnon. Patroclus, Achilles' close friend, comes to console him and they agree that Patroclus shall put on Achilles' armour and go to fight in his name. Patroclus is killed by Hector and, as the Trojans rejoice in their victory, Achilles' blood-curdling voice is heard, swearing vengeance for his friend.

ACT III As the fighting continues outside the city, Andromache and Hecuba wait anxiously in the palace for news. When Helen joins them, they insult her and accuse her of being responsible for the bloodshed, to which she responds with an assertion of her sexual power over men and her godlike qualities. News arrives of Hector's death and Priam, overcome with sorrow, declares that if he had known Paris' survival would have meant the death of Hector, as well as his own, he would willingly have had the baby killed. Paris swears to take revenge by killing Achilles himself and leaves. Priam then goes to Achilles' tent with the body of Patroclus, and begs Achilles to exchange it for that of his son, Hector. The two enemies, united in grief, accept their fates: each will be killed by the other's son. Priam returns to Troy where, overcome by sorrow, he waits for Neoptolemus, Achilles' son, to fulfil his destiny.

Music and Background

The least lyrical of Tippett's operas, *King Priam* is an attempt to recreate epic, classically hard-hitting theatre in music that abandons the luxuriant orchestral richness of the composer's previous scores and speaks instead with an abrasive muscularity. Instead of creating a smooth orchestral blend, the instruments tend to sound in separate departments, with the wind more prominent than the strings. Structurally, the score relies on contrast rather than development – an idea Tippett would pursue in later works – and the vocal style is largely declamatory and hard-edged, although it softens in scenes that reflect the tenderness of the relationship between Achilles and Patroclus.

Highlights

Act I: Priam's motto theme 'a father and a king'; and the arrival of Hermes at the close of the Act. Act II: Achilles' song to Patroclus; Achilles' offstage war-cry. Act III: the scene between Priam and Achilles.

Did You Know?

☙ This war-opera had its first performance at a festival to mark the consecration of the new Coventry Cathedral, built on the site of its predecessor, which had been destroyed by wartime bombs. The premiere took place the day before the premiere of Britten's *War Requiem*.

Recommended Recording

Norman Bailey, Heather Harper, Thomas Allen, Felicity Palmer, Robert Tear, Philip Langridge, London Sinfonietta/David Atherton. Chandos 9406/7. A roll-call of fine British singers, originally collected together in 1980 for Decca but now transferred to Chandos.

The Knot Garden

FORM: Opera in three acts; in English
COMPOSER: Michael Tippett (1905–)
LIBRETTO: Michael Tippett
FIRST PERFORMANCE: London, 2 December 1970

Principal Characters

Faber, an engineer ❧ **Baritone**
Thea, his wife ❧ **Mezzo-soprano**
Flora, their ward ❧ **Soprano**
Denise, Thea's sister, a human rights activist ❧ **Soprano**
Mel, a black writer ❧ **Baritone**
Dov, his lover, a musician ❧ **Tenor**
Mangus, a psychoanalyst ❧ **Baritone**

Synopsis of the Plot

Setting: A high-walled garden; the present

ACT I Confrontation. Mangus, a psychoanalyst, has been invited by Thea and Faber to stay with them in the hope that he can help them with their troublesome adolescent ward, Flora. Mangus soon realises that Flora's problems are symptomatic of much deeper difficulties in the relationship between Thea and Faber. Taking Shakespeare's *The Tempest* as his paradigm, Mangus casts himself as Prospero, the manipulator of men, and suggests a series of games and charades based on characters from the play, through which he hopes to explore the relationships between Faber, Thea and Flora. The action opens with Thea tending her beloved garden, her refuge from unhappiness; refusing help from Mangus, she is interrupted when Flora, screaming and hysterical, rushes into her arms, pursued by Faber. Mangus takes Flora away and Thea accuses her husband of being sexually attracted towards their ward. Left alone, Faber reassures himself that his behaviour towards Flora is not untoward and then goes to his work in the city – his form of escape from domestic unhappiness. A homosexual couple, Mel and Dov, join the group to play the parts of Ariel and Caliban, and they start to perform in front of Flora, who has been tranquilly arranging flowers, but now stands transfixed in front of them. *The Tempest* cast is now complete, with Ferdinand as Faber and Miranda as Flora. Tensions begin to rise as Thea and Mel seem to be attracted to one another, leaving Dov to howl in anguish like a dog. The arrival of Thea's sister, Denise, disfigured by the torture she has suffered in her fight for human rights, heightens the tension between the characters, who do not know how to respond to her vivid account of her sufferings. Finally, Mel begins a blues melody in which all the others gradually join, each using it as a vehicle to express his or her feelings.

ACT II Labyrinth. The garden now represents an intricate maze with a kind of centripetal force in which the characters seem to be caught, almost colliding with each other and briefly connecting, before separating again and disappearing. In this nightmarish vision, Faber imposes himself on Flora and is whipped by Thea; Dov and Mel end their affair; and Mel becomes attracted to Denise. Finally there is calm, and the weeping Flora and heartbroken Dov are left alone.

ACT III Charade. Mangus has persuaded the group to act out charades, drawn from scenes in *The Tempest*. These become infused with the feelings and attitudes of the players, until they are able, to an extent, to come to terms with themselves and with each other. Mangus stops the proceedings and they join with one another to sing of human love, the only force that can truly bind people together.

Music and Background

Playing onstage like an Iris Murdoch novel set to music, the closed world of this domestic piece with just seven characters (no chorus) embraces a rich panorama of contemporary issues – from political freedom-fighting to homosexuality – within a symbolic framework of Jungian psychology and Shakespeare. The very allusiveness of the opera, with all its references taken out, is problematic, and the plot isn't much more than a manipulation and re-ordering of the relationships between the characters, somewhat along the lines of Mozart's *Così fan Tutte*. But the score moves fast, through short scenes that dissolve into each other cinematically; and the musical language mirrors the magpie quality of the text, taking from whatever seems appropriate, including jazz and rock. Tippett's enthusiasm for absorbing popular clichés into his libretto is one of the less comfortable things about the piece, and dates it as a relic of the 1960s. But *The Knot Garden* is probably just getting old enough, now, for such things to sound more period than old-fashioned.

Highlights

Act I: Denise's 'O you may stare in horror' and the powerful blues septet that follows. Act II: the tender exchange of songs between Flora and Dov. Act III: the quotations from Tippett's earlier *Songs for Ariel* which accompany the re-sorting of relationships.

Did You Know?

🎵 *The Knot Garden* contains what is almost certainly the first open representation of a gay relationship in opera.

The Midsummer Marriage

FORM: Opera in three acts; in English
COMPOSER: Michael Tippett (1905–)
LIBRETTO: Michael Tippett
FIRST PERFORMANCE: London, 27 January 1955

Principal Characters

Mark, a young man ∾ Tenor
Jenifer, his fiancée ∾ Soprano
King Fisher, her father ∾ Baritone
Bella, his secretary ∾ Soprano
Jack, her boyfriend ∾ Tenor
Two Ancients, priest and priestess of the temple
∾ Bass, Mezzo-soprano
Sosostris, a clairvoyante ∾ Contralto
Strephon, a dancer ∾ Silent role
Chorus of Mark and Jenifer's friends
∾ Soprano, Alto, Tenor, Bass

Synopsis of the Plot

Setting: Midsummer Day; the present

ACT I Mark and his friends arrive at the clearing in the woods where he has come to celebrate his marriage with Jenifer at the ancient temple there on midsummer morning. But when Jenifer arrives, she tells the baffled Mark that the wedding will not take place, explaining that she is looking for truth, not love. The lovers quarrel, after which Jenifer, saying she is searching for enlightenment, ascends a spiral staircase near the temple and disappears. Mark, distraught, goes into a cavern, whose gates close firmly behind him. At that moment, Jenifer's father, King Fisher, accompanied by Bella, his secretary, comes in search of his errant daughter. Seeing the locked gates, he tells Bella to fetch her mechanic boyfriend, Jack, to open them.

When he has gone, King Fisher turns to Mark's friends, castigating Mark and trying to bribe them, without success, to tell him Jenifer's whereabouts. When Jack arrives, he and Bella first sing of their love for each other, before he tackles the gate. As he raises his hammer for the second time, a warning voice (Sosostris) calls out to King Fisher not to interfere, but he takes no notice. Suddenly Jenifer appears at the top of the staircase and Mark comes to the mouth of the cave. Both are evidently altered by their experiences and the Ancients command the two to tell of what they have encountered: Jenifer's spiritual enlightenment contrasts with Mark's more earthy, sensual knowledge. The two seem farther apart than ever and, searching for further illumination, they resume their spiritual journeys – Mark ascends the staircase and Jenifer retreats into the cave.

ACT II Bella and Jack, accompanied by friends of Mark and Jenifer, return to the temple in the afternoon. Bella and Jack agree to marry and wander away into the woods. Strephon and his dancers perform the traditional three midsummer dances: in the first dance he is a hare, hunted by a hound; in the second, a fish hunted by an otter; in the third, an injured bird hunted by a hawk. Only in the last dance is he captured, prompting Bella to scream out in terror. The dancers disappear and Bella, once more composed, prepares to return to King Fisher.

ACT III Evening has come to the clearing and Mark and Jenifer's friends are enjoying a midsummer party. But King Fisher is still determined to find his daughter and sends them away to bring his personal clairvoyante, Sosostris, to confront and force the Ancients to disclose what has happened to her. The chorus return with a mysterious figure – but this, it transpires, is merely Jack in disguise, carrying a crystal bowl. Then Sosostris herself appears and, reluctantly using her powers, sees a vision of the two lovers in the crystal bowl. Furious, King Fisher smashes the bowl and tells Jack to unveil Sosostris. Jack refuses and King Fisher approaches her himself, in spite of warnings from the Ancients. But when the final veil falls away, it is not a woman but a huge bud-like flower that stands before him. As the petals open to reveal Mark and Jenifer, King Fisher raises his gun to shoot, but before he can act, Mark and Jenifer turn to gaze at him and he falls dead. Strephon performs the final ritual dance, the petals close again round Mark and Jenifer, and Strephon himself is absorbed into the flower, which bursts into flame. When the flames die down the atmosphere becomes cold and dark; the chorus call on the day to break and, with the dawn, come Mark and Jenifer, united and at peace with one another. Jenifer takes Mark's wedding ring and they disappear as the sun rises.

Music and Background

This is Tippett's operatic masterpiece; and although the score is long, rambling and flawed, with an awkwardly obscure libretto (cod-T.S. Eliot) that attracted derision when the piece first appeared, it rises to moments of ravishing, mystical beauty unsurpassed in any modern stage work. Where *The Knot Garden* was a 20th-century take on *Così fan Tutte*, *The Midsummer Marriage* was a lingering reflection on *Die Zauberflöte*, with its modern myth of two pairs of lovers – one exalted, one lowly – in pursuit of self-knowledge; and if the piece has a governing idea, it is the aspiration found in Tippett's earlier oratorio *A Child of Our Time*: 'I would know my shadow and my light/So shall I at last be whole'. The music is the most developed example of Tippett's early style: ecstatic, highly energised, but transcendental, using the traditional resources of opera – big arias, chorus numbers, dance sequences – but in a distinctive way that can best be summed up as 'English Visionary'.

Highlights

Act I: Mark's rapturous opening aria 'Ah . . . the summer morning dances in my heart', leading into his quarrel duet with Jenifer; and King Fisher's address to the chorus 'So you, so you'. Act II: the Ritual Dances (a popular concert piece in their own right). Act III: Sosostris' big set-piece aria; and the final Ritual Dance.

Did You Know?

The first Jenifer was grandly cast with Joan Sutherland.

Recommended Recording

Alberto Remedios, Joan Carlyle, Raimund Herincx, Royal Opera, Covent Garden/Colin Davis. Lyrita SRCD 2217. The only recording, originally released by Philips and superbly conducted by a seasoned Tippett champion.

Giuseppe Verdi

(1813–1901)

Oberto (1839)
Nabucco (1841)
Ernani (1844)
I Due Foscari (1844)
Attila (1846)
Macbeth (1847)
Luisa Miller (1849)
Stiffelio (1850)
Rigoletto (1851)
Il Trovatore (1853)
La Traviata (1853)
Les Vêpres Siciliennes (1855)
Simon Boccanegra (1857, rewritten 1881)
Un Ballo in Maschera (1858)
La Forza del Destino (1861)
Don Carlos (1867)
Aida (1871)
Otello (1886)
Falstaff (1892)

A century after his death, Verdi remains the presiding genius of Italian opera and one of the two or three dominant figures in the whole history of the lyric stage. Twelve of his twenty-eight operas are 'core' repertory; and most of them have ranked high in public popularity from the time they first appeared. However radical he may have been as a composer, Verdi never lost the common touch, or the ability to make an instant impact. Born in humble circumstances in a village near Parma, he studied in Milan and had his first opera, *Oberto*, staged there at La Scala. But his first real success came several years later with *Nabucco*, whose story of lost nationhood acquired peculiar resonance in Risorgimento Italy, where political factions were fighting to create a single state out of a collection of principalities. Overnight, Verdi became a patriotic hero; and the rousing, high-adrenalin (some might say tub-thumping) tunes of his early operas were adopted as popular anthems of the Unification cause. From then on his work was in constant demand, and there followed what Verdi called his 'years in the galley', generating one score after the next in relentless succession. In the 1850s he produced his most popular works – *Rigoletto*, *La Traviata* and *Il Trovatore*, but then the pace slowed down as Verdi settled into the life of a well-heeled country squire and nationally-famous politician (he was made a deputy in the first all-Italian parliament). His mature operas tended to be longer, more complex scores, following the model of French grand opera – notably *Don Carlos* and *Aida*, which promised to be his last work. However, after a long gap he started to compose again in old age, producing three Indian summer operas, all with libretti by the young poet/composer Boito: *Simon Boccanegra* (rewritten from an earlier version), *Otello* and *Falstaff*. Most commentators consider them his greatest works.

Aida

FORM: Opera in four acts; in Italian
COMPOSER: Giuseppe Verdi (1813–1901)
LIBRETTO: Antonio Ghislanzoni; after Mariette and du Locle
FIRST PERFORMANCE: Cairo, 24 December 1871

Principal Characters

The King of Egypt ∽ Bass
Amneris, his daughter ∽ **Mezzo-soprano**
Aida, her slave, an Ethiopian prisoner and daughter of Amonasro
∽ **Soprano**
Amonasro, King of Ethiopia ∽ **Baritone**
Radamès, captain of the Egyptian guard ∽ **Tenor**
Ramfis, the Egyptian high priest ∽ **Bass**

Synopsis of the Plot

Setting: Memphis and Thebes in the time of the pharaohs

ACT I The Ethiopians have invaded Egypt and a new leader for the Egyptian armies is about to be chosen. Radamès, inspired by his love for Aida, a captured Ethiopian slave, longs to be chosen to lead his countrymen to victory so that he can return and claim her as his bride. But Radamès, in turn, is loved by Amneris, the King of Egypt's daughter, who suspects Aida to be her rival. The new leader is about to be chosen and the king and priests enter to await the decision: the great god, Isis, has designated Radamès to be the leader and he is overjoyed. Aida, however, is torn by conflicting emotions – her love for Radamès and loyalty to her father who, unbeknown to the Egyptians, is the Ethiopian king.

ACT II Radamès and his forces have routed the Ethiopians and he is on his way home. Amneris, determined to find out the truth about the relationship between Aida and Radamès, pretends to Aida that he has been killed, thus provoking Aida into admitting her love for him. Amneris scornfully dismisses her slave as an unworthy consort for a great warrior, and prepares herself to greet Radamès. The victor returns, in great splendour, bringing with him several prisoners, among whom is Amonasro, disguised as an ordinary soldier, though immediately recognised by his daughter. Amonasro begs the King to show mercy on the prisoners and, supported by Radamès and the Egyptian people, the King agrees to release them, keeping only Amonasro as a hostage. To the horror of Radamès and Aida, the King then gives his daughter, Amneris, to the warrior as his bride.

ACT III Amneris goes to the temple to ask the gods' blessing on her marriage, as Aida arrives for an assignation with Radamès. But before her lover arrives, Amonasro appears and convinces her that she owes it to her country to find out from Radamès which route the Egyptian forces are planning to use to invade Ethiopia. Reluctantly Aida agrees to do so and she extracts the information from Radamès; just then Amonasro steps forward and reveals his true identity to the stunned warrior, who realises he has betrayed his country. They are overheard by Amneris and Ramfis, the priest, who emerge from the temple; the guards are called but Radamès manages to help Aida and Amonasro to escape before he is taken himself.

ACT IV Amonasro is dead and Aida has disappeared. Amneris, trying desperately to save Radamès, offers to plead for him if he will repent and renounce Aida. Radamès refuses. He is tried, sentenced to be buried alive and taken away. As the walls of his burial chamber are sealed up, Radamès discovers that Aida has concealed herself in the darkness, ready to die with him. To the sound of Amneris' anguished prayers and the chanting of the priests, the lovers prepare to die together.

Music and Background

People will tell you this opera was written for the opening of the Suez Canal, and it isn't true. Nor did it open the new Cairo Opera House. But the piece *was* commissioned by the Khedive of Egypt to premiere at Cairo, and the subject matter *was* fixed by the commission to create something that the Egyptians could adopt as a national opera. But apart from the atmospheric use of harps, flutes, trumpets and a mysterious offstage voice in the score, *Aida*'s music is acually quite conservative, enlarging the sort of thing Verdi put into his popular works of twenty years before with the ceremonial spectacle of French grand opera – especially in Acts I and II where the big moments come. Acts III and IV are more intimate.

Highlights

Act I: Radamès' classic tenor aria 'Celeste Aida' and the following trio, 'Trema o rea', with Amneris and Aida; the grand military march 'Su! del Nilo'; and the Temple Scene with offstage priestess ('Possente Fthà') and belligerent chorus ('La mano tua distendi'). Act II: the opening slave girls' chorus 'Chi mai fra gl'inni'; the mighty choral scene 'Gloria all'Egitto' and its reprise at the end of the act. Act IV: the Radamès/Amneris duet 'Già i sacerdoti'; and the closing section of the Radamès/Aida duet 'O terra, addio'.

Did You Know?

☙ The Cairo premiere of *Aida* was delayed because the sets and costumes had been ordered from Paris and were trapped there by the Franco-Prussian War. Verdi contributed part of his fee for the opera to help the French wounded.

☙ Attending a performance of the opera in 1888, George Bernard Shaw noted Ramfis, Amneris and the royal party being ferried up the moonlit Nile to the temple in a sumptuous royal barge controlled by an oarsman who stood on a prow some five feet high. Unfortunately, when the party disembarked the barge unbalanced and tipped stern over prow. The oarsman, commented Shaw, 'disappeared beneath the waves never to be seen again'.

Recommended Recording

Mirella Freni, José Carreras, Agnes Baltsa, Vienna State Opera/Herbert von Karajan. EMI CMS7 69300-2. Rich in aural splendour and atmosphere, with radiant singing from Freni in the title role.

Un Ballo in Maschera
(*A Masked Ball*)

FORM: Opera in three acts; in Italian
COMPOSER: Giuseppe Verdi (1813–1901)
LIBRETTO: Antonio Somma; after Scribe
FIRST PERFORMANCE: Rome, 17 February 1859

Principal Characters

Riccardo, Governor of Boston/**Gustavus III** ❧ **Tenor**
Renato, Riccardo's secretary and friend/**Anckarstroem** ❧ **Baritone**
Amelia, his wife ❧ **Soprano**
Oscar, a page ❧ **Soprano**
Ulrica, a fortune-teller/**Arvidson** ❧ **Contralto**
Samuele, a conspirator/**Count Ribbing** ❧ **Bass**
Tomaso, a conspirator/**Count Horn** ❧ **Bass**

Synopsis of the Plot

Setting: Boston; late 17th century

ACT I Riccardo, the popular and affable governor, is occupied in studying the guest list for a forthcoming masked ball. He is especially delighted to see that Amelia, the wife of his friend and secretary, Renato, will be coming, for he is in love with her and he allows himself to dream a little of the fulfilment of this love, which he knows is reciprocated. But these reveries are suddenly interrupted by Renato himself, who tells the governor that there are rumours of a plot against him. Riccardo refuses to take this seriously. His next visitor is a judge who has come to ask for an order to banish the fortune-teller, Ulrica, but Oscar, the page, pleads for mercy, and Riccardo decides to test her powers for himself. Riccardo, in the guise of a fisherman, goes to Ulrica's hut and hides as he sees Amelia approaching. Amelia has come to ask for help to quench a guilty love and Ulrica tells her to gather herbs at midnight at the gallows-tree. Amelia resolves to do what she must to exorcise this wrongful love. After she leaves, Riccardo steps forward to have his fortune told. Ulrica warns him that his death is imminent and his murderer will be the next man to shake his hand. Riccardo dismisses these predictions as absurd and, as Renato joins him, grasps him firmly by the hand.

ACT II Amelia has gone to the gallows-tree to look for the herbs, where she is joined by Riccardo. She tries to resist him and keep to her good intentions, but she cannot. Suddenly Renato appears and warns Riccardo that the conspirators are on their way to kill him. The two men exchange cloaks and Riccardo makes Renato promise to escort the heavily-veiled Amelia back to the city. As Riccardo leaves, Amelia and Renato are surrounded by conspirators, her veil slips and, to his shame and humiliation (and the amusement of his companions), Renato recognises his wife. In revenge, he resolves to join the plot against Riccardo.

ACT III The next day, Renato and Amelia are at home. Renato tells her she must die for her faithlessness and she asks him if he will allow her to see their son one last time. Renato agrees but, when she has gone, decides that the blame lies with Riccardo, not Amelia, and he resolves to kill the governor instead of his wife. The two conspirators, Samuele and Tomaso, arrive and the three men draw lots to determine who shall strike the fatal blow. As predicted by Ulrica, Renato will be the one to kill his friend, and the deed will be done at the masked ball later that day. When the evening comes,

Riccardo sits alone, writing an order that will send Renato and Amelia together back to England. Oscar brings a letter to him warning that an attempt on his life will be made at the ball but, as this is the last time he will see Amelia, the governor ignores it and leaves for the ball where he is stabbed by Renato. In his dying words, the governor assures Renato of his wife's virtue and Renato is overcome with remorse.

Music and Background

The idea of a royal assassination on stage was too sensitive for comfort in mid-19th-century Italy, which is why Verdi was prevailed upon to relocate his plot to colonial America, but the result was ludicrous – hence the modern tendency to switch things back to Sweden. With its brilliant writing for the cross-gendered role, Oscar, *Un Ballo in Maschera* is an odd, almost Shakespearian mix of light and dark emotions, which run together at a breathless pace and build into strong encounters, not least the love duet at the very centre of the story. It counts among the best examples of the composer's mature style, with a following which has increased in recent years.

Highlights

Act I: Riccardo's opening cavatina 'La rivedrà nell'estasi', followed by Oscar's 'Volta la terrea'; Riccardo's operetta-like 'Dunque, signori, aspettovi'; and the quintet with Ulrica, 'È scherzo od è follia'. Act II: the Riccardo/Amelia duet 'Teco io sto'; and the mocking chorus after Amelia's self-revelation 'Seguitemi'. Act III: the conspirators' quartet 'Il mio nome'.

Did You Know?

🖎 *Un Ballo in Maschera* is sometimes called Verdi's *Tristan und Isolde* in acknowledgment of the strength of the love duet.

Recommended Recording

Plácido Domingo, Josephine Barstow, Leo Nucci, Vienna State Opera/ Herbert von Karajan. DG 427 635-2. Karajan's last opera recording, made in 1989, with one of Josephine Barstow's rare appearances on disc. Handsomely done.

Don Carlos

FORM: Opera in five acts; in French
COMPOSER: Giuseppe Verdi (1813–1901)
LIBRETTO: Joseph Méry and Camille du Locle;
after Schiller and Cormon
FIRST PERFORMANCE: Paris, 11 March 1867

Principal Characters

King Philip II of Spain ∾ **Bass**
Don Carlos, his son ∾ **Tenor**
Elisabeth de Valois, daughter of the King of France ∾ **Soprano**
Rodrigo, Marquis of Posa ∾ **Baritone**
Princess Eboli ∾ **Mezzo-soprano**
The Grand Inquisitor ∾ **Bass**

Synopsis of the Plot

Setting: France and Spain; about 1560

ACT I France and Spain have long been at war, but Carlos has come to France to see Elisabeth, to whom he is betrothed although he has never met her. They meet in the forest of Fontainebleau and fall in love, and their joy seems to be complete when they hear that, at long last, a peace agreement has been signed between the two warring nations. But then Elisabeth, to her dismay, learns that she is to be married to King Philip of Spain himself, as a pledge of the new peace.

ACT II Carlos, suffering the anguish of his impossible love for Elisabeth, now his stepmother, visits the monastery of St Yuste, near Madrid, in search of peace. Here he encounters his old friend, Rodrigo, Marquis of Posa who has recently returned from Flanders, a Spanish province, and tells Carlos of the hardships and tyranny endured by the people there. Rodrigo, aware of his friend's unhappiness, advises him to go to Flanders and help the oppressed population. Later, Philip and Rodrigo discuss the situation in Flanders and Rodrigo appeals to the king to stop the persecution of the Protestants. The king is impressed by Rodrigo's integrity and force of character, although he warns him to beware of the power of the Inquisition, and he goes on to confide in the young man his suspicions about his wife and his son.

ACT III Carlos receives an anonymous note arranging a secret assignation, which he presumes is from Elisabeth. He meets a veiled figure in the garden and passionately declares his love, before realising it is, in fact, Princess Eboli who is in love with him. The princess quickly understands the real situation and threatens Carlos with exposure. In front of the cathedral an auto-da-fé has been arranged, in celebration of Philip's coronation. A group of Flemish deputies, prisoners of the Inquisition, beg Philip for mercy and are supported by Elisabeth, Rodrigo and most of the crowd. But the king is obdurate and will not relent. Carlos steps forward and asks Philip to appoint him as governor of Flanders but the king refuses and Carlos draws his sword – a treasonable act in the king's presence. Rodrigo disarms Carlos and is rewarded with a dukedom.

ACT IV Philip, alone, is sadly reflecting on his failure to win Elisabeth's love, when the Grand Inquisitor is brought in. The Inquisitor declares that Carlos must die for his crime, together with Rodrigo whom he accuses of plotting against king and country. After he leaves, the king, having found a portrait of Carlos in Elisabeth's jewel box, accuses her of adultery and she collapses. Princess Eboli, who gave the box to the king, now regrets her action and determines to make amends by saving Carlos from the Inquisition. Rodrigo goes to visit Carlos in prison, but he is ambushed and shot; before he dies he tells Carlos that the queen will meet him at St Yuste the next day. The king himself then enters the prison cell; he returns his son's sword and forgives him, but Carlos rejects him. Outside, the people are shouting their support for Carlos and the courtiers are afraid. In the resultant confusion, the disguised Princess Eboli spirits Carlos away, as the Grand Inquisitor frightens the protesters into submission.

ACT V Elisabeth has come to St Yuste, sorrowfully accepting the end of her hopes and dreams, and recalling her happy youth. She is joined by Carlos and they acknowledge that their love can only be fulfilled in heaven, as Philip and his guards arrive to arrest them. Suddenly the tomb of Charles V opens and a ghostly figure, dressed as a monk, emerges. Leaving the onlookers transfixed with terror, the spirit disappears into the depths of the monastery taking Carlos with him.

Music and Background

Written for Paris, where grandeur was the thing, this was an opera where Verdi thought big: so big, at first, that the piece worked out at five hours long and had to be cut and patched before the premiere. He then spent the next seventeen years toying with it, and finally jettisoned Act I, the ballets, and more besides to create the 'Italian' four-act version, premiered in Milan on 10 January 1884. It is anyone's guess what you will get in the opera house, and no one choice is more authentic than another, because *Don Carlos* was always, in a sense, a work in progress. Nevertheless, the epic score flows with near-unbroken momentum, building into great choral scenes, powerful monologues and towering confrontations. That it doesn't get done so often – because of the huge resources it requires – only makes its rare appearances more of an event.

Highlights

Act I: Carlos' romance 'Je l'ai vu et dans son sourire'; the courtiers' march 'O chants de fête'. Act II: the friendship duet between Carlos and Rodrigo,

'Dieu tu semas', reprised at the end of the second scene (and elsewhere in the score); Eboli's Veil Song 'Au palais des fées'; and Posa's celebrated baritone classic 'L'infant Carlos'. Act III: the climax of the auto-da-fé, 'Les flamands sont des infidels'. Act IV: Philip's opening monologue 'Elle ne m'aime pas' (the greatest bass aria in all Verdi); and the entire bass-to-bass encounter with the Grand Inquisitor. Eboli's 'O don fatal'; and Posa's farewell to Carlos, 'C'est mon jour'. Act V: Elisabeth's great set-piece, 'Toi qui sus'; and her following duet with Carlos.

Did You Know?

🔊 However many acts you play in this most ambitious of Verdi's operas, there are good grounds for saying that they should *ideally* be in French, because even the 1884 'Italian' version was first written in French and then translated for its Milan audience.

🔊 The opera was banned in Madrid during the Franco regime.

Recommended Recording

Plácido Domingo, Montserrat Caballé, Ruggero Raimondi, Royal Opera, Covent Garden/Carlo Maria Giulini. EMI CDs 47701-8. All five acts, but sung in Italian, with typically elegant, well-articulated direction from Giulini and largely fine singing.

Falstaff

FORM: Opera in three acts; in Italian
COMPOSER: Giuseppe Verdi (1813–1901)
LIBRETTO: Arrigo Boito; after Shakespeare
FIRST PERFORMANCE: Milan, 9 February 1893

Principal Characters

Sir John Falstaff 🔊 Baritone
Mistress Alice Ford 🔊 Soprano
Ford, her husband 🔊 Baritone
Nannetta, their daughter, in love with Fenton 🔊 Soprano
Mistress Meg Page 🔊 Mezzo-soprano
Mistress Quickly 🔊 Mezzo-soprano
Fenton, in love with Nannetta 🔊 Tenor

Dr Caius, suitor to Nannetta ∼ **Tenor**
Pistol, Falstaff's follower ∼ **Bass**
Bardolph, Falstaff's follower ∼ **Tenor**

Synopsis of the Plot

Setting: Windsor during the reign of Henry IV (1399–1413)

ACT I Falstaff is drinking with his unruly friends in the Garter Inn, and bemoaning his lack of money. He decides that the best way of resolving this situation is to initiate love affairs with the wives of two of the town's most prominent citizens, thereby laying hands on some of their husbands' money. He immediately puts the plan into action by sending identical letters to Alice Ford and Meg Page, arranging assignations with them both. When the letters arrive, the two women, together with Mistress Quickly and Alice Ford's daughter, Nannetta, compare their letters and decide that their overweight admirer should be taught a lesson. Meanwhile, Pistol warns Ford that Falstaff has designs on his wife and Ford decides to investigate the situation for himself.

ACT II Mistress Quickly goes to the inn to tell Falstaff that, although Page keeps a close eye on his wife, rarely letting her out of his sight, Alice Ford would be pleased to see him any afternoon between two and three o'clock. Mistress Quickly reports back to Alice and preparations are made to receive the suitor, who soon arrives and ardently begins to woo the lady. Suddenly, Mistress Quickly interrupts them to announce that Ford is on his way home and Falstaff hides behind a screen, just as Ford bursts in and proceeds to hunt high and low for his rival. As he briefly leaves the room to search elsewhere, Falstaff is hurried from behind the screen and pushed into the laundry basket. Fenton and Nannetta take his place behind the screen and, when Ford returns and triumphantly wrenches it aside, he is furious to find he has been duped. Once again he rushes out and Alice orders the servants to tip the entire contents of the laundry basket into the Thames. Ford returns and Alice takes him to the window to enjoy the spectacle outside.

ACT III Falstaff's spirits are now, understandably, somewhat dampened but, after a tankard of good wine, he recovers so far as to agree to Mistress Quickly's suggestion of a further assignation with Alice in the forest. Meanwhile, Ford has assured Dr Caius that he will be officially engaged to Nannetta that evening. He is overheard by Mistress Quickly who tells Alice and Meg, and they devise a counter-plan to unite Nannetta with her love, Fenton. Falstaff and Alice duly meet in the forest at midnight but his wooing is again interrupted, this time by Nannetta as queen of the fairies, and her entourage, who tease and torment the terrified Falstaff mercilessly until, as their masks begin to slip, Falstaff realises he has been tricked. Ford announces the formal engagement of Dr Caius and the fairy queen, together with that of another masked couple. Once the ceremony is over the masks are removed – and Dr Caius finds he has just become engaged to Bardolph, while Fenton is united with his beloved Nannetta. They all accept the situation with good grace and great hilarity.

Music and Background

Verdi left it late in life to tackle comedy head-on: this was his last piece for the stage, written between the ages of seventy-eight and eighty in the final, Indian-summer burst of creativity inspired by his professional association with the much younger composer/librettist Arrigo Boito. Surprisingly for a last work, it takes on a new direction. More concentrated, less lyrical than any of his other scores, it moves at an astonishing pace and observes little or nothing of the traditional workings of Italian opera. To hear it is to realise the octogenarian Verdi was on the brink of some kind of compositional breakthrough when he finally put down his pen, not least in his use of quasi-Wagnerian leitmotifs: recurring themes associated with a character or idea. *Falstaff* has never been a popular hit on the terms of *Aida* or *La Traviata*, but it ranks high in any musicological assessment of Verdi's output, especially for the inventive brilliance of its orchestration.

Highlights

Act I: Falstaff's comic monologue 'L'Onore'; and the eight-part patter ensemble 'Del tuo barbaro'. Act II: the Falstaff/Ford duet 'Io l'amo'; and the riotous Laundry-basket Scene, with frantic patter surrounding the young lovers' beguiling 'Bella ridente'. Act III: the concluding fugue for the entire cast, 'Tutto nel mondo'.

Did You Know?

⤷ Verdi's other Shakespeare-based operas are *Macbeth* and *Otello*. He planned to set *King Lear* but never got further than initial preparations.

Recommended Recording

Renato Bruson, Katia Ricciarelli, Leo Nucci, Los Angeles Philharmonic Orchestra/Carlo Maria Giulini. DG 410 503-2. A live recording but caught with excellent clarity and Bruson being funnier than you'd expect.

La Forza del Destino
(The Force of Destiny)

FORM: Opera in four acts; in Italian
COMPOSER: Giuseppe Verdi (1813–1901)
LIBRETTO: Francesco Maria Piave;
after the Duke of Rivas and Schiller
FIRST PERFORMANCE: St Petersburg, 10 November 1862;
revised version Milan, 27 February 1869

Principal Characters

Leonora ✎ Soprano
The Marquis of Calatrava, her father ✎ Bass
Don Alvaro, her lover ✎ Tenor
Don Carlo, her brother ✎ Baritone
Trabuco, a muleteer ✎ Tenor
The Father Superior ✎ Bass

Synopsis of the Plot

Setting: Spain and Italy; mid-18th century

ACT I Leonora and Alvaro are in love, but their union has been forbidden by her father, who believes that Alvaro is untrustworthy; determined, nevertheless, to be together, the two lovers decide to elope. But when Alvaro comes for her, Leonora hesitates too long and her father appears with his servants to stop them. In a gesture of surrender, Alvaro throws his gun at the Marquis' feet, but it explodes and kills him. As he dies, the Marquis curses Leonora.

ACT II High in the Spanish mountains, people are gathering at an inn, including Leonora, in disguise, accompanied by the muleteer Trabuco, and her brother, Carlo, also disguised, who is searching for Leonora and Alvaro. Leonora recognises Carlo and is disconcerted when he questions Trabuco about her identity, but the danger passes amid the general hustle and bustle of the inn. Later, outside the village monastery, Hornachuelos, the despondent and exhausted Leonora prays for forgiveness. The Father Superior takes pity on her and she tells him the whole story, after which he suggests that, as a penance, she should become a nun. Leonora, instead, begs him to allow her to live as a hermit in a nearby cave, under the protection of the monastery.

ACT III Alvaro (who believes Leonora is dead) and Carlo, unknown to each other, have both enlisted in the Spanish army, under false names. Alvaro is instrumental in saving Carlo's life and they swear eternal friendship. When Alvaro is severely wounded in battle, he is comforted by Carlo, who tells him he will receive a military honour, the Order of Calatrava. Alvaro's violent reaction to this name arouses Carlo's suspicions and when Alvaro, believing himself to be dying, asks Carlo to destroy, unopened, a box of his personal possessions, Carlo elects to look through them. A portrait of his sister, Leonora, confirms his suspicions and he is further pleased to learn that Alvaro will not die from his wounds, thus allowing him to kill his enemy himself. Once Alvaro is fully recovered, Carlo confronts him, revealing his true identity and telling him that Leonora is still alive, much to Alvaro's joy. Carlo insists on fighting a duel and the two men are only prevented from killing each other by the intervention of their fellow soldiers. As the camp springs to life around him, Alvaro resolves to retreat to a monastery.

ACT IV Several years have passed and Alvaro has become a monk, Father Raffaello, at the Hornachuelos monastery. Carlo has, however, tracked him down and, when Alvaro appears, challenges him to fight. Alvaro refuses until Carlo provocatively strikes him in the face, and the two go off to fight a duel. Leonora, in her lonely hermitage, hears the sound of swordplay then Alvaro bursts in beseeching the 'hermit' to give absolution to a dying man. Leonora calls for the Father Superior and, as Alvaro and she recognise one another, she rushes out to comfort her brother. But Carlo, bent on revenge to the last, fatally stabs her as she bends over him. Alvaro, left alone, curses the forces of destiny but sees, faintly, some hope of redemption for himself.

Music and Background

La Forza del Destino comes between Simon Boccanegra and Don Carlos in Verdi's catalogue, and its improbable Gothic-fantasy manner doesn't quite square up to the consistent strengths of either. An attempt to write an opera of ideas, around the abstract theme of random fate, it proved to be random in structure, with a rambling, panoramic narrative. But at the same time it was an occasion for experiment in the use of recurrent musical themes: especially the theme that represents destiny itself, heard in the overture, at the climax to Act I, and elsewhere.

Highlights

The overture, with its destiny theme. Act II: the Pilgrims Scene with Leonora's 'Padre Eterno'; Leonora's prayer 'Madre pietosa'. Act III: the Alvaro/Carlo duet 'Solenne in quest'ora'. Act IV: the Alvaro/Carlo duet 'Le minaccie', one of the opera's finest melodies; and the final trio 'Non imprecare'.

Did You Know?

The premiere of La Forza del Destino was delayed by nine months after Verdi arrived in St Petersburg and refused to proceed with the Leonora who had already been cast.

Macbeth

FORM: Opera in four acts; in Italian
COMPOSER: Giuseppe Verdi (1813–1901)
LIBRETTO: Francesco Maria Piave; after Shakespeare
FIRST PERFORMANCE: Florence, 14 March 1847;
revised version Paris, 21 April 1865

Principal Characters

Macbeth, a general Baritone
Lady Macbeth, his wife Soprano
Duncan, King of Scotland Silent role
Malcolm, his son Tenor
Banquo, a general Bass
Fleance, his son Silent role
Macduff, a nobleman Tenor

Synopsis of the Plot

Setting: Scotland; mid-11th century

ACT I Macbeth and Banquo, King Duncan's generals, are making their way home after a victorious battle against the enemy, when they are confronted by a group of witches. The women foretell that Macbeth will be king of Scotland (a secret ambition of his), and that Banquo will be the father of future kings. At Macbeth's castle, Lady Macbeth awaits her husband's return, and resolves to use all her powers to help him realise his ambitions, doubting that, without her, he would have the strength of purpose to accomplish great things. When she receives news that Macbeth is bringing the king to lodge with them that night, Lady Macbeth decides that the time has come to act and soon persuades the hesitant Macbeth to kill Duncan, arranging herself for the guards to be incriminated.

ACT II Malcolm, Duncan's son, has fled to England, and Macbeth and his wife, now king and queen, decide that Banquo and his son must also be killed, in order to secure Macbeth's position. But the murderers, attacking Banquo and Fleance, kill only Banquo and allow the boy to escape. Later that day, at a celebratory banquet, the terrified Macbeth sees an apparition of the dead Banquo enter the room and sit in the seat allocated to him. Lady Macbeth tries to calm the guests, but Macbeth's bizarre behaviour arouses suspicion and the company drifts away.

ACT III Macbeth goes in search of the witches and demands that they tell him what will happen to him. They warn him to beware of Macduff, before telling him that he cannot be harmed by a man born of woman and that his position is secure until Birnam Wood comes to his castle at Dunsinane. Macbeth is reassured by this until, finally, they call up a procession of eight future kings, all of Banquo's line, at which Macbeth faints with terror. But, encouraged by his wife, the usurper resolves to destroy both Macduff and Fleance, and thus consolidate his power.

ACT IV Malcolm, Duncan's son, is returning from England at the head of an army, and is joined by Macduff, whose entire family has now been murdered by Macbeth. The men camouflage their approach to Macbeth's castle by cutting branches from the trees in Birnam Wood and advancing under their cover. In the castle, Lady Macbeth is suffering from fits of sleepwalking, during which she mutters about the murders for which she and her husband are responsible, and perpetually tries to wash invisible blood from her hands. Meanwhile, Macbeth, deserted by his friends and on the point of being attacked, rages at his situation. When news comes that his wife is dead and that the wood appears to be advancing on the castle, he and his few remaining men leave to confront Malcolm's forces. Macbeth and Macduff encounter each other on the battlefield and Macbeth triumphantly quotes the witches' prophesy, that he cannot be killed by a man born of woman. But his triumph is shortlived as Macduff responds that he was 'from his mother's womb untimely ripped'. Macbeth is doomed and Malcolm's victorious troops proclaim the liberty of Scotland.

Music and Background

Macbeth was a significant landmark in Verdi's development: his first attempt at Shakespeare. The occasional village-band banality betrays its origins as early work from the 'galley years', but nevertheless transcends all expectations in music that touches dizzy heights of sophistication and strength. The pace is fast, the drama intense, the dealing with the supernatural done with relish, and there is some spectacular writing for Lady Macbeth which great singing actresses like Maria Callas have made their own. Never one of the most popular Verdi operas, *Macbeth* has acquired more of a performance profile in recent years.

Highlights

Act I: the Macbeth/Lady Macbeth duet 'Fatal mia donna!'; and the powerful choral close to scene ii, 'Schiudi inferno'. Act III: Macbeth's second encounter with the witches and his subsequent, half-crazed duet with Lady Macbeth, 'Vi trovo alfin'. Act IV: Lady Macbeth's towering Sleepwalking Scene, 'Una macchia è qui tuttora'; and the final chorus, 'Salgan mie grazie a te'.

Recommended Recording

Renato Bruson, Mara Zampieri, Neil Shicoff, Berlin Deutsche Oper/ Giuseppe Sinopoli. Philips 412 133-2. Highly dramatic with hard-edged singing.

Nabucco
(Nebuchadnezzar)

FORM: Opera in four acts; in Italian
COMPOSER: Giuseppe Verdi (1813–1901)
LIBRETTO: Temistocle Solera;
after Amicet-Bourgeois, Cornu and Cortesi
FIRST PERFORMANCE: Milan, 9 March 1842

Principal Characters

Nabucco, King of Babylon 🔊 **Baritone**
Fenena, his younger daughter 🔊 **Soprano**
Abigaille, his elder daughter 🔊 **Soprano**
Ismaele, a Jew 🔊 **Tenor**
Zaccaria, High Priest of Jerusalem 🔊 **Bass**
High Priest of Baal 🔊 **Bass**

Synopsis of the Plot

Setting: Jerusalem and Babylon; 587 BC

ACT I The Jews, defeated by Nabucco and his Babylonian army, take refuge in the temple and pray to God to save them. As the enemy closes in, Ismaele is left alone with his beloved, the Babylonian hostage Fenena, who is Nabucco's daughter. Suddenly, a group of soldiers burst into the temple, led by Abigaille, Nabucco's elder daughter. She, too, is in love with Ismaele, who was once captured and held prisoner for a time when on a diplomatic mission to Nabucco's court. Abigaille promises to spare the Jews if Ismaele will leave Fenena for her. The next moment the temple is filled with the Jews and their Babylonian conquerors, led by Nabucco himself. Zaccaria, the high priest, threatens to kill Fenena, but is prevented from doing so by Ismaele. Nabucco orders the temple to be plundered as the Jews castigate Ismaele for his actions.

ACT II The Jews are now held captive in Babylon, and Fenena, in the absence of her father, rules as regent. Abigaille, jealous of her sister's power and sympathy with the Jews, receives confirmation that her own birth is illegitimate – her mother was a slave. This serves only to make her more determined to take power for herself, and she gains a valuable ally in the High Priest of Baal, who reveals to Abigaille that her sister has now converted to Judaism. Together they circulate a rumour that Nabucco has been killed and urge support for Abigaille to become queen. But their plans to overthrow Fenena are thwarted by the unexpected return of Nabucco himself who, on his arrival, proclaims himself to be God. For this blasphemy he is struck down by a thunderbolt and the crown falls from his head. While her father babbles incoherently, Abigaille snatches up the crown and puts it on her own head.

ACT III The High Priest of Baal and Abigaille decide to kill all the Jews, including Fenena. Nabucco appears, still clearly unbalanced, and Abigaille first tricks him into signing the order to kill the Jews and then tells him he is her prisoner, before destroying the document that proves her illegitimacy. The once-mighty monarch, completely broken, appeals fruitlessly for her help and sympathy. Outside the palace, Zaccaria encourages the Jews by prophesying the imminent destruction of Babylon.

ACT IV In the palace, Nabucco is roused by the sounds of a procession outside. Seeing that it is his beloved daughter, Fenena, being led to her death, he is suddenly inspired by the realisation that Jehovah is the one and only God and he prays fervently for forgiveness for his sin of pride. The balance of his mind is miraculously restored and he calls on his supporters to follow him. Outside, Fenena and the Jews are preparing for death as Nabucco bursts on the scene; the statue of Baal falls to pieces as the people rejoice and give thanks to God. Abigaille, overcome with remorse, takes poison and dies, appealing to God to forgive her.

Music and Background

Nabucco was Verdi's first real hit – the point where, by his own admission, his career began – but the success was as much a matter of political timing as it was of musical achievement. This was the period of the Risorgimento, the movement for the unification of Italy, and his treatment of the story of the captive Israelites struck resonantly patriotic chords in the hearts of his Italian audience. The abundance of big-boned choral writing, often in unison, might have been designed for popular singing in the streets, and the brassy rawness of the orchestration certainly *was* designed to stir heady emotions, even if today it strikes the ear as crude.

Highlights

Act I: the High Priest's rousing 'Sperate, o figli'. Act II: Abigaille's 'Anch'io dischiuso un giorno'; and Nabucco's fateful 'Non son piu Rè, son Dio'. Act III: the famous Chorus of the Hebrew Slaves, 'Va, pensiero, sull'ali dorate'. Act IV: Fenena's prayer, 'Oh dischiuso è il firmamento!'

Did You Know?

~ The Hebrew chorus 'Va, pensiero' was sung by a crowd of tens of thousands of people who lined the streets at Verdi's funeral.

~ The chorus has featured in an advertisement for British Airways.

Recommended Recording

Piero Cappuccilli, Ghena Dimitrova, Plácido Domingo, Berlin Deutsche Oper/Giuseppe Sinopoli. DG 410 512-2. A fastidious performance that nonetheless captures the vitality and drama of the score.

Otello
(Othello)

FORM: Opera in four acts; in Italian
COMPOSER: Giuseppe Verdi (1813–1901)
LIBRETTO: Arrigo Boito; after Shakespeare
FIRST PERFORMANCE: Milan, 5 February 1887

Principal Characters

Othello, Governor of Cyprus ~ Tenor
Desdemona, his wife ~ Soprano
Cassio, his lieutenant ~ Tenor
Iago, his ensign ~ Baritone
Emilia, Iago's wife and Desdemona's maid ~ Mezzo-soprano
Roderigo, a Venetian gentleman ~ Tenor
Montano, Venetian commander in Cyprus ~ Bass
Lodovico, Venetian ambassador ~ Bass

Synopsis of the Plot

Setting: Cyprus; late 15th century

ACT I Crowds are waiting at the harbour to welcome home the governor, Othello, who brings the good news that the Turks have been defeated. The governor makes his way to the castle and the crowds drift away, leaving Othello's ensign, Iago, and Roderigo alone. The two men both wish for Othello's downfall: Iago because he has been passed over for promotion in favour of Cassio; and Roderigo because he is in love with Desdemona, Othello's wife. The two men join forces. Later, at the victory celebrations, Iago quickly makes Cassio drunk, provoking him to a duel during which Montano, the commander, is accidentally wounded. The ensuing uproar brings Othello to the scene; angrily he dismisses Cassio and appoints Iago in his place as lieutenant. Desdemona comes to find her husband and they reassure each other of their love.

ACT II Iago advises Cassio, as a 'friend', to persuade Desdemona to intercede with Othello for his reinstatement. Cassio does so but, in the meantime, Iago suggests to Othello that the relationship between his wife and Cassio is not as innocent as it seems. Othello dismisses his insinuations, but his suspicions are aroused when Desdemona comes to him to plead Cassio's cause, tossing aside a handkerchief which she offers him and which Iago later retrieves, intending to use it as proof of Desdemona's infidelity. Iago's poison slowly begins to work in Othello's mind and he demands that Iago should give him definite proof of his wife's disloyalty. Iago responds by saying he has overheard Cassio talking about her in his sleep and that he treasures one of her handkerchiefs. Othello, furious, swears vengeance.

ACT III Othello is awaiting the arrival of a deputation from Venice, when Desdemona again comes to plead for Cassio's reinstatement. Her husband's response is to question her about her handkerchief and when she is unable to produce it, Othello insults her and sends her away. He conceals himself as Iago brings in Cassio and encourages him to talk about his mistress, Bianca; Othello thinks he is talking about Desdemona, especially when Cassio unwittingly produces Desdemona's handkerchief. After Cassio leaves, Iago and Othello swear oaths that Desdemona and Cassio shall die that night. Later, when the deputation from Venice arrives, Othello's behaviour causes great concern; he insults his wife, knocks her to the ground and has to be restrained by Lodovico, the ambassador. Othello is soundly castigated by the whole company before they leave and he collapses, unconscious, under the contemptuous gaze of Iago.

ACT IV Othello comes to Desdemona's room and, in spite of her desperate pleas for mercy and denials of any wrongdoing, smothers her. Emilia, Desdemona's maid, runs in to tell her mistress that Cassio, attacked by Roderigo, has killed his adversary. Horrified at what she sees, Emilia raises the alarm. Montano brings news of Roderigo's dying confession and Iago slips away. Othello, realising the truth, snatches up his dagger and, after begging Desdemona's forgiveness, stabs himself and falls, dying, beside her.

Music and Background

Boito's adaptation (and, necessarily, reduction) of Shakespeare is often said to work better on stage than the original play, and it is certainly a masterpiece of high-energy compression. From curtain-up, the drama hurtles forward in a maelstrom of excitement. And the simplification of the story, with its tight focus on the three central characters, is boldly done, turning the piece into an encounter between savage (Othello) and saint (Desdemona), mediated by the devil (Iago). Verdi's penultimate opera, written at the end of his life after a long period of producing nothing absolutely new, *Otello* is very different in style to the composer's previous work. It largely abandons the division between aria, ensemble and recitative, sustaining the musical line in a near-seamless flow which audiences at the time considered 'Wagnerian'. In retrospect that seems like an exaggeration. But the richness of the orchestral sound and sophisticated harmony *do* mark out this opera as belonging to the post-Wagnerian world.

Highlights

Act I: Othello's thrilling entrance from the storm, 'Esultate!', and the subsequent chorus 'Fuoco di gioia!'; Iago's drinking song 'Chi all'esca'; and the love duet 'Già nella notte'. Act II: Iago's 'Credo in un Dio'; the Othello/Desdemona/Iago/Emilia quartet 'Forse perche'; and the Othello/Iago duet scene 'Ora e per sempre'. Act III: Othello's outburst of grief 'Dio! mi potevi'; and the huge finale for soloists and chorus, beginning with Desdemona's 'A terra!'. Act IV: Desdemona's Willow Song, 'O Salce! Salce!', and prayer 'Ave Maria'; and Othello's final 'Niun mi tema'.

Did You Know?

One of the consequences of Boito's adaptation is a greater emphasis on the character of Iago, who gets an entire monologue (his Credo) not in Shakespeare and very nearly got the title of the opera, which was initially intended to be called 'Iago'.

George Bernard Shaw commented, 'The truth is that instead of *Otello* being an Italian opera written in the style of Shakespeare, *Othello* is a play written by Shakespeare in the style of Italian opera.'

The opera was made into a film starring Plácido Domingo and Katia Ricciarelli, and directed by Franco Zeffirelli, in 1986.

Recommended Recording

Luciano Pavarotti, Kiri Te Kanawa, Leo Nucci, Chicago Symphony Orchestra/Georg Solti. Decca 433 669-2. Glorious vivid singing from Pavarotti, touching pathos from Te Kanawa, and a full orchestral sound.

Rigoletto

FORM: Opera in three acts; in Italian
COMPOSER: Giuseppe Verdi (1813–1901)
LIBRETTO: Francesco Maria Piave; after Victor Hugo
FIRST PERFORMANCE: Venice, 11 March 1851

Principal Characters

Rigoletto, the Duke of Mantua's jester ∾ Baritone
Gilda, his daughter ∾ Soprano
Duke of Mantua ∾ Tenor
Count Ceprano ∾ Bass
Count Monterone ∾ Baritone
Sparafucile, an innkeeper and professional assassin ∾ Bass
Maddalena, his sister ∾ Mezzo-soprano

Synopsis of the Plot

Setting: Mantua; 16th century

ACT I The dissolute Duke of Mantua is hosting a magnificent ball at his palace. He extols the pleasures of love and dances openly with Countess Ceprano, one of his conquests, much to her husband's fury. The hunchback, Rigoletto, the Duke's jester, mocks the cuckolded Ceprano who, together with his friends, decides to take revenge on him. Suddenly, Count Monterone bursts in and denounces the Duke for seducing his only daughter, before solemnly cursing both the Duke and the mocking Rigoletto. Later, Rigoletto goes to see his secret daughter, Gilda, whom he keeps closely confined for her own protection, allowing her only to leave the house to go to church. But even here she is not safe, for the Duke has seen her at her devotions and followed her home. Disguised as a poor student, the Duke overhears Rigoletto talking to Gilda in the courtyard. He is astonished to discover she is the jester's daughter, but still determined to pursue her. When Rigoletto goes inside, the Duke quickly goes to her and declares his passion. Gilda responds willingly to his caresses, but the sound of footsteps forces them to part. The footsteps belong to Ceprano's friends who also have discovered Gilda's existence, although they assume she is Rigoletto's mistress and plan to abduct her. Rigoletto joins them and they tell him they are about to kidnap Countess Ceprano, who lives nearby. The jester enthusiastically agrees to join them and, under the pretence of masking him, he is blindfolded and, unwittingly, joins in the ransacking of his own house and the abduction of Gilda.

ACT II The Duke has returned to Gilda's house and, finding it deserted, he believes he has lost her, and returns to the palace. But his dejection vanishes instantly when he is told that she has been kidnapped and is thus now in his power. He quickly leaves in search of her, and Rigoletto arrives, desperately looking for his daughter. However, the jester receives no help from the courtiers and he denounces them for their heartlessness. Gilda herself then appears and tells her father what has happened to her, whereupon Rigoletto's anguish swiftly turns to anger. When he suddenly sees Monterone on his way to prison, Rigoletto turns to the man he had previously scorned and promises revenge for both of them, despite Gilda's pleas for the Duke, whom she genuinely loves.

ACT III Rigoletto has brought Gilda to Sparafucile's shabby inn, where he plans to show her that the Duke is a well-known customer, renowned for his drinking and womanising. The two conceal themselves as the Duke arrives and begins to make advances to Maddalena, Sparafucile's sister. Gilda is distraught and Rigoletto sends her home, telling her to dress as a boy and leave immediately for Verona. After she goes, Rigoletto pays Sparafucile to kill the Duke and put the body in a sack which he will collect at midnight. Maddalena learns of the plan and pleads for the Duke's life, whereupon Sparafucile offers a compromise: if any other male should arrive at the inn before midnight, he will kill him instead of the Duke. Their conversation is overheard by Gilda who, dressed as a boy, has secretly returned to the inn. She decides to sacrifice herself for the Duke and, as a storm breaks overhead, she enters the inn. Rigoletto duly returns for the body but, on hearing the Duke's voice in the house, tears open the sack to reveal his beloved daughter, now dying in his arms. Monterone's curse has been amply fulfilled.

Music and Background

As one of *the* most popular operas in repertory, with a structure where everything seems to fall comfortably (and familiarly) into place, *Rigoletto* no longer presents itself as an innovative or radical piece. But in its own time it caused problems with the Italian censors (who initially found its storyline immoral) and would have struck its first audiences as a clear break with tradition in that it rejects many of the formalities of early 19th-century opera. Like other Verdi scores, it has a distinctive *tinta* or colouring of sound. For example, there are no women's voices in the chorus; and the heroine has only one aria, which comes in something other than the expected form – more like a sequence of variations on a theme, first heard in the orchestral flutes. In some ways *Rigoletto* is a crude piece, with little of the finesse of Verdi's more mature writing. The composer called it a 'melodrama'. But the central character at least is fascinating in his ambiguity: spiteful but loving – a prototype for Britten's Peter Grimes. And however absurd the details of the plot, audiences have learned to read beyond the nonsense and surrender to the drama of the music.

Highlights

Act I : 'Questa o quella', the Duke's first number; Rigoletto's instructions to Gilda's minder 'Ah veglia, o donna'; and Gilda's celebrated and showy coloratura aria 'Caro nome'. Act II: the Duke's 'Possente amor mi chiama'; Rigoletto's feigned indifference to the abduction, leading to his pleas to the courtiers, 'Cortigiani, vil razza dannata', duet with Gilda, and vow of vengeance, 'Sì, vendetta'. Act III: the Duke's famous 'La donna è mobile'; the Duke/Maddalena/Gilda/Rigoletto quartet 'Bella figlia dell'amore'; and the frantic trio for Gilda/Maddalena/Sparafucile 'Se pria ch'abbia'.

Did You Know?

- Verdi originally portrayed the dissolute Duke as a king (Francis I of France), but the Austrian censors in Venice found this unacceptable and the king became an anonymous duke.
- Within ten years of completion, *Rigoletto* had played at 250 opera houses throughout the world.
- 'La donna è mobile' has featured in a television advertisement for Ragù pasta sauce.

Recommended Recording

Renato Bruson, Edita Gruberová, Neil Shicoff, Rome Opera/Giuseppe Sinopoli. Philips 412 592-2. A true coloratura heroine but with emotion, surrounded by voices that balance strength with sympathy.

Simon Boccanegra

FORM: Opera in a Prologue and three acts; in Italian
COMPOSER: Giuseppe Verdi (1813–1901)
LIBRETTO: Francesco Maria Piave and Arrigo Boito; after Gutiérrez
FIRST PERFORMANCE: Milan, 24 March 1881 (see note)

Note: An earlier version of the opera was premiered in Venice in March 1857 but was a failure.

Principal Characters

Simon Boccanegra, a corsair in the service of the Genoese Republic
~ **Baritone**
Jacopo Fiesco (Andrea), a Genoese nobleman ~ **Bass**
Amelia Grimaldi (the young Maria), Boccanegra's daughter and Fiesco's grand-daughter ~ **Soprano**
Gabriele Adorno, a Genoese nobleman ~ **Tenor**
Paolo Albiani, leader of the people's party ~ **Baritone**

Synopsis of the Plot

Setting: Genoa; 14th century

PROLOGUE A new doge (ruler) is about to be chosen. Simon Boccanegra, originally reluctant to be nominated, accepts when it is pointed out to him that, as doge, he can release Maria, the girl he loves and who has been kept prisoner by her father, the present doge, Fiesco, even though she has borne Boccanegra a child. Fiesco comes to Boccanegra and says he will forgive him for seducing his daughter if he lets him have their child, the young Maria. Boccanegra refuses, saying the girl has vanished and, determined to see his beloved Maria once more, enters the palace only to discover, to his great grief, that she has died.

ACT I Twenty-five years have elapsed and Boccanegra is now doge; Fiesco, using the name 'Andrea', is conspiring against him. In the garden of the Grimaldi Palace Amelia, Andrea's ward, meets her sweetheart, Gabriele. She warns him that the intrigues in which he and her guardian are involved may cause serious trouble, but they are interrupted by a messenger from Boccanegra, announcing that he is on his way to see her. Amelia knows that the doge has come to tell her he wishes her to marry Paolo, and to prevent this happening she urges Gabriele to see Andrea and ask his permission for their marriage. Gabriele does so and, even when Andrea reveals that she is not a Grimaldi but an orphan, his love for her remains steadfast. Andrea blesses them and agrees to their marriage. Meanwhile, Boccanegra has arrived at the palace and, as he talks to Amelia, he discovers she is his long-lost daughter, the young Maria. He immediately abandons his mission to persuade her to marry Paolo who, angry at being thus thwarted, plans to abduct her. Later, Boccanegra is presiding over discussions in the council chamber when an angry crowd is heard approaching the building, calling for Boccanegra's death and that of all the ruling nobles. Gabriele and Andrea are dragged in and accused of killing a man called Lorenzino. Gabriele declares that Lorenzino abducted Amelia and goes on to accuse Boccanegra of ordering the abduction himself. Gabriele tries to stab the doge but Amelia herself appears and stops him, amid scenes of uproar and confusion. Finally, Gabriele is taken prisoner for one night, while investigations take place.

ACT II Paolo, determined on revenge, poisons Boccanegra's water and tells Gabriele that Amelia is Boccanegra's mistress. When Amelia enters, Gabriele accuses her of infidelity and, hearing Boccanegra's approach, conceals himself on the balcony, planning to kill the doge at the first opportunity. Amelia confides in her father that she loves Gabriele, but he is distressed to hear this, since Gabriele and his family have long been enemies of his. Amelia leaves and Boccanegra, contemplating what he should do, drinks from the poisoned water and falls asleep. Gabriele emerges and, on the point of stabbing Boccanegra, is prevented by Amelia, who has come back to forestall just such an event. Boccanegra awakes and explains the true nature of his relationship with Amelia to Gabriele, promising him Amelia's hand if he can stop the rioting which is once again heard in the streets.

ACT III The insurrection has been put down and Paolo, who had joined the rebels, is under sentence of death. As the sounds of Amelia's wedding to Gabriele are heard in the distance, Paolo tells Andrea that Boccanegra has been poisoned and, indeed, as he enters, faltering and unsteady, it is clear that he has little time to live. Andrea, revealing his true identity, approaches the doge and the two men are reconciled; Boccanegra explains that Amelia is Maria's daughter, therefore his child and Fiesco's grandchild. Weeping, the two former adversaries embrace each other, as Amelia and Gabriele, now married, join them with the wedding guests. Boccanegra blesses the young couple and, dying, nominates Gabriele as his successor.

Music and Background

This is an opera which has had two lives. Its first, as written in 1856–7 for Venice, was a failed attempt to reduce a rambling and largely unintelligible plot into meaningful music theatre. Its second, nearly a quarter of a century later, involved a rewritten libretto by the young poet/composer Boito who supplied the inspiration for the Indian summer of creativity that enriched Verdi's last years. And in this second version (which has now, for all practical purposes, completely supplanted the first) it marks the beginning of Verdi's ultimate, mature style. It is effectively a prologue to *Otello* and *Falstaff* which followed, again with libretti by Boito. Even in its revised form, *Simon Boccanegra* remains a confusing story that confounds most efforts at rational interpretation. But the score is strong: highly expressive in its depiction of character, evocatively atmospheric in its sense of location (note the sea music of the opening), and channelling most of its energies into powerful duets and ensembles. Simon has just one solo aria: all the more important for its singularity and unarguably effective, but still only one.

Highlights

Act I: 'Figlia! a tal nome io palpito', the duet in which Simon discovers his daughter; Simon's address to the Council, 'Plebe! Patrizi!'; and the concluding quartet 'Il suo commosso'. Act II: the Gabriele/Amelia duet 'Parla in tuo cor virgineo'; and the Gabriele/Amelia/ Doge trio 'Perdon, perdon, Amelia'. Act III: the farewell quartet 'Gran Dio, ti benedici'.

Recommended Recording

Piero Cappuccilli, Mirella Freni, Nicolai Ghiaurov, José Carreras, La Scala Milan/Claudio Abbado. DG 415 692-2. An award-winning issue that ranks among the best Verdi opera ever committed to disc.

La Traviata
(The Woman Led Astray, The Fallen Woman)

FORM: Opera in three acts; in Italian
COMPOSER: Giuseppe Verdi (1813–1901)
LIBRETTO: Francesco Maria Piave; after Dumas
FIRST PERFORMANCE: Venice, 6 March 1853

Principal Characters

Violetta Valéry, a courtesan 🔊 **Soprano**
Flora Bervoix, her friend 🔊 **Mezzo-soprano**
Annina, Violetta's maid 🔊 **Soprano**
Alfredo Germont, her admirer 🔊 **Tenor**
Giorgio Germont, Alfredo's father 🔊 **Baritone**
Baron Douphol, Violetta's admirer 🔊 **Baritone**
Gastone, Vicomte de Letorières, Violetta's friend 🔊 **Tenor**
Dr Grenvil 🔊 **Bass**

Synopsis of the Plot

Setting: Paris; mid-19th century

ACT I Violetta, a successful courtesan, is holding a party for her admirers and friends, one of whom, Gastone, brings with him a young man, Alfredo, who has long worshipped Violetta although he has never before met her. As the company drifts away into the next room to dance, Violetta is shaken by a violent fit of coughing and is consoled by Alfredo, who touches her deeply with the sincerity of his love for her. Once the party is over and the guests have gone, Violetta muses on the possibility of finding a better, purer and simpler life through Alfredo's love.

ACT II Some time has passed, Alfredo has evidently won Violetta's heart and the two are living quietly in the country. But Alfredo's happiness is greatly shaken when he learns that Violetta has been secretly selling her jewels to maintain their life together, and he leaves immediately for Paris to raise the money to buy them back. After he has left, Violetta receives an unexpected visitor, Alfredo's father, Giorgio Germont, who begs her to leave Alfredo as their scandalous relationship is ruining Alfredo's sister's opportunity of making a 'good' marriage. Sadly, Violetta agrees to leave him but, before she can go, Alfredo returns. Violetta pretends she is going away just for a few days and begs him to love her as she loves him. But she also leaves a note for him to read when she has gone, saying that she is returning to her old way of life. Alfredo's father tries to console his son but, distraught, Alfredo vows to take his revenge on Violetta and hastily leaves for Paris. In the next scene Violetta and Baron Douphol arrive at a party held by Violetta's friend, Flora. Alfredo is already there and he joins the Baron in a game of cards, gambling for ever higher stakes. As Alfredo continues to win each hand, tensions rise and a duel seems imminent. Violetta, becoming anxious, advises Alfredo to leave and, to encourage him to go, falsely tells him she loves Douphol. Alfredo, furious, calls the other guests to be his witnesses as he denounces her for her faithlessness and flings his winnings at her feet, saying he has now paid for her 'services'.

ACT III Violetta, now desperately ill with tuberculosis, lies in a bleak room with only the devoted Annina for company. Dr Grenvil reassures her that she will soon be well, but he acknowledges the truth to Annina, and Violetta herself suspects that she has only a few hours to live. Even a letter from Alfredo's father saying that Alfredo now knows the truth and is rushing to her side cannot dispel her bitter thoughts that it is too late, there is no future for her. Alfredo bursts in and sweeps Violetta into his arms, promising to take her away to the country to recover, but Violetta calmly accepts the inevitable and, giving Alfredo a medallion to remember her by, she dies peacefully in his arms.

Music and Background

One of the 1850s trio of Verdi's most popular operas, along with *Rigoletto* and *Il Trovatore*, *La Traviata* is an example of French-influenced romantic realism that was calculated to test the moral tolerance of its contemporary audience. The story was 'modern' – taken from a stage play which had appeared only the previous year – and Verdi wanted the first production to run in modern dress (although, in the event, it didn't). The success of the piece relies on a compact, straightforward plot that pushes forward in a single thrust through the three acts, sweeping Violetta to her inevitable end. The structure isn't flawless: the Spanish ballet in the second Party Scene interrupts the momentum, and the succession of duets in Act II can build into a log-jam as the same characters come and go. But the characters are finely drawn, with brilliant coloratura writing for Violetta and fine, noble numbers for the elder Germont which have classic status in the baritone repertoire.

Highlights

Act I: Violetta's brindisi 'Libiamo ne' lieti calici'; her scene with Alfredo, opening with his 'Un dì felice'; and her climactic 'Sempre libera'. Act II: Germont's 'Pura siccome un angelo' and subsequent 'Di Provenza'; and the ensemble finale of the second Party Scene, beginning with Germont's 'Di sprezzo degno sè stesso'. Act III: Violetta's 'Addio, del passato'; her duet with Alfredo 'Parigi, o cara, noi lasceremo'; and her final, soaring aria 'Se una pudica vergine'.

Did You Know?

❧ When *La Traviata* first played in London, the theatre authorities provided no translation of the text on the grounds that it might cause moral offence.

❧ Franco Zeffirelli directed a film of the opera in 1982, starring Plácido Domingo and Teresa Stratas.

Recommended Recording

Angela Gheorghiu, Frank Lopardo, Leo Nucci, Royal Opera, Covent Garden/Georg Solti. Decca 448 119-2. Taken live from the dazzling Covent Garden performances that turned Gheorghiu into a superstar.

Il Trovatore
(The Troubadour)

FORM: Opera in four acts; in Italian
COMPOSER: Giuseppe Verdi (1813–1901)
LIBRETTO: Salvatore Cammarano and Leone Bardare;
after Gutiérrez
FIRST PERFORMANCE: Rome, 19 January 1853

Principal Characters

Manrico, a troubadour ⁊ **Tenor**
Leonora ⁊ **Soprano**
Count di Luna, in love with Leonora ⁊ **Bass**
Inez, Leonora's maid ⁊ **Soprano**
Ferrando, captain of the guard ⁊ **Bass**
Azucena, a gypsy and Manrico's supposed mother ⁊ **Mezzo-soprano**

Synopsis of the Plot

Setting: Spain; 15th century

ACT I Ferrando, the Count's captain of the guard, is waiting with his men outside the palace where the Count has gone to see Leonora, with whom he is in love. To pass the time, Ferrando tells the story of the Count's father, who had two sons. One morning the old count found a gypsy leaning over the cradle of the younger boy who, shortly after, became ill. Blaming the gypsy for this, the count had her burned at the stake; in revenge the gypsy's daughter, Azucena, is said to have thrown the count's baby on the fire that killed her mother. The scene changes to the palace gardens where Leonora tells Inez, her maid, of her love for a mysterious young man, Manrico, who serenades her here and is even now heard approaching. As she goes to meet him, Leonora stumbles into the Count, who has hidden nearby and heard everything. The Count and Manrico draw their swords as Leonora faints with terror.

ACT II The two men have fought; Manrico is the victor and, although he has been wounded, he has magnanimously spared the Count's life. Manrico returns to the gypsy camp where Azucena, whom he believes to be his mother, tends to his injuries and relates the terrible story of her own mother's death at the stake. She tells Manrico how, in revenge, she intended to throw the old count's son into the flames but, distraught, threw in her own son, of the same age, instead. Manrico, greatly disturbed by this revelation, questions her about his parentage, but she quickly dismisses her own words as nonsense. Suddenly news arrives that Leonora, believing him to be dead, is about to enter a convent and Manrico rushes away to prevent this. The Count, too, has heard of Leonora's intention and has gone to the convent to abduct her. As she approaches with the nuns the two men, with their followers, confront each other; Manrico's forces are the stronger and he takes Leonora away.

ACT III The Count is laying siege to the castle in which Manrico and Leonora have taken refuge. Ferrando announces that a gypsy, wandering nearby, has been arrested as a spy and, as she is dragged in, he recognises her as Azucena. Condemned for the long-ago murder of the baby, she is taken to be burned at the stake. On hearing of this, Manrico immediately leaves the safety of the castle to rescue her.

ACT IV Manrico has been captured and he and Azucena are imprisoned by the Count, under sentence of death. Leonora pleads for Manrico's life and offers herself to the Count if he will free him. The Count agrees, but Leonora secretly takes poison and, finding her way to Manrico's cell, tells him what she has done before dying in his arms. Furious, the Count orders Manrico's immediate execution and, as the sentence is carried out, Azucena turns to him triumphantly saying that in killing Manrico he has murdered his own brother; her mother's death is now avenged.

Music and Background

A bizarre piece with a crazy plot (especially the baby-burning episode) and operatic caricatures rather than characters, Il Trovatore's strength is that it looks vulgarity in the face and makes a virtue of it. This is old-time melodrama with a vengeance and music to match, building slowly through Act I into a hard-driven machine of brazen, crude, bombastic energy. And when it reaches full power, you forgive it everything. The nonsense of it all becomes a justified excuse for singing, with vocal writing that makes enormous demands of the principals (not least, a tenor capable of sustaining repeated top Cs) and strikes the ear with an exhilarating force. The boldness of Verdi's design is evidenced in the extraordinary start to Act IV where elements intended by the librettists to play in sequence – an offstage chorus, an aria for Leonora and a ballad for Manrico – run together, overlaid.

Highlights

Act I: Leonora's 'Tacea la notte placida'; and her trio with Manrico and the Count 'Di geloso amor sprezzato'. Act II: the opening Anvil Chorus 'La zingarella'; Azucena's pyrotechnic 'Stride la vampa!'; and the Count's famous love aria 'Il balen del suo sorriso'. Act III: the soldiers' chorus 'Squilli, echeggi la tromba'; the lovers' duet 'Ah sì, ben mio'; and Manrico's rousing 'Di quella pira'. Act IV: the so-called Miserere Scene, introduced by Leonora's 'D'amor sull'ali rosee' and leading into the lovers' duet 'Non ti scordar'; and the Manrico/Azucena/Leonora scene 'Ai nostri monti'.

Did You Know?

🐦 Caruso famously said that all *Il Trovatore* needed was a quartet of the four greatest voices in the world. By implication, it didn't need too much in the way of acting skills.

🐦 It was a performance of *Il Trovatore* that the Marx Brothers successfully destroyed in their 1935 film *A Night at the Opera*.

Recommended Recording

Leontyne Price, Plácido Domingo, Sherrill Milnes, New Philharmonia Orchestra/Zubin Mehta. RCA RD 86194. High-octane performances all round, with Price in magnificent form and stirring chorus work.

Richard Wagner
(1813–83)

Rienzi (1840)
Der Fliegende Holländer (1841)
Tannhäuser (1845)
Lohengrin (1848)
Das Rheingold (1854)
Die Walküre (1856)
Tristan und Isolde (1859)
Die Meistersinger von Nürnberg (1867)
Siegfried (1871)
Götterdämmerung (1874)
Parsifal (1882)

*A*uden thought him 'the greatest genius of all time'. So did Adolf Hitler. And more than a century after his death, Wagner remains one of the most controversially dominant figures in the cultural history of the modern world, worshipped and despised in equal measure and with equal passion. Ten of his thirteen operas rank among the greatest achievements ever essayed by a human being: towering, monumental works designed to take the artform to its limits (and beyond). But the ideas behind the music range from the crackpot (redemption of the world by vegetarianism) to the repellant (blistering anti-semitism); and while Wagner can't be blamed for the fact that his scores became the theme tunes to the Third Reich, his extra-musical theories certainly helped legitimise its claims.

Born in 1813 (the same year as Verdi) in Leipzig, his early years were spent working in German opera houses until he was forced by unpaid debts to flee to Paris; and much of the rest of his life was spent on the road, pursued by creditors (he lived extravagantly) or the police (he was a political subversive). His first public success was *Rienzi*, an outrageously oversized six-hour score – not that anyone does it in its complete form. But his real achievement began with *Der Fliegende Holländer*, which introduced a trio of transitional scores (the others are *Tannhäuser* and *Lohengrin*) through which he incubated his ideas about the radical reform of opera. His objective was *Gesamtkunstwerk*, a total artform which would combine music, dance, theatre and, through its spiritual transcendence, provide a sort of cultural redemptive therapy for the world. More practically, he was moving towards a method of writing which would abandon once and for all the self-contained forms of 'number' opera – aria, recitative, ensemble, and so on – and substitute a seamless flow of sound which he called *unendliche melodie*. The four great operas of the Ring Cycle (*Das Rheingold, Die Walküre, Siegfried, Götterdämmerung*) are the ultimate expression of that ideal, and the Bayreuth Festival was established by Wagner as a place where they could be presented in accordance with his wishes, as a four-night ceremony of High Art. The erotic, revolutionary *Tristan und Isolde* and endearing (if heavy-going) human comedy *Die Meistersinger von Nürnberg* were written as diversions from the long work on the Ring. And the other-worldy religio-erotic mysticism of *Parsifal* became its coda. Wagner died in Venice, a cult figure and sacred monster without equal.

Der Fliegende Holländer
(*The Flying Dutchman*)

FORM: Opera in three acts; in German
COMPOSER: Richard Wagner (1813–83)
LIBRETTO: Richard Wagner; after Heine
FIRST PERFORMANCE: Dresden, 2 January 1843

Principal Characters

Daland, captain of a Norwegian ship ∾ **Bass**
Senta, his daughter ∾ **Soprano**
The Flying Dutchman ∾ **Bass-baritone**
Erik, a huntsman, in love with Senta ∾ **Tenor**

Synopsis of the Plot

Setting: A Norwegian fishing village; 18th century

ACT I Daland and his crew have been forced by stormy weather to put ashore tantalisingly close to their home port and their loved ones. Leaving a steersman on watch, the captain and his men go below for some welcome rest. The steersman, despite his best efforts, falls asleep and does not see the approach of a ghostly ship which silently anchors close by. Its captain, the Flying Dutchman, comes ashore and recounts the dreadful curse upon him:

many years ago, rounding the Cape of Good Hope in appalling weather, he called on the Devil to help him, the punishment for which is to sail the seas until the Day of Judgement unless he can find a woman who is faithful 'unto death' and who will save him. Every seven years he may come ashore to search for such a woman and now this time has come again. When Daland returns on deck he sees the other ship and encounters the Dutchman, who asks him for shelter at his home. Discovering that Daland has a daughter, the Dutchman asks for her hand in marriage, in return for unbelievable riches, to which Daland eagerly agrees. The storm has now passed and a favourable wind sends the Norwegians joyfully on their way home, leaving the ghostly ship to follow behind.

ACT II At Daland's house, his daughter, Senta, and her companions are busy at their spinning wheels and happily anticipating the return of their menfolk. But Senta, alone, hardly hears them as she is so preoccupied with a portrait on the wall of a pale, bearded man in black – the Flying Dutchman. She recounts the old story of the curse of the Flying Dutchman and, to the horror of her companions, she concludes by saying that she thinks she might be the one to save him. Erik, who has overheard her, then announces that Daland's ship has been sighted and, as the others rush out, he is left alone with Senta, whom he loves. But Senta barely listens to his declarations – she is still immersed in the painting and the story. Erik tells her of a dream he had in which he saw Senta and the Flying Dutchman passionately embrace each other, making Senta even more convinced that it is her fate to save the wandering sailor from the curse. Erik leaves in despair as Daland returns home with his guest. Senta and the Dutchman gaze, transfixed, at each other and, left alone, their mutual love becomes apparent. The Dutchman tells Senta of the terrible consequences she will be forced to bear on his behalf if she promises eternal faithfulness, but her compassion for his evident suffering overrides her fears and strengthens her resolve to save him. When Daland returns, he is delighted to discover that he can announce their engagement.

ACT III The Norwegians are celebrating, their ship festooned with lights, in sharp contrast to the Dutchman's ship, shrouded in darkness. The women take food and drink to the silent ship, but their calls evoke no response and, when the men move towards it, a strange, wild wind suddenly blows up and waves rise round it. The people are frightened and run away and the wind dies down as suddenly as it rose. Senta and Erik emerge from her house and Erik tries to persuade her not to marry the Dutchman, reminding her of the promises she made to him and accusing her of faithlessness. Their conversation is overheard by the Dutchman, who concludes that Senta has betrayed him and makes to leave, in spite of her pleas. Then the Dutchman reveals to Senta who he is, but she responds that she knows already and begs him to let her save him, but to no avail. The Dutchman steps on board his ship and the anchor is weighed; Senta calls out to him and throws herself into the sea, at which the Dutchman's ship disappears into a whirlpool and, transformed, Senta and the Dutchman are seen, hand in hand, ascending into the sky.

Music and Background

The first of the canon of Great Wagner Operas, *Der Fliegende Holländer* is a comparatively conventional grand opera of its time, with stand-alone set-piece numbers and big choral statements. But it signals the composer's growing interest in the *inner* rather than the *outer* lives of his characters, and touches on themes that would colour the rest of his life's work: redemption through the love of a good woman, yearning for death, wandering, and transfiguration. A wanderer himself at the time, living in impoverished exile in Paris, Wagner identified with the Dutchman's plight, and marked the end of the manuscript score with a note to the effect that it had been written 'in need and care'.

Highlights

The Overture. Act I: 'Mit Gewitter und Sturm', the Steersman's song; and 'Die Frist ist Um', the Dutchman's first aria. Act II: the Spinning Chorus 'Summ und brumm'; Senta's ballad 'Johohohe!'; and the Senta/Dutchman duet beginning 'Wie aus der Ferne'. Act III: the sailors' chorus 'Steuermann, lass' die Wacht'; and Erik's reproving 'Willst jenes Tag's'.

Did You Know?

🎵 Wagner initially toyed with the idea of setting the opera in Scotland, with a father called Donald rather than Daland.

🎵 Wagner reputedly sold the original scenario for the opera to the Paris Opéra for 500 francs, money he claimed was necessary for him to rent the piano he needed to continue his work.

Recommended Recording

José van Dam, Dunja Vejzovic, Berlin Philharmonic Orchestra/Herbert von Karajan. EMI CMS7 64650-2. A big reading with big sound and a strong but cleanly-focused title role.

Lohengrin

FORM: Opera in three acts; in German
COMPOSER: Richard Wagner (1813–83)
LIBRETTO: Richard Wagner; after traditional sources
FIRST PERFORMANCE: Weimar, 28 August 1850

Principal Characters

Lohengrin, Knight of the Holy Grail ❧ **Tenor**
Heinrich, King of Germany ❧ **Bass**
Friedrich of Telramund, a Brabantian nobleman ❧ **Bass**
Ortrud, his wife, a sorceress ❧ **Mezzo-soprano**
Elsa, daughter of the late Duke of Brabant ❧ **Soprano**
Gottfried, her brother ❧ **Silent role**
A herald ❧ **Bass**

Synopsis of the Plot

Setting: Antwerp; early 10th century

ACT I King Heinrich of Germany has come to Antwerp to recruit forces from Brabant to help him repel Hungarian invaders, but he is dismayed to find evidence of considerable unrest in the country, and calls on Telramund, a Brabantian nobleman, to explain the reasons for this. Telramund tells him that he was left to care for the late duke's children, Elsa and Gottfried. One day, when alone with Elsa, Gottfried disappeared and Elsa was accused of murdering him to gain the dukedom for herself. As a result, Telramund renounced his right to marry her and instead took Ortrud, daughter of Radbod, Prince of Friesland, as his wife and now claims the dukedom for himself. The king summons Elsa to hear her part of the story, but she can give no satisfactory explanation of these events, telling only of a dream she had in which a knight in shining armour comes to her rescue. Heinrich proclaims that the dispute shall be resolved by single combat between Telramund and any man who will be Elsa's champion. Twice the call goes out for a champion to save her, but there is no response. Then, as Elsa kneels to pray, a white swan is seen on the river, drawing a boat in which there is a knight in full armour. The knight, Lohengrin, steps ashore and agrees to be Elsa's champion, on condition that she never asks him his name or about his origins. Elsa agrees, they pledge mutual love and the fight begins. Lohengrin is the victor but he mercifully spares Telramund's life, leaving only Ortrud to brood menacingly on this unforeseen frustration of her plans to rule with Telramund.

ACT II Telramund and Ortrud decide to persuade Elsa to question Lohengrin about his name and background, and thereby gain their revenge; if this fails, then Ortrud, through witchcraft, can use magic to reduce his powers so that he can be easily wounded. When Elsa appears, her happiness allowing her generously to forgive and pledge her help to Telramund and Ortrud, Ortrud begins cunningly to sow the seeds of doubt in Elsa's mind about the faithfulness of her champion, who, she suggests, might leave her as suddenly as he came. As dawn breaks, the herald announces that Telramund is to go into exile and Brabant will now be ruled by the knight, who will marry Elsa that same day; the next day the new ruler will lead the people into battle. Telramund gathers some disaffected nobles around him and determines to destroy Lohengrin. Later, as Elsa comes to the cathedral for her wedding, Ortrud taunts her for not knowing anything about her future husband and claims he is a traitor. When Lohengrin arrives, Telramund steps forward and demands to know his identity, claiming that otherwise he might be suspected of evil magic. Lohengrin refuses to answer and leads his bride, by now greatly troubled, into the cathedral as Ortrud and Telramund anticipate their coming triumph.

ACT III Alone in the bridal chamber, Elsa and Lohengrin assure each other of their love, but Elsa is sad that she cannot call her husband by his name, and begs him to tell her, pressing him more and more. As their argument reaches a climax, Telramund and his friends burst in; Lohengrin kills Telramund with a single blow and he tells Elsa he will answer her questions before Heinrich and the people, but that their chance of happiness together is now lost. Later, beside the river, Lohengrin tells the king and the assembled Brabantian troops that he cannot now lead them to victory. He reveals that he is Lohengrin, Parsifal's son and a knight of the Holy Grail; the knights are sent to distant lands to achieve heroic deeds, but they must return to the Grail once their identity is known. Elsa, in despair at what she has done, begs him to stay, but the white swan is seen approaching, once more drawing the boat, and Lohengrin hands her a sword, horn and ring to give to her brother, Gottfried, if he should ever return. Ortrud can no longer hide her triumph and she tells Elsa that it was she who made Gottfried disappear, using her magic powers to transform him into a swan. Lohengrin falls to his knees in prayer and a white dove appears over the boat. Suddenly the swan is transformed into Gottfried and Lohengrin proclaims him as the rightful ruler of Brabant, before stepping into the boat which is drawn away by the dove. As Elsa watches him disappear she collapses, lifeless, into her brother's arms.

Music and Background

This is the link between Wagner the German Romantic and Wagner the mature composer of what came to be called 'music drama' as opposed to 'opera' (although Wagner preferred the simple term 'drama'). Based like most of the other Wagner works on mythic history, it shows the first real signs of a concerted attempt to break down the divisions between set-numbers, and run the music in something like a continuous flow. The orchestra begins to acquire a more prominent role in its own right as a player in the drama. And there is a sense of overall design in the score that could reasonably be called symphonic. But even so, *Lohengrin* achieved popularity through the extraction of its component parts as concert items – especially the Bridal Chorus, which became fashionable when a daughter of Queen Victoria had it played at her wedding. That the operatic context of the Bridal Chorus hardly supports the idea of nuptial bliss seems to have been lost on the British royal family, or anybody else who chooses it.

Highlights

Act I: Lohengrin's 'Nun sei bedankt, mein lieber Schwan'. Act II: Friedrich and Ortrud's 'Der Rache Werk'; Ortrud's 'Entweihe Götter'; and Friedrich's interruption of the wedding, 'O König! Trugbetorte Fursten!'. Act III: that fateful Bridal Chorus 'Treulich geführt'; Lohengrin's 'Atmest du nicht' and the next-scene monologue 'In fernem Land'; and Elsa's final 'Mein Gatte!'

Did You Know?

✎ When Franz Liszt conducted the premiere of *Lohengrin* in Weimar, Wagner was not and could not be present. He had left Germany under threat of arrest for revolutionary activities and had been forced into political exile in Switzerland.

✎ George Bernard Shaw commented that *Lohengrin* was 'the first work of Wagner's that really conquered the world and changed the face of music for us'.

Recommended Recording

Plácido Domingo, Jessye Norman, Eva Randová, Dietrich Fischer-Dieskau, Vienna Philharmonic Orchestra/Georg Solti. Decca 421 053-2. Radiantly sung by Domingo, with deliberate but effective direction from Solti. An award-winning set.

Die Meistersinger von Nürnberg
(*The Mastersingers of Nuremberg*)

FORM: Opera in three acts; in German
COMPOSER: Richard Wagner (1813–83)
LIBRETTO: Richard Wagner
FIRST PERFORMANCE: Munich, 21 June 1868

Principal Characters

Walther von Stolzing, a young knight ✎ **Tenor**
Veit Pogner, a goldsmith ✎ **Bass**
Eva, his daughter ✎ **Soprano**
Magdalene, her maid ✎ **Soprano**
David, Magdalene's sweetheart and Sachs' apprentice ✎ **Tenor**

Hans Sachs, a shoemaker ✑ **Bass-baritone**
Sixtus Beckmesser, town clerk ✑ **Bass**

Synopsis of the Plot
Setting: Nuremberg; mid-16th century

ACT I The young knight, Walther von Stolzing, has come to transact some business with Pogner, the goldsmith, and has fallen in love with Eva, Pogner's daughter. He follows her to church where, after the service, Eva sends her maid back to fetch her prayerbook, allowing her a few minutes alone with the handsome Walther, with whom she is in love. But, to his dismay, Walther now learns that Pogner has promised Eva's hand (and his considerable fortune) to the winner of the singing competition, due to take place the next day. Walther has no alternative but to try and get membership of the Mastersingers' Guild without delay, and persuades them to allow him to audition for membership. Pogner is inclined to favour the nobleman's efforts but Beckmesser, the town clerk and singing assessor who is also keen to win Eva, carefully notes down a whole catalogue of errors and triumphantly brandishes aloft his slate, covered in chalk marks. The other masters agree that the song did not accord with the rules – although Sachs maintains that its originality should not be counted against it. But no one listens to him and Walther leaves, deemed to have failed the test.

ACT II Magdalene tells Eva of Walther's failure to become a Mastersinger, and Eva confides their secret love to Sachs. When Eva hears that Beckmesser is coming to serenade her, she persuades Magdalene to impersonate her at her window, while she secretly meets Walther to make plans to elope. Beckmesser arrives but is dismayed to find Sachs still noisily working in his cobbler's shop next door. They agree that Beckmesser can sing, but only if Sachs can take his role as assessor and mark each mistake with a hammer blow. Beckmesser attempts to drown the hammer blows by singing louder and louder, which wakes the whole street, including David, who is furious to find Beckmesser serenading (as he thinks) his sweetheart, Magdalene. In the ensuing uproar Walther and Eva try to escape, but they are thwarted by Sachs, who disapproves of the idea of an elopement and pushes Walther into his shop and Eva into her father's hands, just as the nightwatchman's horn is heard and the crowd disperses.

ACT III Next morning, Sachs is reading quietly in his workshop when Walther arrives and tells him of a song that came to him in his sleep. Sachs encourages him to sing it and transcribes the first two verses for him. After they have left, Beckmesser comes in, finds the song and, still smarting from the previous night's humiliation, he assumes it to be the one that Sachs himself will sing. When Sachs returns he reassures Beckmesser that he is not his rival and generously gives him the song, although without telling Beckmesser who the real author is. Later, at the contest Beckmesser, shaking with nerves, is unable to remember the words and the crowd jeers and laughs at him. In a rage, Beckmesser says that Sachs wrote the song, but

Sachs denies this and calls on Walther, the composer, to sing it himself. Walther does so and, although not a member of the Guild, is acclaimed as the winner of the contest. He is made a Mastersinger and his union with Eva is blessed by her father as the people sing of the glories of German culture.

Music and Background

Die Meistersinger von Nürnberg is unusual in Wagner's output in that it is a comedy (the composer didn't have much of a sense of humour), realistic (as opposed to mythic), busy with action (as opposed to static with reflection) and has comparatively conventional music, tending towards self-contained numbers as against the 'endless melody' of Wagner's mature work, and full of period pastiche like parodies of Lutheran chorales and Baroque-style counterpoint. To that extent, the score reflects the message of the piece, which is about cultural consolidation. Walther's song can only win the competition when it marries innovation with a sense of tradition: renewing the past, as it were, from within. *Die Meistersinger von Nürnberg* is also the most humane and likeable of the Wagner operas, radiant with a benign wisdom that only palls in the final scene, in which Sachs delivers his lecture on Holy German Art (an uncomfortable piece of propagandist nationalism that later played into the hands of Hitler and commended this piece as the official opera of the Nuremberg rallies).

Highlights

The Overture. Act I: Walther's autobiographical 'Am stillen Herd' and his first trial song 'Fanget an!'. Act II: Sachs' so-called Flieder monologue, the ruminative 'Was duftet doch der Flieder' and his Schusterlied or Cobbler's Song 'Jerum! Jerum!'; and the resultant street brawl 'Zum Teufel mit dir'. Act III: the prelude; Sachs' monologue 'Wahn! Wahn!'; Walther's Prize Song 'Morgenlich leuchtend' (the big tune for the whole opera); Eva's 'O Sachs! Mein Freund!' and the subsequent quintet for Eva, Sachs, Walther, David and Magdalene 'Selig, wie die Sonne' (the most beautiful moment in the opera); the municipal chorus of greeting for the Mastersingers 'Wach auf'; Walther's Prize Song 'Morgenlich leuchtend' in its ultimate and most resplendent form.

Did You Know?

❧ Beckmesser is sometimes said to be an example of Wagnerian anti-semitism: a parody of Jewish musicianship. It isn't clear whether that was really intended. But the character certainly *was* meant to be a parody of Eduard Hanslick, a famous music critic who refused to fall at Wagner's feet.
❧ The real Hans Sachs (1494–1576) was a shoemaker and lived in Nuremberg; he is said to have written over six thousand poems.

Parsifal

FORM: Opera in three acts; in German
COMPOSER: Richard Wagner (1813–83)
LIBRETTO: Richard Wagner; after traditional sources
FIRST PERFORMANCE: Bayreuth, 26 July 1882

Principal Characters

Parsifal ~ Tenor
Amfortas, ruler of the Knights of the Holy Grail ~ **Baritone**
Titurel, his father and former ruler ~ **Bass**
Gurnemanz, an older knight ~ **Bass**
Kundry, a sorceress ~ **Soprano**
Klingsor, a former knight, now a magician ~ **Bass**

Synopsis of the Plot

Setting: Spain; 10th century

ACT I Amfortas, the ruler of the Knights of the Holy Grail, comes to bathe in the lake near the Knights' castle. He has a painful wound that will not heal and Kundry, the sorceress, brings a phial of ointment from Arabia for him. Amfortas tells of a prediction that an 'innocent fool' who achieves wisdom through compassion will one day heal him and become their leader himself. Amfortas takes Kundry's phial and goes, leaving Gurnemanz, an older knight, to recount the history of the Knights of the Holy Grail, telling how the Holy Spear (which pierced Christ's side) and the Cup (used at the Last Supper) came into Titurel's hands. Titurel founded the Knights to guard them and now his son, Amfortas, has that responsibility. But one knight, Klingsor, was refused membership of the brotherhood and, in revenge, he lured Amfortas into his magic garden where the ruler was seduced by a beautiful woman while Klingsor stole the Holy Spear. Klingsor thrust the Spear through Amfortas' side and the wound will never heal, except through the actions of an 'innocent fool' whose wisdom comes through pity. Just then a young man, Parsifal, is brought in; he has shot and killed a swan, which disturbs the knights as all life is sacred to them. The contrite Parsifal is questioned by Gurnemanz, but he seems to know nothing of his own background and he is taken away to the castle of the Grail. In the great hall, the reluctant Amfortas is forced by Titurel to unveil the Holy Cup and distribute the bread and wine to the Knights, who sing of its powers of redemption. But there is no relief for the suffering Amfortas, whose agonies are merely increased by the ceremony. Parsifal, although moved by what he sees, seems baffled by its meaning and Gurnemanz sends him away.

ACT II Parsifal is on his way to attack Klingsor in his castle. Klingsor summons Kundry, over whom he has considerable power, and orders her to seduce Parsifal in his magical garden. Kundry is reluctant to obey him, but she has no choice; transformed into a beautiful woman she tries everything in her power to ensnare the youth, but still he resists her, aided by a recollection of Amfortas' wound and a vision of the Holy Grail. Kundry begs him to save her, saying that the terrible curse that she brought upon herself by mocking Christ himself can be lifted if she can spend just one hour in his arms. Parsifal, however, stands firm and, enraged, Kundry curses him. Immediately Klingsor appears and aims the Holy Spear at Parsifal but, miraculously, Parsifal seizes it in mid-air and makes the sign of the cross; instantly Klingsor's castle crumbles to dust and the garden becomes a desert.

ACT III Years have now passed. One day Gurnemanz, now a very old man and living as a hermit, finds the half-dead Kundry near his hut; he takes care of her and she revives. Parsifal, dressed in black armour and carrying the Holy Spear, enters and Gurnemanz, who does not recognise him, tells him that no man can come into the domain of the Holy Grail if he is armed, especially not today which is Good Friday. Parsifal takes off his armour and Gurnemanz recognises him as the 'innocent youth'. Parsifal tells the old man that he has long been searching for the way back to the Knights' castle, but Kundry's curse has prevented him from finding it. Gurnemanz tells Parsifal that the knights need him desperately: Amfortas refuses to unveil the Grail and, without its redemptive powers, Titurel has died. Parsifal is deeply grieved at this and Gurnemanz and Kundry recognise him as the new ruler; together they celebrate the redeeming power of the beautiful Good Friday morning. In the great hall of the Knights' castle, the Knights are pleading with the sick and weary Amfortas to unveil the Grail, but he refuses, longing only for death. At that moment Parsifal enters, carrying the Holy Spear and wearing the cloak of a Knight of the Holy Grail. Parsifal takes the spear and touches Amfortas' wound with it; instantly it is healed. Amfortas' sin, of allowing himself to be seduced and losing the Holy Spear, is now absolved and he acknowledges Parsifal as the new ruler of the Knights. Parsifal orders the unveiling of the Grail and blesses the Knights who kneel before him as Kundry, redeemed at last, falls lifeless to the floor.

Music and Background

The most provocative and questionable of all Wagner's operas, *Parsifal* is a heady, *fin de siècle* brew of fetishist religion, racial supremacy and sex which

Wagner claimed to have received as a vision on Good Friday 1857 although neither the libretto nor the music was written until twenty years later. For some it is a work of sublime spirituality; for others it is a pretentious and repellent example of pseudo-religiosity with an underlying message of anti-semitism. Take your pick – because no one could definitively say what the piece is about. The only certainty is that at its heart is an idea of redeeming the world through *Mitleid* or compassion: an idea derived from the philosopher Schopenhauer and associated with denial of the human will. Wagner's response to Schopenhauer was vague and self-contradictory; but he undoubtedly thought of *Parsifal* as a kind of ritual through which the world might be redeemed. He called it a 'stage consecration play'. And his intention was that it should only ever be performed at the shrine of Bayreuth, his own newly-built festival theatre. As with all the mature Wagner scores, its musical world is peopled by leitmotifs, or recurring themes, that represent an object, a person or an idea. Most of them are prefaced in the opening Prelude, and the most conspicuous is the motif of the Holy Grail.

Highlights

The Prelude (listen for the leitmotifs). Act I: Gurnemanz's narration 'Schuf sie euch Schaden je?'; the nature music of Gurnemanz's later 'Du konntest morden'; and the male chorus with bells 'Zum letzten Liebesmahle' during the Grail Scene. Act II: the flowermaidens' 'Komm, komm , holder Knabe!'; Kundry's 'Dich nannt' ich' and attempted seduction 'War dir fremd'. Act III: the Prelude; the ritual preparation of Parsifal and the Good Friday music; the bell-accompanied procession to the Grail Hall; and the final chorus 'Hochsten Heiles Wunder!'

Did You Know?

↝ One of the ironies of this deeply Aryan (and by implication anti-semitic) work is that its first performance involved, against Wagner's wishes, a Jewish conductor, Jewish designer and Jewish stage manager.
↝ In one performance at Bayreuth, the (stuffed) swan shot by Parsifal landed on a chorus member's head, knocking him unconscious.

Recommended Recording

Peter Hofmann, Kurt Moll, Dunja Vejzovic, Berlin Philharmonic Orchestra/ Herbert von Karajan. DG 413 347-2. One of the finest Wagner opera sets ever issued, with Kurt Moll assuming centrality to the score, and gorgeously alluring orchestral sound.

Der Ring des Nibelungen
(The Ring of the Nibelung)

FORM: A stage-festival play for three days and a preliminary evening
COMPOSER: Richard Wagner (1813–83)
LIBRETTO: Richard Wagner; after traditional sources
FIRST PERFORMANCE: (Complete) Bayreuth, 13–17 August 1876

The four operas that collectively make up Wagner's Ring Cycle amount to something like fifteen hours of music and one of the most awesome creations ever attempted by human hands. The aural equivalent of several Sistine Chapels or the *Encyclopaedia Britannica*, they dominated the composer's life for thirty years, from the 1840s when he began work on the libretti until 1876 when the whole cycle had its first complete performance. And during that time, Wagner's ideas about the cycle changed: which is why the narrative is so messily inconsistent and why no one can definitively say what it's about (although apologists will tell you that ambiguity is essential to the nature of myth). Starting off as a dungeons and dragons fantasy but maturing into a more human-based soap opera (albeit on an epic scale) you could broadly argue that the myth of the Ring (which Wagner largely invented himself, with help from a 13th-century epic poem) concerns the history of the world and everything in it. *Das Rheingold* describes the creation of a world order based on an error of judgement. *Die Walküre, Siegfried* and *Götterdämmerung* chart various attempts to put things right. And since, at the very end, things *are* put right (i.e. the Ring is returned to the Rhinemaidens) the big question is: Why is the world destroyed? There is no truly convincing answer to this question. Wagner would have said it was emotionally appropriate and that his work concerned inner feelings rather than external action. Certainly, the pace of the Ring is slow and the music heavy if sublime, written for a massive orchestra that only massive *helden* (or heroic) voices can compete with. Keeping concentration through the long tracts of *unendliche melodie* (seamless arioso-like singing, not divided into set-piece numbers) can be difficult. But Wagner provides aural landmarks in the form of a hundred (or more) leitmotifs which recur throughout the four parts and signal the presence on stage (or in someone's mind) of a person, object or idea. The enormous demands of a Ring Cycle make it the greatest challenge any opera company can take on. A complete performance is invariably An Event.

Part One: Das Rheingold
(*The Rhine Gold*)

FORM: One act; in German
FIRST PERFORMANCE: Munich, 22 September 1869

Principal Characters

Woglinde, a Rhinemaiden ❧ **Soprano**
Wellgunde, a Rhinemaiden ❧ **Soprano**
Flosshilde, a Rhinemaiden ❧ **Mezzo-soprano**
Alberich, Ruler of the Nibelungs ❧ **Bass-baritone**
Mime, a Nibelung, Alberich's brother ❧ **Tenor**
Wotan, Ruler of the Gods ❧ **Baritone**
Fricka, his wife ❧ **Mezzo-soprano**
Freia, Goddess of Youth, her sister ❧ **Soprano**
Froh, God of Joy and Youth, Freia's brother ❧ **Tenor**
Donner, God of Thunder, Freia's brother ❧ **Bass**
Erda, Goddess of the Earth ❧ **Contralto**
Loge, God of Fire ❧ **Tenor**
Fasolt, a giant ❧ **Bass**
Fafner, a giant ❧ **Bass**

Synopsis of the Plot

Setting: In and around the River Rhine and the caves of Nibelheim;
mythological times

SCENE 1 In the depths of the river Rhine, the three Rhinemaidens cruelly
tease the dwarfish Alberich, who is much taken by their beauty and
fruitlessly pursues each one in turn. Suddenly, a shaft of sunlight pierces the
water, illuminating the gold that the Rhinemaidens guard. Wellgunde
unwisely tells Alberich that whoever steals the gold and makes it into a ring
will possess incalculable power – but only if the thief is prepared to make a
terrible sacrifice, to renounce love forever. Alberich, with hardly a moment's
pause, feverishly seizes the gold and vanishes.

SCENE 2 High in the mountains, Wotan gazes with great satisfaction at
the magnificent fortress the giants have built for the gods. But his wife,
Fricka, reminds him of the bargain he made with the giants, Fasolt and
Fafner: in return for building the castle Wotan agreed to give them Fricka's
sister, Freia. Wotan replies that he never intended to keep this bargain and
he is expecting help from Loge to trick the giants. Then Freia herself runs in,
pursued by the giants, who claim their payment in terms of the contract.
Wotan temporises and Froh and Donner, Freia's brothers, arrive to protect
her, followed at last by Loge, who brings news of Alberich's theft of the
Rhinegold and the extraordinary powers of the Ring he has made from it. As

430

Loge had hoped, the giants are tempted by the idea of the gold and agree to accept it instead of Freia, whom they take away as a hostage until the gold is delivered to them that evening. As soon as Freia, the Goddess of Youth, has gone, the gods visibly age and Wotan determines to go to Nibelheim, the land of the Nibelungs, to take the gold.

SCENE 3 Deep in the Nibelungs' caves, Alberich, master of the Ring, has become a tyrant, hated and feared by his people. He forces his brother, Mime, to give him a helmet, the Tarnhelm, which Mime has skilfully fashioned from the Rhinegold and which bestows magical powers on its wearer. Placing it on his head, Alberich becomes invisible and starts brutally to whip his brother before he goes out. Wotan and Loge arrive and Mime describes his brother's terrible powers before Alberich himself reappears, driving a group of Nibelungs, laden with treasure, before him. Alberich proudly boasts of his powers before the gods, particularly that of the Tarnhelm, which allows the wearer to change his shape and form. Prompted by Loge, who pretends scepticism, Alberich transforms himself into a dragon, then a toad, whereupon Wotan puts his foot on him and he is easily captured.

SCENE 4 Alberich is taken to the mountains, where he is forced, in return for his freedom, to surrender all his treasure, including the Tarnhelm and the Ring, which Wotan himself wrenches from the dwarf's finger. Before he goes, the bitter Nibelung curses whoever might wear it in future. Fasolt and Fafner return with Freia and insist that the pile of treasure given in exchange for her must be sufficient to conceal her completely. The gold is piled up but even the Tarnhelm and the Ring must be surrendered to complete the bargain. Wotan refuses to part with the Ring and the giants refuse to conclude the bargain. Then, suddenly and mysteriously, Erda, Goddess of the Earth, appears and tells Wotan to relinquish the Ring, reminding him of Alberich's curse. Wotan flings the Ring onto the pile and immediately the curse begins to take effect as the giants fight over the gold and Fafner clubs his brother to death, before leaving with the Ring, Tarnhelm and the treasure. Donner, God of Thunder, strikes a mighty hammer blow, the clouds part and a rainbow bridge is revealed, leading to the new castle, Valhalla. The gods cross the bridge in triumph as Loge watches them cryptically and the sad voices of the Rhinemaidens rise from the depths of the river.

Music and Background

This is the shortest of the Ring operas and was conceived by Wagner as a lighter-weight introduction to the serious business of the other three. The opening bars, with their deep sustained E flat on the lower strings, are famous as a sound portrait of the creation of the world, and Wagner intended that they should play in darkness, out of which the music and the staging should slowly emerge, borne on the swirling waters of the Rhine. Wagner also intended that the whole opera should play without an interval between the scenes in, as it were, a single (massive) breath, but this is rarely done. *Das Rheingold* introduces some of the key leitmotifs of the Ring, including that for the gold itself, for the curse, and for Valhalla.

Highlights

The opening prelude and flow of the Rhine into the Rhinemaidens' hymn 'Heiajaheia'; Alberich's foreswearing of love, 'Der Welt Erbe'; Loge's narration about the ring, 'Umsonst sucht' ich'; the orchestral music covering the scene-shift down to Nibelheim; Alberich's capture, 'Reisen-Wurme winde sich ringelnd', and curse 'So verfluch ich die Liebe '; Erda's warning song 'Wie alles war'; Donner's invocation of the Rainbow Bridge 'Schwüles Gedünst'; and the closing scene as the Rhinemaidens lament their lost gold and the gods progress to Valhalla.

Did You Know?

The orchestration requirements include sixteen anvils for the Nibelheim Scene.

Recommended Recording

George London, Kirsten Flagstad, Vienna Philharmonic Orchestra/Georg Solti. Decca 414 101-2. Solti's Ring Cycle was arguably the great landmark in the history of opera recording, and this opening chapter is alive with the promise of what was to come.

Part Two: Die Walküre
(*The Valkyrie*)

FORM: Three acts; in German
FIRST PERFORMANCE: Munich, 26 June 1870

Principal Characters

Siegmund, Wotan's son by a mortal **Tenor**
Sieglinde, his twin sister **Soprano**
Hunding, Sieglinde's husband **Bass**
Wotan, Ruler of the Gods **Baritone**
Fricka, his wife **Mezzo-soprano**
Brünnhilde, Wotan's daughter, a Valkyrie **Soprano**
Eight Valkyries **Four Sopranos, Four Mezzo-sopranos**

Synopsis of the Plot

Setting: A forest hut and a mountainside; mythological times

ACT I A man staggers through the door of a forest hut and collapses on the floor. Sieglinde, hearing the noise comes, in some trepidation, to see if it is her husband, Hunding, who has taken her by force to be his wife. She gives the stranger water and begs him to stay with her, even though he tells her that he will only bring her bad luck. Hunding returns and begins to question the stranger, who reveals that his mother was killed and his twin sister abducted when he was young and, since then, he has wandered from place to place, misfortune always accompanying him. His present predicament came about, he adds, because he tried to help a young girl who was being forcibly abducted; he fought, and killed, her attackers but is now being hunted down by their families. Hunding, who has listened to this story with increasing fury, reveals that he is one of the stranger's pursuers himself; he will allow his enemy to rest that night in his hut, in accordance with the laws of hospitality, but they must fight to the death the following day. Hunding and Sieglinde leave the room and the stranger wonders how he will fight since all his weapons are lost. Then he recalls his father's promise to provide him with a sword in the moment of his greatest danger. Later, Sieglinde returns, having given Hunding a sleeping potion, and shows the stranger a sword deeply embedded in the trunk of a huge ash tree, which stands in the centre of the hut. She tells him how, during her wedding feast, an old, one-eyed man, a stranger, thrust it into the trunk and no one has yet been able to withdraw it. The two, much attracted to each other, ardently embrace as the doors burst open to reveal a beautiful moonlit night. Eagerly they exchange information about each other and realise that they are from the same family, the Wälsungs. Siegmund then pulls the sword from the tree and, joyfully, Sieglinde recognises him as her long-lost brother. Passionately, as lovers, the two embrace.

ACT II On a wild mountainside Wotan is instructing his daughter, Brünnhilde, a Valkyrie, to take his son Siegmund's part in the forthcoming fight with Hunding, in spite of Brünnhilde's warning that Fricka, Wotan's wife and the guardian of marriage vows, is on her way to try and prevent Siegmund's victory. When Fricka arrives, she castigates the incestuous Wälsungs and argues that if, as Ruler of the Gods, Wotan was seen to be supporting this forbidden relationship and the betrayal of Hunding, the gods would be reviled and scorned by all mankind and their downfall would quickly follow. In vain Wotan explains to her that he needs Siegmund to try and regain Alberich's Ring so that he can return it to the Rhinemaidens and thus lift Alberich's curse. But Fricka is adamant and reluctantly Wotan agrees to allow Hunding to triumph. Fricka leaves and Brünnhilde returns to find her father sunk in sadness and despair, foreseeing the demise of the gods. He explains to her that she cannot now help Siegmund and he orders her to protect Hunding, much to her disapproval. Shortly after they leave, Siegmund and Sieglinde enter, pursued by Hunding and his men, and with

Sieglinde in a state of collapse. Brünnhilde appears to Siegmund and tells him he is to die in the forthcoming fight and she, as a Valkyrie, will bear his body to the heroes' eternal home, Valhalla. Siegmund asks her if Sieglinde will be there too, and on learning that she cannot join him he refuses to go, threatening to kill both Sieglinde and their unborn child rather than leave them defenceless in the world. Brünnhilde is very moved by Siegmund's great love for Sieglinde and promises that she will defy her father and save Siegmund, not Hunding, in the fight. Hearing Hunding's horn, Siegmund goes to meet him in single combat. Brünnhilde protects Siegmund with her shield but a furious Wotan intervenes and Notung, Siegmund's sword, shatters, allowing Hunding to pierce him through the heart. As Sieglinde falls senseless at the sight of the dead Siegmund, Brünnhilde gathers her up, together with the broken sword, and rides off on horseback. Wotan, angry at his daughter's disobedience, causes Hunding to fall lifeless to the ground before riding after her.

ACT III Brünnhilde and Sieglinde arrive on a rocky mountaintop, where they join Brünnhilde's Valkyrie sisters, each carrying a dead hero on her horse, on the way to Valhalla. The Valkyries are disturbed when Brünnhilde tells them what has happened and, afraid of Wotan, are reluctant to help her. Wotan is heard approaching and Brünnhilde tells Sieglinde to go to a forest in the east, where she will safely give birth to a son, Siegfried, a great and noble hero who will reforge the broken Notung. Sieglinde leaves, taking the broken shards of the great sword with her. After she has gone, Wotan arrives and punishes Brünnhilde by condemning her to lie in an endless sleep, to be broken only by the first man to kiss her and thus remove her immortality. The Valkyries are horrorstruck and gallop away. Brünnhilde kneels penitently before her father and tells him of Sieglinde's child, the hero for whom Wotan has been waiting. But Wotan is adamant, the punishment must stand. Finally, however, he accedes to her request that her rocky resting place will be surrounded by a magic fire which only a great hero, fearless and free, will be able to penetrate. Wotan's kiss sends his daughter into a deep sleep; he covers her with her shield and summons Loge, God of Fire, to encircle her with flame.

Music and Background

This is the point where the Disney fantasy of the Ring story acquires human interest, and many listeners find it the easiest point of entry into the whole Cycle, with vividly-created sound worlds for the Storm Scene at the start, the the Magic Fire Music at the end, and the passionate exchanges of incestuous love in the middle. Wotan's Act II retelling of past history (for anyone who missed *Das Rheingold*) can be frustratingly tiresome, but the Spring Song and the Ride of the Valkyries are among the most glorious and exhilarating music Wagner ever wrote. And by introducing Brünnhilde, the Valkyrie of the title, it supplies the one wholly sympathetic character in all four operas: a hugely demanding role and, along with Isolde in *Tristan und Isolde*, the one by which Wagnerian sopranos are measured.

Highlights

Act I: the Prelude, a fierce orchestral storm leading to Sieglinde's tender encounter with Siegmund 'Ein fremder Mann?'; Siegmund's 'Ein Schwert verhiess mir der Vater', and Spring Song 'Winterstürme wichen dem Wonnemond'; and the sword motif, resplendent as Notung is extracted from the tree. Act II: the Valkyries' 'Hojotoho's; Fricka's demand of Wotan 'Deiner ew'gen Gattin'; Brünnhilde's address to Siegmund 'Siegmund! Sieh' auf mich' and defiance of Wotan 'Halt ein, Wälsung'. Act III: the Ride of the Valkyries; Sieglinde's ecstasy motif 'O hehrstes Wunder!'; The Valkyries' pleading with Wotan for mercy 'Halt ein, o Vater'; Brünnhilde's appeal to Wotan 'Soll fesselnder Schlaf' and Wotan's farewell 'Leb wohl, du kuhnes'; and the concluding Magic Fire Music.

Did You Know?

🎵 The incest and adultery apparently condoned in *Die Walküre* would have shocked contemporary audiences, but extra-marital amour was central to Wagner's life at the time. During the composition of this opera he was having an affair with the married Mathilde Wesendonck, and he included no fewer than seventeen coded messages to her in the original draft.

🎵 'The Ride of the Valkyries' was used in the 1979 film *Apocalypse Now*.

Recommended Recording

Birgit Nilsson, Régine Crespin, Christa Ludwig, Hans Hotter, James King, Vienna Philharmonic Orchestra/Georg Solti. Decca 414 105-2. Featuring one of the great Brünnhildes in Nilsson and maybe the greatest of all Wotans, Hotter.

Part Three: Siegfried

FORM: Three acts; in German
FIRST PERFORMANCE: Bayreuth, 16 August 1876

Principal Characters

Siegfried, son of Siegmund and Sieglinde 🎵 **Tenor**
Brünnhilde, Wotan's daughter, formerly a Valkyrie 🎵 **Soprano**
Wotan, Ruler of the Gods 🎵 **Baritone**
Alberich, Ruler of the Nibelungs 🎵 **Bass-baritone**

Mime, a Nibelung, Alberich's brother ❧ **Tenor**
Fafner, a giant ❧ **Bass**
A Woodbird ❧ **Soprano**
Erda, Goddess of the Earth ❧ **Mezzo-soprano**

Synopsis of the Plot

Setting: A forest and a mountainside; mythological times

ACT I Mime is at work in his cave, forging a sword and complaining that he can never make one too strong for Siegfried to break. Then Siegfried himself comes in and insists that Mime tells him who his real parents are. Mime explains that he was found as a baby lying beside his dying mother, who entrusted him to Mime, saying his name was Siegfried, and passing on to the dwarf the broken shards of Siegmund's sword. Siegfried, excited by this story, commands Mime to reforge the sword, Notung, so that he can leave the Nibelung (whom he despises) for good and never return. Mime is struggling unsuccessfully to repair the sword when he is joined by the mysterious, cloaked Wanderer (Wotan in disguise). The two begin a riddling game, with the loser to forfeit his head. Mime cannot answer Wotan's final question – who will reforge the sword? – and Wotan tells him that only one who knows no fear will do so and Mime will lose his head as a consequence. Mime is terrified and when Siegfried returns to see how work on the sword is progressing, the Nibelung suddenly realises that in bringing up Siegfried he has forgotten to teach him fear. He tries, belatedly, to convey this concept to Siegfried, but the young man cannot understand him and, impatiently, takes over the work on the sword himself. Mime, anxiously observing the new sword emerging in Siegfried's hands, plans to turn the situation to his own advantage: he will take Siegfried to the giant, Fafner, possessor of the Rhinegold; the young man is sure to defeat the giant, with the aid of Notung, after which Mime will poison Siegfried and keep the treasure for himself. He looks on, delighted with his own cunning, as Siegfried raises the mighty sword and splits the anvil in two.

ACT II Fafner, in the form of a dragon, guards his treasure deep in the forest. Alberich, who first stole the Rhinegold from the Rhinemaidens, keeps watch outside Fafner's cave. He is joined by the Wanderer, whom he recognises as Wotan, and who warns him that a young man is on his way to kill Fafner and take the treasure. Siegfried and Mime arrive with the dawn and the dwarf leaves Siegfried alone to rest. Siegfried, hearing the birds singing around him, tries to communicate with them using his reed pipe, but eventually takes up his silver horn and blows several times on it. The noise wakes Fafner and they fight; Siegfried plunges his sword into the dragon's heart and, as the creature falls dying, he warns Siegfried of Mime's plans. Glancing at his hands, Siegfried sees that he has dragon's blood on his fingers; he licks it off and immediately finds he can understand the song of the Woodbird, who tells him of the Rhinegold hidden in the cave, and Siegfried disappears inside just as Alberich and Mime appear. When he emerges, carrying the Tarnhelm and the Ring, the Woodbird warns him of

Mime's treachery and the dragon's blood enables him to understand what Mime is thinking, not just saying. Knowing now that the cup Mime offers him is poisoned, Siegfried kills Mime to the sound of Alberich's mocking laughter. Again the Woodbird speaks to Siegfried, telling him about Brünnhilde and leading the fearless hero towards her fiery rock.

ACT III In a remote, rocky place close to Brünnhilde's rock, Wotan summons Erda from her deep sleep. He asks her how he can stop the fulfilment of destiny, the downfall of the gods. Erda, who wants only to sleep again, has no answers and Wotan accepts that his downfall, and that of all the gods, is inevitable, but that they will be replaced by a new dynasty, led by Siegfried, which will be founded on human love and will end the Nibelung's curse. Erda returns underground and Wotan waits for Siegfried, who arrives as dawn is breaking. Wotan challenges the young man, who uses Notung to split Wotan's spear with a single blow, at which the god vanishes. Siegfried sounds his horn and hurls himself into the flames, making his way up the mountain to Brünnhilde. The flames die down as he reaches the summit and, kissing her, releases her from sleep. Overcome by their strong feelings for each other, they both suffer conflicting emotions: for Siegfried it is bewilderment, touched with fear, at what he feels; for Brünnhilde it is joy at awakening and desire for Siegfried, together with regret at the loss of her immortality and her independence. But all these doubts slip away as they acknowledge their love for each other and, anticipating their joyful union, they embrace passionately.

Music and Background

The musical language of this score changes significantly between the beginning and end, because Wagner broke off composition half way through and spent twelve years composing other works (*Tristan und Isolde* and *Die Meistersinger von Nürnberg*) before he returned to it. Commentators vary on exactly why this temporary abandonment took place, but Wagner was certainly having problems with the central character, who remains almost impossible to cast. A golden-locked Teutonic youth with the unselfconscious, ruddy vigour to make boorish behaviour vaguely acceptable, Siegfried is expected to have the sort of *helden* vocal stamina normally found in singers who are neither golden, vigorous nor youthful but who instead are men in portly middle age. They accordingly look ridiculous and make the character unsympathetic.

Highlights

Act I: the Prelude; Siegfried's bear-story 'Nach bessrem Gesellen'; and the forging song 'Notung! Notung!'. Act II: the Prelude; the Forest Murmurs Music that comes before the battle with the dragon; the Woodbird's 'Hei! Siegfried'; Siegfried's meditation 'Da lieg auch du' and his conversation with the Woodbird. Act III: Wotan's oration 'Du bist nicht' and his exchanges with Siegfried 'Was lachst du mich aus?'; the orchestral transition to Brünnhilde's rock; Siegfried's awakening of Brünnhilde 'Das ist kein Mann' and their subsequent duet 'O Heil der Mutter'; Brünnhilde's Siegfried Idyll quote 'Ewig war ich'; and the final love duet 'Dich lieb' ich'.

Did You Know?

One of the toughest requirements of Siegfried is that having spent most of the opera on stage, singing against the dead weight of a massive orchestra and killing dragons, dwarves, etc. into the bargain, he then has to hold his own in a forty-five minute duet with Brünnhilde who comes on fresh of voice, not having previously sung a note.

Recommended Recording

Wolfgang Windgassen, Birgit Nilsson, Hans Hotter, Vienna Philharmonic Orchestra/Georg Solti. Decca 414 110-2. Probably the best of the Solti Ring Cycle instalments, with Joan Sutherland making for exquisite ornithology in the small part of the Woodbird.

Part Four:
Götterdämmerung
(The Twilight of the Gods)

FORM: Prologue and three acts; in German
FIRST PERFORMANCE: Bayreuth, 17 August 1876

Principal Characters

Siegfried ~ Tenor
Brünnhilde ~ Soprano
The three Norns, daughters of Erda, Goddess of the Earth
~ **Contralto, Mezzo-soprano, Soprano**
Gunther, Lord of the Gibichungs ~ **Baritone**
Gutrune, his sister ~ **Soprano**
Hagen, their half-brother and Alberich's son ~ **Bass**
Alberich, Ruler of the Nibelungs ~ **Bass-baritone**
Waltraute, a Valkyrie ~ **Mezzo-soprano**
Woglinde, a Rhinemaiden ~ **Soprano**
Wellgunde, a Rhinemaiden ~ **Soprano**
Flosshilde, a Rhinemaiden ~ **Mezzo-soprano**

Synopsis of the Plot

Setting: A rocky mountainside, the Gibichungs' Castle
and a forest beside the Rhine

PROLOGUE The Norns, daughters of Erda, spin the rope of world destiny and tell of the history of the gods, of Alberich's theft of the Rhinegold and the unleashing of the curse (the renunciation of love forever), now causing the gradual collapse of Wotan's power. Suddenly the rope begins to fray as the curse takes effect and, in spite of their best efforts to prevent it, it snaps, breaking the continuity between past and future. Holding the broken rope, the Norns know that their wisdom has now come to an end and they vanish back to their mother, the earth. Brünnhilde and Siegfried emerge from the cave, where they have consummated their love, and sing of their feelings for each other. Siegfried, however, knows he must leave her to fulfil his destiny and Brünnhilde accepts this. Siegfried gives her the Ring, as a token of his love and, in return, Brünnhilde gives him her horse, Grane. Siegfried mounts and rides away, the sound of his horn ringing in the distance. Brünnhilde, meanwhile, is to mount her fire-ringed rock until Siegfried's return.

ACT I In the great hall of the Gibichungs' castle by the Rhine, Gunther, his sister Gutrune and their half-brother Hagen, Alberich's son, are discussing the best way to augment the family's power and prestige. Hagen suggests that Gunther should marry Brünnhilde and Gutrune should take Siegfried as a husband. Hagen, whose prime motive is to regain the Ring for his father, suggests that he gives Siegfried a magic potion which will make him fall in love with Gutrune; as the only man who can penetrate the flames surrounding Brünnhilde's rock, he can then go to her and bring her back to Gunther. Siegfried's horn is heard in the distance and soon he is welcomed into the great hall. He tells Gunther and Hagen of his fight with Fafner and of the Rhinegold, and shows them the Tarnhelm he carries at his waist. Gutrune returns with the potion which Siegfried drinks and, as Hagen predicted, falls instantly in love with Gutrune, forgetting Brünnhilde completely. He eagerly agrees to Hagen's plan to win Brünnhilde for Gunther and sets off for Brünnhilde's rock. Meanwhile, Brünnhilde sits alone on the mountainside, meditating on the Ring and on her love for Siegfried. Waltraute, one of her Valkyrie sisters, comes to tell her of how Wotan sits morosely in Valhalla, sorrowfully contemplating the loss of the Ring. Waltraute begs Brünnhilde to return the Ring to the Rhinemaidens, but Brünnhilde refuses and Waltraute leaves, bitterly disappointed. Just then Siegfried's hunting horn is heard and Brünnhilde rushes joyfully to meet him only to see, to her dismay, a man in Gunther's form (Siegfried has used the Tarnhelm to disguise himself), who wrenches the ring from her finger and forces her into the cave where, preparing for sleep, he lays down his sword between them as a sign of his loyalty to Gunther.

ACT II Hagen, asleep in the Gibichungs' castle, sees a vision of his father, Alberich, who urges him to regain the Ring from Siegfried and thus complete the overthrow of the gods. As day dawns Alberich vanishes and

Siegfried returns, ahead of Gunther and Brünnhilde. He tells Hagen of the successful outcome of their plans, and Hagen calls the Gibichung servants to prepare a great wedding feast. Gunther and Brünnhilde arrive and Brünnhilde is astonished and bewildered to see Siegfried, who does not recognise her; when she sees the Ring on his finger she bitterly accuses him of betraying her, but Siegfried denies any treachery and goes out, leaving Brünnhilde, Hagen and Gunther (who is beginning to suspect Siegfried of duplicity) alone. At Hagen's prompting, the three swear revenge on Siegfried and Brünnhilde reveals that Siegfried's back is not protected by magic, as he would never have turned it on an enemy. To protect themselves, Hagen suggests they should make Siegfried's death look like a hunting accident.

ACT III Siegfried, on the banks of the Rhine, rejects the Rhinemaidens' pleas to return the Ring to them and they swim away, leaving him to his fate. He is joined by his hunting companions and begins to tell them the story of his adventures with Fafner and the Rhinegold. Hagen offers him a drink into which he has put an antidote to the earlier potion; Siegfried's memory returns and he recalls Brünnhilde and his love for her. Gunther, astonished, realises the true nature of Siegfried's relationship with Brünnhilde for the first time, and Hagen, having listened to Siegfried talking of the Woodbird, whose language he understood, asks him if he can understand the two ravens (harbingers of death) nearby. As Siegfried turns to look at them, Hagen stabs him in the back and he falls, dying. The horrified Gunther orders his servants to take the body back to the castle. Meanwhile, Gutrune has been greatly disturbed by strange dreams and, when she sees Siegfried's body carried in, she turns on her brother. Gunther blames Hagen, who demands the Ring, and the two men fight, leaving Gunther fatally wounded. Hagen tries to wrench the ring from Siegfried's finger, but the dead hand rises menacingly to prevent him. Brünnhilde, now understanding everything, orders Siegfried's body to be placed on a great pyre; she takes the Ring from his finger and places it on her own. Sending the two ravens to Wotan, to tell him what has happened, she lights the pyre and, mounting her horse, Grane, rides into the flames, united with Siegfried in death. Suddenly the waters of the Rhine rise up and pour over the flames, bringing with them the Rhinemaidens who draw Hagen away into the depths and retrieve the Ring, now purified by fire. Brünnhilde's sacrifice has lifted the curse, bringing with it the dawning of a new age, the triumph of love. But for this to come about, the old gods must die and, high in the sky, a bright glow indicates the destruction of Valhalla and the end of the gods.

Music and Background

This is the longest of the Ring operas, with a running time of roughly six hours (including intervals) and a first Act long enough to contain the whole of *La Bohème* or *Tosca*. Its pyrotechnic conclusion brings the Cycle – and the whole world as Wagner envisages it – to a spectacular end. But the end is also equivocal in that the composer leaves it up to you (or more particularly, the stage director) to decide if it's an optimistic or pessimistic outcome. The orchestra, always prominent in Wagner, repeatedly takes centre stage in the score; and the final scene of cataclysm is effectively a great symphonic reprise of leading leitmotifs in which voices play no part.

Highlights

Prologue: the Siegfried/Brünnhilde duet 'Zu neuen Taten'; Siegfried's orchestral journey down the Rhine. ActI: the arrival of Siegfried (disguised as Gunther) at the circle of fire and Brünnhilde's capture 'Wer ist der Mann'. Act II: Hagen's summons to the vassals 'Hoiho!'; Brünnhilde's reproach 'Ha! Dieser war es'; and the final Gunther/Hagen/Brünnhilde trio 'Was riet mir mein Wissen?'. Act III: the Rhinemaidens' song 'Frau Sonne sendet Lichte'; Siegfried's death and funeral march; Brünnhilde's instructions for the funeral pyre and burning of Valhalla, climaxing on 'Fliegt heim ihr Raben!'; and the orchestral close.

Did You Know?

George Bernard Shaw countered criticism that Wagner's work was 'too remote' with the claim that, 'Everybody can enjoy the love music, the hammer and anvil music, the clumping of the giants, the tune of the young woodsman's horn, the trilling of the bird, the dragon music and nightmare music, the profusion of simple melody, the sensuous charm of the orchestration: in short, the vast extent of common ground between *The Ring* and the ordinary music we use for play and pleasure.'

Recommended Recording

Birgit Nilsson, Wolfgang Windgassen, Dietrich Fischer-Dieskau, Vienna Philharmonic Orchestra/Georg Solti. Decca 414 115-2. Incomparable sound with singers at their peakdelivering a benchmark performance which has never yet been bettered on disc.

Tannhäuser

FORM: Opera in three acts; in German
COMPOSER: Richard Wagner (1813–83)
LIBRETTO: Richard Wagner; after traditional sources
FIRST PERFORMANCE: Dresden, 19 October 1845

Principal Characters

Tannhäuser, knight and minstrel ✿ **Tenor**
Venus, Goddess of Love ✿ **Soprano**
Elisabeth, the Landgrave's niece ✿ **Soprano**
Wolfram von Eschenbach, knight and minstrel ✿ **Baritone**
The Landgrave of Thuringia ✿ **Bass**

Synopsis of the Plot

Setting: Thuringia; 13th century

ACT I Tannhäuser is tiring of his life in the Venusberg, the mountain in which Venus, Goddess of Love, holds her court and claims the souls of men through an endless round of sensuous lusts and pleasures. He comes to the goddess and tells her of his longing to rejoin the human world, with all its pains and troubles, and begs her to let him go. Venus tries to persuade him to stay, but he is adamant and, finally, she angrily dismisses him. Tannhäuser calls on the Virgin Mary to help him, Venus and the mountain vanish and he finds himself in a valley near Wartburg Castle. A group of chanting pilgrims passes by, prompting Tannhäuser to fall to his knees and pray fervently for forgiveness for his past sins. The sound of hunting horns is heard and the Landgrave and his knights arrive. They do not at first recognise Tannhäuser, a former member of their company, but he is soon welcomed back joyfully. They urge him to return with them but, at first, he is reluctant to do so, feeling the weight of his sins pressing upon him. However, when Wolfram tells him how much the Landgrave's niece, Elisabeth, still misses him, he changes his mind and goes back to Wartburg.

ACT II In the castle Elisabeth and Tannhäuser are joyfully reunited, although the knight's refusal to be anything more than deliberately vague about the reasons for his long absence disturb her. Meanwhile, the Landgrave has announced a singing contest to take place at the castle, in which each competitor must define the nature of love in his song; the winner will receive whatever he asks from Elisabeth. Tannhäuser eagerly agrees to take part in the competition and the great hall is filled with knights and their ladies drawn from far and near. The contest begins and the first competitors sing of the purity and holiness of love, much to the approval of the assembled company. But when it is Tannhäuser's turn, he sings of the pleasure of physical love and the joys of sexual fulfilment. The company is scandalised, the ladies rush out and Tannhäuser is surrounded by a threatening circle of knights and minstrels, their swords drawn. Only Elisabeth's intervention saves his life and Tannhäuser is commanded to make a pilgrimage to Rome to expiate his sins.

ACT III Time has passed and Elisabeth, longing hopelessly for Tannhäuser's return, prays to the Virgin to release her from her misery by allowing her to die. Wolfram, who loves Elisabeth, is distraught at her longing for death, but she leaves him, insisting that she must be alone. As the knight sits miserably in the gathering dusk, he is joined by the returning

Tannhäuser, weary and ragged, who brings the news that the Pope refused him absolution for his sins, saying that his cause was hopeless; it was as likely that the Pope's wooden staff should grow leaves as that Tannhäuser should be forgiven. There is, therefore, nowhere else for him to go but back to Venus and, as he says her name, her voice is heard, calling him to return to her. Tannhäuser struggles with himself, invoking Elisabeth's name and, as he does so, a funeral procession comes in, bearing her body: she has sacrificed her life to save Tannhäuser. Venus, defeated, vanishes and Tannhäuser falls, dying, beside Elisabeth's body. As the day breaks a group of pilgrims comes by, carrying the Pope's staff, now bearing leaves: Tannhäuser's soul has been saved.

Music and Background

The kitsch religiosity with which Wagner saturates this medieval German legend is the more outrageous when you consider that Wagner had little in the way of true Christian belief and was the last person to be delivering lectures on the ideal of chastity. As a result, *Tannhäuser* rings hollow and in recent years it has fallen from the popularity it once enjoyed, although the melodies remain among the best-known in the Wagner canon. A transitional score, it edges Wagner's technique forward while still clinging to the basic organisational method of 'numbers' linked by something like recitative. Its dimensions were enlarged in 1860 when the Paris Opéra agreed to stage it – on condition that Wagner added a ballet, as was customary in all Paris Opéra productions. Unfortunately he put the ballet in the wrong place: during Act I instead of Act II, where fashionable Parisians (who rarely arrived until the interval) expected to find it. The consequence was a riot in the auditorium on the opening night, at which young aristocrats from the Jockey Club drowned out the singers with dog-noises. This later enlargement is known as the Paris version, in contrast to the original Dresden version.

Highlights

Act I: the Overture and ballet music for the Venusberg orgy; Tannhäuser's set-piece song 'Dir töne Lob!'; The Pilgrims' Chorus 'Zu dir wall ich'; the subsequent accumulation of horn-calls; and Wolfram's address 'Als du in kühnem Sange'. Act II: Elisabeth's greeting aria 'Wie jetzt mein Busen'; the trumpet-announced Grand March; Tannhäuser's song 'Dir, Gottin der Liebe'; and the chorus and ensemble 'Ein Engel stieg'. Act III: the Pilgrims' Chorus (again); Elisabeth's prayer 'Allmächt'ge Jungfrau'; Wolfram's so-called Star of Eve 'O du, mein holder Abendstern'; and the male chorus 'Ihr ward der Engel'.

Did You Know?

⌘ The Paris Opéra had never encountered anything quite like *Tannhäuser*, with its (unrealised) demands for twenty-four horns, etc., and it took 163 rehearsals to get the piece into shape for its opening night there.

⌘ Tannhäuser was an actual 13th-century minstrel.

Tristan und Isolde

FORM: Opera in three acts; in German
COMPOSER: Richard Wagner (1813–83)
LIBRETTO: Richard Wagner; after traditional sources
FIRST PERFORMANCE: Munich, 19 June 1865

Principal Characters

Isolde, an Irish princess   Soprano
Brangäne, her attendant   Mezzo-soprano
Tristan, a knight   Tenor
Kurwenal, his squire   Baritone
King Marke of Cornwall   Bass
Melot, a courtier   Tenor

Synopsis of the Plot

Setting: Legendary Brittany and Cornwall

ACT I Escorted by Tristan, Isolde is being taken by ship from Ireland to
Cornwall, a reluctant bride for the ageing King Marke. As the Cornish coast
comes into view, Isolde sends her attendant, Brangäne, to ask Tristan to
come and see her, but the young knight refuses. Angry and insulted by his
behaviour, Isolde tells Brangäne how, having fought and killed her lover,
Tristan had come to her, as a practitioner of the healing arts, to nurse his
injuries. At first she wanted to kill him, in revenge for her lover's death, but
found herself falling in love with him instead. Now she feels he has betrayed
her by bringing her to a loveless marriage. Brangäne tries to comfort Isolde
by reminding her that she has brought with her her mother's powerful love
potion – but Isolde's eye is drawn to the other phial in the casket, a deadly
poison. Isolde tells Brangäne to prepare poisoned drinks for herself and
Tristan, then sends for him again. When Tristan finally comes to her
apartments, she offers him a toast, to mark their reconciliation, and they
drink. Tristan, in love with Isolde as she is with him, and knowing this love to
be impossible, suspects poison and drinks willingly. But Brangäne has

exchanged the poison for the love potion and the two fall passionately into each other's arms. As the ship docks, Brangäne realises the consequences of her actions and Isolde faints in her lover's arms.

ACT II King Marke is away on a hunting expedition while, in the palace, Isolde is anxiously preparing for a secret assignation with her love. Brangäne confides in her mistress that she suspects Melot, Tristan's close friend, of betraying them. Isolde scornfully dismisses Brangäne's doubts and, when Tristan arrives, they fall rapturously into each other's arms. Suddenly Kurwenal, Tristan's faithful servant, rushes in, warning them that, led by Melot, King Marke is on his way and urging Tristan to save himself. But it is too late: Melot draws his sword and challenges Tristan who, allowing his guard to drop, is seriously wounded.

ACT III The faithful and grief-stricken Kurwenal has brought Tristan back to his homeland, Brittany, to try and rouse him from a deep sleep. Slowly Tristan awakes, but his only thoughts are for Isolde, and Kurwenal comforts him by saying he has sent for her and she will soon be with him. At last the shepherd's pipe gives the sign that she has arrived and Kurwenal leaves his master to go and meet her. Tristan, transformed, leaps from his bed and tears away his bandages. But, in his weakened condition, his excitement is too much for him and, as Isolde enters, he collapses, dying, in her arms. A second ship has brought King Marke and his knights to Brittany and they burst in; swords are drawn and Kurwenal kills Melot, before collapsing and dying beside his master. Brangäne tells her mistress that the king has come to forgive her – she has told him about the love potions – but Isolde no longer hears her. Movingly expressing her love for Tristan and her grief at his death, Isolde falls, lifeless, on her lover's corpse; the lovers are united in death.

Music and Background

This was the Great Leap Forward that took 19th-century harmony to its limits and beyond, with heavily chromatic writing that undermined the established way of organising music around key signatures and laid the foundations for the twelve-note, serial method of composition with which Schoenberg would later revolutionise musical thinking. The whole sound world of the score is miraculously summarised in the opening chord – the 'Tristan Chord' – which must be the most exhaustively debated and profoundly influential group of four notes ever put to paper. Twentieth-century music effectively begins (fifty years before its time) with these notes, and they form part of the central leitmotif of the score, representing the love potion and the theme of irresistible desire which governs the story. In fact, the entire score is an attempt to re-create in music the erotic charge of heightened sexual passion, and for its 19th-century audience it was accordingly X-certificate material, an unprecedented example of the power of art to stir potent and potentially dangerous emotions. The two central roles make enormous demands of power and stamina, which makes them very hard to cast. Isolde is arguably the toughest female part in all opera.

Highlights

Act I: the Prelude with that all-important 'Tristan Chord'; the
unaccompanied Sailor's Song; Isolde's fury 'O blinde Augen!' and first
address to Tristan, 'Nicht da war's'; the drinking of the potion, the
acknowledgment of the lovers, 'Tristan . . . Isolde', and their passionate duet
'Wehe! Weh!', leading to a suddenly busy close of act. Act II: the Prelude; the
great love duet 'Isolde! Geliebte!' and then 'Lausch Geliebter!' Act III: the
Prelude; Tristan's delirious 'O diese Sonne!'; and Isolde's mighty and
concluding Liebestod (Love-death) 'Mild und leise'.

Did You Know?

☞ The 'Tristan Chord' is so instantly recognisable that it has been quoted
in numerous scores by other composers – often comically, as in Britten's
Albert Herring, where it accompanies the lacing of the lemonade.
☞ The emphasis on physical passion in the work caused considerable
controversy in polite 19th-century society. The young Duchess Sophie of
Bavaria, for example, although a married woman, was prohibited from
attending the premiere out of reservations as to its suitability.
☞ Wagner admitted that his secret passion for a married woman,
Mathilde Wesendonck, was an important influence behind the work.

Recommended Recording

Jon Vickers, Helga Dernesch, Christa Ludwig, Berlin Philharmonic
Orchestra/Herbert von Karajan. EMI CMS7 69319-2. Made in 1972, with
Vickers at his most powerfully *helden* and Dernesch powerfully alluring.

William Walton

(1902–83)

Troilus and Cressida (1954)
The Bear (1967)

Born in humble circumstances in Oldham, Walton's early-flowering genius attracted the attention of the Sitwell family who effectively adopted him as a teenager and set him up as their own in-house *enfant terrible*, notorious for his settings of Edith Sitwell's *Façade*. More seriously, he built a career through the 1930s with his First Symphony, his Viola and Violin Concertos, and the oratorio *Belshazzar's Feast*. Opera hardly featured in his thinking: it was widely assumed that British composers had no instinct for such things, and they certainly had no real precedent. But the success of Britten's *Peter Grimes* in 1945 stirred Walton's interest; and the result, nine years later, was *Troilus and Cressida* – a large-scale, late-Romantic score which cost Walton dear in terms of toil and grief. By this time he was married and living on the Neapolitan island of Ischia, and a distinct Mediterranean ambience had filtered into his music. His only other opera was the short, comic one-acter *The Bear*, taken from Chekhov and exploiting the wry lightness of touch that endured throughout his work.

Troilus and Cressida

FORM: Opera in three acts; in English
COMPOSER: William Walton (1902–83)
LIBRETTO: Christopher Hassall; after Chaucer and other sources
FIRST PERFORMANCE: London, 3 December 1954

Principal Characters

Troilus, a Trojan prince ~ Tenor
Cressida ~ Soprano/Mezzo-soprano
Calkas, the High Priest, her father ~ Bass
Pandarus, Cressida's uncle ~ Tenor
Antenor, a Trojan officer ~ Baritone
Evadne, Cressida's servant ~ Mezzo-soprano
Diomede, a Greek prince ~ Baritone

Synopsis of the Plot

Setting: Troy and Greece; mythological times

ACT I The Trojan war has lasted ten years and there is still no sign of victory for either side. Calkas, the High Priest of Troy, publicly announces that the Delphic Oracle has advised the Trojans to surrender to the Greeks, but the people reject this and turn on him, accusing him of treachery. But Calkas is supported and protected by Prince Troilus, the son of the Trojan king Priam, who is in love with Cressida, Calkas' daughter, a war widow whose only consolation now is taking care of the altar in the temple. Pandarus, Cressida's uncle, a rich, foppish courtier, tells a willing Troilus that he will intercede with Cressida on his behalf. Meanwhile, Calkas has secretly deserted to the Greeks and the young Trojan officer, Antenor, who denounced him earlier, has been take prisoner by the enemy. Troilus vows to rescue him and, sending for Calkas to bless his sword, discovers, to his anger, that Calkas has betrayed and deserted him. Cressida, worked upon by her uncle, has left her red scarf as a love token for Troilus.

ACT II Pandarus has invited Cressida to his house for the evening. A violent thunderstorm breaks and Pandarus persuades her to stay the night, secretly sending a servant for Troilus to join her. The two consummate their love but their joy is interrupted the next day by the arrival of Diomede, a Greek prince, who announces that Cressida must now join her father, in exchange for the release of Antenor. Troilus promises Cressida that he will keep in touch with her constantly and will, somehow, effect her release. Before they part, he returns her scarf to her, the symbol of their love.

ACT III Weeks have gone by and the captive Cressida has received no message from Troilus. Her servant, Evadne, advises her mistress to forget him and concentrate on Diomede, who loves her, and to whom Cressida is herself attracted. Cressida finally capitulates and, as a token, gives Diomede her red scarf, which he wears on his helmet. When she learns of Cressida's promise to marry Diomede, Evadne destroys the last of Troilus' messages, all of which, on Calkas' orders, she has intercepted and hidden. Meanwhile, during a brief truce, Troilus and Pandarus come to the Greek camp as Troilus has arranged a ransom for Cressida's release. The two meet: Troilus is aghast to see Cressida in her wedding clothes and Cressida, distraught, begs him to tell her why he sent her no message. When Diomede appears, with Cressida's scarf on his helmet, Troilus claims her as his own and attacks Diomede; but Calkas stabs him in the back and he falls, dying. Diomede orders Calkas to be returned to Troy in chains and Cressida, who rejected Diomede's order to spurn her lover, is condemned to stay in Greece, a prostitute for the common soldiers. Hearing this, Cressida seizes Troilus' sword and stabs herself, falling across her lover's body as she dies.

Music and Background

The product of his 'second' life in Italy and of his marriage to a young woman of fiery Latin origin, *Troilus and Cressida* is a luscious, late-Romantic score that glows with Mediterranean warmth but staggers slightly under the dead weight of a dated English libretto. From the start it was a problem piece, conservative in idiom and written for a soprano (Elisabeth Schwarzkopf) who never sang it on stage. Difficulties with casting a second production caused Walton to rewrite the female lead for a mezzo rather than a soprano, so that Janet Baker could sing it. But the most recent production (at Opera North in 1996) restored the role to its original pitch. The secondary but important role of Pandarus was written for Peter Pears and its music suggests a sly parody of Britten.

Highlights

Act I: Cressida's first aria 'Slowly it all comes back'; and the recurrent 'scarf' motif. Act II: Cressida's second aria 'At the haunted end of the day' (the most celebrated number in the score); and the love duet and graphic orchestral interlude that describe the couple's love-making.

Recommended Recording

Judith Howarth, Arthur Davies, Opera North/Richard Hickox. Chandos 9370/1. The cast of the most recent British production, led with spirit by Hickox, who reinstates a dramatic soprano in the title role.

Carl Maria von Weber

(1786–1826)

Der Freischütz (1821)
Euryanthe (1823)
Die Drei Pintos (1824, abandoned)
Oberon (1826)

Weber was *the* significant figure of German Romantic (and by the same token, German Nationalist) opera, taking the genre from its first, isolated flowering in Beethoven's *Fidelio* to the point where it was ready to receive the early works of Wagner. Born and raised in the theatre (his father ran a touring company), Weber began to write German *Singspiels* at an early age, receiving sporadic tuition from composers like Michael Haydn in Salzburg. His output was subsequently limited by the amount of time he spent performing as a concert pianist and running the musical life of various opera houses: Breslau, Prague, Dresden. But with *Der Freischütz* he scored an immediate and lasting success. None of the other operas managed to repeat it: *Die Drei Pintos* was abandoned and only completed after Weber's death by Gustav Mahler. Weber died in London, where he was staying to supervise the first performances of *Oberon*, a commission from Covent Garden.

Der Freischütz
(The Marksman with the Magic Bullets)

FORM: Opera in three acts; in German
COMPOSER: Carl Maria von Weber (1786–1826)
LIBRETTO: Johann Friedrich Kind; after Apel and Laun
FIRST PERFORMANCE: Berlin, 18 June 1821

Principal Characters

Max, a young woodsman 〰 **Tenor**
Agathe, daughter of the head ranger 〰 **Soprano**
Caspar, a young woodsman 〰 **Bass**
Ännchen, Agathe's cousin 〰 **Soprano**
Prince Ottokar 〰 **Baritone**
Samiel, a devil 〰 **Spoken role**

Synopsis of the Plot

Setting: Bohemia; 1760s

ACT I Max has been beaten in a shooting contest and he is worried that this may mean that he cannot become the next head ranger after Cuno, and fulfil his dream of marrying Cuno's daughter, Agathe. As he sings of his concern, he is observed by the demon, Samiel. Later, Max meets another forester, Caspar, who has secretly made a pact with Samiel. Caspar promises to help Max; he gives him his gun and tells him to fire a shot at a bird high in the sky. Max does so, and an eagle falls dead at his feet. Caspar explains that he fired a magic bullet, one that always hits its mark. Max agrees to meet Caspar later that night in a lonely part of the forest, Wolf's Glen, so that they can make more bullets.

ACT II Agathe and Ännchen are at home, and Agathe is feeling sad, despite her cousin's attempts to cheer her up. Max comes to see her but, on a pretext and despite her pleas, soon leaves to meet Caspar in the forest. Meanwhile, his friend is already in the Wolf's Glen, with its terrifying sounds, sights and chorus of invisible spirits; he has summoned the demon, Samiel, and offered him Max as a substitute victim. Samiel accepts and Caspar waits for Max to arrive. When he comes they begin to forge the bullets, making seven in all, as the supernatural manifestations increase in their ferocity. Finally the bullets are finished: six will go where the marksman wishes, the seventh will go where Samiel wishes.

ACT III Max has used three of his bullets while out hunting, leaving the last for the next shooting contest; Caspar has used all of his. The day of the shooting competition and of Agathe's marriage to the winner has arrived, but she is sad and disturbed because of a bad dream she has had, in which she was a white dove, shot by Max. Ännchen scoffs at Agathe's worries but is, nevertheless, deeply shocked when a box arrives and, instead of the bridal bouquet, she finds a funeral wreath inside. The contest begins and the Prince orders Max to shoot at a white dove. Agathe begs him not to, saying that she is the dove, but he shoots nevertheless and Agathe falls to the ground. The observers are convinced that Max has shot Agathe, but she has only fainted while Caspar, who was hiding behind the tree on which the dove was resting, has been mortally wounded, and dies cursing, to be claimed by Samiel. The shaken Max makes a full confession, is pardoned by the Prince and the wedding goes ahead.

Music and Background

A paradigm of German Romanticism, *Der Freischütz* is a fireside story of the supernatural that could easily be creaky nonsense but in fact carries the potential for real and chilling theatre, simply because the music is so effective. Weber was a master of dramatic and atmospheric effect, as well as a brilliant craftsman of orchestral colour. The Wolf's Glen Scene is Hammer House of Horror to perfection, and the use of speech (this is a German *Singspiel*, mixing spoken text and song) is judiciously sparing. Note that Weber experiments here with key symbolism, associating F sharp minor and C minor with Samiel, and C major with the victory of goodness over evil.

Highlights

Act I; the Overture and teasing chorus 'Schau der Herr mich an als König'; the chorus 'Das wild in Fluren' and following Tyrolean waltz; and Caspar's drinking song 'Hier im ird'schen Jammerthal'. Act II: Agathe's 'Wie nahte mir der Schlummer'; the farewell trio 'Wie? Was? Entsetzen!'; and the entire Wolf's Glen Scene, especially the orchestral accompaniment to the casting of the bullets. Act III: the hunting interlude; Agathe's wedding song 'Und ob die Wolke'; the hunting chorus 'Was gleicht wohl auf Erden'; Agathe's 'return' to life 'Ich atme noch'; and the final sextet.

Did You Know?

🎵 Part of the reason for the success of *Der Freischütz* was that its nationalist spirit caught the mood of the moment, as Germans celebrated the defeat of Napoleon and patriotic fervour was the order of the day.

🎵 During a performance of *Der Freischütz*, Hector Berlioz responded to 'a wild sweetness in the music which I found intoxicating'.

Recommended Recording

Gundula Janowitz, Edith Mathis, Peter Schreier, Dresden Opera/Carlos Kleiber. DG 415 432-2. Kleiber's first big recording project and as superb as you'd expect, with vivid but sensitive singing.

Kurt Weill

(1900–50)

Die Dreigroschenoper (1928)
Happy End (1929)
Aufstieg und Fall der Stadt Mahagonny (1929)
Der Silbersee (1933)
Die Sieben Todsünden (1933)
Knickerbocker Holiday (1938)
Lady in the Dark (1941)
One Touch of Venus (1943)
The Firebrand of Florence (1945)
Street Scene (1946)
Love Life (1948)
Lost in the Stars (1949)

The Jewish son of a Dessau cantor, Kurt Weill's life was divided in two by the rise of Nazism. He first found fame as a composer of astringently Expressionist German music theatre, much of it written in collaboration with Bertolt Brecht and employing shock tactics to make what would be sober moral points but for the exuberance of the accompanying score. Then in 1933, after persistent attacks on his work by Nazi polemicists, he fled the country, ending up in America where he settled and wrote Broadway musicals, to the enduring contempt of some European critics who still see his late career as a surrender to commercialism. In fact, Weill was always commercially minded. Most of his German works played on the Berlin equivalent of Broadway, and their populist tone, incorporating elements of cabaret and street song, was not wholly determined by left-wing political idealism. Weill was never the committed communist that Brecht became. He simply believed in writing for the widest possible audience, and in doing so he bridged the gulf between serious and popular culture with a degree of success that few composers since have managed to reproduce. He died young, aged fifty.

Aufstieg und Fall der Stadt Mahagonny
(*Rise and Fall of the City of Mahagonny*)

FORM: Opera in three acts; in German
COMPOSER: Kurt Weill (1900–50)
LIBRETTO: Bertolt Brecht
FIRST PERFORMANCE: Leipzig, 9 March 1930

Principal Characters

Leokadja Begbick ∽ Mezzo-soprano
Fatty ∽ Tenor
Trinity Moses ∽ Baritone
Jenny Hill ∽ Soprano
Jim Mahoney ∽ Tenor
Bill ∽ Baritone
Joe ∽ Bass
Toby Higgins ∽ Tenor

Synopsis of the Plot

Setting: A desolate place in contemporary America

ACT I A large, battered truck arrives on the scene and comes to a spluttering halt. Its three occupants, Leokadja Begbick, Trinity Moses and Fatty – all on the run from the police – emerge and, seeing that the truck has finally broken down, decide to stay where they are and found a new city, devoted to money and pleasure since life elsewhere is so miserable. The city, Mahagonny, quickly rises and news of its existence travels fast, attracting many new residents from all over the world, including Jenny Hill and her six fellow prostitutes, and the Alaskan, Jim Mahoney, with his lumberjack friends. But soon the residents become disillusioned and start to leave Mahagonny, including Jim, who is bored and disappointed with the city's harmonious atmosphere, although, at the last minute, he is persuaded by his friends to stay on. Then news of an approaching hurricane sends the people into a panic, except for Jim, who looks forward to some excitement and uses the occasion to propound his theory that Mahagonny is too restricted by its regulations and should, instead, be founded on total permissiveness: everyone should be able to do exactly as he or she pleases, bearing only in mind that each one must take the consequences of their choices – 'you make your own bed and lie on it'.

ACT II The danger from the hurricane has passed, Jim's philosophy has been acted upon and, in the next four scenes, we see some of the consequences: the lumberjack Jake dies from over-eating; lust is represented by Mrs Begbick presiding over her brothel; violence by a boxing match in which the lumberjack Joe is unevenly matched with Trinity Moses and is killed in the ring; finally, there is alcohol and we see Jim buying a round of drinks from Mrs Begbick, which he cannot pay for. Now penniless, Jim is spurned by all his old friends and arrested, as Jenny echoes his own words – 'you make your own bed and lie on it'.

ACT III Trinity Moses sells tickets for the court proceedings, in a tent, presided over by Mrs Begbick as judge. The first case, a charge of murder against Tobby Higgins, is dropped when the accused hands over a considerable sum to the bench. Jim asks his friend, Bill, for a loan so that he can arrange just such a satisfactory outcome for his own case, but Bill refuses – their past friendship is not worth the money. Jim is found guilty on five charges, ranging from breach of the peace to singing during the hurricane, but the most serious is lack of money. Unable to buy himself off, he is sentenced to death by electric chair and dies, unrepentant and without regrets. After his death people take to the streets to demonstrate and counter-demonstrate against the rising cost of living, while the city burns around them. Jim's remains are carried in procession but, as the company points out to the audience, there is nothing they can do to help Jim, themselves, the audience or, indeed, anybody at all!

Music and Background

This abrasively didactic piece grew out of a sequence of songs to Brechtian texts – *The Mahagonny Songspiel* – which tell much the same story in much the same cabaret-style music. The larger work is not well organised: it rambles through long tracts of secondary inspiration. But the big set-piece moments come with memorable impact and unforgettable tunes that ride across raunchy, dance band-brash accompaniments. Resonant with parody (including a cheerful take on the Bridesmaids' Chorus from *Der Freischütz*), *Mahagonny*'s musical invention compensates for its heavy-handed (and now stale) political moralising.

Highlights

Act I: Jenny's Alabama Song ('Oh show us the way to the next whisky bar'); the Hurricane Scene; and Jim's song 'As you make your bed'. Act II: the Mandalay Song; and the chorus 'If you had five bucks a day'. Act III: the Benares Song sung by the male ensemble; and the chorus anticipating the arrival of God.

Recommended Recording

Anja Silja, Wolfgang Neumann, Anny Schlemm, Cologne Radio Symphony Orchestra/Jan Latham-Koenig. Capriccio 10 160/61. The competition here is an old recording that features Lotte Lenya (Weill's wife) but which has questionable sound. Silja is a more than adequate alternative, and the sound is better.

Die Dreigroschenoper
(*The Threepenny Opera*)

FORM: Play with music in a Prologue and three acts; in German
COMPOSER: Kurt Weill (1900–50)
LIBRETTO: Bertolt Brecht; after Gay
FIRST PERFORMANCE: Berlin, 31 August 1928

Principal Characters

Mr Peachum ✒ Baritone
Mrs Peachum ✒ Mezzo-soprano
Polly Peachum, their daughter ✒ Soprano
Macheath (Mac the Knife), a highwayman ✒ Tenor
Jenny Diver, a prostitute ✒ Soprano
Tiger Brown, Chief Constable of London ✒ Bass
Lucy, his daughter ✒ Soprano
A ballad singer ✒ Tenor

Synopsis of the Plot

Setting: Victorian London

PROLOGUE Various underworld characters are gathered at a fair in Soho and are entertained by a ballad singer, who tells the story of Mac the Knife, a notorious criminal who always seems to evade capture.

ACT I Mr and Mrs Peachum, organisers of a successful business in robbery and petty crime, are concerned that the absence of their daughter, Polly, may mean that she has eloped with the highwayman Macheath, the infamous Mac the Knife. This is indeed the case as the next scene reveals their wedding celebrations, in a stable full of stolen goods, and the guest list includes members of Macheath's gang, a cleric and the police chief, Tiger Brown, an old schoolfriend of the groom. Afterwards, Polly goes back to her parents' shop and tries to explain how much she loves her new husband, but Mr and Mrs Peachum are unimpressed and determine to have Macheath arrested and hanged. In the First Threepenny Finale, the three sing of the misery of living in such an unreliable and untrustworthy world.

ACT II Polly warns Macheath that her parents are setting a trap for him and Mrs Peachum bribes Jenny Diver, a prostitute, to betray Macheath to the police. In prison, Macheath is visited by Lucy Brown, Tiger's daughter, who rails at him for jilting her and, when Polly comes to visit her husband, the two women regard each other with undisguised venom. Mrs Peachum arrives and drags her daughter away and the impressionable Lucy helps Macheath to escape from his cell – much to the delight of his friend, Tiger, until Mr Peachum reminds the chief constable that he will be held responsible for allowing it to happen. The act closes with the Second Threepenny Finale, lamenting the exploitation of man by his fellow man.

ACT III The coronation of the new king is about to take place and Peachum is organising his team of thieves and pickpockets to take full advantage of this special opportunity. Tiger Brown arrives to arrest Peachum and stop his gang from operating in the streets, but Peachum bribes him to leave him alone by telling him that Macheath is at the house of another prostitute, Suky Tawdry. Macheath is again arrested, but this time he cannot escape and Polly and his gang are unable to raise enough money to bribe his jailer into letting him go. The hanging is imminent and Macheath takes a bitter farewell of the world. Then Peachum, turning to the audience, announces in the Third Threepenny Finale that he and the company have thought up a different ending: Tiger Brown rides in bringing not only a reprieve for Macheath but also a knighthood, a pension and a country estate! The company join in an ironic commentary on the ways of the world and their consequences.

Music and Background

As John Gay's *The Beggar's Opera* was a populist reaction against the exquisiteness of Handelian opera seria, so *Die Dreigroschenoper* (devised loosely around Gay) was a populist reaction against Wagner. Its set-piece speech-with-songs style revisited the old traditions of German *Singspiel* through the modern ones of cabaret, and its sardonic celebration of low-life values was meant to shock. A huge and instant success after its Berlin premiere, it was suppressed by the Nazis but entered a new life in English translation, made by the composer Marc Blitzstein for a New York production in 1954. The piece exists in varying forms – it developed as it went along and as Brecht's political stance became more firmly Marxist – and performances today bear little resemblance to the way it would originally have appeared. One abiding question is with regard to the kind of performers it should use and to what extent they should or shouldn't sound 'operatic'.

Highlights

Prologue: the Overture and opening Ballad of Mac the Knife, 'Und der Haifisch' – Weill's most famous tune. Act I: Peachum's hymn 'Wach auf'; the Ballad of Pirate Jenny, 'Meine Herren'; and the Cannon Song 'John war darunter'. Act II: Polly's regretful 'Hubsch als es wahrte'; Mrs Peachum's Ballad of Sexual Dependency, 'Da ist nun einer schon'; and the finale, 'Ihr Herrn, die ihr uns lehrt'. Act III: Peachum's Ballad of the Insufficiency of Human Endeavour, 'Der Mensch lebt durch den Kopf'.

Did You Know?

Some measure of the phenomenal pre-war success of *Der Dreigroschenoper* can be drawn from the fact that licences for 133 separate productions had been granted before Weill fled the country in 1933.

Recommended Recording

René Kollo, Ute Lemper, Milva, Helga Dernesch, Berlin Radio Symphony Orchestra/John Mauceri. Decca 430 075-2. An odd mix of opera and cabaret stars that sort of works and is no more uncomfortable than the piece itself.

Street Scene

FORM: Opera in two acts; in English
COMPOSER: Kurt Weill (1900–50)
LIBRETTO: Elmer Rice and Langston Hughes
FIRST PERFORMANCE: Philadelphia, 16 December 1946

Principal Characters

Anna Maurrant ~ Soprano
Frank Maurrant, her husband ~ Baritone
Rose Maurrant, their daughter ~ Soprano
Sam Kaplan, in love with Rose ~ Tenor
Jennie Hildebrand ~ Soprano
Harry Easter ~ Baritone
First Nursemaid ~ Soprano
Second Nursemaid ~ Mezzo-soprano
Steve Sankey ~ Spoken role

Synopsis of the Plot

Setting: A bleak New York tenement block

ACT I It is a sweltering hot evening in early June and the inhabitants of the block gradually drift out onto the pavement for some air. They complain about the heat, chat about their lives and gossip about the other residents. Anna Maurrant expresses her disillusionment with life and her secret longings – her affair with Steve Sankey is known to all the other residents, but not yet to her husband, Frank, although his suspicions are soon aroused. Jennie Hildebrand comes cheerfully home from her graduation ceremony, but the other residents' happiness for her is marred by the fact that they know that Jennie and her family, deserted by her father, will tomorrow be evicted for rent arrears. Anna Maurrant's daughter, Rose, is escorted home by a married colleague from her office, Mr Easter, who tries to tempt her into becoming his mistress, using the age-old promise of a Broadway career, but, after a moment's hesitation, Rose rejects him, preferring her own ideals of love and romance. Easter leaves, Rose turns to Sam and they sing of their dreams of a better life together, before saying goodnight.

ACT II The next morning tensions are rising between Anna and Frank Maurrant; Rose appeals to her father to be kinder to her mother but he rejects her and leaves for work. Rose tells Sam about her problems with Mr Easter and they decide to go away together, to take responsibility for their own lives. Meanwhile, Mr Easter comes to take Rose to an office funeral and Anna invites Steve Sankey up to her flat. Frank comes home unexpectedly, shots are heard and Frank runs out. Returning to find a crowd of excited onlookers outside the tenement, Rose finds Sankey dead and her dying mother being carried into an ambulance. Meanwhile, the Hildebrands' belongings are being carried out and set on the pavement by the bailiffs. It is not long before the scene of the double murder becomes a magnet for sightseers, including two nursemaids from the other side of the town, who walk their charges past the grisly scene. Frank Maurrant is arrested but, before he is taken away, he tells Rose that he loved her mother, he shot her only because he was terrified of losing her. Rose and Sam talk again of their plans, but her parents' tragedy has confused and troubled her; she no longer feels able to commit herself to Sam and realises she must go away by herself. Rose leaves as prospective tenants come to view the Hildebrands' flat and the residents come out again to sit on the pavement and complain about the heat.

Music and Background

This is a piece of socialist-realism as veristic and as dark as Mascagni or Leoncavallo, and its tragically unresolved ending was a brave choice for something that was intended to play commercially on Broadway. *Street Scene* was at one point called by Weill a 'Broadway Opera', and its idiom mixes the ingredients of conventional European operatic writing with the packaged song style of American musical theatre. To that extent it marks the common ground between Weill's native and adoptive worlds. But it also carries forward the experiment of George Gershwin's *Porgy and Bess* (a conscious model) to later composers like Bernstein and Sondheim, whose work straddles the popular/classical divide.

Highlights

Act I: the opening ensemble 'Ain't it awful, the heat?'; Mrs Maurrant's big aria 'Somehow I never could believe'; the Ice Cream Sextet ; the graduation ensemble 'Wrapped in a ribbon'; Sam's 'Lonely house'; Rose's 'What good would the moon be?'; and the concluding love duet for Rose and Sam. Act II: Sam and Rose's 'We'll go away together'; the comic nursemaids' duet 'Sleep, baby dear'; and the finale and reprise of 'Ain't it awful, the heat?'

Did You Know?

෨ Kurt Weill considered *Street Scene* to be his most important work.

Recommended Recording

Josephine Barstow, Samuel Ramey, Jerry Hadley, Scottish Opera/John Mauceri. Decca 433 371-2. A starry cast that some will find too grand for their roles, although they give the score the vocal quality it deserves.

Bernd Alois Zimmermann
(1918–70)

Die Soldaten (1965)

Born near Cologne, Zimmermann belonged to the generation of
German composers who learned their craft under the Third
Reich and spent the next twenty years coming to terms with the fact. His
training in the immediate post-war period steered him towards
Serialism but he developed a method of writing that borrowed freely
from many different sources, mixing styles, techniques and direct
quotations from other composers into what he called 'collages' of sound.
His only completed opera, *Die Soldaten*, is a prime example. Never quite
in the forefront of the European avant-garde, Zimmermann acquired a
high profile in Germany during the 1960s – largely through *Die
Soldaten* but also through theatre and radio work, and his *Requiem for a
Young Poet*. He taught at Cologne University until his death, by suicide,
at the age of fifty-two.

Die Soldaten
(The Soldiers)

FORM: Opera in four acts and fifteen scenes; in German
COMPOSER: Bernd Alois Zimmermann (1918–70)
LIBRETTO: Bernd Zimmermann; after Lenz
FIRST PERFORMANCE: Cologne, 15 February 1965

Principal Characters
Wesener, a merchant in Lille ⮞ Bass
Marie, his daughter ⮞ Soprano
Charlotte, her sister ⮞ Mezzo-soprano
Their grandmother ⮞ Contralto
Stolzius, a draper in Armentières ⮞ Baritone
His mother ⮞ Contralto

Desportes, a French officer ⚘ **Tenor**
His servant ⚘ **Spoken role**
Eisenhardt, French army chaplain ⚘ **Baritone**
Major Haudy, French officer ⚘ **Baritone**
Major Mary, French officer ⚘ **Baritone**
Captain Pirzel, French officer ⚘ **Tenor**
Countess de la Roche ⚘ **Mezzo-soprano**
The Young Count, her son ⚘ **Tenor**
Andalusian waitress ⚘ **Dancer**

Synopsis of the Plot

Setting: French-speaking Flanders; yesterday, today and tomorrow

ACT I Scene 1 (Strofe) Marie is at home in her father's house in Lille, writing a letter to Mrs Stolzius in Armentières, with whom she has recently been staying and with whose draper son she has fallen in love.
Scene 2 (Ciacona I) Armentières. Marie's letter arrives and, when his mother eventually shows it to him, does much to cheer up the downcast Stolzius who reciprocates Marie's affection, although his mother evidently does not approve of the liaison.
Scene 3 (Ricercari I) Lille. Followed by a short interlude (Tratto I), the scene opens with Marie receiving a visit from Desportes, a young French nobleman and army officer, who begins extravagantly to woo her. He invites her to the theatre, but her father refuses to let her go, justifying his decision on the grounds that she is his only joy in life and he must protect her.
Scene 4 (Toccata I) Armentières. A group of French officers and their chaplain discuss whether sermons or theatrical performances provide the most effective platform for discussing moral issues and, more particularly, whether the theatre has a detrimental moral influence on army officers, encouraging them to seduce respectable girls. Major Haudy is adamant – 'A whore will always be a whore' – but Eisenhardt's response is that no woman became a prostitute without being made one.
Scene 5 (Nocturno I) Lille. Marie shows her father a love poem Desportes has sent to her and Wesener advises her to encourage him – but also to keep Stolzius in the background as a possible husband if Desportes fails to propose. After he leaves her, Marie sings passionately of her love for Stolzius.

ACT II Scene 1 (Toccata II) Armentières. The officers have gathered at a café and, after an elaborate dance led by the attractive Andalusian waitress, during which the soldiers tap out rhythms on glasses, cups, teaspoons and tabletops, the soldiers fall to teasing Stolzius about Marie's relationship with Desportes in Lille. Stolzius denies all knowledge of this and soon leaves.
Scene 2 (Capriccio, Chorale and Ciacona II) Lille. Marie has received a reproachful letter from Stolzius and, in tears, hands it to Desportes when he comes to see her. The officer seizes upon her temporary emotional vulnerability as an opportunity to seduce her and, as the seduction

continues we see, simultaneously, Marie's grandmother foreseeing Marie's eventual fate and Stolzius, in Armentières, reading a letter from Marie (dictated by Desportes), in which she breaks off their association. Stolzius vows to avenge himself on his rival.

ACT III Scene 1 (Rondino) Armentières. The chaplain and Captain Pirzel are involved in one of their endless philosophical discussions; Eisenhardt asks Pirzel the reasons for Major Mary's recent move to Lille, but Pirzel shows little interest or concern.

Scene 2 (Rappresentazione) Lille. Major Mary receives a visit from Stolzius (whom he does not know), dressed as a soldier. Stolzius applies to become Mary's batman and is taken on.

Scene 3 (Ricercari II) Lille. Desportes is away and Marie willingly accepts the attentions of Mary, in spite of her sister Charlotte's disapproval. Mary arrives to take the sisters for a drive and they remark on the strange resemblance between Mary's batman and Stolzius.

Scene 4 (Nocturno II) Lille. The Countess de la Roche is waiting for her son, the Young Count, to return home and muses on the pain sons cause their mothers through their behaviour. When he arrives, the Countess upbraids him for associating with a girl like Marie Wesener, whose social station precludes her from being a suitable wife for him, and undertakes to take care of the girl herself.

Scene 5 (Tropi) Lille. The Countess goes to see Marie, who has apparently now been abandoned by Mary, as well as Desportes, and, rather patronisingly, offers her a place in her own household.

ACT IV Scene 1 (Toccata III) Armentières. In a series of scenes, played simultaneously, we see the various stages of Marie's gradual downfall. Using three levels on the stage and three projection screens, Zimmermann deploys singers, doubles, dancers and film to show how Marie runs away, is raped by Desportes' servant (with his master's connivance) and becomes a prostitute. On learning what has happened, Stolzius buys rat poison.

Scene 2 (Ciacona III) Armentières. Desportes and Mary are dining together in Mary's rooms. Desportes relates to his friend how he arranged for Marie to be 'taken care of' by his servant. Mary is disgusted at this and says he would have married Marie himself if the Young Count had not interfered. Stolzius, who has overheard their conversation, puts the poison in Desportes' soup and, as the officer writhes in agony, shrieks Marie's name into his face. As Desportes dies, Stolzius takes poison himself and collapses.

Scene 3 (Nocturno III) A road beside the River Lys. Marie, now miserable and destitute, begs money from her father, Wesener, who does not recognise her. He hesitates then, reflecting on his own daughter's fate, gives her a coin and she sinks to the ground. Simultaneously there is a collage of scenes and voices from the action, from soldiers in the café and the chaplain praying, to film of soldiers of all nationalities marching relentlessly on. Finally, the concept of endless marching, with its hypnotic rhythms, dominates both aurally and visually, becoming louder and louder until it is overwhelming.

Music and Background

A testament to post-war German conscience, *Die Soldaten* is also a monument to the musical tastes of the 1960s; a big, abrasive score that builds massive, complicated textures from the 'collage' of disparate materials, including borrowings from Bach chorales and Richard Strauss. The staging is meant to incorporate collage techniques as well, with different scenes taking place simultaneously and intercut with film sequences. Hailed in its own time as the most significant German opera since Berg's *Lulu*, it no longer seems to make such a strong claim. But the comparison with Berg is valid in that however brazen and cacophonous the music may seem, it is actually organised into strictly controlled, quasi-symphonic movements that bear classical names like 'nocturno' and 'toccata'. The central character Marie – a hugely demanding role that requires a wide range of accomplishments, including good old-fashioned coloratura – is clearly conceived in terms of Berg's two leading ladies.

Highlights

Act I: Marie's closing love aria and the following orchestral postlude. Act II: the seduction of Marie and the two other scenes with which it simultaneously plays. Act III: the Straussian all-female trio for the Countess, Marie and Charlotte. Act IV: the rapid opening sequence that charts Marie's downfall.

Did You Know?

ちゃ. The 18th-century playwright, Lenz, took the theme of his play from a real incident involving one of his friends and the daughter of a jeweller in Strasbourg.

ちゃ. Zimmermann's original intention was to stage *Die Soldaten* with twelve separate acting areas, each having its own instrumental ensemble. The idea was abandoned as impractical.

Recommended Recording

Nancy Shade, Milagro Vargas, Stuttgart Opera/Bernhard Kontarsky. Teldec 9031-72775-2. Taken from a staged production with performances that really feel 'worked in', which is just as well, because this is the only version you'll find at the moment.

Glossary

ACT
A main section of an opera, usually having an integral form of its own and ending with a suitable highpoint in the plot. Early operas and 17th- and 18th-century French operas generally had five acts, though in 19th-century Italy three-act operas became common. Particularly in the 20th century, there has been a growth in the number of one-act operas, e.g. Richard Strauss' *Elektra* and Bartók's *Duke Bluebeard's Castle*.

ADAGIO
Italian. Music to be played and sung at a slow pace.

AIR: See aria

ARIA
Italian. A lyrical piece for one voice, generally used to illustrate a character's state of mind at a specific point in an opera and to show the singer's virtuosity. Arias were used in the earliest operas and were still common in the mid-19th century. Well-known examples are 'La donna è mobile' from Verdi's *Rigoletto* and 'Dove sono' from Mozart's *Le Nozze di Figaro*. An arietta is a shorter and less complicated aria.

BALLAD OPERA
A form of opera prevalent in England in the 18th century, in which spoken dialogue alternates with popular songs of the time set to traditional tunes. Gay's *The Beggar's Opera* is a prime example.

BALLET
A story told through dance with musical accompaniment. Ballet originated in the 16th century and was used in the form of interludes in French court operas, before developing into a main component of 19th-century French *grand opéra*. Verdi amended a number of his operas, e.g. *Macbeth*, to incorporate ballet for their first French productions.

BARCAROLLE
A piece with a lilting rhythm and reminiscent of the songs of Venetian gondoliers. The best-known example is that which appears in Offenbach's *Les Contes d'Hoffman*.

BARITONE
A moderately low male voice pitched higher than bass and lower than tenor. Famous baritones include Thomas Allen, Dietrich Fischer-Dieskau, Tito Gobbi, Thomas Hampson and Bryn Terfel.

BAROQUE
In music, the time between roughly 1600 and 1750, and incorporating the works of Monteverdi and Handel.

BASS
From Italian *basso*, meaning 'low'. The lowest male voice. Famous basses are Boris Christoff, Ruggero Raimondi, John Tomlinson and Willard White.

BASS-BARITONE
The male voice covering the range of both the bass and the baritone voices.

BEL CANTO
Italian. Meaning 'beautiful singing'. A style of singing common in the late 18th and early 19th centuries in Italy, intended to display the singer's tone and virtuosic vocal ability to the best advantage. Rossini, Donizetti and Bellini are the best-known composers in this style.

CASTRATO
A male singer, castrated prior to puberty in order to retain a soprano or, more commonly, a contralto range. Castrati were popular in the 17th and 18th centuries, and were originally used in operas by, among others, Handel and Mozart.

CAVATINA
Italian. A short aria common in the 18th century, of which 'Una voce poco fa' from Rossini's *Il Barbiere di Siviglia* is a well-known example.

CHORUS
An ensemble of singers of voice types soprano, contralto, tenor and bass, the number varying with the requirements of the opera, used to comment on the action or be involved in crowd scenes. Gluck was the first composer to use the chorus as an integral part of the drama. In the 19th century choruses featured increasingly in their own set-pieces, famous examples of which are The Chorus of the Hebrew Slaves from Verdi's *Nabucco* and The Pilgrims' Chorus from Wagner's *Tannhäuser*.

CHROMATICISM
A type of composition using sharpened and flattened notes that don't belong to any obvious key signature. An essentially 19th-century development in harmony, it is particularly evident in the music of Wagner.

CLASSICAL
In music, specifically the time between about 1750 and 1830, and encompassing the work of Haydn, Mozart and Beethoven.

COLORATURA
A type of singing that demands exceptional range, ability and lightness, as heard in such highly decorative roles as The Queen of the Night in Mozart's *Die Zauberflöte* and Lucia in Donizetti's *Lucia di Lammermoor*.

COMIC OPERA
An opera of a light nature, often with a spoken dialogue element. In its different forms it is known in Italy as opera buffa, in France as *opéra comique*, in Germany as *Singspiel* and in Spain as zarzuela. It sometimes crosses into the territory of operetta.

COMMEDIA DELL'ARTE
Originating in 16th-century Italy, and using comedy, masks, and stock characters such as Harlequin and Pulcinella to act out different scenarios, commedia dell'arte has been incorporated in such operas as Mozart's *Le Nozze di Figaro* and Richard Strauss' *Ariadne auf Naxos*.

CONTINUO
Used up until the end of the 18th century, this is a continuous, accompanimental bass part, played usually on a sustaining instrument, e.g. double bass, bassoon, and a harmonic instrument, e.g. harpsichord.

CONTRALTO
The lowest female voice. It was in this range that castrati generally sang.

COUNTERPOINT
Two or more musical lines placed against each other.

COUNTERTENOR
Nowadays used to denote a male alto singing music originally written for castrati in Baroque opera. Famous countertenors are Alfred Deller and James Bowman.

DA CAPO
Italian. Meaning 'repeat from the beginning'. Arias of the Baroque and Classical periods often took this form, with the repeat featuring much vocal and instrumental decoration.

DISSONANCE
The use of two or more notes to create an uncomfortable or unpleasant sound.

DUET
Italian. In opera, a piece for two singers. A famous example is 'Au fond du temple saint' from Bizet's *Les Pêcheurs de Perles*.

ENTR'ACTE
French. Originally music to be played between the acts of a play, and following the same use in opera, particularly in the works of Lully and, much later, *Pelléas et Mélisande* by Debussy.

EXPRESSIONISM
Music which describes a character's psychological state, composed mainly in Germany in the early 20th century by, for example, Richard Strauss, Berg and Schoenberg.

GESAMTKUNSTWERK
German. Meaning 'total work of art', and used by Wagner to describe the uniting of music, drama, painting and poetry to create a brand-new art form.

GRAND OPÉRA
Nowadays used to describe any large-scale opera, e.g. *La Forza del Destino*. In the 19th century *grand opéra* was the term used for works produced at the Paris Opéra, often with a libretto by Scribe, and generally with five acts, plus lavish sets, a ballet and an epic plot. Examples are *La Juive* by Halévy, *Les Huguenots* by Meyerbeer and *Le Cid* by Massenet. Operas written by Italians for production at the Paris Opéra which can be classed as *grand opéra* are Donizetti's *La Favorite* and Rossini's *Guillaume Tell*.

HELDENTENOR
German. Meaning 'heroic tenor'. The heavier and more taxing tenor roles of the German repertory, such as those of Wagner, require this voice type.

IMPRESSIONISM
Taking its name from the art movement of the late 19th century, Impressionism when related to music concerns the composer's desire to convey mood and emotion. Debussy's *Pelléas et Mélisande* is an example of Impressionistic music.

INTERMEZZO
Italian. Either a short comic opera placed between the acts of an 18th-century Italian opera seria, the best-known example being Pergolesi's *La Serva Padrona*, or a short orchestral piece between two scenes, such as the celebrated example in Mascagni's *Cavalleria Rusticana*.

LARGO
Italian. A direction for the music to be played and sung at a broad, slow pace.

LEITMOTIF
German. Meaning 'leading motive'. A short fragment of music which can be harmonic, melodic or rhythmic, associated with a particular character, object or idea. Wagner used the leitmotif extensively in *Der Ring des Nibelungen*.

LIBRETTO
Italian. Meaning 'little book'. The words of an opera or operetta. Famous librettists include Lorenzo da Ponte (for Mozart), Arrigo Boito (for Verdi) and Hugo von Hofmannsthal (for Richard Strauss).

LIED, LIEDER
German. Meaning 'song, songs'. Generally a song based on poetry sung to a piano accompaniment, in opera the term applies to simple, solo numbers in 19th-century German works.

MADRIGAL
In operatic terms, a contrapuntal (see counterpoint) piece for several voices, the style of composition originating in the 16th century in Italy and then spreading to England.

MASQUE
A form of entertainment combining music, dance and lavish costumes with plots often based on mythological subjects, which was popular in the courts of Italy, France and Britain in the 16th and 17th centuries.

MEZZO-SOPRANO
Italian. Literally 'half soprano'. The middle female voice range, below soprano and above contralto. Well-known mezzo-sopranos are Cecilia Bartoli, Teresa Berganza, Kathleen Ferrier and Tatiana Troyanos.

MINIMALISM
A form of composition in which the same fragment of music is repeated almost indefinitely, with only very small differences in rhythm and key. Philip Glass' opera *Akhnaten* is an example of its use.

NEOCLASSICISM
A form of composition using 17th- and 18th-century models in a reaction against the perceived excesses of the late-Romantic music of the late 19th and early 20th centuries. Stravinsky's *Oedipus Rex* is an example of a Neoclassical opera.

OPERA
Italian. Literally 'work'. An abbreviation of *opera in musica*, used to refer to a drama set to music and employing one or more singers, the whole being performed in appropriate costumes and stage settings. An opera is distinct from a musical in having music which is integral rather than incidental.

OPERA BUFFA: See comic opera

OPÉRA COMIQUE: See comic opera

OPERA SEMI SERIA
Italian. Meaning 'half-serious work'. An opera of mainly, though not exclusively, light tone popular from the mid-18th century.

OPERA SERIA
Italian. Meaning 'serious work'. The main operatic form of the 17th and 18th

centuries, incorporating a plot based on a mythological subject with elaborate display arias. A well-known example is *Idomeneo* by Mozart.

OPERETTA
Italian. Meaning 'little work'. In its strictest sense, operetta is a play with an overture, songs and dances, generally in a comic idiom. Nineteenth-century composers of operetta include Offenbach, Sullivan and Johann Strauss II, while Noël Coward's 'musical comedies' can also be considered as operetta.

ORATORIO
A religious text set for solo voices, chorus and orchestra, generally performed in either a church or concert hall without costumes or sets.

ORCHESTRATION
The art of writing music for an orchestra.

OVERTURE
From French *ouverture*, meaning 'opening'. A piece of purely instrumental music preceding an opera and often including melodies to be heard later in the work. Famous operatic overtures include those to Rossini's *Il Barbiere di Siviglia*, Verdi's *La Forza del Destino* and Glinka's *Ruslan and Lyudmila*.

PARLANDO
Italian. Meaning 'speaking'. An instruction to a singer to make the vocal tone approximate to that of ordinary speech.

PRELUDE
From Latin *praeludium*, meaning 'before-game'. A short piece of music functioning as an introduction to an act in an opera. The prelude to Act III of Wagner's *Lohengrin* is one of the best-known examples.

PRIMA DONNA
Italian. Meaning 'first lady'. Originally used to denote the main female role in an opera, the title is nowadays given to mean a leading female singer.

QUARTET
Italian. In opera, a piece for four singers. The quartet 'Mir ist so wunderbar' in Beethoven's *Fidelio* is a famous example.

QUINTET
Italian. In opera, a piece for five singers. An example is 'Wie? Wie? Wie? Ihr an diesen Schreckens-ort?' in Act II of Mozart's *Die Zauberflöte*.

RECITATIVE
Declamatory speech-like singing which advances the plot of an opera and is used between the formal, more reflective, numbers such as arias. It is mainly found in music composed before Wagner.

RESCUE OPERA
An opera in which the plot revolves around the rescue of a principal character from a life-threatening situation. The best-known example is Beethoven's *Fidelio*.

ROMANCE
A piece of music, generally slow in pace, with a lyrical and tender quality.

ROMANTICISM
In opera, the time between about 1830 and 1900, and including the works of Weber and Verdi.

SCENE
A subdivision of an act in an opera, in which the setting and/or the number of singers remains the same. In Italy it is known as a scena.

SCORE
The written down, and generally printed, vocal and orchestral notation for an opera. Purely vocal scores are also available with piano accompaniment.

SERIALISM
A style of composition developed at the beginning of the 20th century by Schoenberg, in which all twelve notes in an octave (five black and seven white notes when played on a piano) have equal importance, as opposed to the traditional major/minor key system.

SEXTET
Italian. In opera, a piece for six singers. The sextet 'Chi me freno in tal momento' from Donizetti's *Lucia di Lammermoor* is probably the best-known example.

SINGSPIEL: See comic opera

SOPRANO
From Italian *sopra*, meaning 'above'. The highest female voice range. Victoria de los Angeles, Montserrat Caballé, Maria Callas, Jessye Norman and Joan Sutherland are all famous sopranos.

TEMPO
Italian. Meaning 'time'. The pace of the music.

TENOR
From Italian, meaning 'hold'. The highest natural male voice. The term comes from the Middle Ages when the tenor voice 'held' the melody while the other voices sang in counterpoint to it. Jussi Björling, José Carreras, Plácido Domingo, Beniamino Gigli and Luciano Pavarotti are all famous tenors.

THEME
An arrangement of notes which play an important part in a composition.

TREBLE
The highest range of girl's and unbroken boy's voice. Roles which require these voices are Miles and Flora in Britten's *The Turn of the Screw* and Amahl in Menotti's *Amahl and the Night Visitors*.

TRIO
Italian. In opera, a piece for three singers. 'Soave sia il vento' from Mozart's *Così fan Tutte* is a well-known example.

TWELVE-TONE SYSTEM: See Serialism

VERISMO
Italian. Meaning 'realism'. A style of opera pioneered in late-19th century Italy by Mascagni which aimed to depict real life, rather than mythological or historical subjects. Popular verismo operas are *I Pagliacci* by Leoncavallo and *La Bohème* by Puccini.

ZARZUELA: See comic opera

Index of Operas and Operettas

Index of Composers